From the Nation's Leading Social Studies Educator

Adventures

ENHANCE YOUR TEACHING AND HAVE MORE FUN HELPING

GRADE 2

GRADE 1

in

YOUR STUDENTS TO BECOME

GRADE 3

Time

GRADE K

21ST CENTURY CITIZENS &

GRADE 4

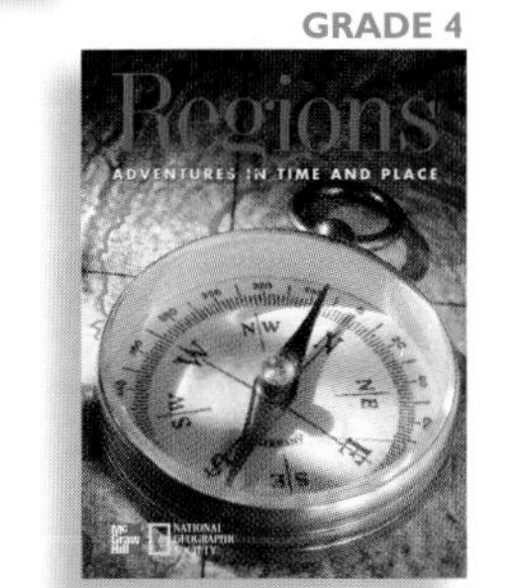

and

GRADE 5

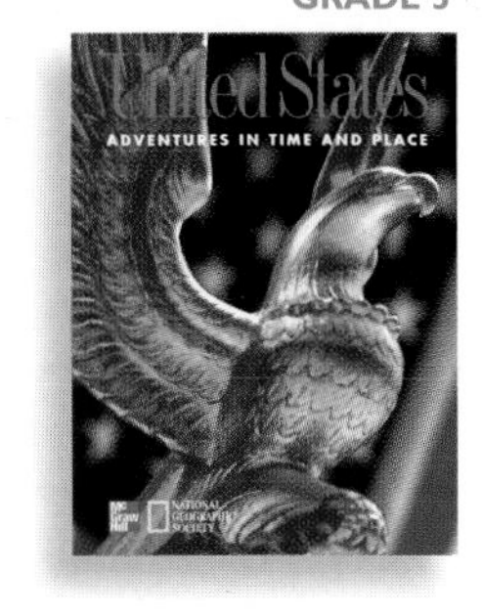

GRADE 6/7

GEOGRAPHY-LITERATE EXPLORERS

Place

GRADE 6/7

& HISTORY-SMART ADVENTURERS

GRADE 6/7

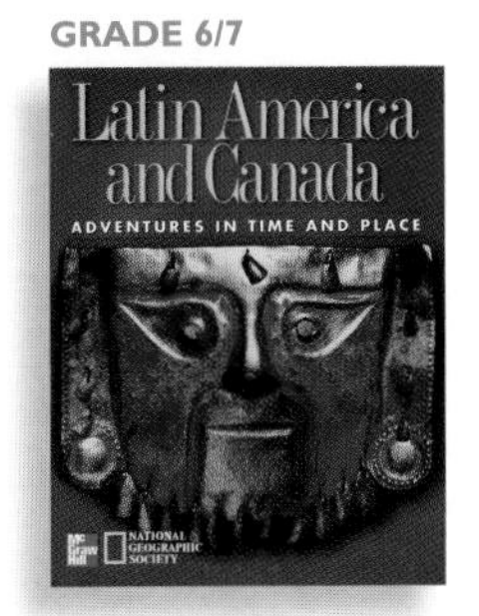

McGRAW-HILL

McGraw-Hill invites you to experience the

Adventures in

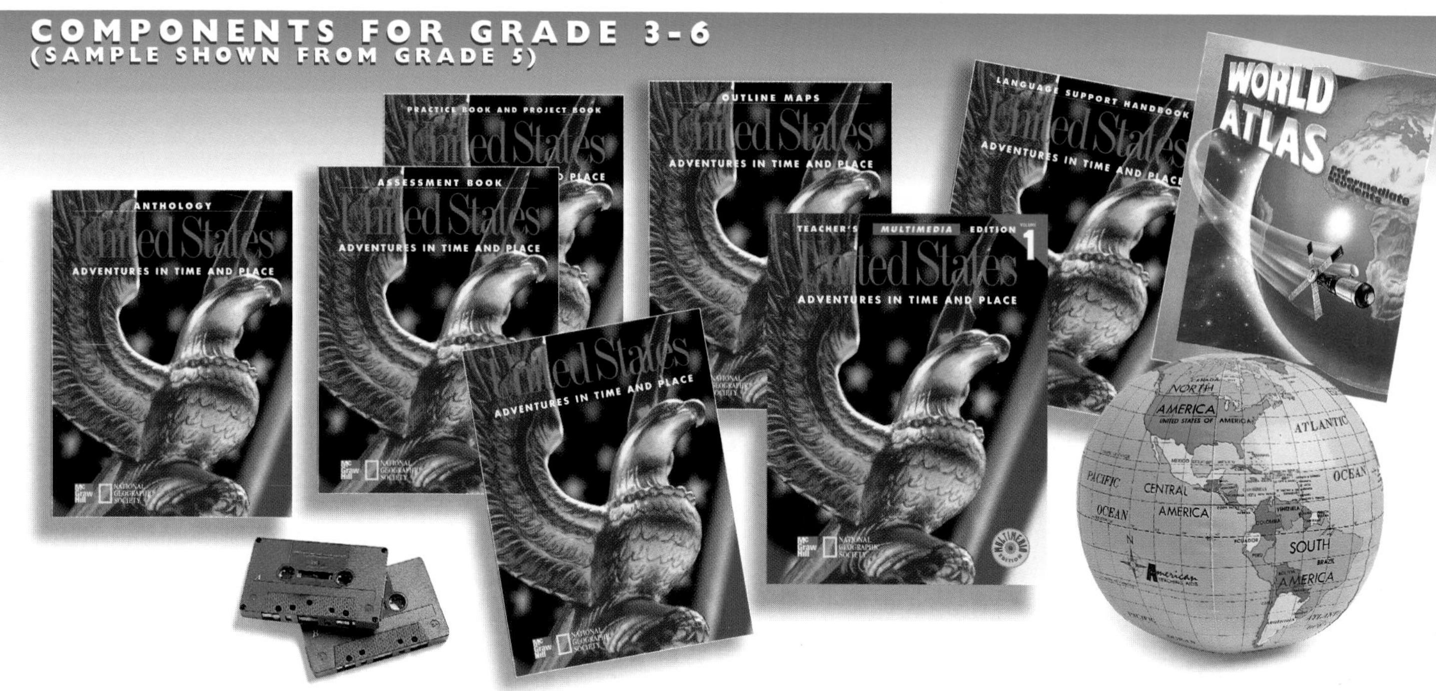

Choices in easy-to-use materials

GRADES K–2

You have these options to choose from:

- Teach with Big Books (K–2)
- Teach with Pupil Edition (1–2)
- Teach with a combination (1–2)

Use the same manageable Teacher's Edition for all three options. Choose the activities that meet your needs, in your setting, to fit your classroom style!

6 theme big books for group instruction

A Teacher's Multimedia Edition to support your approach

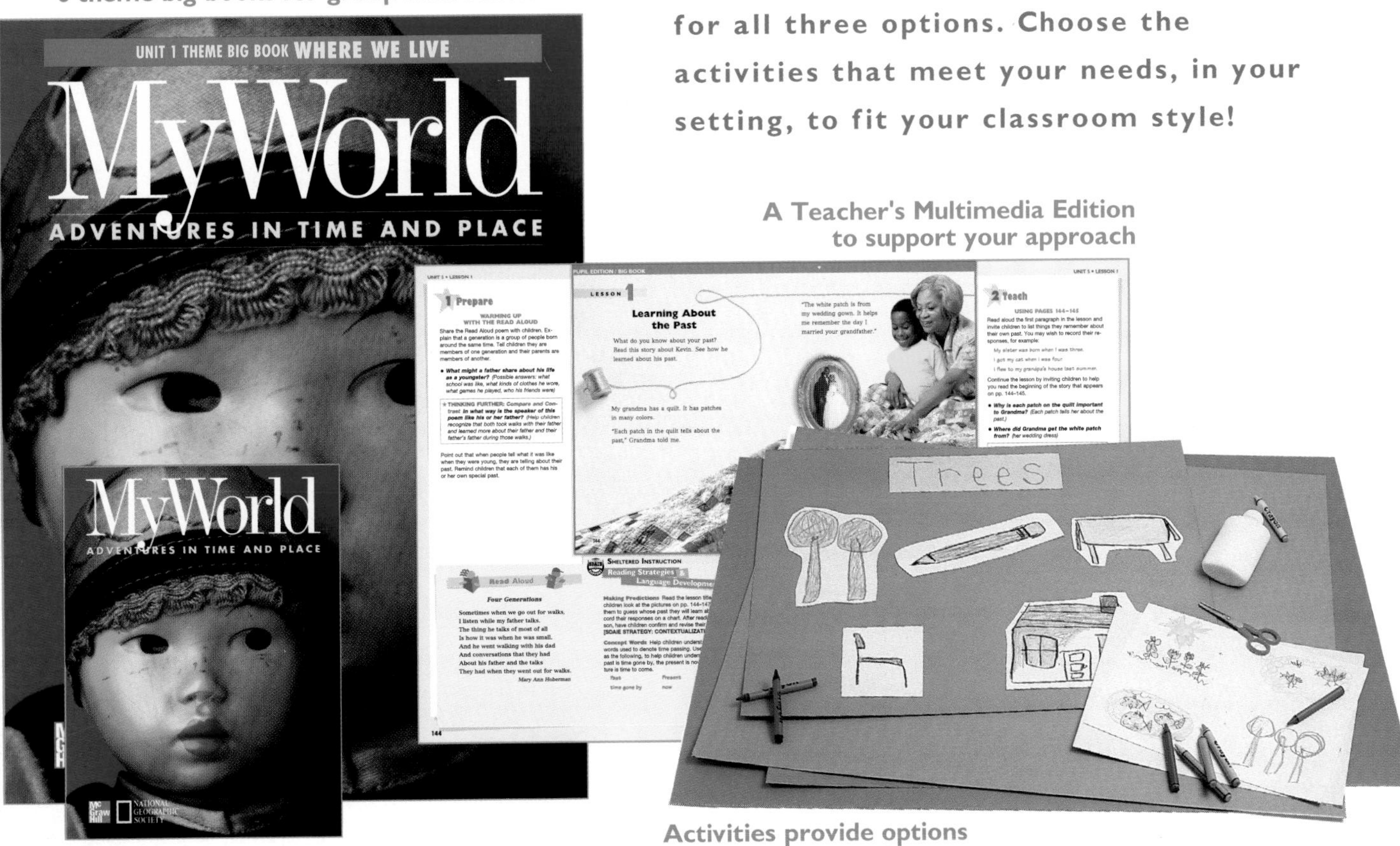

A Pupil Edition for individual teaching

Activities provide options for hands-on learning

Choices help you meet your needs and reach your goals

AT EVERY GRADE

The rich content is supported by hands-on activites and brought to life through motivating primary sources and diverse perspectives. Your teaching is supported with a 3-Step Lesson Plan — 1 PREPARE, 2 TEACH, 3 CLOSE — that's easy to use and easy to manage.

Program Philosophy

Each and every one of the educators, authors, editors, and designers who created McGraw-Hill's Adventures in Time and Place share a deep commitment to provide

- **rich, relevant content** in all areas of social studies at every grade level
- **geographic literacy skills** for all students, created in partnership with the National Geographic Society
- **easy-to-use teaching materials** with choices to accommodate diverse student learning styles and support various teaching styles

Program Authorship

National Geographic Society, the world's premier authority on

NATIONAL GEOGRAPHIC SOCIETY

geography and geography education, joins the same team that created the best-selling McGraw-Hill Social Studies Program THE WORLD AROUND US to bring you a brand new program...

Adventures in Time and Place.

DR. BARRY BEYER
George Mason University
Fairfax, VA

DR. JAMES BANKS
University of Washington
Seattle, WA

JEAN CRAVEN
Albuquerque Public Schools
Albuquerque, NM

DR. GLORIA CONTRERAS
University of North Texas
Denton, TX

DR. MARY MCFARLAND
Parkway Public Schools
Creve Coeur, MO

DR. WALTER PARKER
University of Washington
Seattle, WA

DR. GLORIA LADSON-BILLINGS
University of Wisconsin-Madison
Madison, WI

Designed for teacher-friendly classroom management

COMPONENTS CHART

	K HERE I AM	1 MY WORLD	2 PEOPLE TOGETHER	3 COMMUNITIES	4 REGIONS	5 UNITED STATES	4/5 A YOUNG NATION	5/6 A NATION GROWS	6/7 WORLD	6/7 LATIN AMERICA AND CANADA	6/7 WORLD REGIONS
PUPIL EDITION		✔	✔	✔	✔	✔	✔	✔	✔	✔	✔
PUPIL EDITION ON CASSETTE		✔	✔	✔	✔	✔	✔	✔	✔	✔	✔
TEACHER'S MULTIMEDIA EDITION	✔	✔	✔	✔	✔	✔	✔	✔	✔	✔	✔
COLOR MAP TRANSPARENCIES		✔	✔	✔	✔	✔	✔	✔	✔	✔	✔
GRAPHIC ORGANIZERS				✔	✔	✔	✔	✔	✔	✔	✔
THEME BIG BOOKS	✔	✔	✔								
STICKERS FOR THEME BIG BOOKS	✔	✔	✔								
LITERATURE BIG BOOKS	✔	✔	✔	✔							
GEO BIG BOOK	✔	✔	✔	✔							
VOCABULARY/WORD CARDS	✔	✔	✔	✔							
PRACTICE BOOK		✔	✔	✔	✔	✔	✔	✔	✔	✔	✔
PROJECT BOOK	✔	✔	✔	✔							
GEOADVENTURES/ DAILY GEOGRAPHY ACTIVITIES		✔	✔	✔	✔	✔	✔	✔	✔	✔	✔
FLOOR MAP	✔	✔	✔	✔							
DESK MAPS	✔	✔	✔	✔	✔	✔	✔	✔	✔	✔	✔
OUTLINE MAPS		✔	✔	✔	✔	✔	✔	✔	✔	✔	✔
INFLATABLE GLOBE	✔	✔	✔	✔	✔	✔	✔	✔	✔	✔	✔
STUDENT ATLAS	✔	✔	✔	✔	✔	✔	✔	✔	✔	✔	✔
SOCIAL STUDIES ANTHOLOGY	✔	✔	✔	✔	✔	✔	✔	✔	✔	✔	✔
ANTHOLOGY CASSETTE	✔	✔	✔	✔	✔	✔	✔	✔	✔	✔	✔
CLASSROOM LIBRARY TRADE BOOKS	✔	✔	✔	✔	✔	✔	✔	✔	✔		
CLASSROOM LIBRARY TEACHER'S GUIDE	✔	✔	✔	✔	✔	✔	✔	✔	✔		
ADVENTURE BOOKS	✔	✔	✔	✔	✔	✔			✔	✔	✔
LANGUAGE SUPPORT HANDBOOK	✔	✔	✔	✔	✔	✔			✔		
POSTERS	✔	✔	✔	✔	✔	✔	✔	✔	✔		✔
UNIT TESTS		✔	✔	✔	✔	✔	✔	✔	✔	✔	✔
CHAPTER TESTS				✔	✔	✔	✔	✔	✔	✔	✔
PERFORMANCE ASSESSMENT	✔	✔	✔	✔	✔	✔	✔	✔	✔	✔	✔
VIDEODISCS	✔	✔	✔	✔	✔	✔	✔	✔	✔		✔
VIDEOTAPES	✔	✔	✔	✔	✔	✔	✔	✔	✔		✔
CD-ROM				✔	✔	✔	✔	✔	✔	✔	✔
INTERNET PROJECTS		✔	✔	✔	✔	✔	✔	✔	✔	✔	✔

Adventures in Time and Place...

COME ALONG AND BRING YOUR STUDENTS TO JOIN IN ON THE ADVENTURE!

excitement of their new Social Studies Program

Time and Place

Choices for assessment and accountability

Adventures in Time and Place provides a variety of methods to check both students' recall of factual information and their application of that knowledge. It's your choice:

- **Standardized Test Format**
- **Written Response Format**
- **Performance Assessments with Scoring Rubrics**

There's a way to get an accurate assessment — a real grade — for every child, whichever approach you use for evaluation.

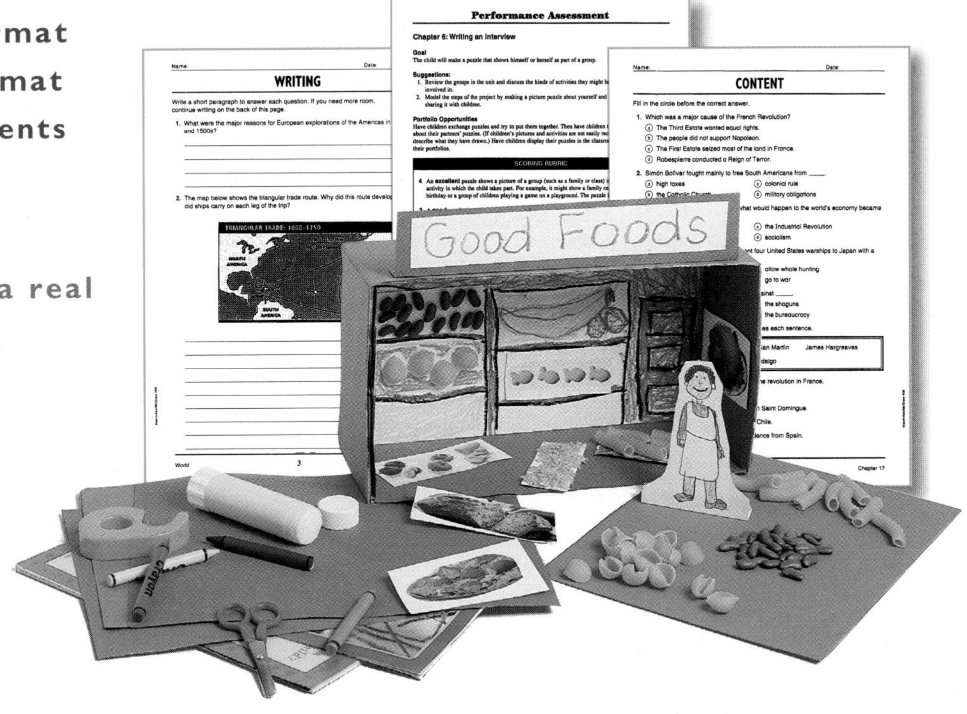

Choices in technology support

Multimedia technology options, correlated directly to the program, are easy extensions at your fingertips. You have the widest variety of choices available to meet your needs.

• Videodiscs • CD-ROM • Videotapes

Barcoded lessons on videodisc make enriching your teaching a breeze. These same lessons are also available on videotape to add to your flexibility. And best of all, it's all at point-of-use in your Teacher's Edition.

CD-ROM technology adds sight-and-sound power through an enhanced atlas and searchable database. The correlation to the program's lessons and activities makes this a useful research tool for all students.

National Geographic Technology is now available through McGraw-Hill to support your teaching. Direct correlations of these resources in Adventures in Time and Place ensure that you have the options to support all your students' needs and your teaching style.

Adventures in Rich, Relevant Content

1 History lessons link past and present in ways that make sense for all students — at all grade levels.

- More solid content at grades 1 and 2, with a narrative style that puts the "story" back in history, and lets you teach real history at primary grade levels.
- "Many Voices" from meaningful primary sources and literature are integrated in text features to bring history alive in words and pictures.
- Historical figures of many backgrounds, both famous and ordinary, provide reflections on our past from diverse perspectives.

FROM GRADE 3 PUPIL EDITION

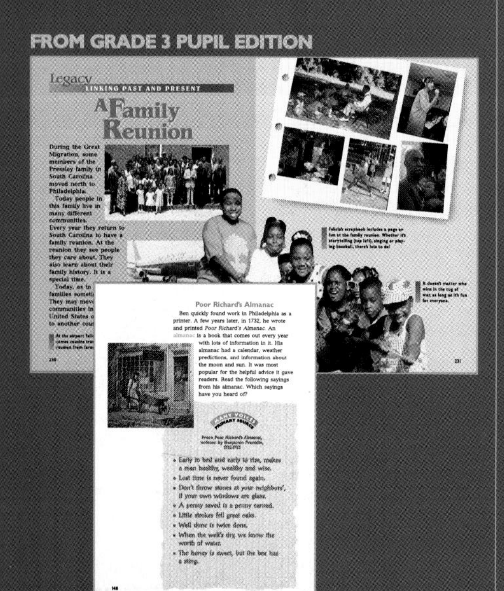

2 Geographic Literacy for all students is assured through the co-authorship of the National Geographic Society.

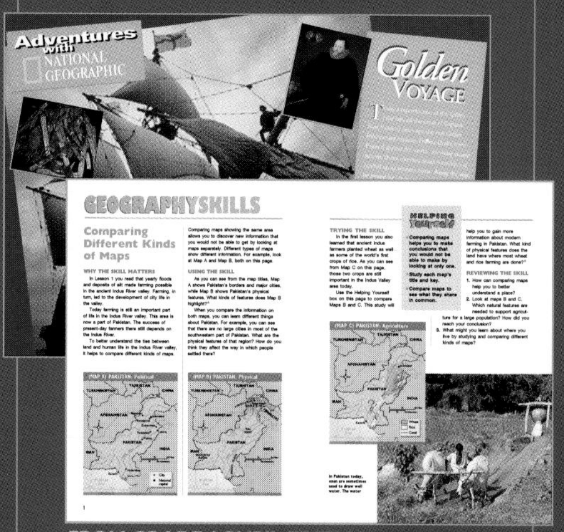

FROM GRADE 6 PUPIL EDITION

- Geography's impact on history is emphasized to teach students the connection between them.
- Geography's five fundamental themes are the focus of skill lessons and features that support the ties among past and present people, places, and events.
- Map skills are developed systematically for use in real life situations and for standardized test-taking.

3 Active Citizenship is taught through skill lessons, interactive activities and concrete examples.

- Citizenship and Thinking Skills lessons help form the ideas and thought processes needed by citizens of the 21st century.
- "Making a Difference" introduces everyday people who practice good citizenship in their communities.

CITIZENSHIP MAKING A DIFFERENCE
Bringing Back the Prairie

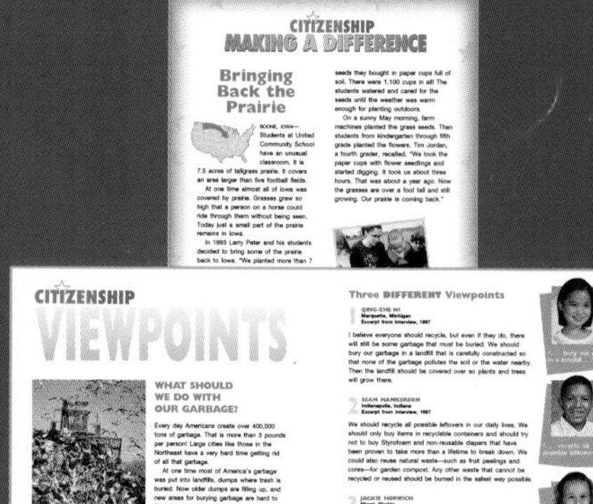

FROM GRADE 4 PUPIL EDITION

- "Viewpoints" in grades 3–6 allow students to discover and appreciate many different points of view — and to learn to handle differences.

TABLE OF CONTENTS FOR TEACHER INTRODUCTION

Here I Am

ADVENTURES IN TIME AND PLACE

Program Authors and Historians/Scholars for Adventures in Time and Place

PROGRAM AUTHORS

Dr. James A. Banks
Professor of Education and Director of the Center for Multicultural Education
University of Washington
Seattle, Washington
Related Publications: *An Introduction to Multicultural Education,* Allyn & Bacon, ©1994; *Multiethnic Education: Theory and Practice,* Allyn & Bacon, © 1981
Honors: Teachers of English to Speakers of Other Languages, Inc. 1998 Presidents' Award; National Association of Multicultural Education for the Handbook of Research on Multicultural Education

Dr. Barry K. Beyer
Professor Emeritus,
Graduate School of Education
George Mason University
Fairfax, Virginia
Related Publications: *Hints for Improving the Teaching Thinking in Our Schools: A Baker's Dozen* (Montclair State College: Institute for Critical Thinking) Resource Publication, Series 1#4, 1988; *Using Inquiry in the Social Studies Guidelines for Teaching,* Cooperative Center for Social Science Education, Ohio University, 1968; Guest editor, "Critical Thinking Revisited," Social Education, April 1985; Co-editor, Values of the American Heritage, 46th (Bicentennial) Yearbook of the National Council for the Social Studies, 1976

Dr. Gloria Contreras
Professor of Education
University of North Texas
Denton, Texas
Related Publications: Editor, *Latin American Culture Studies Handbook* Austin, Texas: The University of Texas Institute for Latin American Studies, 1988
Awards: University of North Texas Student Association Honor Professor Award, 1997; "Professing Women" Award, UNT Women's Studies Roundtable, 1996

Jean Craven
District Coordinator of Curriculum Development
Albuquerque Public Schools
Albuquerque, New Mexico
Related Publications: *Teacher's Manual for Government in the United States,* Macmillan Publishing, ©1984
Advisory Boards: Editorial Review Board, The Social Studies, 1994-1997; National Commission on Social Studies in the Schools, 1989-1990

Dr. Gloria Ladson-Billings
Professor of Education
University of Wisconsin
Madison, Wisconsin
Related Publications: *Dictionary of Multicultural Education,* Oryz Press, 1997; *The Dreamkeepers: Successful Teachers of African American Children,* Jossey Bass, 1994
Awards: Mary Ann Raywid Award for Distinguished Scholarship in Education, Society of Professors of Education, American Educational Research Association, 1997; Outstanding Educator Award Research Focus in Black Education, 1996

Dr. Mary A. McFarland
Instructional Coordinator of Social Studies, K-12, and Director of Staff Development
Parkway School District
Chesterfield, Missouri
Grants: Author of Block Grant Project in Social Studies, 1990; Director of Missouri Committee for the Humanities Project, 1985

Dr. Walter C. Parker
Professor and Program Chair for Social Studies Education
University of Washington
Seattle, Washington
Related Publications: *Social Studies in Elementary Education,* 10th ed. Merill/Prentice-Hall, 1997; editor, *Educating the Democratic Mind,* SUNY Press, 1996; *Renewing the Social Studies Curriculum;* Association for Supervision and Curriculum Development, 1991

NATIONAL GEOGRAPHIC SOCIETY
Washington, D.C.

HISTORIANS/SCHOLARS

Dr. John Bodnar
Professor of History
Indiana University
Bloomington, Indiana
Related Publications: *Remaking America: Public Memory, Commemoration, and Patriotism in the Twentieth Century,* (Pulitzer Prize Nominee) Princeton University Press, 1992
Awards: Teaching Excellence Award, Indiana University, 1997; Florence Chair in American History, Florence, Italy (selected by the Fulbright Commission)

Dr. Sheilah Clarke-Ekong
Professor, Department of Anthropology
University of Missouri, St. Louis
St. Louis, Missouri
Related Publications: "Ghana's Festivals: Celebrations of Life and Loyalty" *Journal of African Activist Association,* Vol. 23, 1997; "Traditional Festivals in the Political Economy," *Journal of Social Development in Africa*

Dr. Carlos E. Cortés
Professor Emeritus of History
University of California
Riverside, California
Related Publications: co-author: Beyond Language: *Social and Cultural Factors in Schooling Language Minority Students;* three-book series: *The Mexican American, The Chicano Heritage, and Hispanics in the United States;* books-in-progress: *The Mass Media and Multicultural Education; A History of Multicultural 21st Century America*
Awards: Hilda Taba Award of the California Council for the Social Studies, 1995; Smithsonian Institution Public Lecturer, 1994
Grants: Fulbright Travel Grant to Yugoslavia, 1980

Council on Islamic Education
Fountain Valley, California
Related Publications: *Muslim Holidays; Muslim Women Through the Centuries; The Crusades from Medieval European and Muslim Perspectives; Images of the Orient: 19th-century European Travelers to Muslim*

Lands; Beyond A Thousand and One Nights, A Sampler of Literature from Muslim Civilization; The Emergence of the Renaissance: Cultural Interactions Between Europeans and Muslims

Dr. John L. Esposito
Professor of Religion and International Affairs
Georgetown University
Washington, D.C.
Related Publications: *The Islamic Threat: Myth or Reality,* Oxford University Press, 1992; Editor-in-Chief, *Encyclopedia of the Modern Islamic World,* 4 vols., Oxford University Press, 1995; *Islam: The Straight Path,* Oxford University Press, 1988

Dr. Darlene Clark Hine
John A. Hannah Professor of History
Michigan State University
East Lansing, Michigan
Related Publications: *A Shining Thread of Hope: The History of Black Women in America,* Broadway Books, 1998; *Speak Truth to Power: Black Professional Class in United States History,* Carlson Publishing, Inc. 1995
Awards: Doctor of Humane Letters, University of Massachusetts, 1998; Avery Citizenship Award, Avery Research Center, College of Charleston, 1997

Dr. Gary Manson
Department of Geography
Michigan State University
East Lansing, Michigan
Related Publications: *New Perspectives on Geographic Education: Putting Theory Into Practice,* Kendall-Hunt Publishing Company, 1977 (editor)
Grants: National Science Foundation, 1982

Dr. Juan Mora-Torrés
Professor of Latin American History
University of Texas at San Antonio
San Antonio, Texas
Related Publications: *The Making of the Mexican Border: The State, Capitalism and Society, Nuevo Leon,* 1848-1970 (in progress)

Honors: Visiting Scholar, University of Chicago, Center for Latin American Studies, 1999

Dr. Valerie Ooka Pang
Professor, School of Teacher Education
San Diego State University
San Diego, California
Related Publications: Editor, *Struggling To Be Heard: The Unmet Needs of Asian Pacific American Children,* 1998, State University of New York
Awards: Senior Fellow, Annenberg Institute for School Reform, Brown University 1998-2000; Distinguished Scholar Award, American Educational Research Association, 1997

Dr. Curtis Roseman
Professor of Geography
University of Southern California
Los Angeles, California
Related Publications: *Human Spatial Behavior, A Social Geography,* Duxbury Press, 1976; editor, *EthniCity, Geographic Perspectives on Ethnic Change in Modern Urban Areas,* Rowman & Littlefield, 1996
Awards: National Councillor, Association of American Geographers, 1998; National Science Foundation, Geography and Regional Science Review Panel, 1992-1994

Dr. Joseph Rosenbloom
Professor, Classics Department
Washington University
St. Louis, Missouri
Related Publications: *Conversion to Judaism: From the Biblical Period to the Present,* Hebrew Union College Press, 1978; *The Dead Sea Isaiah Scrolls: A Literary Analysis,* William B. Eerdsmans Publishing Company, 1970

Dr. Robert Seltzer
Professor of Jewish History
Hunter College
City University of New York
Related Publications: *Jewish People, Jewish Thought: The Jewish Experience in History,* Macmillan, 1980; editor, *Judaism: A People and its History,* Macmillan, 1989

Dr. Robert M. Senkewicz
Professor of History
Santa Clara University
Santa Clara, California
Related Publications: *Vigilantes in Gold Rush San Francisco,* Stanford University Press, 1985; editor & translator, *The History of Alta California: A Memoir of Mexican California,* University of Wisconsin Press, 1966

Dr. Peter Stearns
Dean, College of Humanities and Social Studies
Carnegie Mellon University
Pittsburgh, Pennsylvania
Related Publications: *The Industrial Revolution in World History,* Westview, 1998; *World History: Patterns of Change and Continuity,* HarperCollins, 1998
Awards: 1998 finalist History Book of the Year Award; Robert Doherty Educational Leadership Award, Carnegie Mellon, 1995

Dr. Clifford E. Trafzer
Professor of History
Department of Ethnic Studies and History
University of California, Riverside
Related Publications: *Blue Dawn, Red Earth,* Doubleday/Anchor Books, 1996; *Chief Joseph's Allies: The Palouse Indians and the Nez Perce War of 1877,* Sierra Oaks Publishers, 1992
Honors: Vice-Chair, California Native American Heritage Commission, 1992-98; Rockefeller Foundation National Endowment Research Fellowship, 1995

KINDERGARTEN SOCIAL STUDIES READINESS

THE PURPOSE OF THESE ACTIVITIES IS TO INTRODUCE YOUNG CHILDREN TO CONCEPTS THAT ARE BASIC TO UNDERSTANDING SOCIAL STUDIES. YOU MAY ALSO WISH TO USE THESE ACTIVITIES TO REINFORCE THE CORRESPONDING LESSONS IN THE UNIT THEME BIG BOOKS.

Learning about Alone and Together (Corresponds to Unit 1, Lesson 2, *Our Busy Classroom*, Unit 1 Theme Big Book, pp. 8—9; Teachers Edition, pp. 15—18)

Objective: To distinguish between doing things alone and doing things together. Be sure children understand that *alone* means by oneself, not with anyone else, and that *together* means with others. Introduce the concepts of *alone* and *together* by brainstorming with children things they have done alone (answers will vary: brush teeth, draw a picture, walk, sing a song) and things they have done together. (answers will vary: draw a picture with classmates, play ball, have dinner with family) Then distribute copies of *Alone and Together* worksheet, page C7. Tell children to look at the pictures. Familiarize them with the pictures by asking where they might take place. (at a camp; at a park) Point out the group of children playing basketball. Say that these children are playing *together.* Tell children to draw a circle around them. Point out the child playing basketball *alone*. Tell children to draw a line under him. Have children repeat the procedure of circling the pictures of people doing things together and underlining the pictures of people doing things alone with (a) the children eating together, and the child eating alone, and (b) the children playing the blindfold game together, and the child playing with a doll and doll clothes alone. You may wish to have children find examples in the classroom of things that are done alone and things that are done together.

Learning about Left and Right (Corresponds to Unit 1, Geography Skills, *Finding Where Things Are,* Unit 1 Theme Big Book, pp. 10—11; Teachers Edition, pp. 19—22.)

Objective: To determine left and right. Introduce the subject of left and right to children by asking them alternately to raise only their right hands, then only their left. Continue until they can do this quite easily. Then distribute copies of *Left and Right* worksheet, page C8. Make sure that the worksheet is positioned straight up and down in front of them. Tell children to look at the two identical flowers at the top of the paper. Have them decide which of the two flowers is on the *right* side of the paper. Tell them to draw leaves on this flower. Give children time to complete this step. Repeat this procedure with the remaining pictures—drawing whiskers on the cat located on the *left* side of the paper, drawing candles on the birthday cake located on the *right* side of the paper, and drawing a handle on the umbrella located on the *left* side of the paper.

Learning about Families (Corresponds to Unit 2, Lesson 1, *Our Special Families,* Unit 2 Theme Big Book, pp. 4—5; Teachers Edition, pp. 47—50)

Objective: To recognize that every family is unique. Invite children to share their ideas about *families* with you. Lead children to recognize that "family" means people who love and care for each other. Discuss with children that every family is different. For example, some members of a family may live together in the same house and some may live in other places. Then distribute copies of *Families* worksheet, page C9. Explain that Jan's family lives in the apartment house on the left side of the worksheet. Point out that Jan has a younger sister. Explain that Anna's family lives in the house on the right side of the worksheet. Point out that Anna's grandfather lives with her. Ask children which family has more pets. (Anna's) Ask which family lives in an apartment building. (Jan's) Ask children to draw a picture of another family in the space provided at the bottom of the worksheet.

Learning about Needs & Wants (Corresponds to Unit 2, Lesson 5, *Needs and Wants,* Unit 2 Theme Big Book, pp. 14—15; Teachers Edition, pp. 67—70)

Objective: To determine the difference between needs and wants. Explain to children that *needs* are things you must have in order to survive, like food, shelter, love and care; *wants* are things that would be nice to have, but are not necessary. Brainstorm with children on things that are needs and things that are wants. Write the words *needs* and *wants* on the chalkboard and help children to categorize examples that they call out. Distribute copies of *Needs and Wants* worksheet, page C10. Tell children to look at the two arrows that point at *needs.* Have children tell you why one arrow is pointing at the child getting hugged (we need love and caring to live) and why the other arrow points to a house. (we need a place to live) Ask children to pick out the other two pictures of *needs.* (a healthy plate of food—we need food to live; shirt and pants—we need clothing to live) Tell them to draw an arrow pointing from the child to each of these two needs. Discuss with children why the television, ice cream cone, toy car, and basketball are wants rather than needs. (they are nice to have, but not necessary)

Learning about Alike & Different (Corresponds to Unit 2, Thinking Skills, *Finding Alike and Different,* Unit 2 Theme Big Book, pp. 16—17; Teachers Edition, pp. 71—74)

Objective: To identify things that are alike and things that are different. Explain to children that things that are *alike* are the same in some way, and things that are *different* are not the same in some way. Have them look around the classroom and point out two things that are *alike* and tell you why. (accept all answers that support the concept— it could be two objects that are both the same color or two windows that are shaped alike, etc.) Next have them look around the classroom and point out two things that are different and tell you why they are different. Distribute copies of *Alike and Different* worksheet, page C11. Tell children to look at the first picture on the lesson page. Ask them why they think the three animals are circled together and one is left out. (accept all answers that support the concept of alike and different; the three animals are dogs and the one left out is a turtle—three are alike and one is different) Next ask children to look at the middle picture. Ask them which three are alike and which one is different. (accept all answers that support the concept of alike and different; three flowers are alike and the car is different) Tell them to draw one circle around the three flowers and another circle around the car. Now have children look at the last picture. Ask them which three are alike and which one is different. (accept all answers that support the concept of alike and different; the three children are young and the man is old) Tell them to draw a circle around the three that are most alike and draw a circle around the one that is most different.

Learning about the Four Seasons (Corresponds to Unit 3, Lesson 1, *The Seasons Around Us,* Unit 3 Theme Big Book, pp. 4—5; Teachers Edition, pp. 87—90)

Objective: To distinguish between the four different seasons as traditionally depicted. Introduce children to the *four seasons* by telling them that one year is divided into four different periods— summer, fall, winter, and spring. You may wish to explain that the seasons follow one another each year in the same order. Write the four seasons left to right across the chalkboard and ask the following questions: Which season is the coldest? Which season is the warmest? Then for each season, ask children what kind of things happen, and what kind of things they do in each of the four seasons. List any answers under the correct season. For children in year-round warm climates it may be necessary to explain which parts of the U.S. have these seasonal changes. Distribute copies of *Four Seasons* worksheet, page C12. Ask children to look at each numbered picture. Discuss each picture by pointing out one of them and asking the following questions: How are the children dressed? What are they doing? This season is called __________. Ask them to color the picture of that season.

Learning about the Map of the United States of America (Corresponds to Unit 4, Lesson 1, *This is Our Country,* Unit 4 Theme Big Book, pp. 4—5; Teachers Edition, pp. 127—130)

Objective: To examine the map of the United States of America. Introduce the children to the 50 states by asking them the question: Where do we live? Starting with living at home, guide them through the hierarchy of home all the way up to country to recognize that they live in the United States. Do this by helping them to locate themselves as living in: a home; home is in a neighborhood; neighborhood is in a community; community is in a town or city; town or city is in a state; state is one of the 50 states that all together make up our country, which is called the United States of America. Ask children if they can name any of the states. Then distribute copies of *Map of the United States of America* worksheet, page C13. Tell children that there are 50 States on the map. Point out the state in which the children live. Have them circle the name of their state on the map. Point out that Alaska and Hawaii are states, but they are not connected to the other 48 states. Tell them that the state of Washington is known for tall trees. Have children find the tall trees on the map and color the state of Washington green. Explain that Florida is known for growing oranges. Have children find the oranges on the map and color Florida orange. Tell them that Kansas is known for growing wheat. Have them locate the wheat and color Kansas yellow. You may wish to explain to children that wheat is a kind of grass. The seeds from wheat are used to make flour for bread and for other foods like cereal.

Learning about Earth (Corresponds to Unit 4, Lesson 3, *Looking at Land and Water,* Unit 4 Theme Big Book, pp. 10—11; Teachers Edition, pp. 139—142)

Objective: Determine that Earth is round and is made of water and land. Discuss with children that Earth is the planet on which we live. Explain that it is round, shaped like a ball, and is made of water and land. Distribute copies of Earth worksheet, page C14. Help children identify the area which is water and color the water blue. Remind children that the rest of Earth is made of land. Have children color the land brown. Children may wish to draw fish in the water, and trees or mountains on the land. To reinforce their understanding that Earth is shaped like a ball, show children a globe of the Earth.

Learning about Months, Weeks, and Days (Corresponds to Unit 5, Study Skills, *Looking at Calendars,* Unit 5 Theme Big Book, pp. 8—9; Teachers Edition, pp. 171—174)

Objective: To recognize months, weeks, and days of the year. Introduce calendars to children, showing them that there are 12 months in a year, by holding up a real calendar and turning the pages, displaying each of the 12 months, asking children to count them aloud with you. Explain to children that each of the 12 months has its own name. Open the calendar again to show them just the month of November before distributing copies of *Months, Weeks, and Days* worksheet, page C15. Explain that they now have their own page of the month of November. Ask children to find the word "November" at the top of the page. Let children color the name "November." Have children run their fingers across a row of seven blocks. Tell them that each square represents one day, and that seven days make up one week. Have them color the whole row of seven squares the color yellow. Remind them that the seven yellow squares all together make up one week. Explain that each day has its own name. Recite aloud the days of the week with children. Choose a new row and have children point to each square, left to right, calling out the name of each day. Then have them color each square (day) a different color, according to your instructions ("Color Sunday blue . . . now color Monday red . . . " etc.) Ask children if they can guess why there is a turkey in one of the squares (it is Thanksgiving Day.)

Alone and Together

Name: ______________________ Date: ______________

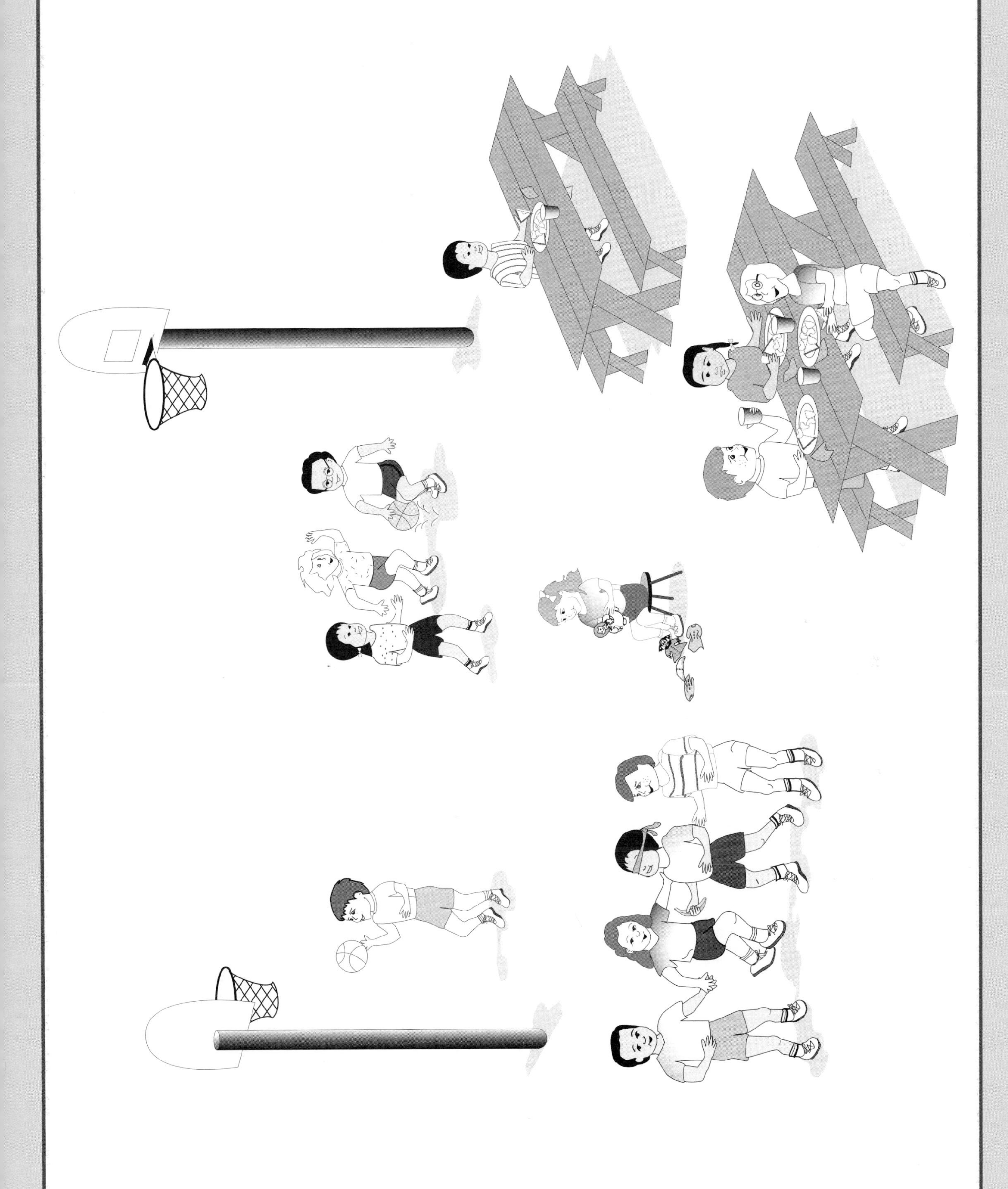

Left and Right

Name: ______________________ Date: __________

Families

Name: ______________________ Date: ______________

Needs and Wants

Name: ______________________________ Date: ______________

Alike and Different

Name: ______________________ Date: ______________

Four Seasons

Name: ______________________________ Date: ______________

1.

2.

3.

4.

Map of the United States of America

Name: ______________________________ Date: ______________

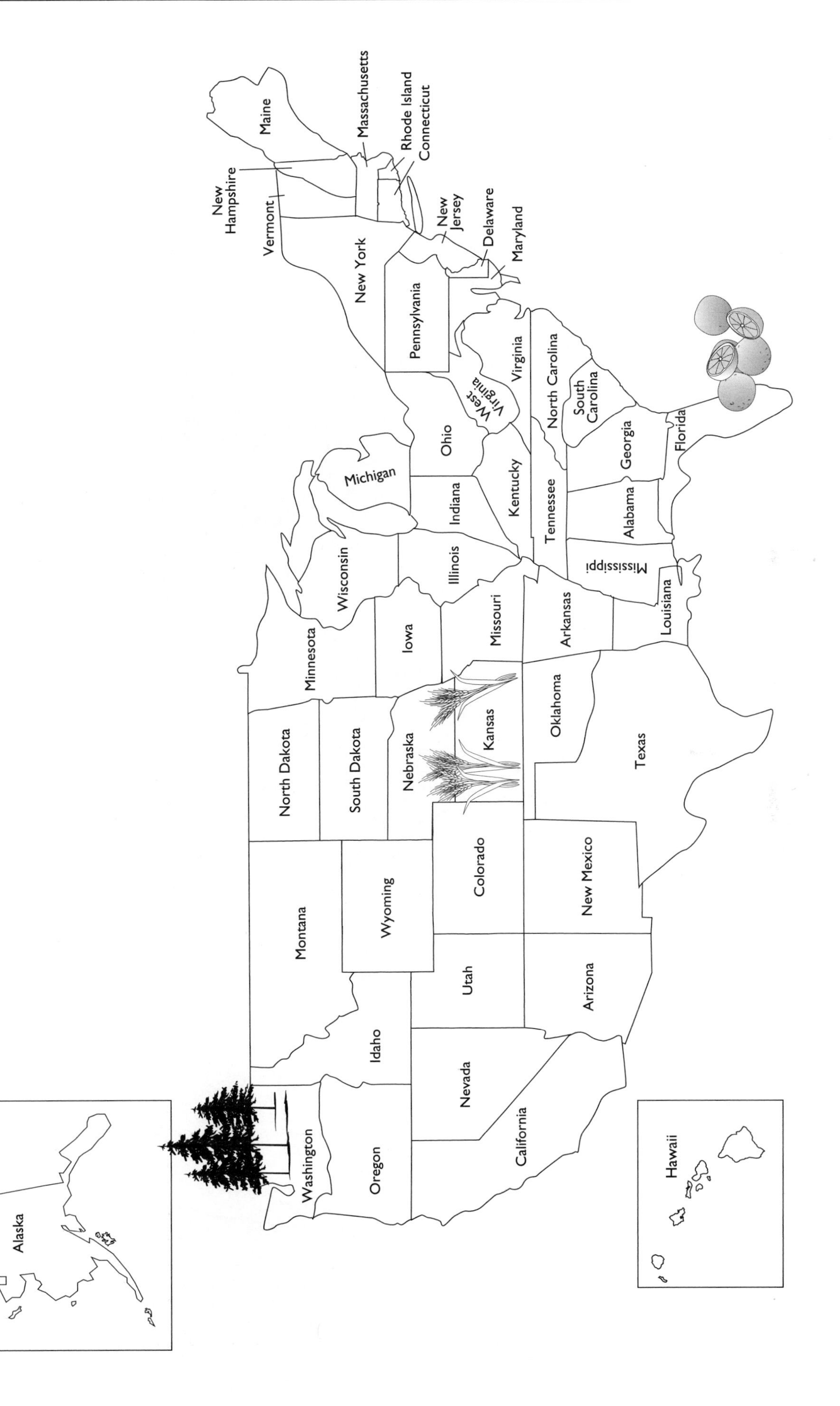

Earth

Name: ______________________________ Date: ______________

Name: ______________________ Date: ____________

November

SUNDAY	MONDAY	TUESDAY	WEDNESDAY	THURSDAY	FRIDAY	SATURDAY
	1	2	3	4	5	6
7	8	9	10	11	12	13
14	15	16	17	18	19	20
21	22	23	24	25 Thanksgiving	26	27
28	29	30				

Ensuring Success For All Learners

Facilitating a Child's Learning and Understanding of English

by Janice Wu

Student Achievement Specialist, Sacramento City Unified School District

Today, nearly one of every five students in the United States entering school (2.5-3.5 million children per year) knows a language other than English. Nearly half of these students are limited in English-language proficiency. According to demographers, in the near future, language-minority students and those acquiring a second language will compose an even larger proportion of our school-age population.

Many English Language Learners (ELL) come into the classroom with a wealth of prior knowledge and a strong oral language base. But some do not experience success in school. Many students who speak a language other than English face barriers that inhibit their learning. As a result, the role of the teacher as facilitator becomes one of nurturing and building upon what a child already knows.

In accessing the curriculum in ***Adventures in Time and Place/Aventuras a través del tiempo***, you need to be skillful in utilizing the text to meet the needs of every individual learner. The instruction you provide your students will facilitate the understanding of the curriculum for English Language Learners. As you structure an environment that builds on students' strengths and English language learning, you will make learning a rewarding and meaningful experience for all your students. The information provided below will help you utilize the many resources available in ***Adventures in Time and Place/Aventuras a través del tiempo*** so that you can effectively meet the needs of every individual learner.

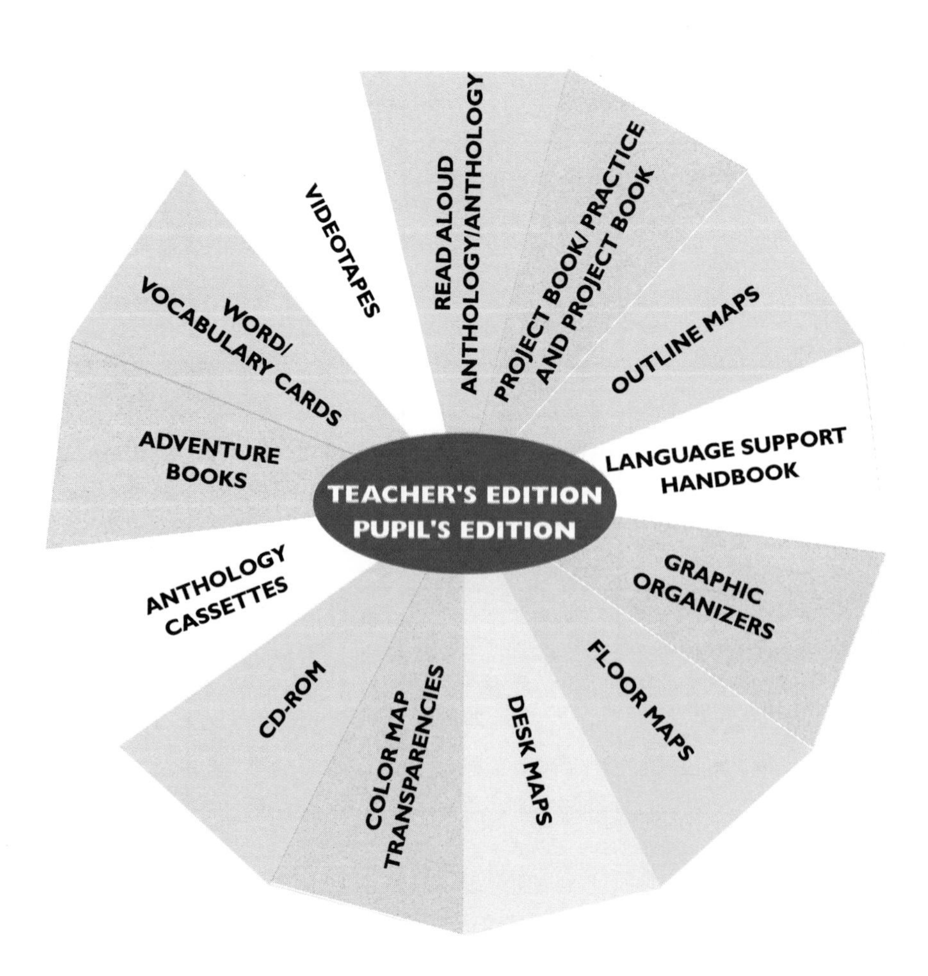

I TEACHER'S EDITION

The ***Adventures in Time and Place/Aventuras a través del tiempo*** Teacher's Edition provides a variety of features that complement content lessons by offering teacher support and strategies for English Language Learners. These features include:

- **Specially Designed Academic Instruction in English (SDAIE)/Sheltered Instruction** is presented to you to help engage students in active learning. The focus of SDAIE is to provide curriculum content for all students—especially, but not only, those challenged by less than proficient English skills.
- **Second Language Support** offers strategies to help you customize instruction for the English Language Learner. These strategies are designed to help you contextualize the lessons to make them more understandable and meaningful to students who are acquiring English and to help you present lesson content while providing linguistic and conceptual support.
- **Meeting Individual Needs** allows you to re-teach, extend, and enrich the instruction for every child. Scaffolding the instruction for English Language Learners in this manner will foster positive and successful learning experiences in Social Studies.
- **Reading Strategies and Language Development** provides you with teaching suggestions aimed at understanding and clarifying concepts and vocabulary that could be confusing to the English Language Learner.
- **Extending the Lesson Activities** in Grades 1–2 and **Getting Ready for the Chapter** in Grades 3-6 provide activities in a variety of learning styles, such as auditory, kinesthetic, and visual, to satisfy the learning needs of students who are talented in art, language, and physical activity and who may better understand history/social science concepts connected to their own areas of interest.
- **Visual Literacy** is the integration of text with visuals. This integration is especially helpful to the English Language Learner. The Teacher's Edition offers strategies that provide you with opportunities for the teaching of important history/social science concepts by utilizing photographs, artwork, and maps in ***Adventures in Time and Place/Aventuras a través del tiempo.***
- **Ongoing Unit Projects** set the stage for all learners by inviting them to participate in a cooperative setting that encourages language development in a natural environment. These projects also engage English Language Learners in high interest, hands-on experiences.

II ADVENTURES IN TIME AND PLACE/AVENTURAS A TRAVÉS DEL TIEMPO COMPONENTS

In addition to the ***Adventures in Time and Place/ Aventuras a través del tiempo*** Teacher's Edition features mentioned above, there are a variety of supplementary program components that provide teacher support and strategies for English Language Learners. A description of these resources, in addition to suggested ELL classroom activities, is listed below:

• ADVENTURE BOOKS (Grades K-6)

Description: Adventure Books are supplementary "easy readers" that provide additional literacy experiences tailored to specific students' needs and interests. The range and simplicity of the stories allows for independent reading related to the Social Studies content. Students will read about special people, places, and events that reflect many people and cultures around the world.

ELL Strategy: Building Comprehension Skills

To encourage independent reading, set up a student reading center with the Adventure Books. Allow English Language Learners to select from the various stories and report on their favorite readers by making posters or charts with illustrations. Students at different levels of language proficiency in English can label and/or write brief descriptions retelling the story.

• ANTHOLOGY CASSETTES (Grades K-6)

Description: Students will be exposed to a variety of literature selections, songs, and poems that are read in an engaging and entertaining style.

ELL Strategy: Facilitate Listening Comprehension in English

Listening to songs and poetry read by others is a powerful way to provide models of fluent and dramatic reading. Set up a "Listening Post" or "Listening Center" for a small group of students. Model the use of the listening area with your class and assign a student monitor who will be in charge of rotating the cassettes as needed.

• CD-ROM (Grades 3-6)

Description: *The Adventure Time!* CD-ROM enables students to travel the world, meet people, and explore places. Students can experience historical events through photographs, maps, movies, charts, and climographs. The *Adventure Time!* CD-ROM program makes geography fun, puts history in context, and motivates children to learn map and globe skills.

ELL Strategy: Paired Reading

With a click of the computer mouse an English Language Learner can see, hear, and take world tours and experience environments from images on a CD-ROM. Pair an English Language Learner with an English-proficient learner and ask them to read the text in each frame together. Partners should take turns reading. At the end of each frame, the listener should relate back the main ideas of the text. Discussions can also include descriptions of sounds and visuals they are experiencing. Encourage students to work together to discuss these responses.

• COLOR MAP TRANSPARENCIES (Grades 1-6)

Description: Map transparencies support a student-centered map program and encourages active, hands-on geography practice. These maps are from Reviewing Geography Skills lessons, Skills Lessons, and the Atlas in the Pupil's Edition.

ELL Strategy: Using Visuals

The use of visuals like map symbols provides important support in building comprehension and establishing the context-rich environment that fosters language acquisition. Using an overhead projector, have students identify the different map symbols on each Map Transparency. Then have them describe the symbols shown on each map.

• DESK MAPS (GRADES 1-6)

Description: Students will gain a greater understanding of their community and the world around them by using Desk Maps of the United States and the world. These maps are useful in teaching map and globe skills in meaningful and concrete ways.

ELL Strategy: Building Geography Skills

Use of the Desk Maps will encourage students to develop their geography skills. Prompt students to work alone or in groups to use lesson content and other maps to search the text for illustrations and information to help them place details on the map, such as mountain ranges, deserts, oceans, etc. Encourage students to use as many details as possible. Pairing English Language Learners with partners that are fluent English speakers encourages mastery of the English language in a non-threatening environment.

• FLOOR MAPS (Grades K-3)

Description: Students can use a floor map as a base for building three-dimensional models of different types of communities or environments. Floor maps can help English Language Learners move from understanding simple, concrete materials to understanding more difficult and abstract concepts.

ELL Strategy: Using Manipulative Materials

Divide students into groups of four to six students. To encourage rich dialogue include students of different levels of English proficiency in each group. Have each group create simple three-dimensional buildings, cars, people, etc. to place on the floor maps in order to create a community. Students should describe the objects that they have created and discuss where they should be placed on the floor map. Encourage students to use geography and map-related terms and concepts to describe their community.

• GRAPHIC ORGANIZERS (Grades 3-6)

Description: Graphic Organizers provide visual tools to help English Language Learners organize the relationships between and among words, concepts, ideas, and events.

ELL Strategy: Organizing Information Using a Visual Tool

Have students organize information about the natural resources of their community. Encourage them to list on the chart some of the resources they have learned about and whether they are renewable or nonrenewable. Have students display and discuss their completed charts in class.

• LANGUAGE SUPPORT HANDBOOK (Grades K-6)

Description: In working with the English Language Learner it is important to recognize that each child enters the classroom with different levels of oral language proficiency. This means that the production of language may be receptive (absorbing the language but not producing verbally) or productive (verbally producing some English words or phrases). To help you have a better understanding of the various stages of second language acquisition, the Language Support Handbook lists the stages of language production with student behaviors and effective teaching strategies.

ELL Strategy: Shared Reading

It is important for English Language Learners to hear English read by a fluent English speaker. A useful strategy is to read aloud while students are able to read and follow along silently with their own text copies. Ask students to take notes as important concepts are discussed. They can then work with others to write a brief summary of the most important information they have learned.

• OUTLINE MAPS (GRADES 1-6)

Description: Outline Maps offer students the opportunity to improve their basic map skills, such as understanding hemispheres, using cardinal and intermediate directions, and identifying map keys and symbols.

ELL Strategy: Understanding Personal Perspectives

Have students use Outline Maps to locate their community in relation to their state and country. Then have them use the World Map to locate their community in relation to the country that they, or their parents or friends, may have come from. By understanding different geographic perspectives, English Language Learners can gain understanding and confidence in learning about different cultures and places.

• PROJECT BOOK (Grades K-3) PRACTICE AND PROJECT BOOK (Grades 4-6)

Description: Your students will be actively involved in constructing a variety of projects related to the Social Studies content in their Pupil's Edition. These activities include tracing family ties, connecting their home to their communities, and understanding important dates and events relevant to them.

ELL Strategy: Facilitating Cooperative Learning and Interaction

Set aside an area in the classroom for a work station or center called "Our Projects." This work station should have ample working room for a group of four or five students to design and create projects listed in the Project Book. Projects can then be displayed in this area, as well as in other areas of the classroom. This activity encourages friendly dialogue and discussions among students and encourages positive language learning. Students of all language levels of proficiency will benefit.

• READ ALOUD ANTHOLOGY (Grades K-3) ANTHOLOGY (Grades 4-6)

Description: Anthologies are rich resources filled with literature, stories, songs, poems, folk-tales, and more. They are useful in supporting lesson content and themes taught in the Pupil's Edition.

ELL Strategy: Paired Reading

Pair each English Language Learner with a fluent English partner. Tell each pair to choose a character from an Anthology selection in whose voice they will speak or write. Ask them to search the text and illustrations for pertinent information, then have them introduce them-selves to their partners and talk about their experiences. Prompt them to expand their sto-ries by suggesting a series of basic questions to which they can respond: *What is your name? Where do you live? What has been happening around you? What do you think will happen next?*

• VIDEOTAPES (Grades K-6)

Description: Videotapes of rich and relevant content covering topics such as communities and geographic location are available at every grade level. These short video presentations provide the teacher and students with another means of "experiencing" events in history.

ELL Strategy: Previewing/Reviewing

A preview/review strategy will facilitate students' understanding of the curriculum. Identify significant concepts and vocabulary that will be used in the video and teach them to stu-dents. After watching the video, check student comprehension by asking questions related to the initial concepts and vocabulary presented during the preview lesson. This activity will help reinforce concepts, build vocabulary, and expand students' knowledge.

• WORD/VOCABULARY Cards (Grades K-3)

Description: Word/Vocabulary cards are used to help teach challenging vocabulary words or phrases that appear in the Social Studies Pupil's Edition. Each word or phrase appears on one side of a card. A definition of the word or phrase appears on the other side of the card.

ELL Strategy: Building Vocabulary Skills

Select five important words from the appropriate Pupil's Edition lessons that might be diffi-cult for the English Language Learner to comprehend. Write these words on the chalkboard. Then hand out five blank index cards to each student. Next, use gestures, props, illustrations, etc. to act out the meaning of the word for the students. Students should then write the word you are describing on their index cards. On the backs of the cards they should draw pictures or illustrations to help them remember the meaning of the word. Repeat this process for all five words. Students can learn the definitions of these words by using their index cards as flashcards.

III TIPS FOR CREATING AN EFFECTIVE LEARNING ENVIRONMENT FOR THE ENGLISH LANGUAGE LEARNER

School experiences are long-lasting and set the stage for future performance. By creating a positive, sensitive, and interactive learning environment, you can make a critical difference in preparing English Language Learners for the future. Remember that success for these students means more than acquiring good grades and high test scores. It also means having a positive image of themselves and confidence in their ability to embrace a second language and a new culture. Following is a list of useful tips for helping you create an effective learning environment for the English Language Learner.

- **Praise Students' Efforts Regularly**

  Accept the "half rights" and "yes" and "no" responses from your English Language Learners. A nod of the head in agreement or a simple "yes" response from you will let your students know that they are on the right track.

- **Accelerate Students' Learning**

  Maintaining high expectations for all English Language Learners will accelerate learning. Conveying the belief that all students have the ability and desire to succeed is your responsibility. Provide multiple opportunities for students to "take charge" and be responsible for the work that they produce.

- **Encourage Students To Preview Or "Picture Walk"**

  Students will be eager and excited to learn about the lesson when they are allowed to explore and select information (e.g. picture, caption, word or phrase) that piques their interest. Direct students to share their findings in English or their primary language with a partner or partners. Sampling a lesson in this manner will lower the student's affective filter and make for a more comfortable and positive experience.

- **Minimize Structural Error Correction**

  As students participate in class discussions, modeling appropriate structural responses can be done in a manner that does not directly bring attention to the error. For example, student states, "My country Central America. She country North America." Teacher may respond by modeling, "Yes, your country is in Central America," and "her [for "she"] country is in North America."

- **Allow For Appropriate "Wait Time"**

  English Language Learners need "wait time" to process the information being taught. Give students sufficient time for a response. Keep in mind that responses will vary depending on the students' levels of oral language proficiency. A simple facial expression, physical gesture or short phrase may serve as a response.

- **Use A Total Physical Response Approach**

  Use gestures and facial expressions (as dramatic as you need to be) to assist students in comprehending what is being conveyed. Allow students to respond in the same manner.

- **Practice The 3 R's Of Instruction**

  Revisit, Review, and Repeat the material being taught as much as possible in different ways. Approaching the instruction from a different perspective provides the student with another opportunity to acquire the content being taught. When Social Studies content is familiar it allows students to be freed up to attend to new and challenging content.

- **Speak Naturally**

  Students benefit greatly from having the teacher explain challenging content in clear and simplified speech. Clear enunciation and brief pauses assist the English Language Learner in hearing distinct pronunciation of vocabulary.

- **Summarize Content Taught Frequently**

  For English Language Learners it is important to summarize the content at point of use. Briefly stating in simple sentences the content after one, two, or three paragraphs is a strategy that benefits all students by allowing them to reflect on what they have just read and enables you to check for understanding.

- **Sheltered English Strategies**

  In order to make the content matter meaningful to students, it is important to provide many examples of the concepts being taught. Simplifying the language when presenting a concept is crucial, as is providing visuals (video clip, semantic web, or graphic organizer) to demonstrate the concept. For example, when teaching the concept of "community," rather than just defining the term, you might encourage students to draw, take photographs, or cut clippings from magazines or newspapers to construct a collage or mural of what they perceive as a community.

- **Allow Students to Speak Their Native Languages**

  Encourage students to communicate with their peers who are speakers of the same language. Allow students to write in their primary language and seek others who are literate in that language to translate and provide feedback. Provide primary language resources such as dictionaries, storybooks, videos, audiocassettes, and computer software. Having access to resources that they can read and use independently builds students' confidence in learning.

- **Word Walls to Build Vocabulary**

  A word wall is a designated wall in the classroom that displays a collection of words. Social Studies word walls provide a place to display important vocabulary words with illustrations to clarify definitions and concepts. The word wall can include important words from the curriculum as well as often-used words and/or commonly misspelled words that students can access and use when they write. Students should be encouraged to contribute to the "Social Studies Word Wall" whenever they feel that there are important words that they want clarified.

- **Provide Opportunities for Students to Work Together**

  English Language Learners benefit from working in cooperative learning groups. Working in mixed ability groups, English Language Learners have the opportunity to use language for real communication as they solve problems assigned by the teacher. As English Language Learners work together they learn academic language while investigating new topics or exploring content areas.

- **Encourage Classroom Participation**

  Give students opportunities to talk and interact. Also encourage them to express ideas, feelings, and opinions. Students' self-esteem and motivation are enhanced when teachers elicit their experiences in classroom discussions and validate what they have to say.

- **Cross-Age Tutoring and Peer Tutoring**

  Research indicates that learning is enhanced both for those who are tutored and for the tutors themselves. English Language Learners working one-on-one with tutors develop listening, communication, and problem-solving skills. The tutor develops personal responsibility and self-esteem as he or she works to ensure the success of another child. The tutor becomes a model of success. Pairing intermediate grade students with primary grade students makes for positive and lasting friendships.

By utilizing the resources in the ***Adventures in Time and Place/Aventuras a través del tiempo,*** the instruction you provide will facilitate learning for English Language Learners. As you structure an environment that builds on students' strengths and English Language Learning, you will make the classroom experience rewarding and meaningful for all your students.

TEACHER'S MULTIMEDIA EDITION

Here I Am

ADVENTURES IN TIME AND PLACE

James A. Banks

Barry K. Beyer

Gloria Contreras

Jean Craven

Gloria Ladson-Billings

Mary A. McFarland

Walter C. Parker

NATIONAL GEOGRAPHIC SOCIETY

THE TEDDY BEAR IS NAMED AFTER TEDDY ROOSEVELT, 26TH PRESIDENT OF THE UNITED STATES.

McGraw-Hill School Division

New York Farmington

PROGRAM AUTHORS

Dr. James A. Banks
Professor of Education and Director of the Center for Multicultural Education
University of Washington
Seattle, Washington

Dr. Barry K. Beyer
Professor Emeritus, Graduate School of Education
George Mason University
Fairfax, Virginia

Dr. Gloria Contreras
Professor of Education
University of North Texas
Denton, Texas

Jean Craven
District Coordinator of Curriculum Development
Albuquerque Public Schools
Albuquerque, New Mexico

Dr. Gloria Ladson-Billings
Professor of Education
University of Wisconsin
Madison, Wisconsin

Dr. Mary A. McFarland
Instructional Coordinator of Social Studies, K–12, and Director of Staff Development
Parkway School District
Chesterfield, Missouri

Dr. Walter C. Parker
Professor and Program Chair for Social Studies Education
University of Washington
Seattle, Washington

NATIONAL GEOGRAPHIC SOCIETY
Washington, D.C.

CALIFORNIA SENIOR CONSULTANT

Dr. Carlos E. Cortés
Professor Emeritus of History
University of California
Riverside, California

CALIFORNIA PROGRAM CONSULTANTS

Diane Bowers
Former Assistant Director of Education for the Yurok Tribe
Klamath, California

Dr. Susan L. Douglass
Affiliated Scholar, Council on Islamic Education
Fountain Valley, California

Dr. Karen Nakai
Lecturer of History-Social Science
Department of Education
University of California
Irvine, California

Shelly Osborne
Teacher-Literacy Mentor
Franklin School
Alameda, California

Dr. Valerie Ooka Pang
Professor, School of Teacher Education
San Diego State University
San Diego, California

Lyn Reese
Director, Women in History Project
Berkeley, California

Dr. Curtis C. Roseman
Professor of Geography
University Of Southern California
Los Angeles, California

Dr. Robert M. Senkewicz
Professor of History
Santa Clara University
Santa Clara, California

Evelyn Staton
Librarian
San Francisco School District
Member, Multiethnic Literature Forum for San Francisco
San Francisco, California

PROGRAM CONSULTANTS

Dr. John Bodnar
Professor of History
Indiana University
Bloomington, Indiana

Dr. Sheilah Clark-Ekong
Professor, Department of Anthropology
University of Missouri, St. Louis
St. Louis, Missouri

Dr. Darlene Clark Hine
John A. Hannah Professor of History
Michigan State University
East Lansing, Michigan

Dr. John L. Esposito
Professor of Religion and International Affairs
Georgetown University
Washington, D. C.

Dr. Gary Manson
Department of Geography
Michigan State University
East Lansing, Michigan

Dr. Juan Mora-Torrés
Professor of Latin American History
University of Texas at San Antonio
San Antonio, Texas

Dr. Joseph Rosenbloom
Professor, Classics Department
Washington University
St. Louis, Missouri

Dr. Robert Seltzer
Professor of Jewish History
Hunter College
City University of New York

Dr. Peter Stearns
Dean, College of Humanities and Social Studies
Carnegie Mellon University
Pittsburgh, Pennsylvania

CONSULTING AUTHORS

Dr. James Flood
Professor of Teacher Education, Reading and Language Development
San Diego State University
San Diego, California

Dr. Diane Lapp
Professor of Teacher Education, Reading and Language Development
San Diego State University
San Diego, California

GRADE-LEVEL CONSULTANTS

Sherry Betche
Kindergarten Teacher
Townview Elementary School
Dayton, Ohio

Laura Campbell
Kindergarten Teacher
Sierra View Elementary School
North Highlands, California

Sandy Curren
Kindergarten Teacher
Linda Vista Annex Elementary School
San Diego, California

Denise Graham
Kindergarten Teacher
Travis Heights Elementary
Austin, Texas

Helen Horton
Kindergarten Teacher
Rosecrans School
Compton, California

Mattie Olds
Kindergarten Teacher
Sawyer Elementary
Chicago, Illinois

Diane Railsback
Kindergarten Teacher
Kingston Elementary School
Hesperia, California

Nancy Rustige
Kindergarten Teacher
Calcedeaver Elementary School
Mt. Vernon, Alabama

CONTRIBUTING WRITER

Catherine M. Tamblyn
Little Silver, New Jersey

McGraw-Hill School Division
A Division of The McGraw-Hill Companies

McGraw-Hill School Division
Two Penn Plaza
New York, New York 10121

Printed in the United States of America

ISBN 0-02-148857-6 / K

1 2 3 4 5 6 7 8 9 042 03 02 01 00 99 98

CONTENTS Teacher's Edition

UNIT 3 *Let's Explore*

UNIT 4 *Our Country, Our World*

UNIT 5 *Hooray for Special Days!*

Using the Literature Big Books

Holidays

Stickers

CONTENTS

UNIT ONE

THEME BIG BOOK

Starting School

UNIT TWO

THEME BIG BOOK

Meeting Families

UNIT THREE

THEME BIG BOOK

Let's Explore

UNIT FOUR

Our Country, Our World

THEME BIG BOOK

UNIT FIVE

Hooray for Special Days!

THEME BIG BOOK

NATIONAL GEOGRAPHIC

LOOK AT YOUR WORLD

UNIT 1 THEME BIG BOOK, PAGES 2–3

Tell children that some of the things they will be learning about this year include land, water, plants, and animals. Explain to children that all of these things are part of *nature,* or the world around us. In addition, let children know they will learn about some of the ways in which people live and work in nature. Point out the photographs on Unit 1 Theme Big Book pp. 2–3.

- ***What are some of the places you see in the photographs?*** *(hills, forests, oceans)*
- ***What types of growing things do you see in the photographs?*** *(tall trees and other kinds of plants, children, and fish)*
- ***What are the children in the water looking at?*** *(fish)*
- ***Which photograph shows something mov ing across the land?*** *(the photograph with the truck)*
- ***What are some of the people in the pho tographs doing?*** *(They are walking in the woods, planting a garden, looking at a map, and exploring the ocean.)*

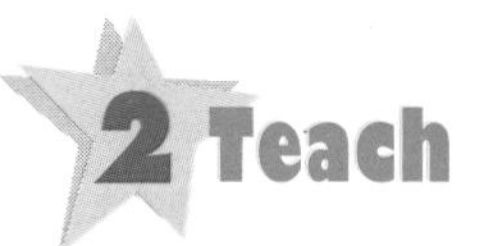

Tell children that as they continue looking through the Theme Big Books, they will learn that the world in which we live is very large. Explain to them that our world has many different people and places, but that in many ways these people and these places are alike.

Discussing the Five Themes Discuss the definitions of the five themes of geography with the children. *Region* is an area with common features that set it apart from other areas; *Human /Environment Interaction* is the relationship between people and the land on which they live; *Place* is a description of what an area is like based on various features (natural or built by people); *Location* is the exact measurement of where something can be found. Location can be described absolutely (often using numbers, such as longitude and latitude) and relatively (where one place is described in relation to another place); *Movement* is the movement of people, goods, and ideas around the world as well as how patterns of movement affect people and the way in which communities develop.

THEMES of GEOGRAPHY

Geography encompasses all the places and people in the world and all the interconnections among them. To help organize and convey geographic knowledge, the five themes of geography—*Region, Human/Environmental Interaction, Place, Location,* and *Movement*—were introduced in 1984. The popularity of the themes set the stage for a more comprehensive framework—the National Geography Standards.

On these pages, the truck on a Nevada highway represents *Movement;* the trees in the Redwood National Park in California represent *Region;* the boys snorkeling in the water represent *Place;* the girl planting pumpkin seeds represents *Human/Environmental Interaction;* and the girl reading the map represents *Location.*

To order a copy of *Geography for Life: National Geography Standards 1994,* contact: National Geographic Society, P.O. Box 98171, Washington, D.C., 20013-8171.

- ***How are the trees and the other plants in the photographs alike?*** *(Possible answer: They all grow in the ground and outdoors.)*
- ***How are some of the photographs on these pages alike?*** *(Possible answers: They show children, they show things in nature, they show growing things.)*
- ***What things in the pictures were made by people? What things are found in nature?*** *(People made the truck, the shovel, the map, the clothes on the children, the diving masks, and the packet containing the seeds; the trees, the other plants, the water, the fish, the seeds, and the hills can be found in nature.)*

3 Close

EVALUATE

Ask children why they think learning about the people, land, and water in our world is important. (Accept all reasonable answers.)

Note that the background map shows the 48 contiguous states. Students can turn to pp. R2–R3 in the ***GEO BIG BOOK,*** or pp. 4–5 in the Unit 4 Theme Big Book to see a map of all 50 states.

Background Information

DEVELOPING GEOGRAPHY SKILLS

You may wish to use the following activity to help children become familiar with some geography skills:

- Have children think of three places they have visited or would like to visit. Record children's answers on the chalkboard.
- Identify on a wall map or a globe some of the places that children have chosen.
- Encourage children to describe the places they chose by answering the following questions:

    Which place is farthest from your home?

    How might you get to each place?

    What kind of weather will you find in each place during winter? during summer?

    How does each place look?

    What will you do in each place?

Starting School
PLANNING GUIDE
Pupil Edition and Unit 1 Theme Big Book Pages 4–39

INTRODUCTION
SUGGESTED PACING: 3 DAYS

Begin With The Literature Big Book, pages 7, 206–207

Using The Unit Opener
pp. 8–10

PROJECT IDEAS
- Getting to Know You / ART
- Make a Model School Hallway / ART
- Enriching with Multimedia
- Our School Favorites / MATHEMATICS
- Become the "Friend of the Day" / ART

LESSON 1
SUGGESTED PACING: 1–2 DAYS

Meeting Our Class pp. 11–14

KEY CONCEPTS
school, class, special

PROJECT IDEAS
- Make a Teddy-Bear Class / ART
- Sing "Teddy Bear, Teddy Bear" / MUSIC / MOVEMENT
- Make a Class Jigsaw Puzzle / ART

RESOURCES
Project Book, pp. 4–5 • Big Book Stickers Sheet 1 • Anthology, p. 44

LESSON 2
SUGGESTED PACING: 1–2 DAYS

Our Busy Classroom
pp. 15–18

KEY CONCEPTS
activities, before, after, group, work, senses

PROJECT IDEAS
- Making Busy-Bee Pendants / ART
- Making an Eye Chart / SCIENCE
- Ten Little Firemen / DRAMA / MATH

RESOURCES
Project Book, p. 6 • Big Book Stickers Sheet 1

GEOGRAPHY SKILLS
SUGGESTED PACING: 1–2 DAYS

Looking At Maps pp. 23–26

KEY CONCEPTS
map, model

PROJECT IDEAS
- Make a Hand Map / ART
- Make a Classroom Map / ART
- Create a Neighborhood on a Floor Map / ART

RESOURCES
Project Book, pp. 8; 65–76 • Big Book Stickers Sheets 2, 3, 4 • Floor Map • Word Cards • TECHNOLOGY Videodisc

LESSON 3
SUGGESTED PACING: 1–2 DAYS

School Rules pp. 27–30

KEY CONCEPTS
rules

PROJECT IDEAS
- Make a Safety Badge / ART/DRAMA
- Make a Traffic Light / ART
- Play by the Rules / MOVEMENT

RESOURCES
Project Book, p. 9 • Big Book Stickers Sheet 4

CITIZENSHIP
SUGGESTED PACING: 1–2 DAYS

Making Choices: Working Together pp. 31–34

KEY CONCEPTS
working together, share

PROJECT IDEAS
- Make a Partner Picture / ART
- Make Music Together / MUSIC / ART
- Create a Group Collage / ART

RESOURCES
Project Book, pp. 10–11 • Anthology, p. 40 • TECHNOLOGY Videodisc/Video Tape 1

UNIT ASSESSMENT
SUGGESTED PACING: 1 DAY

pp. 38–39

OBSERVATIONAL/PORTFOLIO ASSESSMENT, p. 38
- Draw Favorite School Activities
- Draw Schoolrooms
- Identify School Rules

OBJECTIVES CHECKLIST, p. 39

McGRAW-HILL SCHOOL DIVISION'S HOME PAGE at http://www.mhschool.com contains on-line student activities related to this unit.

GEOGRAPHY SKILLS

SUGGESTED PACING: 1–2 DAYS

Finding Where Things Are pp. 19–22

KEY CONCEPTS

left, right, above, below, inside, outside, in front of, behind, top, middle, bottom

PROJECT IDEAS

Make Left and Right Signs / ART
Play "Hide-and-Seek" / LANGUAGE ARTS
Sing "Hokey Pokey" / MUSIC/MOVEMENT

RESOURCES

Project Book, pp. 7 • Big Book Stickers Sheets 2–3 • Word Cards

CLOSE WITH A POEM

SUGGESTED PACING: 1–2 DAYS

At School pp. 35–37

PROJECT IDEAS

Make Classroom Puppets / DRAMA

RESOURCES

Project Book, p. 12 • Anthology

SHELTERED INSTRUCTION

Reading Strategies & Language Development

Bridging, p. 8

Second-Language Support

Drama, p. 12
Using Visuals, p. 25

Meeting Individual Needs

McGraw-Hill Adventure Books

Assessment Opportunities

Ongoing Unit Project: Make a Model School Hallway, p. 9
Observational and Portfolio Assessment, p. 38
Objectives Checklist, p. 39
Evaluate, pp. 13, 17, 21, 25, 29, 33

FOR FURTHER SUPPORT

- Language Support Handbook
- Social Studies Readiness

Unit 1 Bibliography and Resources

MCGRAW-HILL ADVENTURE BOOKS Easy-to-Read Books

Bryant, Tamera. ***We Are Friends.*** Children meet their teacher and classmates, and become familiar with the classroom and its routines on the first schoolday.

Evans, Mary. ***A Picture.*** A series of words and drawings act as clues to a mystery picture.

CLASSROOM LIBRARY

McMillan, Bruce. ***Mouse Views: What the Class Pet Saw.*** New York: Holiday House, 1993. Colorful and intriguing photos will entertain children as they follow the antics of a pet mouse that escapes in school.

READ ALOUD BOOKS

Ahlberg, Janet, and Allan Ahlberg. ***Starting School.*** New York: Viking Kestrel, 1988. All of the routines and activities involved in starting school are described with engaging text and detailed illustrations.

Ashley, Bernard. ***Cleversticks.*** New York: Crown Publishers, Inc., 1991. Ling Sung, a new boy in school, happily discovers something he can teach others while he tries to adjust to a different culture.

Baer, Edith. ***This Is the Way We Go to School.*** New York: Scholastic Inc., 1994. This informative and lively presentation about how children around the world go to school is accompanied with charming illustrations.

Fanelli, Sara. ***My Map Book.*** New York: HarperCollins, 1995. A variety of maps provide views into a child's room, school, playground, and other places in a child's world.

Johnson, Dolores. ***What Will Mommy Do When I'm at School?*** New York: Macmillan Publishing Company, 1990. A young girl becomes anxious when she wonders what her mother will be doing while she's in school.

Schwartz, Amy. ***Annabelle Swift, Kindergartner.*** New York: Orchard Books, 1988. Amy's sister tries to prepare her for her first day in kindergarten.

Senisi, Ellen. ***Kindergarten Kids.*** New York: Scholastic Inc., 1994 One class's activities in kindergarten are described with colorful photos.

Serfozo, Mary. ***Benjamin Bigfoot.*** New York: Margaret McElderry Books, 1993. With the help of a very patient teacher, a young boy discovers why it is not a good idea to wear his father's shoes on his first day of school.

Slate, Joseph. ***Miss Bindergarten Gets Ready for Kindergarten.*** New York: Dutton's Children's Books, 1996. Students and teacher get ready for the first day of kindergarten; each introduced in alphabetical order.

Sweeney, Joan. ***Me on the Map.*** New York: Crown Publishers, 1996. This playful introduction to maps helps children locate themselves in the world and on a map.

TEACHER BOOKS

Raines, Shirley C., and Robert J. Canady. ***Story Stretchers for the Primary Grades: Activities to Expand Children's Favorite Books.*** Mt. Rainier, MD: Gryphon House, 1992. This resource is filled with activity suggestions for extensions of popular literature for the kindergarten classroom.

Scott, Louise Binder. ***Rhymes for Learning Times: Let's Pretend Activities for Early Childhood.*** Minneapolis, MN: T.S. Denison & Co., Inc., 1983. This book offers rhymes appropriate for the kindergarten classroom that will be useful throughout the school year.

TECHNOLOGY MULTIMEDIA

Let's Begin: Starting School. Video. RB811 (18 min). From school bus to classroom, children can learn about the people who help run the school and its daily activities. Rainbow Educational Media. (800) 331-4047.

Off to School I Go! (4 sound filmstrips) S20670-SATC. "My First Day of School," "My Class," "Recess," and "We Go on a Field Trip" are topics that will help acquaint students with new school experiences. Society For Visual Education. (800) 829-1900.

FREE OR INEXPENSIVE MATERIALS

For a copy of "Good Teaching Practices for 4- and 5-Year-Olds" #522, write to: National Assoc. for the Education of Young Children, 1509 16th Street, N.W., Washington, DC 20036-1426.

BEGIN
WITH THE
LITERATURE BIG BOOK

LINKING SOCIAL STUDIES AND LITERATURE

Introduce Unit 1 with the **Literature Big Book, *Someone Special, Just Like You.*** The story acts as a springboard to support these Social Studies concepts:

- Each of us is special.
- People are alike and different in their interests, feelings, and abilities.
- School is a place where children learn.

Literature Big Book

ABOUT THE STORY

A full instructional plan, along with the complete text of the story, appears on pages 206–207.

The wonderful photographs in *Someone Special, Just Like You,* show young children, physically and mentally challenged, discovering the world around them at home, school, and in places throughout the community.

This book shows us that all children, with or without disabilities, have the desire to love, learn, play, and to be accepted.

ABOUT THE AUTHOR

Tricia Brown taught for several years in the New York City school system. She has reported for the *Sacramento Union* as well as for United Press International. Her published works include poetry, short fiction, articles, and a novel.

ABOUT THE PHOTOGRAPHER

Fran Ortiz, an award-winning photojournalist, has photographed for many magazines including *National Geographic, Time, Life, and Harper's Bazaar.* In 1981, he was nominated for the Pulitzer Prize for his social documentary on the Mono Indians.

USING THE Unit 1 Opener

USING BIG BOOK PAGES 4–5

Read aloud the unit title. Then introduce the kindergartners. Point to the children in turn, left to right, while saying each name—Tanya, Joey, and Amy. Tell children they will see Amy again in other pages of the book. Children can preview the unit as they look for Amy in the lessons.

DEVELOPING KEY CONCEPTS

In this unit children will meet a class of kindergartners and learn about school activities, rules, and ways to work alone and together. They will explore the school environment, and solve problems. They also look at a model and map of a school. Introduce these concepts:

class *A class is a group of people in a school.*
school *School is where people go to learn.*
model *A model is a copy of something real.*

USE BIG BOOK STICKERS, SHEET 4

Affix these ***Sticker*** labels on the appropriate places in the picture and then read them aloud.

class | school | model

Sheltered Instruction

Eliciting children's prior knowledge and experience will help them link what they are learning to their personal lives. Explore their familiarity with the unit concepts by brainstorming to create a web on chart paper that reflects their ideas about school. **[SDAIE STRATEGY: BRIDGING]**

BULLETIN BOARD

Getting to Know You

Use your bulletin board to help children become familiar with the members of your class.

- Cover the bulletin board with plain paper. For the center of the bulletin board, you can make a simple-looking schoolhouse out of construction paper. Take a snapshot of each child's face. As an alternative, invite each child to draw a self-portrait. Help children write their names beneath their pictures.
- Enlist children's cooperation in placing the pictures on the bulletin board.
- As an ongoing project, add more information every week about each child. Children can suggest details to add about themselves or about each other. If you notice something helpful one day done by a particular child, demonstrate your appreciation by adding your observation to the board.

ABOUT THE PHOTOGRAPH

Draw attention to the rooms of a model school that the kindergartners are working together to create.

Item 1 Point to and read the label on Tanya's model of her school library. Then identify the cutouts of the door, window, and books. Children might share what they know about their school library.

Item 2 Point to and read the label on Joey's model of his classroom. Have children identify the things in his model classroom. Have children name other things found in classrooms.

Item 3 Point to and read aloud the label on Amy's model of the nurse's office in her school. Also identify the eye chart and scale. Children might share what they know about this room in their school.

Directions for making this Ongoing Unit Project can be found at the bottom of this page.

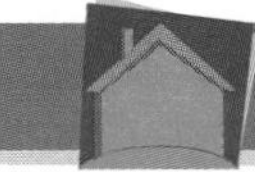

SCHOOL-TO-HOME

My New Friends

- Parents or guardians can help with their child's adjustment to school by knowing more about their child's classroom.
- For each child, make a list of classmates' names to take home. If possible, you can copy-reduce photographs of each child to create a little yearbook. Be sure to add *your* name!
- As children tell about their classmates and their school day, family members can record information on the list or yearbook.

ONGOING UNIT PROJECT

GROUP

Make a Model School Hallway

CURRICULUM CONNECTION **Art**

After children have studied the model of the school in the skills lesson on pp. 24–25, assign groups rooms in your hallway to prepare as models.

Advance Preparation: Collect one large cardboard box for each room in your hallway. Allow children to paint the boxes. Also make a label for each room.

1. Give each group the label of its assigned room and have the group locate the room as you tour your school hallway. Children should count the number of doors and windows in the rooms and identify other items to include in their room models.
2. Children can make their own cutouts for their models as well as use cutouts from ***Project Book*** pp. 2–3 and p. 43 for a cutout of a flag. Help each group make and glue the cutouts and labels on the boxes.
3. Assist children in placing the finished rooms side by side completing the model of your school hallway.
4. This model can be used to practice locational terms, to identify rooms children may need to visit, and to trace and identify routes.

Assessment Suggestion

Signs of Success

- Each group should be able to name its assigned room model and tell about its contents.
- Children should be able to identify other room models by their contents.
- Children should be able to use appropriate locational terms as they identify the location of rooms in relation to one another.
- Children should recognize that the room models together create a model of their school hallway.

TECHNOLOGY CENTER

Enriching with Multimedia

RESOURCE: *Videodisc*

- Enrich Unit 1 with the Glossary map.

Search Frame 5432

RESOURCE: *Videodisc/Video Tape 1*

- Enrich Unit 1 with the Videodisc segment on *Sharing*.

Search Frame 10556, Play to 16280

MATHEMATICS LEARNING CENTER

LEARNING STYLE: VISUAL

Our School Favorites

ON YOUR OWN

15 TO 30 MINUTES

Materials: 3 sheets of oaktag, markers, crayons

1. Talk with children about things they like to do and places they like to go to in school. As children respond, draw a small picture on the chalkboard to represent each suggestion and identify each one.
2. Then copy each picture onto one of the three large sheets of oaktag prepared with graph grids, labeled "Show and Tell," "Things to Do," and "Places to Go." Place the graphs in the Mathematics Learning Center.
3. Invite children to visit the Mathematics Learning Center and color in a square next to each thing on the graph that they like.
4. Work together to tally the graph squares. Encourage children to use location words as they discuss the items on the graphs.

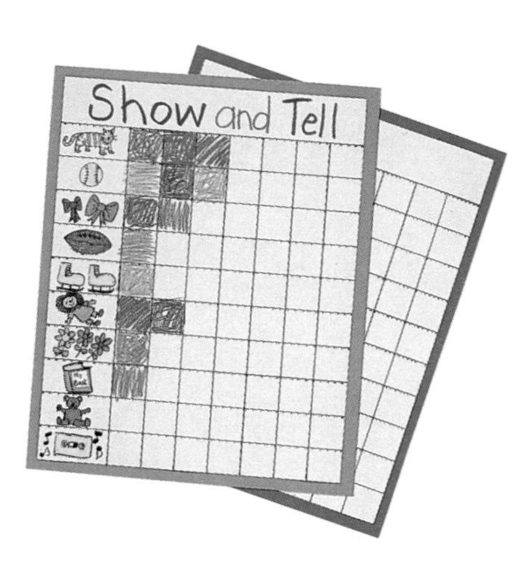

TEACHER EXCHANGE

Thanks to: Sherry Betche, Townview Elementary, Dayton, Ohio

Become the "Friend of the Day"

GROUP

30 MINUTES OR LONGER

Materials: oaktag, markers, yarn, scissors, hole puncher, construction paper, shoebox

1. Discuss with children different ways they can be a friend to someone. Then explain they will each get a chance to be "friend of the day."
2. Have children help you create a "friend of the day" sign from oaktag that can be posted on a chair.
3. Have children create a necklace out of yarn and construction paper. Each child can cut out a piece of paper and draw on it. Help them punch a hole at the top of each piece and string the pieces of paper onto a length of yarn.
4. Collect the necklace and place it in a shoebox. Select a child to be "friend of the day" according to the order on your attendance folder.
5. The chosen child picks the necklace from the box and sits in the specially marked chair. Other children are called upon to tell how they will be this child's friend today.

UNIT 1
LESSON
1

Meeting Our Class

UNIT 1 THEME BIG BOOK, PAGES 6–7

LESSON OVERVIEW

School is a place for learning and for meeting others. People have characteristics that make them special.

LESSON OBJECTIVES

- Recognize that we can learn about others in school.
- Determine that each person is special.
- Identify that people have varied interests and talents.

KEY CONCEPTS

school class special

RESOURCE REMINDER

Project Book
pp. 4–5

Stickers Package
Sheet 1

Anthology
Special, p. 44

GETTING READY

Make a Teddy-Bear Class

CURRICULUM CONNECTION Art

Objective: To become familiar with the teddy-bear motif of the units, to meet classmates, and to realize people have favorite colors that make them special.

Resource: *Project Book* pp. 4–5

Materials: dinner-size and snack-size paper plates, scissors, crayons or colored pencils, glue, metal fasteners or paper clips, tape, string

1. Provide each child with a dinner-size and a snack-size paper plate. Have children tape the plates together to form the head and body of the bear.
2. Distribute a copy of ***Project Book*** p. 5 to each child. Help children write their names on the name tags, cut them out, and glue them onto the larger plates. Then have children draw the eyes, nose, and mouth of the teddy-bear faces. Tell children to select their favorite colors to color in the faces. Have children share their favorite colors with the class. Then have children cut out the faces and glue them onto the smaller plates.
3. Using ***Project Book*** p. 4, have children color and cut out the paws and feet. Help children connect them to the plates with metal fasteners or paper clips.
4. Make a loop of tape behind each bear. Run a string through the tape and then tape the string along the wall to make a chain of teddy bears.

Project Book
pp. 4–5

1 Prepare

WARMING UP WITH THE READ ALOUD

Tell children that many students are excited about coming to school on the first day. They wonder who they will meet, what they will be doing, and how they will find their way in a new place. Share the poem in the Read Aloud. Encourage children to listen for similar concerns they may have had about coming to school.

- ***What did the child in the poem wonder about before the first day of school?*** *(if his/her drawing would be good enough, if people would like him/her, what the teacher would look like, if the puppy would miss him/her)*
- ***What things did you wonder about before starting school?*** *(Children may name new things, concerns mentioned by you, or those stated in the poem.)*

2 Teach

USING BIG BOOK PAGES 6–7

Point out Amy, the girl holding the bear, as the girl introduced in the Unit Opener.

USE BIG BOOK STICKERS, SHEET 1

Use these ***Stickers*** throughout the lesson.

LESSON 1

Meeting Our Class

6

Read Aloud

First Day of School

I wonder
if my drawing
will be as good as theirs.
I wonder
if they'll like me
or just be full of stares.
I wonder
if my teacher
will look like Mom or Gram.
I wonder
if my puppy
will wonder
where I am.

Aileen Fisher

Using the Anthology

Special, page 44 This poem names physical characteristics, behavior, and feelings as qualities that make children special. After you have shared the poem, have children identify the qualities named in the poem. You might have children note each other's special smiles. To point out individuality in their voices, have the class face away from five volunteers. Invite one of the volunteers to speak and ask the class to name that child. Have children suggest other ways they are special such as their names and fingerprints. Afterwards you may wish to take a photograph of each child to put on the "Getting to Know You" bulletin board described on p. 8.

Second-Language Support/Dramatization To make the idea of being special concrete for children needing second-language support, dramatize suggestions or look at names and fingerprints while pointing out their unique characteristics.

What do you like to do?

7

Tell children that Amy is part of a kindergarten class and the class is having "show and tell." Explain that "show and tell" is a way for children to tell others in the class what makes them special. Place the ***Sticker*** of the word *special* on Amy in the Big Book. Define the word as meaning "not like anyone or anything else." Tell children each of them is special. As they answer the following questions, have children use the *X* ***Stickers*** to identify the things the children in the Big Book are holding that make them special.

- ***What does Amy like that makes her special?*** *(teddy bear)*

★**THINKING FURTHER:** ***Making Conclusions*** ***What do you think the other children enjoy doing?*** *(Possible answers: Eric likes animals because he has a photo of a dog, Zoe likes to play sports because she has a soccerball, etc.)*

You may wish to have children match some of the objects the children are holding in the photo with the objects surrounding the photo by using the *X* ***Stickers.*** Explain to children that people have different talents—or things that they are good at doing. Talents also make people special. Explain to children that the things that make them special can make them feel good about themselves.

3 Close

LESSON SUMMARY

Read the lesson question with children, pointing to each word as you read. Have children name things that they like to do.

EVALUATE

Draw Self-Portraits Using oaktag, have children draw and color a self-portrait of their faces, focusing on drawing their special features, such as hair length. Have children cut out their self-portraits and use masking tape to attach the drawings to craftsticks to make masks. Children can share their masks with the class and tell something about themselves.

Background Information

ABOUT TOPIC SENSITIVITY

- A class discussion of individuality relating to specialness may be a sensitive topic for some children. For children who seem uncomfortable revealing information about themselves, allow participation to be voluntary.
- One way to help children to relate to the topic of individuality is to show photographs of children from different racial, ethnic, and cultural backgrounds with a diversity of interests.
- To make children more comfortable with the topic, you may wish to invite to the class guests who have special talents to talk about themselves.

MUSIC/MOVEMENT CONNECTION

LEARNING STYLE: AUDITORY/KINESTHETIC

Sing "Teddy Bear, Teddy Bear"

GROUP

15 TO 30 MINUTES

Objective: To practice word recognition and to review the things children do in school.

Materials: chart paper, marker

Advance Preparation: On large sheets of chart paper, write out the rhyme "Teddy Bear, Teddy Bear." Illustrate the chart.

Teddy Bear, Teddy Bear, turn around,

Teddy Bear, Teddy Bear, touch the ground.

Teddy Bear, Teddy Bear, read the news,

Teddy Bear, Teddy Bear, shine your shoes.

1. Have the class stand in a circle. Teach children the words and have them act them out as they say them.

2. Encourage children to make up their own verses about things they do in the classroom. For example:

Teddy Bear, Teddy Bear, write your name,

Teddy Bear, Teddy Bear, play a game.

ART CONNECTION

LEARNING STYLE: VISUAL

Make a Class Jigsaw Puzzle

GROUP

15 TO 30 MINUTES

Objective: To work cooperatively to make a class portrait.

Materials: four large sheets of oaktag, pencils, crayons or paint, hand mirrors or large mirrors, tape

Advance Preparation: Children will work in four groups to assemble jigsaw puzzles of their portraits. On the oaktag sheets, draw a simple puzzle of four pieces (or however many children are in each group). Then cut out the pieces.

1. Tell children that they will be working together to make a picture of the entire class. Divide the class into four groups. Give each group an oaktag puzzle (broken into pieces). Tell children to draw and color their portraits on their pieces of the puzzle. Have them look at their faces in large or small mirrors placed around the classroom.

2. As each group completes its portraits, help children to print their names below their faces. Help each group complete their jigsaw puzzle. Tape pieces of the completed puzzle together.

3. When all of the groups have completed their puzzles, make sure all pieces are firmly taped together. Then assemble a class portrait on the wall.

UNIT 1

LESSON

2

Our Busy Classroom

UNIT 1 THEME BIG BOOK, PAGES 8–9

LESSON OVERVIEW

During a school day, children participate in a series of activities for learning and having fun.

LESSON OBJECTIVES

- Recognize kindergarten activities and the sequence in which they take place during a typical school day.
- Identify activities that involve working together.
- Identify activities that can be done alone.

KEY CONCEPTS

activities before after
group work senses

RESOURCE REMINDER

Project Book
p. 6

Stickers Package
Sheet 1

GETTING READY

Make Busy-Bee Pendants

CURRICULUM CONNECTION Art

Objective: To understand the concept of a busy classroom.

Resource: *Project Book* p. 6

Materials: picture of honeybees, construction paper, glue, crayons or markers, scissors, string, hole puncher

1. Using a picture of honeybees, explain that bees are very busy insects. Bees have many activities, and they work together to build their hive and to make honey. Discuss with children the ways they are "busy as bees" in the classroom.
2. Using the picture of honeybees as a reference, have children color the bee on ***Project Book*** p. 6. Then have children glue the page onto a sheet of construction paper.
3. Tell children to cut out their bees. Help them punch a hole at the top of the bee and then pull a piece of string through it. Have children wear their bees as pendants when they are busy with classroom activities.

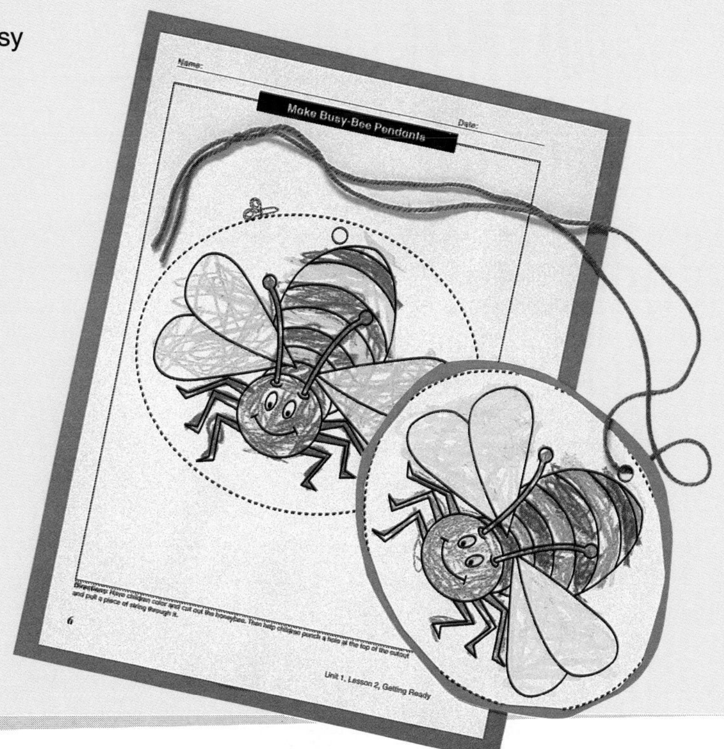

1 Prepare

WARMING UP WITH THE READ ALOUD

Introduce children to the idea of a busy classroom with the Read Aloud.

- ***What are some of the things the children do at school?*** *(Possible answers include talk, sing, jump, climb, paint, build, work, and play.)*
- ***Which days of the week do the children work?*** *(Monday, Tuesday, Wednesday, Thursday, Friday)*

2 Teach

USING BIG BOOK PAGES 8–9

Invite children to name some activities that they have already done at school today. As they name activities, use the words before and after to tell when certain activities took place in relation to each other.

USE BIG BOOK STICKERS, SHEET 1

Use these ***Stickers*** throughout the lesson.

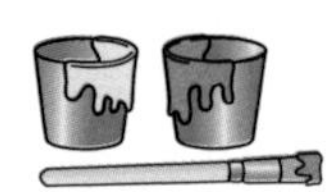

Read Aloud

from *I'm Busy, Too*

Children coming into school,
teachers waiting for the children,
ready for the busy workday,
ready to be busy, busy.

Talking
singing,
jumping
climbing,
painting
building.
Indoors
outdoors,
outdoors
indoors,
working
playing,
playing
working,
all
day
long.

Work on Monday,
work on Tuesday.
Wednesday
Thursday
Friday
workdays.

Children, teachers,
teachers, children,
busy, busy,
working hard.

Norma Simon

Have children use the ***Stickers*** representing kindergarten activities to identify activities in the Big Book. Point out to children that most of the children in the photographs are doing their activities in groups. Other children may work alone. Point out that the photo of the child creating a painting shows a child working alone. Have children place the *X* ***Stickers*** on activities in the Big Book that are the same as those that they do. Compare ways children in the Big Book are working with the ways your class does things.

- ***Which activities do you do by yourself in our class?*** *(Possible answers include drawing, writing, and coloring.)*
- ***Which activities in our class do you do in groups?*** *(Possible answers may include cleaning up, playing games, and playing music.)*

★**THINKING FURTHER:** ***Compare and Contrast*** ***What things do you see in this classroom photo that are the same as in our classroom?*** *(Answers should reflect items that are the same, such as the piano or the computer.)*

Tell children that they use their five senses to help them do activities at school. They can listen, look, touch, smell, and taste things to explore and learn about them. Stress to children that it is important to taste only things we know are safe. Have children identify the senses the children in the Big Book classroom are using to do activities.

3 Close

LESSON SUMMARY

Read the lesson question with children, pointing to each word as you read. Then have volunteers name an activity the class does.

EVALUATE

Draw Favorite School Activities Invite children to draw and color pictures of their favorite school activities. Write children's sentences about their art on their papers. Use the pictures in a bulletin-board display titled "Our Busy Classroom." For assessment suggestions, see p. 38.

Curriculum Connection

Mathematics A time skill may be used with this lesson. You may wish to introduce a calendar for the month of September. The Study Skill, Looking At Calendars, appears on pp. 8–9 of the Unit 5 Theme Big Book and pp. 172–173 in this Teacher's Edition.

Using a September calendar, you might help children to count the number of days in the month. After children learn how to use a calendar, they can help you to record special classroom activities such as guest speakers, field trips, holiday parties, and other events.

SCIENCE CONNECTION

LEARNING STYLE: VISUAL

Make an Eye Chart

ON YOUR OWN

15 TO 30 MINUTES

Objective: To become familiar with the five senses and better understand the notion of a busy classroom.

Materials: index cards; paper; construction paper; glue; crayons; photographs of a pair of eyes, an ear, a mouth, a nose, hands

Advance Preparation: On an index card, draw a picture of an eye. Do not color it. Then duplicate and cut out enough copies for the class. Alternately have each child draw an eye on an index card.

1. One by one, hold up the photographs and ask children to identify the parts of the body shown. Discuss with children that we use our senses to see, hear, taste, smell, and feel things.
2. Prop the photographs along a chalkboard. Then tell children that you will describe some items in their busy classroom that they might associate with certain senses, such as a drawing or a drum. Have volunteers point to the photograph of the sense that goes with the item you describe.
3. Give each child a blank eye. Children should color the eye and then glue it onto a piece of construction paper to make a chart. Beneath the eye have children draw something they do with their eyes in the classroom.

DRAMA/MATH CONNECTION

LEARNING STYLE: AUDITORY/KINESTHETIC

Have Fun with Fingerplays: Ten Little Firemen

GROUP

15 TO 30 MINUTES

Objective: To become acquainted with activities of some busy people and to practice counting.

Advance Preparation: Write out the words of the poem "Ten Little Firemen" on a large piece of chart paper. Illustrate the chart.

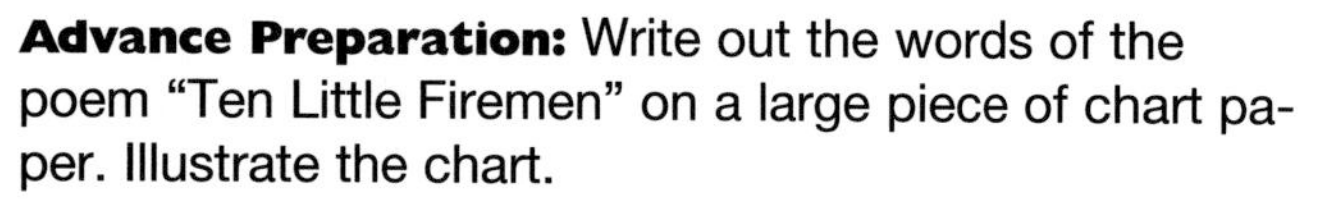

Ten Little Firemen

Ten little firemen
Sleeping in a row;
(Extend both hands, fingers curled, to represent sleeping men.)
Ding, dong goes the bell,
(Pull bell cord with one hand.)
And down the pole they go.
(Close both fists, put one on top of other, slide them down pole.)
Off on the engine, oh, oh, oh,
(Steer engine with hands.)
Using the big hose, so, so, so.
(Make nozzle with fist.)
When all the fire's out, home so-o slow.
(Steer engine with hands.)
Back to bed, all in a row.
(Extend both hands, fingers curled.)

Fingerplay movement by Marion F. Grayson

1. Discuss with the class the different activities people outside of school do. Talk about how these people are busy just like the children are.
2. Help children count their ten fingers before learning the poem. Then have them follow the directions for the finger and hand motions.

Finding Where Things Are

UNIT 1 THEME BIG BOOK PAGES 10–11

LESSON OVERVIEW

The location of items in a picture can be identified through the use of position words.

LESSON OBJECTIVES

- Distinguish between *left* and *right.*
- Use position words *above, below, inside, outside, in front of, behind, top, middle,* and *bottom* to identify the location of things.
- Explore the school environment.

KEY CONCEPTS

left	right	above	below
inside	outside	in front of	behind
top	middle	bottom	

RESOURCE REMINDER

Project Book
p. 7

Stickers Package
Sheets 2–3

Word Cards

GETTING READY

Make Left and Right Signs

ON YOUR OWN

15 TO 30 MINUTES

CURRICULUM CONNECTION Art

Objective: To become familiar with the position words *left* and *right.*

Resource: ***Project Book*** p. 7

Materials: crayons or markers, scissors, craft sticks, glue

Advance Preparation: You may wish to prepare left and right signs to serve as an example.

1. Distribute a copy of ***Project Book*** p. 7 to each child. Tell children to outline the word *left* with a blue crayon or marker and the word *right* with a red crayon or marker. Then have them color in the background of each sign with a color of their choice.
2. Have children cut out both signs and glue each one to a craft stick.
3. Ask children to hold the left sign in their left hand and the right sign in their right hand.

Project Book p. 7

Name: Date:

Make Left and Right Signs

RIGHT

LEFT

Directions: Have children trace the words on the signs. Then have children color the signs and cut them out.

Unit 1, Geography Skills 1, Getting Ready 7

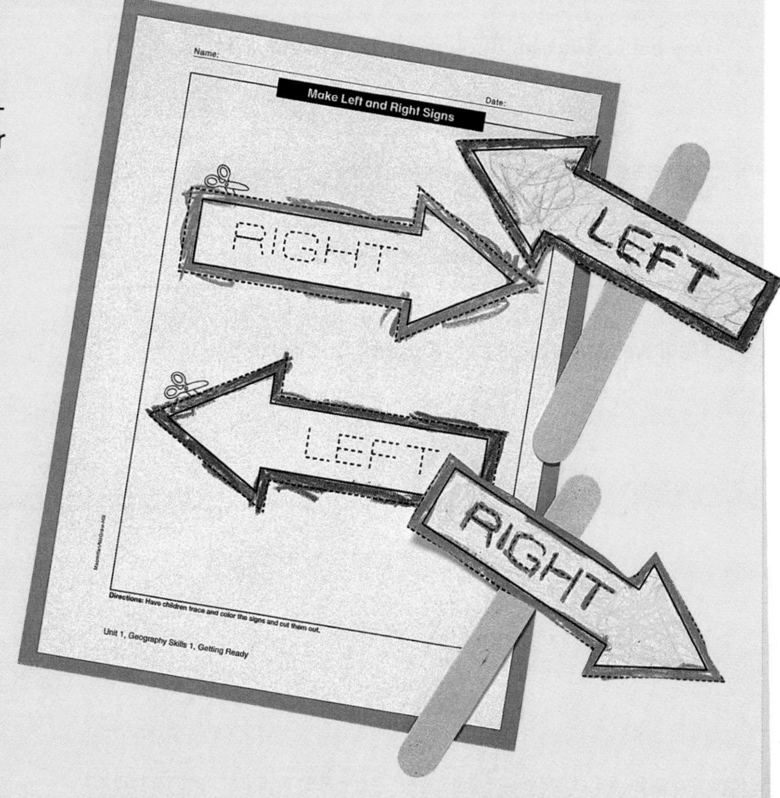

WARMING UP WITH THE READ ALOUD

Write the words left and right on the chalkboard and read them aloud. Show children which side is on their left and which side is on their right. Explain to children that their left hand is always on their left no matter which way they move. Have children point to show the meaning of the terms above and below. Then share the Read Aloud with children.

- ***What things in this classroom are to your right? What things are to your left?*** *(Children should name appropriate classroom items.)*

> ★ **THINKING FURTHER:** ***Making Conclusions***
> ***Why is it important to know left and right?***
> *(Possible answers: to understand where you are, to give directions, to find things and places.)*

USING BIG BOOK PAGES 10–11

Explore the school and its environs as well as the landscape in the neighborhood including its topography, street, transportation systems, and human activities.

USE BIG BOOK STICKERS, SHEETS 2–3

Use these ***Stickers*** throughout the lesson.

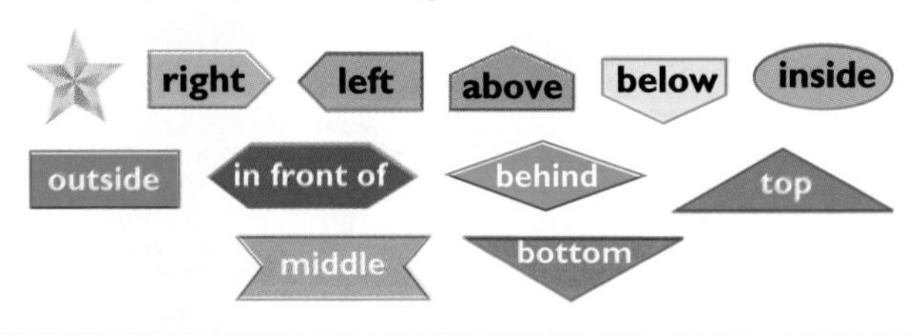

Review with children the steps in the Helping Yourself box on p. 21.

UNIT 1 THEME BIG BOOK

Point to the Right

Point to the right of me,
(Use both arms and follow action slowly as rhyme indicates.)
Point to the left of me,
Point up above me,
Point down below.
Right, left, up,
(Increase speed in pointing.)
And down so slow.
(Decrease speed.)

Marion F. Grayson

HELPING YOURSELF

- There are ways to tell where something is.
- It may be to the right or to the left.
- It may be above or below.
- It may be inside or outside.
- It may be in front of or behind.
- It may be at the top, middle, or bottom.

Have children use ***Stickers*** to identify things in the drawing that are left, right, above, below, inside, outside, in front of, behind, and at the top, middle, and bottom.

- ***Amy is outside her school. What else is outside?*** *(Possible answers include trees, duck, park, squirrel, bus, bird, flag, playground, bike, bike rack, stop sign, grass, bushes, flowers, street, mailbox, and sky.)*

★**THINKING FURTHER:** ***Using Prior Knowledge*** ***Choose a building in the picture and tell what you might see inside.*** *(Accept all reasonable answers.)*

3 Close

LESSON SUMMARY

Read the lesson question with children, pointing to each word as you read. Have children name items that are to Amy's left and right.

EVALUATE

Use Word Cards Use the ***Word Cards*** or write on separate cards or strips of paper the words *left, right, above, below, inside, outside, in front of, behind, top, middle,* and *bottom.* Hand the cards to volunteers and invite them one at a time to stand in front of the classroom. Read each child's card. Invite the seated children to use the words to describe where things are located in your classroom. For example, "Susan's desk is behind Jose's desk." After each description, have the child holding the card tell whether or not the word was used correctly.

Print Awareness

Making Associations Children are introduced to a large number of new words in this lesson. To help them make the association between the printed word and the content, only display one ***Sticker*** at a time as each position is discussed. Remove the ***Sticker*** before discussing the next concept.

Focusing on Words Children may have difficulty focusing on words when they are presented with an engaging illustration. An effective strategy for helping children focus on words or sentences is to use a word mask that allows you to isolate the word from the illustration or photographs. You can create your own word masks by cutting various sizes of "windows" from pieces of poster board.

LANGUAGE ARTS

LEARNING STYLE: AUDITORY/KINESTHETIC

Play "Hide-and-Seek"

GROUP

30 MINUTES OR LONGER

Objective: To become more familiar with the position words *left and right.*

Materials: small objects suitable for hiding, such as a crayon, stone, or paper clip

1. Tell children they will take turns finding something that is hidden.
2. Ask a child to turn his or her back to the classroom while you have a volunteer hide the object.
3. Have the child turn around and look for the object. The class will help give clues by telling the child that he or she should turn to the left and walk, or turn to the right and walk. The class may also give additional clues using position words, such as, "It is behind [something]" or "It is on top of [something]."

MUSIC/MOVEMENT CONNECTION

LEARNING STYLE: AUDITORY/KINESTHETIC

Sing "Hokey Pokey"

GROUP

15 TO 30 MINUTES

Objective: To practice the concept of *left and right.*

Materials: chart paper, marker

Advance Preparation: Write the words to the song "Hokey Pokey" on a large sheet of chart paper. Illustrate the chart.

[Verse:]
You put your right foot in,
You put your right foot out,
You put your right foot in
and you shake it all about;
[Chorus:]
You do the Hokey Pokey
and you turn yourself around.
That's what it's all about!
[Remaining verses include:]
You put your left foot in . . .
[Chorus]
You put your right hand in . . .
[Chorus]
You put your left hand in . . .
[Chorus]
You put your whole self in . . .
[Chorus]

Have children form a circle, face into the circle, and act out the verses.

Looking at Maps

UNIT 1 THEME BIG BOOK, PAGES 12–13

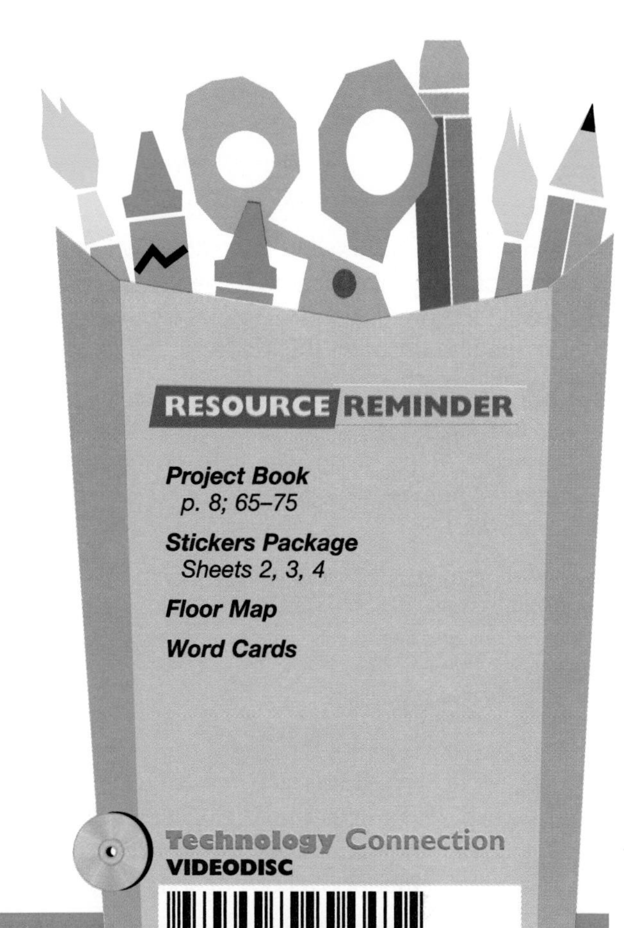

Search Frame 5432

LESSON OVERVIEW

A map can show the location of rooms and hallways in a school.

LESSON OBJECTIVES

- Locate rooms and hallways on a model and a map of a school.
- Recognize that a map is a drawing of a place.
- Trace routes on a map.
- Identify different school workers.

KEY CONCEPTS

map model

GETTING READY

Make a Hand Map

ON YOUR OWN

15 TO 30 MINUTES

CURRICULUM CONNECTION Art

Objective: To understand that a map is a drawing that shows where things are and how things are shaped.

Resource: ***Project Book*** p. 8

Materials: pencils or crayons

1. Have children place their left or right hand, palm down, inside the frame on ***Project Book*** p. 8. Tell them to trace their hand, using a pencil or crayon. Explain that people usually use their right or their left hand to do certain things. In this way, they are right-handed or left-handed.
2. Tell children to draw fingernails for their fingers and thumbs. Have them sketch curved lines for their knuckles and draw any marks, scratches, rings, or bandages they might have on their hands.
3. Help children to print the word *left* or *right* at the base of the palm. Then help them write their names on the pages and label parts, like *nail, ring, thumb,* etc. Discuss with the class that they have made a map of their hand.

Project Book p. 8

Name: Date:
Make a Hand Map
Directions: Have each child trace a hand inside the frame.
8 Unit 1, Geography Skills 2, Getting Ready

1 Prepare

WARMING UP WITH THE READ ALOUD

Define map as "a drawing that shows where places or things are located." Then share the poem in the Read Aloud. Show children examples of maps and describe the places or things shown on each.

- ***What kinds of maps does the poem name?*** *(Possible answers include maps of rooms, homes, schools, yards, and buried treasure.)*
- ***Who can use maps?*** *(everyone)*

2 Teach

USING BIG BOOK PAGES 12–13

Have children compare the model of the school on page 12 with the map of the school on page 13. Explain that a model is a copy of something real.

USE BIG BOOK STICKERS, SHEETS 2, 3, 4

Use these ***Stickers*** throughout the lesson.

Share these tips to help children read maps.

HELPING YOURSELF

- A map is a drawing of a place.
- A map can help you find your way around a place.
- Things that are next to each other on a map will be next to each other in the real place.
- Things that are far from each other on a map will be far from each other in the real place.

GEOGRAPHY SKILLS

Looking at Maps

12

Read Aloud

Maps

Maps are helpful and maps are fun.
They can be used by everyone!
Maps of rooms or homes or schools,
Some of yards with swimming pools,
Even maps with buried treasures
Take us on incredible adventures.
Maps show us where to run and play.
Some even help us find our way.
Maps are helpful and maps are fun.
They're exciting for everyone!

Catherine M. Tamblyn

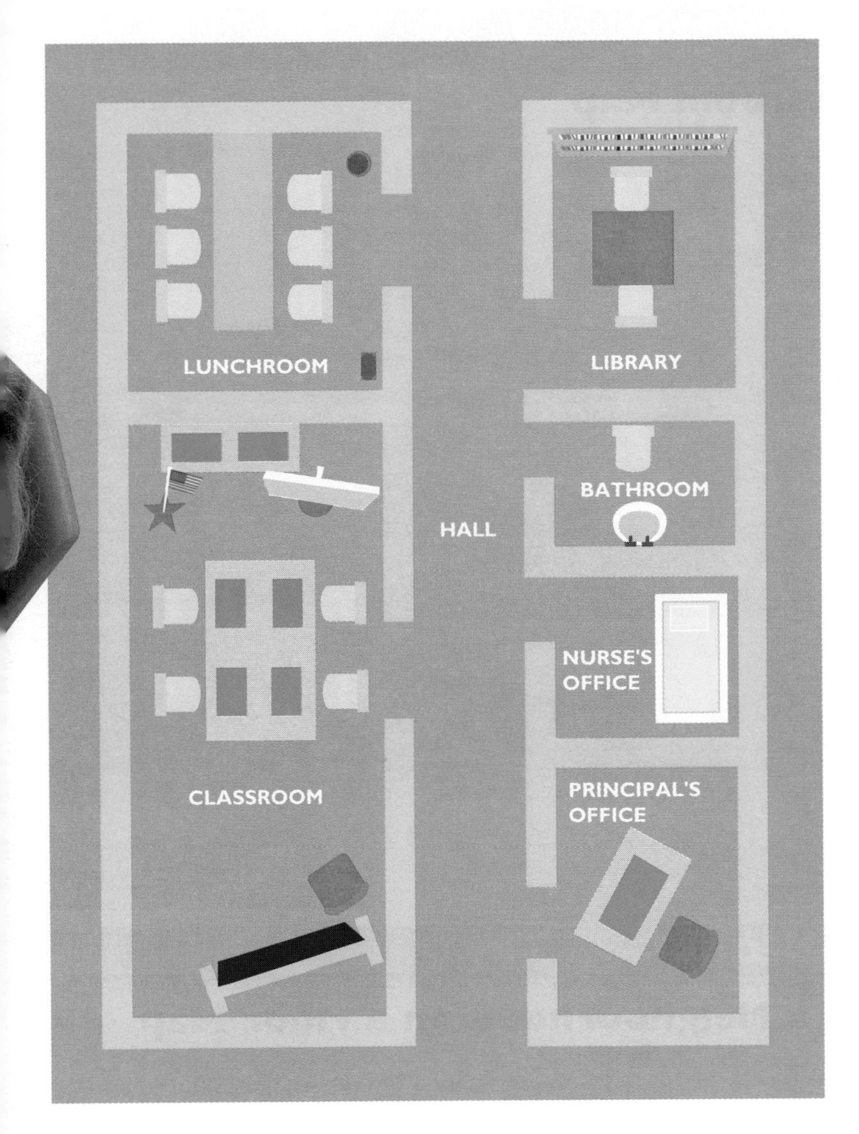

What rooms does this map show

13

Have children use the ***Stickers*** of schoolroom symbols to identify the rooms in the school model. For example, the principal's office is near the nurse's office. Encourage children to use terms such as *near, far from, next to, to the left* and *to the right* to locate things in the model. Then place the ***Sticker*** of the word *model* near the model and the ***Sticker*** of the word *map* near the map. Point out that maps are flat.

- ***What rooms are in this school? What activities might take place in these rooms?*** *(Children should name the rooms on the map and tell appropriate activities for each.)*

★**THINKING FURTHER: *Compare and Contrast* *How are the model of the school and the map the same?*** *(They show the same rooms in the school.)* ***How are they different?*** *(A map is flat. A model is a copy of the real thing in a solid form.)*

Have volunteers place the ***Stickers*** of school workers in the appropriate rooms on the map. Have them name the worker and the job he or she does.

Tell children that maps are helpful because they let us view the school in one look. We can also use them to find our way from one place to another. Name different routes and have children use the ***Stickers*** of children and arrows to show routes on the map. Have children identify routes to nearest EXITS for fire safety.

Technology Connection

VIDEODISC

Enrich the skills lesson with the *map* entry in the Glossary on Frame 5432.

See the bar code on p. 23.

Second-Language Support

Using Visuals As you explain what a map is, make a simple drawing of your schoolroom according to children's directions. For children needing second-language support, visual representation of the concrete objects in your room will provide them with the context they need to understand the rest of the lesson. Begin by inviting a volunteer to point out a desk or table in your room. On chart paper or the chalkboard, draw that object on your "map." Continue to ask children to name objects in the room and draw them on the map. While you are drawing, talk about where you are placing the objects, incorporating positional words that were introduced on p. 20 in the section, *Using Big Book Pages 10–11.* You may wish to use ***Word Cards*** to reinforce word recognition.

3 Close

LESSON SUMMARY

Read the lesson question with children, pointing to each word as you read. Ask volunteers to name the rooms on the map.

EVALUATE

Draw Schoolrooms On drawing paper have each child illustrate a room along your hall. If your class completed the earlier project, "Make a Model School Hallway," on page 9, have children draw illustrations of their room models. Help children to label their illustrations with the names of the rooms. While children work, draw a large map of your hall on mural paper. Invite children to tape their illustrations in or near the corresponding rooms on the map. For assessment suggestions, see p. 38.

ART CONNECTION

LEARNING STYLE: KINESTHETIC

Make a Classroom Map

GROUP

30 MINUTES OR LONGER

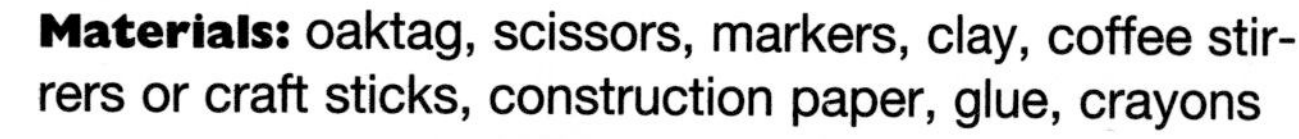

Objective: To develop map skills.

Materials: oaktag, scissors, markers, clay, coffee stirrers or craft sticks, construction paper, glue, crayons

Advance Preparation: Use a large sheet of oaktag to represent your classroom. Cut out a square of construction paper to represent your desk and glue it on the map in its appropriate place. Cut out small triangles from construction paper.

1. Have children look at the map of the classroom. Tell them that the square represents your desk. Then have the class brainstorm a list of different items they see in the classroom that can be added to the map, such as tables or shelves.
2. Have each child select an item from the list and draw it on a construction-paper triangle. Help each child glue the triangle to a coffee stirrer to make a pennant. Have children place their pennants in a small amount of clay so that they stand upright.
3. Invite children to guide you as you decide where on the map each item should be placed.

ART CONNECTION

LEARNING STYLE: KINESTHETIC

Learning Center: Create a Neighborhood on a Floor Map

GROUP

30 MINUTES OR LONGER

Objective: To create a neighborhood map and practice using directions.

Resources: ***Project Book*** pp. 65–75, ***K–1 Floor Map***

Materials: empty 1/2-gallon milk and juice cartons or shoe boxes, small model cars, construction paper, crayons, scissors, glue

1. Brainstorm with children some places near your school or places you might find near a school, such as a park, a post office, and a grocery store.
2. Have children go to the Art Learning Center to cut out and glue buildings from ***Project Book*** pp. 67–69, 71, 74, and 76 onto bands of construction paper. Glue construction paper with patterns onto cartons or boxes to make buildings.
3. Invite groups of children to position their buildings near the illustrated school on the ***Floor Map*** to create a school neighborhood.
4. Discuss where the school and other buildings are located using terms such as *to the left, to the right, near, far from, next to.* For further application, use ***Project Book*** pp. 65, 66, 70, 72, 73, and 75 to have children add cars and other small items to the ***Floor Map*** and discuss their locations in relationship to the buildings.

UNIT 1

LESSON 3

School Rules

UNIT 1 THEME BIG BOOK, PAGES 14–15

RESOURCE REMINDER

Project Book
p. 9

Stickers Package
Sheet 4

LESSON OVERVIEW

School rules are necessary for order and fairness, as well as for children's safety and health.

LESSON OBJECTIVES

- Recognize the need and importance of rules in and around school.
- Identify rules in and around your own school.
- Recognize the consequences of not following school rules.

KEY CONCEPTS

rules

GETTING READY

Make a Safety Badge

GROUP

15 TO 30 MINUTES

CURRICULUM CONNECTION **Art/Drama**

Objective: To act out a rule that children are familiar with.

Resource: *Project Book* p. 9

Materials: crayons or colored pencils, scissors, tape, yarn, hole puncher

1. Distribute a copy of ***Project Book*** p. 9 to each child. Have children color and cut out the safety badge.
2. Help children tape their badges around their arms. If badges are not long enough to fit around children's arms, create extensions by threading yarn through holes punched at both ends of the badge. Help children tie badges around their arms.
3. Divide the class into four groups. Have children in each group take turns acting as a safety patrol leader, helping the other children in the group to cross "the street." The rest of the group can pretend to wait "at a street corner" until the safety patrol leader tells them it is safe to cross.

Project Book
p. 9

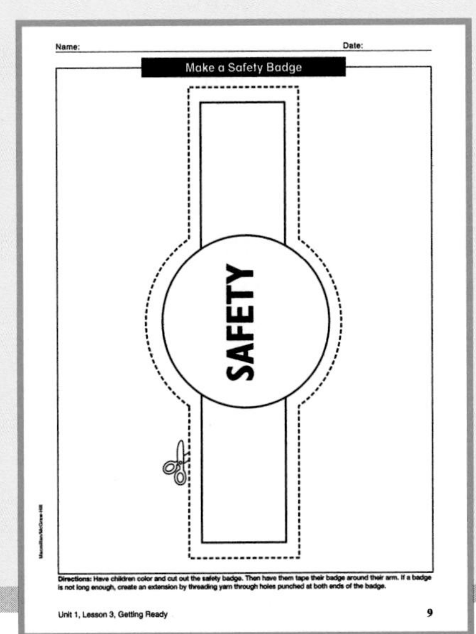

Name: Date:

Make a Safety Badge

SAFETY

Directions: Have children color and cut out the safety badge. Then have them tape their badge around their arm. If a badge is not long enough, create an extension by threading yarn through holes punched at both ends of the badge.

Unit 1, Lesson 3, Getting Ready 9

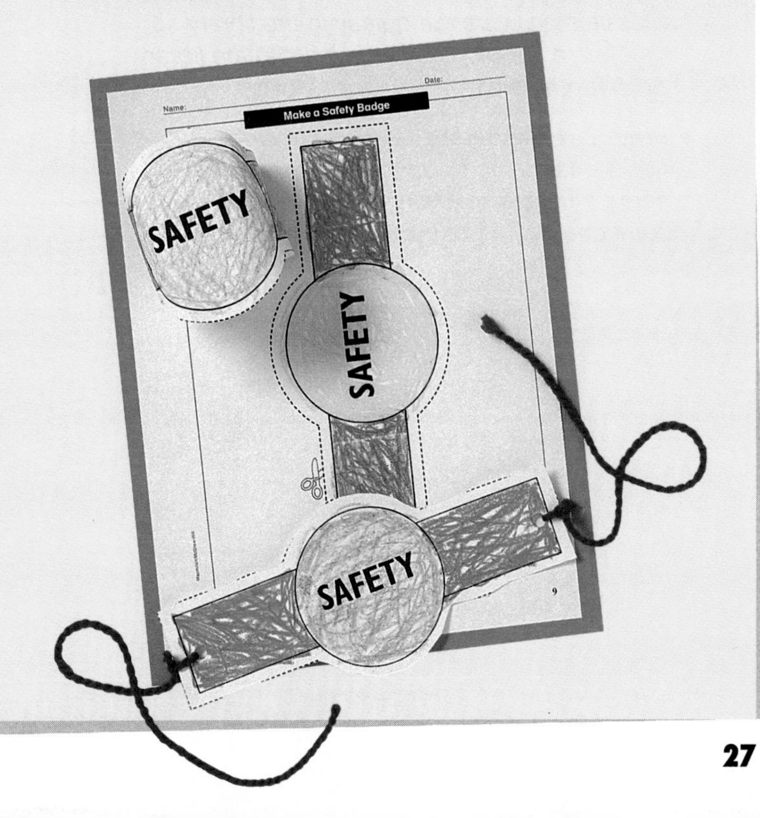

1 Prepare

WARMING UP WITH THE READ ALOUD

Tell children that today they will be learning about rules. Define rule as "something that tells us what we should and should not do." Read the nursery rhyme in the Read Aloud to begin the discussion.

- ***What was the rule in Mary's school?*** *(Possible answer: No animals or pets at school.)*

★ **THINKING FURTHER:** ***Making Conclusions***
Why do you think schools have rules that do not allow children to bring pets to school? *(Possible answers: Pets would be distracting; some children might be afraid of or allergic to certain pets.)*

2 Teach

USING BIG BOOK PAGES 14–15

Read the lesson title with children and have a volunteer tell the meaning of the word *rules*. Point to the first photograph. Have volunteers name rules associated with crossing a street and explain their importance. (Cross with a crossing guard or when the sign says WALK for safety.) Discuss the other photographs highlighting the rule and its importance as children answer the questions.

- ***What rule is being followed in the picture of the trash can? Why is this rule important?*** *(Clean up after yourself by putting litter in the can; the world would be a messy place if people did not clean up after themselves.)*
- ***What rule are the children following in the library? Why is this rule important?*** *(Possible answers: Sit quietly in the library so others are not disturbed, be quiet in the library so that others can enjoy their books.)*
- ***Why is it important to wait for your turn?*** *(It's the fair thing to do; people might argue about whose turn it is; if people push in line, someone might get hurt.)*

UNIT 1 THEME BIG BOOK

Read Aloud

Mary Had a Little Lamb

Mary had a little lamb,
Its fleece was white as snow;
And everywhere that Mary went
The lamb was sure to go.

It followed her to school one day,
That was against the rule;
It made the children laugh and play
To see a lamb at school.

Nursery Rhyme

Discuss with children the rules in your classroom that pertain to working together, caring for and using classroom materials, and listening to the teacher.

You may wish to discuss with children that sometimes rules may change to adjust to a situation or because the rule may not be fair to everyone.

USE BIG BOOK STICKERS, SHEET 4

Use these ***Stickers*** throughout the lesson.

Have children use the ✓ ***Stickers*** to identify rules in the Big Book that they follow in your classroom.

3 Close

LESSON SUMMARY

Read the lesson question with children, pointing to each word as you read. Have each child name a rule that he or she follows at school. As each child names a rule, invite others to give reasons to explain why the rule is necessary.

EVALUATE

Identify School Rules Encourage children to think of a school rule and to illustrate it. Then on sentence strips, write children's dictated sentences about their rules. On other sentence strips, write the consequences of not following the rules. Children's drawings and sentence strips can be shared in a display on a bulletin board, or in a special book that can be reviewed throughout the year. Children can match the rules and consequences to the appropriate pictures. For assessment suggestions, see p. 38.

Field Trip

Prior to going on a field trip around your school, discuss field trip rules such as: holding your partner's hand, staying together, and listening to and following directions.

- You might invite older children to discuss what it is like to go on a field trip and discuss field-trip rules. Have children create some rules to follow on their trip and explain the reasons for the rules. Take children around the inside and outside of your school to note various rules being enforced by teachers, parents, your principal, crossing guards, and school patrols. Also point out any printed rules that you see along the route. Encourage children to identify others who are following school rules.
- You might take children on a walk through the school neighborhood. Help children to read road signs or to decipher the pictures on signs they see and to identify the related rules. Also point out rules on signs at places of business. Explain to children that pictures on signs with a line through them mean "No."

ART CONNECTION

LEARNING STYLE: VISUAL

Make a Traffic Light

ON YOUR OWN

15 TO 30 MINUTES

Objective: To become familiar with rules of the road.

Materials: construction paper; green, red, and yellow crayons or markers; glue

Advance Preparation: Draw a blank traffic light on a sheet of construction paper. Next to each circle, write a double write-on line for children to use. Duplicate enough copies for the class.

1. Discuss with children the function of a traffic light. Mention the different colors on it and what each one means. Write the words *stop, caution,* and *go* on the chalkboard. Explain to children that *caution* means "be very careful" because the light will soon turn red.
2. Give each child a traffic light. Have children color each circle its correct color.
3. Next to each circle help children write either the word *stop, caution,* or *go.* Children can then cut out their traffic lights and glue them onto construction paper.

MOVEMENT CONNECTION

LEARNING STYLE: AUDITORY/KINESTHETIC

Play by the Rules

GROUP

15 TO 30 MINUTES

Objective: To appreciate the importance of following rules.

1. Discuss with children some of the rules that they have learned to follow at school. Write down their responses on the chalkboard. Talk about why the rules are important and what other activities involve rules, such as going to a movie or swimming in a pool.
2. Ask children if they have ever played the game "Simon Says." Write down the different rules of the game on the chalkboard.
3. Invite the class to play, with you as the leader. Then ask other volunteers to be Simon.

Working Together

UNIT 1 THEME BIG BOOK, PAGES 16–17

LESSON OVERVIEW

Children will examine common problems in working with others and will discuss possible solutions.

LESSON OBJECTIVES

- Identify problems children face in working together.
- Determine ways to solve problems.
- Recognize that children have choices.

KEY CONCEPTS

working together share

RESOURCE REMINDER

Project Book
pp. 10–11

Anthology
The More We Get Together, p. 40

Technology Connection
VIDEODISC/VIDEO TAPE 1

Search Frame 10556, Play to 16280

GETTING READY

Make a Partner Picture

PARTNER

15 TO 30 MINUTES

CURRICULUM CONNECTION Art

Objective: To demonstrate the need for working together with other people.

Resource: *Project Book* pp. 10–11

Materials: crayons or colored pencils, scissors, tape, construction paper

1. Divide the class in half. If there is not an even number of children, then you will need to become part of the odd-numbered group. Distribute a copy of ***Project Book*** p. 10 to the children in one group and a copy of ***Project Book*** p. 11 to the other group.
2. Tell children that they are to make a whole picture of the clown by finding a partner in the other group who has the other half of their picture.
3. Once children find a partner, have the partners color and cut out their clown. Then they should tape the two sides of the picture together onto a piece of construction paper. Children may choose to name their clown. Help them write the clown's name on the page.

Project Book pp. 10–11

1 Prepare

WARMING UP WITH THE READ ALOUD

Tell children that they will be talking about how children work with each other and ways they can work together better at school. To begin the discussion, share the poem in the Read Aloud.

- ***What are the children in the poem working together to create?*** *(a crayon drawing of a house)*
- ***What colors are the house?*** *(red and blue)*

Technology Connection

VIDEODISC/VIDEO TAPE 1
Enrich the Citizenship lesson with *Sharing* on Frame 10556.

See the bar code on p. 31.

UNIT 1 THEME BIG BOOK

Read Aloud

Working Together

I'll take the red.
You take the blue.
Together we'll crayon
a house for us two.

A window for me.
A window for you.
We're working together
to make something new!

Wendy Vierow

Using the Anthology

The More We Get Together, page 40 Children will enjoy singing and dancing to this spirited German folk song. To teach the song you may wish to write the words on word or sentence strips and place the strips in a pocket chart. Point out the repetition of words and phrases. Invite children to tell what the song says about getting together. Help them to understand that people feel happier when they spend time with friends.

When children are proficient singing the song, have them sing and dance to the tune. Have children join hands in a circle and move to the right singing the first and third lines and move to the left singing the second and fourth lines.

2 Teach

USING BIG BOOK PAGES 16–17

Tell children that the kindergartners in the picture are each making drawings. Explain to children that the kindergartners must work together and share the drawing markers.

Which children in the group are not thinking about the rights of others? How do you know? *(the boy in the green shirt because he is scribbling on the drawing of the girl in the red shirt; the girl in the yellow shirt because she is taking the marker of the boy in the white shirt)*

★ **THINKING FURTHER:** ***Making Predictions***
How else might the group be able to work together? *(Possible answers: The boy in the green shirt can color on his own paper; the girl in the yellow shirt can share the markers instead of taking them from others; the children can listen to the teacher and share her attention.)*

You may wish to take this opportunity to talk about racial, cultural, and ethnic prejudices and the need to get along and work together.

3 Close

LESSON SUMMARY

Read the lesson question with children, pointing to each word as you read. Invite volunteers to name things they do to work with others in your class.

EVALUATE

Perform School Skits Encourage all children to take part in acting out situations in school which involve choices, such as a child cutting in line, someone leaving a mess on a table, or someone being noisy. Invite those watching to tell what they viewed and to name different ways the situations could be handled.

CITIZENSHIP

A part of classroom citizenship for children is recognizing the small, yet ordinary things they do and can do to help make the classroom run smoothly and help classmates work together. To accomplish this goal, invite children to help you make a poster for the classroom titled "Ways We Work Together."

Children might suggest and illustrate the following elements of citizenship: We share; we take turns; we help each other; we are kind; we follow rules; we listen to others; we are fair; we think of each other's feelings.

When conflict arises in your classroom, remind children of their poster.

MUSIC/ART CONNECTION

LEARNING STYLE: AUDITORY/ KINESTHETIC/VISUAL

Learning Center: Make Music Together

Objective: To learn about a variety of musical instruments and to play cooperatively.

Materials: crayons or markers, glue, glitter, construction paper, chart paper, oatmeal boxes, wooden spoons, boxes filled with rice or beans, large paper, tape

Advance Preparation: Write out the words to a song you wish to teach the class on chart paper. You may wish to use the song "The Bear Went Over the Mountain" or "Mary Had a Little Lamb." Illustrate the song.

1. Teach the class the song you chose. Then divide the class into three groups to make instruments. As each group goes to the Music Learning Center, encourage one group to make drums (empty oatmeal boxes/spoons), another to make maracas (boxes filled with rice or beans), and the last group to make trumpets (large paper rolled into thick cones and sealed with tape).
2. As groups complete making the instruments, have them visit the Art Learning Center to decorate them, eventually making all three instruments.
3. Have each group play a different instrument (drums, maracas, or trumpets) while they sing your chosen song. Discuss with the class how they worked together to create music.

ART CONNECTION

LEARNING STYLE: KINESTHETIC/VISUAL

Create a Group Collage

Objective: To work together toward a common goal.

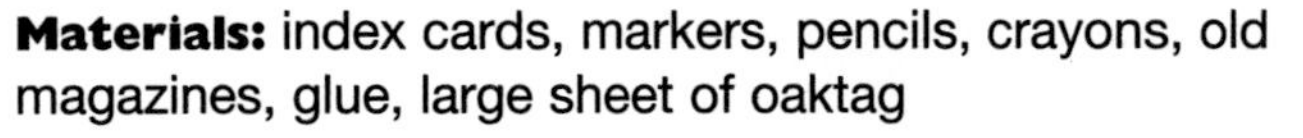

Materials: index cards, markers, pencils, crayons, old magazines, glue, large sheet of oaktag

1. Have each child write his or her name on an index card. Invite children to decorate their cards.
2. Then divide the class into groups and have each child cut out from a magazine one picture that reflects or means something special to that child.
3. Each group can then glue their index cards with their magazine pictures beneath them onto the large sheet of oaktag.
4. Encourage each group to present their collage to the class. Have them explain how they had to work together to complete the collage.

CLOSE WITH A POEM

LINKING SOCIAL STUDIES AND LITERATURE

Bring Unit 1 to a close with the poem "At School" from pages 18–19 of the Big Book. The poem supports these Social Studies concepts:

- School is a busy place where children learn many important things.
- Kindergartners work and play together.

ABOUT THE POEM

A full instructional plan, along with the poem, appears on the following two pages.

This poem by Louise Binder Scott describes some activities of a kindergarten classroom while exploring the idea that it is not unusual to forget things learned at the beginning of the school year.

This poem reinforces the idea that school is a busy and exciting place, where children work and play together.

ABOUT THE POET

Louise Binder Scott has taught as an associate professor of special education at California State University and as a speech-language-hearing-reading specialist in the San Marino, California, schools. She has written extensively for the primary grades. Her publications include the popular *Rhymes for Fingers and Flannelboards* (with J.J. Thompson), *Learning Language Skills*, and *Language Experiences for Young Children: Singing Fun.*

INTRODUCE

Using Prior Knowledge Encourage children to talk about the many different things that they have learned so far in kindergarten. You can list their responses in a chart:

What We Have Learned

- The ABC's
- Numbers
- How to Read Words
- All About Each Other

Previewing Read aloud the title of the poem and the name of the poet. Invite children to look at the picture that accompanies the poem. Guide them to understand that the picture shows a school classroom. Point out the children in the picture who are listening to the teacher while she reads a story. Tell them that the children are sharing the teacher's attention with each other. Point out the group of children sitting around the table making paper-bag puppets. Discuss the importance of considering the rights of others in the use and care of art supplies. Ask what the children near the toy cash register appear to be doing.

UNIT 1 THEME BIG BOOK

Second-Language Support

Using Dialog Invite children to point to an activity you name that is mentioned in the poem and shown in the picture. Then develop a simple conversation. For example, for the grocery store area, you might say, "Right. That's the grocery store. Where are the shelves in the store? Do you see any apples?" The child might simply repeat what you have said, or name another item. Some children may be able to say something about the activity (They're playing grocery store.). Show you understand by restating whatever the child says in your own words.

Curriculum Connection

Mathematics Have children demonstrate the meaning of "three sets of three" found in the poem.

- Provide children with plastic counters or other small manipulatives.
- Have partners work together to make three sets of three with the manipulatives.
- Ask the partners to count the manipulatives to find out how many there are in all. *(9)*

READ

USING BIG BOOK PAGES 18–19

Read aloud the poem, stressing the rhythm and rhyme in the language. Encourage children to follow along in the Big Book as you point to the words. Then read the poem again, inviting children to join in whenever they can.

At this time, you may wish to play the poem on the ***Anthology Cassette***.

SHARE

Use questions such as the following to help prompt a discussion of the poem:

What are the children doing at the left side of the picture? (playing store)

What are the children doing at the right side of the picture? (making puppets)

Which of these things have we done in our own classroom? (Answers will vary.)

Tell children that the school year begins in September in many places around the country. Invite them to think about what they learned at the beginning of the school year. Is there anything they may have forgotten since then? Then talk with them about what makes this poem fun to hear and say.

EXTENDING THE LITERATURE WITH DRAMA

LEARNING STYLE:
AUDITORY/KINESTHETIC/VISUAL

Make Classroom Puppets

GROUP

Objective: To make and use puppets to represent the class.

30 MINUTES OR LONGER

Resource: *Project Book* p. 12

Materials: crayons, scissors, large craft sticks, glue

- Remind children that the children in the poem made puppets from a bag. Then invite them to make another type of puppet that they can use to act out scenes from their own class.
- Give each child a copy of ***Project Book*** p. 12. Read aloud the directions. Have children color, cut out, and glue the puppets onto craft sticks.
- Have small groups of children use the puppets to act out typical classroom activities. Encourage them to improvise appropriate dialogue.

Project Book p. 12

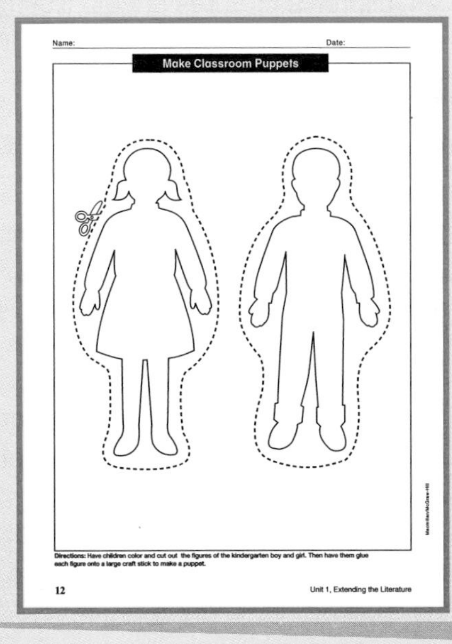
Name: Date:
Make Classroom Puppets
Directions: Have children color and cut out the figures of the kindergarten boy and girl. Then have them glue each figure onto a large craft stick to make a puppet.
12 Unit 1, Extending the Literature

UNIT 1 ASSESSMENT

Assessment Opportunities

The CLOSE section of each lesson includes an EVALUATE activity. This page provides suggestions for using selected EVALUATE activities to integrate your assessment program with each day's lesson plan. The next page lists the main objectives of the unit and some of the activities that reinforce them. You may wish to make a copy of the checklist for each child.

EVALUATE Signs of Success

LESSON 2, Our Busy Classroom
EVALUATE: Draw Favorite School Activities, p. 17

OBSERVATIONAL ASSESSMENT

- Children should be able to distinguish between activities they do alone and those they do with a group as well as activities they perform at home and in school. You may wish to ask them questions such as, "Is this an activity that you would do by yourself?"
- You may wish to record children's answers.

PORTFOLIO ASSESSMENT

The drawings can be part of children's portfolios.

- The drawings should show a favorite school activity accurately.
- Children's dictated sentences should refer to the activity in a positive way. Children should be able to name one thing they like about their favorite activity.

GEOGRAPHY SKILLS, Looking at Maps
EVALUATE: Draw Schoolrooms, p. 25

OBSERVATIONAL ASSESSMENT

- As they are drawing, ask children questions such as, "Is this room next to the library?" You may wish to tape-record their conversations while they draw and answer your questions about their pictures.

PORTFOLIO ASSESSMENT

The illustrations can be part of children's portfolios.

- Children's pictures should illustrate a room located along a hall in your school.

LESSON 3, School Rules
EVALUATE: Identify School Rules, p. 29

OBSERVATIONAL ASSESSMENT

- Children should be able to demonstrate their understanding of what a rule is. You may wish to ask questions such as, "Why is your rule important?" You might tape-record their conversations as well as the answers to your questions.

PORTFOLIO ASSESSMENT

Copies of the drawings and sentence strips can be part of children's portfolios.

- The drawings should illustrate children's rules accurately.

UNIT I OBJECTIVES Checklist

1. Recognize that people have varied interests and talents that make them special.
2. Identify activities that involve working alone and together.
3. Identify activities perfomed in school.
4. Identify the locations of things.
5. Recognize that a map is a drawing of a place.
6. Recognize what a rule is.
7. Recognize the need for school rules.
8. Recognize the importance of working together with others.

Name ______________________ Class ______________________

LESSON	ACTIVITY	PAGE	UNIT I OBJECTIVES	✔
LESSON 1	Make a Teddy-Bear Class	11	1, 2	
LESSON 1	Sing "Teddy Bear, Teddy Bear"	14	3	
LESSON 1	Make a Class Jigsaw Puzzle	14	2	
LESSON 2	Make Busy-Bee Pendants	15	3	
LESSON 2	Make an Eye Chart	18	3, 4	
LESSON 2	Have Fun with Fingerplays	18	1	
GEOGRAPHY SKILL 1	Make Left and Right Signs	19	4	
GEOGRAPHY SKILL 1	Play "Hide-and-Seek"	22	4	
GEOGRAPHY SKILL 1	Sing "Hokey Pokey"	22	4	
GEOGRAPHY SKILL 2	Make a Hand Map	23	4, 5	
GEOGRAPHY SKILL 2	Make a Classroom Map	26	4, 5	
GEOGRAPHY SKILL 2	Create a Neighborhood on a Floor Map	26	4, 5	
LESSON 3	Make a Safety Badge	27	6, 7	
LESSON 3	Make a Traffic Light	30	6, 7	
LESSON 3	Play by the Rules	30	6, 7	
CITIZENSHIP	Make a Partner Picture	31	2, 8	
CITIZENSHIP	Make Music Together	34	2, 8	
CITIZENSHIP	Create a Group Collage	34	1, 2, 8	

Meeting Families

PLANNING GUIDE

Pupil Edition and Unit 2 Theme Big Book Pages 40–79

INTRODUCTION

SUGGESTED PACING: 3 DAYS

Begin With The Literature Big Book, pages 43, 208–209

I Go with My Family to Grandma's

Using The Unit Opener pp. 44–46

PROJECT IDEAS
- Family Quilt / ART
- Make a Family Picture / ART
- Enriching with Multimedia
- A Family Story / LANGUAGE ARTS
- Make Job Fold-Outs / ART

LESSON 1

SUGGESTED PACING: 1–2 DAYS

Our Special Families pp. 47–50

KEY CONCEPTS
family, family member, change

PROJECT IDEAS
- Draw a Special Group / ART
- Make Family Circles / ART
- Chart Family Sizes / MATHEMATICS

RESOURCES
Project Book, p. 14 • Sticker Package Sheet 5, Anthology, pp. 29, 24–25

LESSON 2

SUGGESTED PACING: 1–2 DAYS

Where Families Live pp. 51–54

KEY CONCEPTS
home, neighborhood, address, street

PROJECT IDEAS
- Find Homes for Animals / ART
- Make Pocket Homes / ART
- Building Homes and Addresses / ART

RESOURCES
Project Book, p. 15, 65–76 • Big Book Stickers Sheet 6 • Anthology, p. 3 • Floor Map

AROUND THE WORLD

SUGGESTED PACING: 1–2 DAYS

Families Are Everywhere pp. 59–62

KEY CONCEPTS
world, country

PROJECT IDEAS
- Write a Postcard / ART
- Try Fruit from Around the World / HOME ECONOMICS
- Sing "Frère Jacques" ("Are You Sleeping?") / MUSIC

RESOURCES
Project Book, p. 17 • Big Book Stickers Sheet 7 • Inflatable Globe • TECHNOLOGY Videodisc/Video Tape 2

LESSON 4

SUGGESTED PACING: 1–2 DAYS

At Work pp. 63–66

KEY CONCEPTS
job, workers

PROJECT IDEAS
- Make a Worker Puppet / ART/DRAMA
- Make a Worker's Alphabet Book / LANGUAGE ARTS
- Use Worker Play-Kits / DRAMA

RESOURCES
Project Book, p. 18 • Big Book Stickers Sheet 7 • Anthology, pp. 30–31, 52

LESSON 5

SUGGESTED PACING: 1–2 DAYS

Needs And Wants pp. 67–70

KEY CONCEPTS
needs, food, clothes, shelter, love, money, wants

PROJECT IDEAS
- Make a Piggy Bank / MATHEMATICS
- Make Cards that Hug / ART
- Shop in Our General Store / MATHEMATICS/DRAMA

RESOURCES
Project Book, p. 19 • Big Book Stickers Sheet 8 • Anthology, pp. 14–16, 46–51

CLOSE WITH A POEM

SUGGESTED PACING: 1 DAY

Four Generations pp. 75–77

PROJECT IDEAS
- Make a Walking Partners Picture / ART/LANGUAGE ARTS

RESOURCES
Project Book, p. 21

UNIT ASSESSMENT

SUGGESTED PACING: 1 DAY

pp. 78–79

OBSERVATIONAL/PORTFOLIO ASSESSMENT, p. 78
- Make a Family Word Web
- Perform Family Skits
- Draw Country Pictures

OBJECTIVES CHECKLIST, p. 79

McGRAW-HILL SCHOOL DIVISION'S HOME PAGE at http://www.mhschool.com contains on-line student activities related to this unit.

LESSON 3

SUGGESTED PACING: 1–2 DAYS

Together As A Family

pp. 55–58

KEY CONCEPTS

fun, play, help, work, rules

PROJECT IDEAS

Make a Chart / MATHEMATICS
Make Helping Handprints / ART
Sing a Helping Song / MUSIC/MOVEMENT

RESOURCES

Project Book, p. 16 • Stickers Package Sheet 6 • Anthology, pp. 32–34

THINKING SKILLS

SUGGESTED PACING: 1–2 DAYS

Finding Alike And Different

pp. 71–74

KEY CONCEPTS

alike, different

PROJECT IDEAS

Create a Place Mat / ART
Find Alike and Different / LANGUAGE ARTS
Paint Alike and Different / ART/LANGUAGE ARTS

RESOURCES

Project Book, p. 20 • Big Book Stickers Sheets 4, 8, 16

SHELTERED INSTRUCTION

Reading Strategies & Language Development

Modeling, p. 44

Second-Language Support

Using Visuals, p. 60

Meeting Individual Needs

McGraw-Hill Adventure Books

Assessment Opportunities

Ongoing Unit Project: Make a Family Picture, p. 45

Observational and Portfolio Assessment, p. 78
Objectives Checklist, p.79
Evaluate, pp. 49, 53, 57, 61, 65, 69, 73

FOR FURTHER SUPPORT

- Language Support Handbook
- Social Studies Readiness

Unit 2 Bibliography and Resources

MCGRAW-HILL ADVENTURE BOOKS Easy-to-Read Books

Kono, Juliet S. ***The Pancake Place.*** Everyone in the family helps out when the family business is a restaurant.

Miranda, Anne. ***The Elephants Have a House.*** A family of elephants wants to build a house.

CLASSROOM LIBRARY

McMillan, Bruce. ***Grandfather's Trolley.*** Cambridge, MA: Candlewick Press, 1995. A young girl recalls the excitement of riding the trolley when her grandfather was the conductor.

READ ALOUD BOOKS

Bang, Molly. ***Goose.*** New York: Scholastic Inc., 1996. A baby goose adopted by woodchucks leaves home to find where she belongs.

Barton, Byron, reteller. ***The Little Red Hen.*** New York: HarperCollins Publishers, 1993. A little red hen grows grain and tends to it without any help from her friends.

Bunting, Eve. ***Flower Garden.*** San Diego: Harcourt, Brace & Company, 1994. A girl and her father make a windowsill flower garden as a birthday surprise for Mom.

Dorros, Arthur. ***This Is My House.*** New York: Scholastic Inc., 1992. Text and illustrations depict different kinds of houses lived in by children and their families all around the world.

Hoberman, Mary Ann. ***Fathers, Mothers, Sisters, Brothers: A Collection of Family Poems.*** Boston, MA: Little, Brown & Co., 1991. This collection of poems focuses on family life.

McBratney, Sam. ***Guess How Much I Love You.*** Cambridge, MA: Candlewick Press, 1994. Little Nutbrown Hare demonstrates his love for his father in a bedtime game.

Morris, Ann. ***The Daddy Book.*** Parsippany, NJ: Silver Press, 1996. Fathers and their children are featured around the world in this photoessay.

Morris, Ann. ***Loving.*** New York: Lothrop, Lee & Shepard Books, 1990. Families around the world are shown in colorful photographs.

Reiser, Lynn. ***The Surprise Family.*** New York: Greenwillow Books, 1994. A hen's family is not what she expects them to be, but she loves them just the same.

Rotner, Shelley, and Shelia M. Kelly. ***Lots of Moms.*** New York: Dial Books for Young Readers, 1996. Photographs show a variety of mothers, everywhere, engaged in activities with their children.

Ryan, Pam Muñoz. ***One Hundred Is a Family.*** New York: Hyperion Books for Children, 1994. Families are shown in all sizes doing many family activities.

TEACHER BOOKS

Jenness, Aylette. ***Families: A Celebration of Diversity, Commitment, and Love.*** Boston, MA: Houghton Mifflin Co., 1990. Text and photos combine to depict the lives of diverse families.

Seltzer, Isadore. ***The House I Live In.*** New York: Macmillan Publishing Co., 1992. The various kinds of houses in America are described with full-page, colorful illustrations.

TECHNOLOGY MULTIMEDIA

All About Me. 4 Interactive Discs. (MS-DOS/WINDOWS). Students can construct family trees and explore family history and relationships. HarperCollins Publishers. (800) 242-7737.

Understanding Our Families. Video. S95564-HAVT. Families are explored in a series of videos that includes: "What is a Family?/Families Have Needs and Wants" and "Families Have Responsibilities/Families Change." Society For Visual Education. (800) 829-1900.

FREE OR INEXPENSIVE MATERIALS

For a brochure that explains how children with healthy eating habits learn better, write to: International Reading Association, Dept. EG, 800 Barksdale Road, P.O. Box 8139, Newark, DE 19714-8139.

BEGIN WITH THE LITERATURE BIG BOOK

LINKING SOCIAL STUDIES AND LITERATURE

Introduce Unit 2 with the **Literature Big Book**, ***I Go with My Family to Grandma's***. The story supports these Social Studies concepts:

- Every family is unique.
- Family members love and care for each other.
- Recognize how families lived long ago.

Literature Big Book

ABOUT THE STORY

A full instructional plan, along with the complete text of the story, appears on pages 208–209.

One hundred years ago in New York City, 24 children and ten parents travel by trolley, wagon, ferry, train, and bicycle-built-for-two to Grandma's house for a boisterous reunion and a family photograph.

ABOUT THE AUTHOR

Riki Levinson was an art director for half of her career, then took up writing. Her first book, *Watch the Stars Come Out*, also with Diane Goode, won many awards. She has always lived in New York City.

ABOUT THE ILLUSTRATOR

Diane Goode credits her love of books and art to childhood visits to Europe. She has illustrated 27 books for children, and now lives in Rhode Island.

USING THE
Unit 2 Opener

USING BIG BOOK PAGES 2–3

Read aloud the unit title. Have volunteers share what they know about *families.* Introduce Susan and Jim. Tell children they will see Jim again in other pages of the book. Let children preview the unit as they look for Jim in the lessons.

DEVELOPING KEY CONCEPTS

Children will study families, homes, activities, and needs and wants. They also learn the concepts *alike* and *different.* Ask volunteers to define these words.

family *A family is a group of people who love and care for each other.*

family member *A family member is a person in a family.*

home *A home is a place to live.*

BIG BOOK STICKERS, SHEETS 5–6

Affix these ***Sticker*** labels near the home. Discuss how the words relate to the photograph.

home

SHELTERED INSTRUCTION

Giving children examples of similarities and differences provide them with cues to determine what is similar and different about the families and homes in the text. For example, two families may be the same or different in size. **[SDAIE STRATEGY: MODELING]**

UNIT 2 THEME BIG BOOK

BULLETIN BOARD

Family Quilt

Turn your bulletin board into a patchwork family quilt.

- Cover the bulletin board with plain paper. Distribute square pieces of construction paper to each child.
- Tell children that some family quilts are made from pieces of material that were once special but have since been discarded or are no longer needed, such as a baby blanket or a favorite old shirt.
- Ask children to decorate their squares for a family quilt. Each square should show a favorite picture or pattern that has meaning for the child's family. Possibilities include the design on a favorite old shirt, tablecloth, or curtain from home. Children can also draw pictures of their family or family pet.
- Have children work together to piece the squares together like a quilt on your bulletin board. Encourage a discussion about how all families are different.

ABOUT THE PHOTOGRAPH

Point out that Susan and Jim are working together with a picture of a type of home called an apartment building. Tell children that they made this picture by gluing photographs, drawings of families, and other cutouts to a sheet of cardboard. Have children name things they see in or near the building. Explain that an apartment building is a home for more than one family. Count together the number of families living in the building.

Directions for making this Ongoing Unit Project can be found at the bottom of this page.

SCHOOL-TO-HOME

My Family

- In this unit, children will learn about many families. Encourage parents or guardians and children to work together at home to explore their own families.
- Make a fill-in-the-blanks paragraph as a springboard for home discussion. The paragraph can include information such as: The members of my family are named ___. Some things we do together are ___.

ONGOING UNIT PROJECT

GROUP

Make a Family Picture

CURRICULUM CONNECTION Art

During this unit, children will work in small groups to create homes that will display photographs or drawings of families or things important to families.

Advance Preparation: Gather for each group a large sheet of foam core or cardboard cut from appliance boxes.

1. Tell the groups they will be using the cardboard to make a home, such as the one shown in the opener photograph. Direct them to paint the cardboard any color and allow it to dry.
2. Have children draw pictures of their families or bring a family photograph to school. Children uncomfortable with this task can draw a picture of someone who is important to them, a family pet, or something else that means family to them.
3. Have each group member color and cut out a window box from ***Project Book*** p. 13. Collectively have the members color the door and a set of numbers for each home.
4. Assist children in gluing the pictures or photographs and accessories to the homes. The homes can be further decorated with paint or markers.

Assessment Suggestions

Signs of Success

- Each child should be able to draw a picture or provide a photograph of his or her own family or something that signifies family to him or her.
- On a volunteer basis, children should be able to identify members of the family or something symbolic of family in their drawing or photograph.

TECHNOLOGY CENTER

Enriching with Multimedia

RESOURCE: *Videodisc/Video Tape 1*

- Enrich Unit 2 with the video segment *Learning About Money.*

Search 16286, Play to 20640

RESOURCE: *Videodisc*

- Enrich Unit 2 with *Types of Money.*

Search Frame 23958

LANGUAGE ARTS LEARNING CENTER

LEARNING STYLE: AUDITORY/VISUAL

A Family Story

ON YOUR OWN

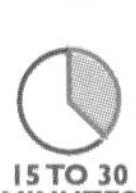

15 TO 30 MINUTES

Materials: drawing paper, crayons, pencils

1. Talk with children about groups they belong to, including family and friends. Encourage them to talk about what makes each group special.
2. Let children know that they are going to create their own family picture stories. Tell them that the story may be about their families, a family they have read about, or a family they may create.
3. Have them work in the Language Arts Learning Center to create their stories. Encourage them to include details that show where the family lives and what each member does inside and outside the home.
4. Invite children to share their stories, and encourage them to write or dictate captions or sentences about their pictures. Display the stories in the Language Arts Learning Center.

TEACHER EXCHANGE

Thanks to: DeAnn A. Kemp, Windridge Elementary, Kaysville, Utah

Make Job Fold-Outs

ON YOUR OWN

15 TO 30 MINUTES

Materials: construction paper, crayons, pencils

1. Discuss with children what jobs they might like to do when they grow up. Ask children what type of clothes they would need to wear while doing each kind of job.
2. Distribute a piece of construction paper to each child. At the top, help children write "I want to be a ________." Have them fold their papers into three sections and label the sections: "My Face," "My Body," and "My Legs."
3. In each section, invite children to draw a part of their body as if they were working in their chosen job.
4. Then children can fold their paper back up in three sections forming a job fold-out. Ask volunteers to share their fold-outs with the class.

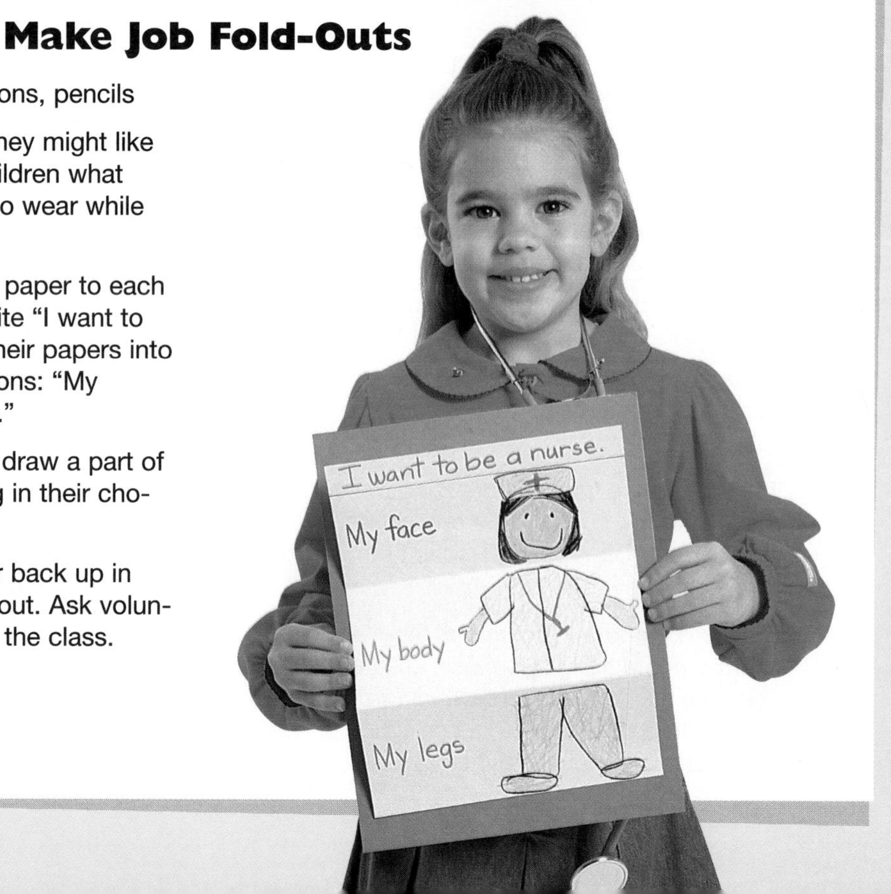

UNIT 2

LESSON 1 Our Special Families

UNIT 2 THEME BIG BOOK, PAGES 4–5

LESSON OVERVIEW

Families are special in their size, composition, and in the ways they change.

LESSON OBJECTIVES

- Recognize that families vary in size and in composition.
- Recognize that families change.
- Realize that each of us is part of a family.

KEY CONCEPTS

family   family member   change

RESOURCE REMINDER

Project Book
p. 14

Stickers Package
Sheet 5

Anthology
Andre, p. 29
Something for Everyone, pp. 24–25

GETTING READY

Draw a Special Group

ON YOUR OWN

15 TO 30 MINUTES

CURRICULUM CONNECTION Art

Objective: To explore different types of groups.

Resource: *Project Book* p. 14

Materials: crayons, pencils

1. Using ***Project Book*** p. 14, ask volunteers to name what is shown on the frame. Elicit from children that the pictures show different groups. Tell them that a group is made up of people who work, play, or live together. Explain that groups are made up of more than one person. A group can be made up of animals, too. Have children name the groups shown on the ***Project Book*** page.
2. Have children draw inside the frame a group to which they belong, such as a family or cub scout troop.
3. In the space below the frame, write children's dictated sentences about their drawings.
4. Invite children to share their drawings. Discuss the different characteristics of each group.

Project Book
p. 14

Name: Date:

Draw a Special Group

Directions: Have children draw a picture of a group they belong to. Write their dictated sentence below the picture.

14 Unit 2, Lesson 1, Getting Ready

Name: Date:

Draw a Special Group

I am part of a reading group.

14 Unit 2, Lesson 1, Getting Ready

1 Prepare

WARMING UP WITH THE READ ALOUD

Tell children that each of them is part of a special group called a family. To help define a *family,* share the poem in the Read Aloud.

- ***Who makes up a family?*** *(Children and parents including step-parents, grandparents, fosterparents, brothers, sisters, aunts, uncles, and cousins. Other answers may include animal and storybook families.)*

★ **THINKING FURTHER: *Classifying* *What kinds of families does the poem name?*** *(human, storybook, and animal families)*

2 Teach

USING BIG BOOK PAGES 4–5

Define *family* as "a group of people who love and care for each other." Introduce the word *families* in the lesson title. Tell children that people can be part of a family even when they do not live together.

Point out Jim, the boy introduced in the Unit Opener. Tell children that Jim is part of the family in the photograph.

USE BIG BOOK STICKERS, SHEET 5

Use the following ***Stickers*** throughout the lesson.

3 3 4 5

Our Special Families

4

Read Aloud

What Is a Family?

What is a family?
Who is a family?
One and another makes two is a family!
Baby and father and mother: a family!
Parents and sister and brother: a family!

All kinds of people can make up a family
All kinds of mixtures can make up a family

What is a family?
Who is a family?
The children that lived in a shoe is a family!
A pair like kanga and roo is a family!
A calf and a cow that go moo is a family!

All kinds of creatures can make up a family
All kinds of numbers can make up a family

What is a family?
Who is a family?
Either a lot or a few is a family;
But whether there's ten or there's two in *your* family,
All of your family plus *you* is a family!

Mary Ann Hoberman

Have children place the ***Stickers*** of the word *family* on the families on pp. 4–5. Identify the people in the families as family members. Have volunteers place the ***Sticker*** of the word *family member* on people in the photographs, naming who they think each person might be such as father or mother. Have children use the ***Sticker*** numerals to identify the different sizes of the families on pp. 4–5.

Point out the photograph album on the table on p. 4. Tell children that photos can show how people and families change over time. Define change as "to become different."

- ***What are the families in the photographs doing?*** *(reading together, playing music, playing with the baby, pouring orange juice)*
- ***In what ways might families change?*** *(Possible answers: New children might be born or adopted as in the picture on p. 4; older members could leave home to go to school, to work, or to get married; relatives could move in; parents could separate, get divorced, remarry, or die; children could move in with guardians.)*

3 Close

LESSON SUMMARY

Read the lesson question, pointing to each word as you read. Elicit from children that families consist of different numbers of people who may or may not be related to each other, who care for each other, and who often live together.

EVALUATE

Make a Family Word Web Have children make illustrated word webs about their families or a family they have read about. Provide children with paper, crayons, and labels for the words *family, family members, change,* and *size.* Tell children to place the word *family* in the center of their drawings, and the words *members, change,* and *size* branching from the center. Direct them to illustrate information about the families under the headings. Children can place their work in their portfolios. For assessment suggestions, see p. 78.

Background Information

ABOUT TOPIC SENSITIVITY You may wish to alert parents in advance that you will be teaching a unit on families. Invite parents and guardians to express concerns they may have about information that they consider private and do not want their child to discuss. To make children more comfortable, allow participation in revealing family sizes and relationships to be voluntary. Display pictures of families of different compositions and sizes. Gather stories with the topics of divorce, adoption, remarriage, single parents, stepparents, foster families, and deceased and dying family members.

Using the Anthology

Andre, page 29 Read the poem. Ask children to give reasons that Andre selected the parents whom he already had.

You can also use **Something for Everyone, pp. 24–25** with Lesson 1

ART CONNECTION

LEARNING STYLE: VISUAL

Make Family Circles

ON YOUR OWN

15 TO 30 MINUTES

Objective: To demonstrate family size and composition.

Materials: white and colored construction or drawing paper, pencils, scissors, tape or glue, crayons, markers

Advance Preparation: Cut sheets of construction or drawing paper in half lengthwise and accordian-fold each half into eight sections. Then draw a form of a person on the folded paper as shown.

1. Tell children that they will be making family circle chains, showing their family or families they know about. Cut out the form of the person or have children carefully cut it out. Each half will make four connected family members. Children with fewer than four family members can cut their chains down and give the additional sections to children with larger families. Any additional sections can be attached with tape or glue.
2. Have children color their family members on the front and back. At the bottom of the chain, help children to write the names of each family member.
3. Children can tape together the arms at the ends of the chain to form a family circle.
4. Children also can glue their chains onto construction paper. At the bottom of the paper, write children's dictated sentences about their families.

MATHEMATICS CONNECTION

LEARNING STYLE: VISUAL

Chart Family Sizes

GROUP

15 TO 30 MINUTES

Objective: To chart and compare size in different families.

Materials: lined chart paper, marker

Advance Preparation: On a sheet of chart paper, write the title "Family Sizes." Then write the numbers 2 to 10 up the left of the sheet as shown. Be sure to allow space between each number so that illustrations can be added.

1. Tell children that they are going to work together to make a chart that will show the sizes of their families or families they know about. Read the title and the numbers with children. Next to each number, you or the children can draw the appropriate number of stick figures.
2. Ask children to draw an *X* on the chart to indicate the number of people in the families. When the chart is complete, have volunteers count the number of *X*s in each row to determine the smallest, largest, and most common size of family.

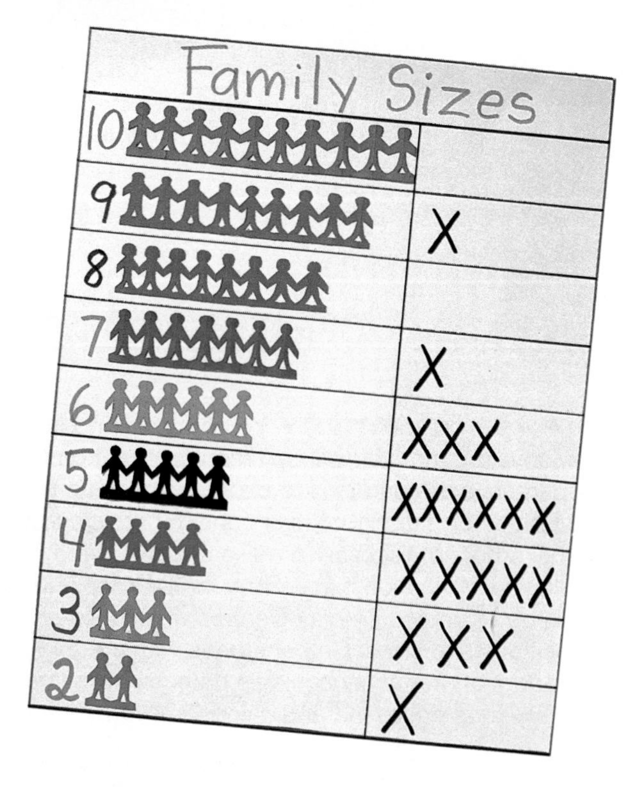

UNIT 2

LESSON

Where Families Live

UNIT 2 THEME BIG BOOK, PAGES 6–7

LESSON OVERVIEW

Families live in many kinds of homes in neighborhoods.

LESSON OBJECTIVES

- Recognize that families live in many kinds of homes.
- Recognize the reasons that families live in homes.
- Identify that a neighborhood is a place where families live.
- Recognize that homes have addresses.

KEY CONCEPTS

home neighborhood address street

RESOURCE REMINDER

Project Book
pp. 15, 65–76

Stickers Package
Sheet 6

Anthology
My Street, p. 3

Floor Map

GETTING READY

Find Homes for Animals

ON YOUR OWN

15 TO 30 MINUTES

CURRICULUM CONNECTION Art

Objective: To recognize that animals have homes.

Resource: ***Project Book*** p. 15

Materials: crayons, scissors, glue, construction paper

1. Have children identify the kinds of homes shown in the boxes at the top of ***Project Book*** p. 15. Ask them to tell what materials the homes may be made from. Children might also identify which homes are made by people and which are made by animals in nature. Next have children name the kinds of animal families shown in the boxes at the bottom of the page.
2. Direct children to color the homes and the animals.
3. Then have children cut out the homes and glue them to a piece of construction paper. Then children should cut out the animals and glue them next to their corresponding homes.

Project Book
p. 15

Name: Date:

Find Homes for Animals

Directions: Have children color the pictures. Then have them cut out the pictures at the bottom and tape or glue them to their correct home.

Unit 2, Lesson 2, Getting Ready 15

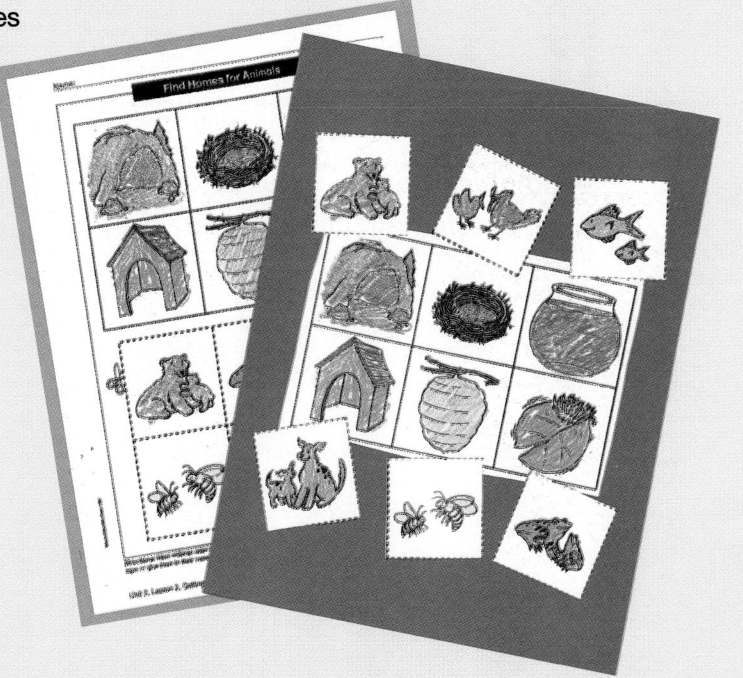

1 Prepare

WARMING UP WITH THE READ ALOUD

Begin the discussion about homes by sharing the poem in the Read Aloud. You may wish to display pictures of creatures and the homes in which they live.

- ***Whose homes does the poem name?*** *(homes of birds, ants, and people)*
- ***Where are the three places you can find homes in the poem?*** *(in the sky or above, underground or below, in-between or in the middle)*

2 Teach

USING BIG BOOK PAGES 6–7

Tell children that families live in many types of homes that are in many different places. You may wish to identify the photos from left to right in the Big Book as an apartment house in New York, a farm in Wisconsin, a mobile home in Pennsylvania, and a house in New Mexico.

USE BIG BOOK STICKERS, SHEET 6

Use the following ***Stickers*** throughout the lesson.

home **neighborhood**

UNIT 2 THEME BIG BOOK

LESSON 2

Where Families Live

6

Read Aloud

Homes

Birds are busy in the sky,
Building sturdy homes up high.

Ants are digging underground,
Making homes with little mounds.

People's homes are in-between,
At least as far as I have seen!

Wendy Vierow

Using the Anthology

My Street, page 3 Share the poem with children. Encourage them to listen for things the poet sees on a street in the neighborhood. As children recall the poem, write the features on the chalkboard under the headings *people, places,* and *things.* Compare these features to the photographs and pictures in the Big Book and add any additional items to the lists. Ask children to name things that they see in their own neighborhoods and add these items to the lists. To help convey meaning, display pictures of the words listed.

Curriculum Connection

Mathematics To give children practice in identifying shapes and colors play "I Spy" as you walk. Ask them to look for colors, and shapes such as rectangles, circles, and squares on homes, buildings, and signs.

Place the ***Sticker*** of the word *home* on the photograph of the apartment building on p. 6. Explain that some homes have one or more families while others are for one family. Ask volunteers to place the other ***Stickers*** of the word *home* on the other pictures. Tell children that the homes we live in make up places called neighborhoods. Affix the ***Sticker*** of the word *neighborhood* near the attached houses. Define *neighborhood* as "a place where people live, work, and play."

Elicit from children the reasons families need homes, such as protection from the weather, a place to sleep, and a place to keep possessions. Tell children that some families are homeless or may live in shelters, where they can sleep and get food.

- ***Which of these homes is for more than one family?*** *(apartment house)*

> ★**THINKING FURTHER:** ***Compare and Contrast*** ***In what ways are these homes the same?*** *(Possible answers: They all have walls and windows, and families live in them.)*

Explain that most homes in towns and cities have an address which includes the number of the home and the name of the street where the home is. Tell children that addresses help us to find places. Have a volunteer place the ***Sticker*** of the letter over the letter that Jim is mailing in the photograph. Explain that letters have addresses so that postal workers can deliver them.

3 Close

LESSON SUMMARY

Read the lesson question with children, pointing to each word as you read. Have them name places and kinds of homes in which families live.

EVALUATE

Make a Neighborhood Word Web Have children prepare an illustrated word web about homes and neighborhoods. Provide children with paper, crayons, and labels that say *home, neighborhood people, neighborhood places,* and *neighborhood things.* Help them place the label *home* in the center of their paper with the other labels branching out from the center. Have children draw a picture of the place where they live or another place they are familiar with or have read about. They should draw relevant illustrations about the neighborhoods under the corresponding headings. Children can include their illustrations in their portfolios.

Field Trip

Help children understand the relationship between the printed words *home, address, street, and neighborhood.* Make a drawing on chart paper of a house with a number on the front door, on a street with a name sign on the corner. Clarify the concepts of address. Then have the children suggest buildings and businesses that might make a neighborhood and add them to the drawing.

Second-Language Support/Using Visuals Use the drawing as a way to introduce vocabulary about a home, address, street, and neighborhood. For example, you might talk about the features of the items in the drawing, such as their size and color.

ART CONNECTION

LEARNING STYLE: VISUAL

Make Pocket Homes

ON YOUR OWN

15 TO 30 MINUTES

Objective: To recognize that homes have addresses.

Materials: drawing paper, crayons, tape, index cards, glue

1. Tell children that they will be making "pocket homes" that will hold a card with their address on it. Begin by having children position the paper vertically in front of them. Help children fold down the top corners of the paper so that a point is formed. Have them tape the edges to secure the point. (For apartment buildings with a flat roof, have children fold down the top of their paper about 1 inch and secure the fold with tape or glue.) Next have children fold up the bottom and tape the edges to form a pocket. Then have children tape the sides of the pocket closed.
2. Write children's addresses on index cards. Place the index cards inside their pocket homes.
3. Have children color their pocket homes. Suggest that they write their house or building numbers on the front.

ART CONNECTION

LEARNING STYLE: KINESTHETIC

Learning Center: Building Homes and Addresses

GROUP

15 TO 30 MINUTES

Objective: To identify different types of homes and addresses.

Resources: ***Project Book*** pp. 13, 65–76, ***K-1 Floor Map***

Materials: Assorted sizes of empty milk and juice cartons, small boxes, crayons, markers, construction paper, scissors, glue, tape

1. Make available ***Project Book*** pp. 65–76 and the ***K-1 Floor Map*** in the Art Learning Center, where groups of children will build homes for families.
2. Discuss with children what kinds of homes they would like to make. For example, a small group of children might work together to make an apartment house using a 1/2 gallon milk container. Individual children could make trailer homes, placing empty quart containers on their sides, or single homes using small boxes or pint containers.
3. First have children cover the cartons and boxes, by gluing construction paper over them. Then have them cut out and tape or glue patterns from the ***Project Book,*** or using markers or crayons, help children draw doors, windows, and roofs onto the covered containers.
4. Help children print numbered addresses on their homes or have them use the numbers found on ***Project Book,*** p. 13. Then help them name the streets, write the names onto construction paper and tape them onto the map.

5. When finished placing the homes on the map, ask children if they can tell what the address is of each home by looking first at the number and then at the street name.

UNIT 2

LESSON

3

Together as a Family

BIG BOOK PAGES 8–9

LESSON OVERVIEW

Family members share household jobs, follow rules, help each other, and enjoy spending time together.

LESSON OBJECTIVES

- Identify family members working together.
- Identify family rules.
- Recognize that families have fun and share special times.
- Recognize that families solve problems.

KEY CONCEPTS

fun play help

RESOURCE REMINDER

Project Book
p. 16

Stickers Package
Sheet 6

Anthology
Home Place
pp. 32–34

GETTING READY

Make a Chart

ON YOUR OWN

15 TO 30 MINUTES

CURRICULUM CONNECTION Mathematics

Objective: To identify activities performed alone and those performed with others in groups.

Resource: *Project Book* p. 16

Materials: scissors, glue, crayons

1. Discuss with children the meaning of the words *alone* and *together.* Have volunteers share activities they do alone and things they do with others.
2. Talk about what the people are doing in each picture on ***Project Book*** p. 16. Have them think about whether people are doing the activities alone or in groups. Read with children the labels at the bottom of the page.
3. Have children color the pictures and cut out the labels. Then direct them to glue the labels under the corresponding pictures showing people doing things alone and together. Point out the family picture that shows a grandfather playing with his grandchildren.

Project Book p. 16

Name: Date:

Make a Chart

alone together

alone together

Directions: Have children color the pictures. Then have them cut out the words at the bottom and glue them below the appropriate pictures.

16 Unit 2, Lesson 3, Getting Ready

1 Prepare

WARMING UP WITH THE READ ALOUD

Tell children that they will be talking about things family members do together. To identify one family activity, read the poem in the Read Aloud. Then teach children the hand movements.

- ***What is the poem about?*** *(celebrating a birthday)*

> ★**THINKING FURTHER:** ***Using Prior Knowledge*** ***Besides visiting, what other things might families do to celebrate a birthday? How do you know?*** *(Possible answers: They might give cards or presents, sing the birthday song, eat cake, or have a party; children may know this from personal experience or the media.)*

2 Teach

USING BIG BOOK PAGES 8–9

Tell children that the Big Book shows Jim's mother sharing her childhood dollhouse with him. They are both having fun because they have decided to play with the dollhouse. Explain that the dollhouse family consists of a mother, father, and two children. Visiting the dollhouse family for dinner are an aunt, uncle, two cousins, grandmother, and grandfather.

UNIT 2 THEME BIG BOOK

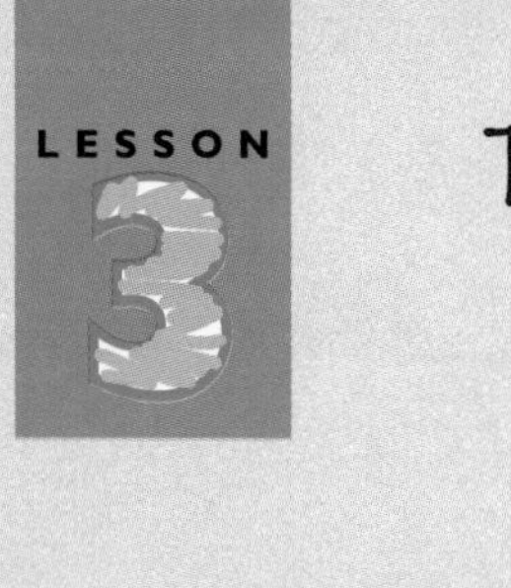

Together as a Family

8

Read Aloud

My Day

One day of the year is a special one.
(Point finger up)
If you are a daughter or a son.
(Hands out holding skirt, hands in pockets)
Sometimes this day is very quiet or very loud.
(Pointer finger over mouth, hands over ears)
But because it's our day we're very, very proud.
(Thumbs under underarms)
And friends and relatives come over to say.
(Fingers on both hands inverted, doing walking motion on lap)
Congratulations to you and Happy Birthday!!
(Hands up high)

Rebecca Boynton

Using the Anthology

Home Place, pages 32–34 The narrator of this gentle poem happens on some blooming daffodils near the remains of an old house and imagines the family that used to live there.

Before you read the story, you might want to explain that daffodils grow from bulbs. Each spring the same bulbs make more flowers.

Ask children if they have ever seen something for sale that was old, like old furniture or old toys. Then ask them to think about the people who once owned those things. Encourage volunteers to make up a story about an old book they saw in a store window. Did a boy or girl own the book? In what kind of house or apartment did the child live? What did the child look like, and so on.

Some family members have decided to help each other and work together to get ready for dinner. Explain that families also follow rules to work and play together. Tell children that families sometimes have problems that they need to solve together.

USE BIG BOOK STICKERS, SHEET 6

You can use the following ***Stickers*** throughout the lesson.

Children can use the ***Stickers*** of the rings to circle the correct answers as they answer the questions.

- ***Which family members in the dollhouse are working together? What are they doing?*** *(A mother and child are making a bed, and another mother and child are preparing dinner.)*
- ***Why is sharing work and helping one another important?*** *(Possible answers: It is only fair to share tasks; it is nice to help others.)*

★**THINKING FURTHER:** ***Using Prior Knowledge*** ***What rules do families need to follow? How do you know?*** *(Possible answers include rules when playing or working together and safety rules; children may say they know about these rules from personal experience or the media.)*

3 Close

LESSON SUMMARY

Read the lesson question with children, pointing to each word as you read. Have them name things families do together.

EVALUATE

Perform Family Skits Invite pairs or small groups of children to take turns dramatizing things family members do together, such as playing a game, drying dishes, or washing a pet. Have the other class members guess what the groups are dramatizing and tell if the groups are dramatizing work or play. For assessment suggestions, see page 78.

CITIZENSHIP

Family Citizenship In this lesson, children have identified and discussed some things that families do together. Children should also be aware that a big part of everyday life at home is the ability to get along with other family members. To help facilitate a discussion about family citizenship, you may wish to post and discuss some ideals for good citizenship such as *share, help, be kind, work together, play as friends, be fair,* and *follow rules.* Children should recognize that if they and other family members try to follow ideals such as these, everyone can get along better. You may wish to point out that the same ideals apply to your classroom. A good way to discuss each ideal is to ask questions such as "What do children do to share at home? Why is it good to share? What rules do children follow at home? Do rules ever change? Why or why not?" and "How can rules help your family to get along better?"

ART CONNECTION

LEARNING STYLE: VISUAL

Make Helping Handprints

ON YOUR OWN

Objective: To recognize ways in which children can help at home.

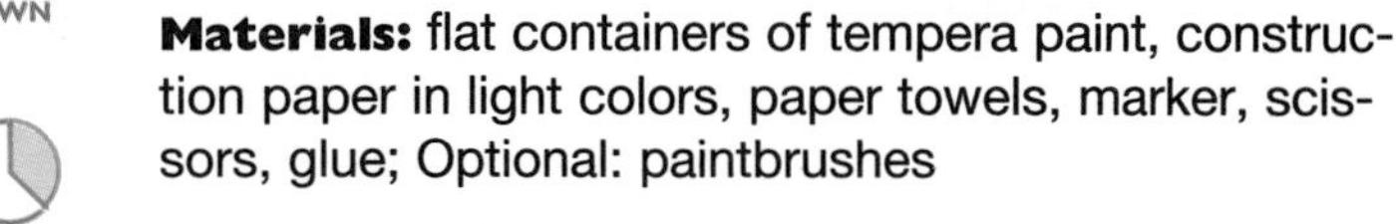

Materials: flat containers of tempera paint, construction paper in light colors, paper towels, marker, scissors, glue; Optional: paintbrushes

15 TO 30 MINUTES

1. Tell children that they will be making handprints to show ways they help at home. Provide children with a sheet of construction paper and flat containers of different color tempera paints. (Unused styrofoam vegetable or meat trays make excellent containers for paint.) Have children make left and right handprints onto the construction paper using different color paints for each palm. When the paint is dry, help children cut out their handprints and glue them onto a large sheet of construction paper.
2. Below each handprint, use a marker to write children's dictated sentences about jobs they can do to help out at home. Ask children to identify which job is done alone or with other family members.

MUSIC/MOVEMENT CONNECTION

LEARNING STYLE: AUDITORY/KINESTHETIC

Sing a Helping Song

GROUP

Objective: To sing about the ways in which children can help their families.

15 TO 30 MINUTES

1. Elicit from volunteers the ways in which children help out at home every day. Write their answers on the chalkboard and discuss when and how often children may do these jobs and the reasons that each is important. As an alternative, you may wish to create a list about ways families have fun.
2. Tell children they are going to use the chalkboard list to make up a song about working together and helping at home. Sing or teach children the chorus to "The Mulberry Bush" prior to singing children's verses.
3. Children will enjoy pantomiming their own verses and verses such as these.
   1. This is the way we make our bed . . .
   2. . . . pick up our toys . . .
   3. . . . set our table . . .
   4. . . . clear our table . . .
   5. . . . wash our dishes . . .
   6. . . . water our plants . . .
   7. . . . walk our dog . . .
   8. . . . feed our pet . . .

Families Are Everywhere

UNIT 2 THEME BIG BOOK, PAGES 10–11

LESSON OVERVIEW

Families around the world live in homes and share family activities.

LESSON OBJECTIVES

- Recognize that families live in many countries.
- Identify activities of families in other countries.
- Compare and contrast families and activities in other countries.

KEY CONCEPTS

world   country

RESOURCE REMINDER

Project Book
p. 17

Stickers Package
Sheet 7

Inflatable Globe

Technology Connection
VIDEODISC/VIDEO TAPE 2

Search Frame 32911, Play to 35216

GETTING READY

Write a Postcard

PARTNER

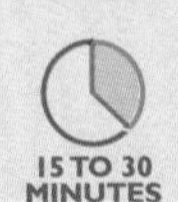
15 TO 30 MINUTES

CURRICULUM CONNECTION Art

Objective: To identify activities children do with families.

Resource: *Project Book* p. 17

Materials: crayons, pencils, glue

1. Using ***Project Book*** p. 17, ask the children if they have ever received or sent a postcard to someone.
2. Children should then cut out the postcard. On the blank side, have children draw a picture of a family doing an activity. Invite them to color the stamp. Pair up children and have them write the name of their partner on one line of the card. You may want children to write the number of their classroom or the name of their school on the other line.
3. Make a bulletin board of the postcards after children have exchanged them with their partners. Later in the unit, you can use the postcards to compare what families in the United States do with activities of families around the world.

Project Book
p. 17

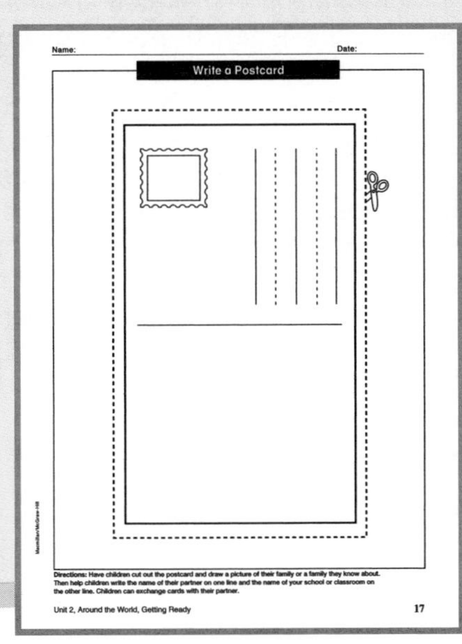

Name: Date:

Write a Postcard

Macmillan/McGraw-Hill

Directions: Have children cut out the postcard and draw a picture of their family or a family they know about. Then help children write the name of their partner on one line and the name of your school or classroom on the other line. Children can exchange cards with their partner.

Unit 2, Around the World, Getting Ready 17

1 Prepare

WARMING UP WITH THE READ ALOUD

Have children recall what they learned about families in regard to their members, homes, and activities. Then share the poem in the Read Aloud to begin a discussion about families around the world. If possible, display pictures of the kinds of homes named to give meaning to the words.

- ***What kinds of homes does the poem name?*** *(Possible answers include: houses, houseboats, apartments, castles, caves, trailers, cabins, condos, tents, and igloos.)*

★ **THINKING FURTHER:** ***Compare and Contrast*** ***Which homes are like those that you have seen?*** *(Answers will vary.)*

2 Teach

USING BIG BOOK PAGES 10–11

Tell children that people live all around the world.

USE BIG BOOK STICKERS, SHEET 7

You can use the following ***Stickers*** throughout the lesson.

Mexico | Canada | South Africa | South Korea | The Netherlands

Read Aloud

A World of Homes

A world full of families, live in all kinds of places
On big city streets and in wide open spaces.
Some live in the mountains, some near the sea,
Deep in the forests or in small towns like me.
In houses on stilts and in houseboats that float,
In sky-high apartments and in castles with moats,
In caves made of rock and in trailers that go,
In cozy wood cabins and also condos.
In tents that fold and in igloos of ice
All homes of families are particularly nice.

Catherine M. Tamblyn

Second-Language Support

Using Visuals As you discuss the concept, *Families Are Everywhere*, incorporate the varied backgrounds of your children. Mention their countries of origin and invite them to show letters or postcards from family members in those countries when you are showing the world map. Create an enlarged version of "A World of Homes." Illustrate it with pictures of the homes and settings described in the poem. Then invite children to draw other kinds of homes in which families around the world live. Have children add these to the earlier drawings and say something about each one. Restate any incomplete or ungrammatical statements correctly.

Define country as "a land and the people who live there." You may wish to use the ***Inflatable Globe*** to locate the United States as well as the countries of Mexico, Canada, South Africa, South Korea, and the Netherlands. Point out that the letters and pictures are from families who live in these countries. Page 10 shows a Mexican family in Mexico City and a Canadian family at Jasper National Park in Alberta. Page 11 shows a South African family in Johannesburg, a South Korean family at dinner, and a Dutch family in Amsterdam. As you discuss each photograph, affix the ***Sticker*** with the country's name.

- ***In what ways are these families like your family or families you know?*** *(Possible answers: They are doing things together or they have the same composition of people.)*

★**THINKING FURTHER:** ***Classifying*** ***Which photographs show families doing activities outside? Which photographs show families doing activities inside?*** *(outside: Mexico, Canada, and the Netherlands; inside: South Africa and South Korea)*

Technology Connection

VIDEODISC/VIDEO TAPE 2
Enrich the Around the World Lesson with the video segment *Our Nation's Neighbors,* Search Frame 32911.

See the bar code on p. 59.

3 Close

LESSON SUMMARY

Read the lesson question with children, pointing to each word as you read. Have them name things the families are doing such as taking a walk or sightseeing, canoeing, working together, eating, or planting flowers together.

EVALUATE

Draw Country Pictures Tell children that the countries they learned about and others make up the countries of the world. Have children illustrate something they have learned about one of the countries on pp. 10–11. Display children's work around the room. Children can add their work to their portfolios. For assessment suggestions, see p. 78.

Background Information

About the Countries Most people in these countries live in urban areas.

Mexico Mexico's people have both Indian and Spanish roots. Spanish is the official language of Mexico.

Canada Canada's people come from many different backgrounds including Asian, African, Native American, Inuit, and European. English and French are the official languages.

South Korea South Korea and North Korea once made up Korea. Now South Korea is its own country, also called the Republic of Korea. The official language is Korean.

South Africa The official languages of South Africa are Afrikaans and English. Blacks make up the largest part of the population today.

The Netherlands Also known as Holland, almost all people in this country are of Dutch ancestry. The official language is Dutch.

HOME ECONOMICS CONNECTION

LEARNING STYLE: KINESTHETIC/ VISUAL

Try Fruit from Around the World

GROUP

30 MINUTES OR LONGER

Objective: To learn about food that is grown and eaten in other countries.

Resource: ***Inflatable Globe***

Materials: photographs from magazines of tropical fruit including bananas, kiwi fruit, mangos, papaya, and pineapple; optional: a variety of fresh tropical fruits, knife (for the teacher), small paper plates, plastic forks; or tropical fruit juices

1. Inform the class that different kinds of foods are grown and eaten in different parts of the world. Explain that families in nearly every country eat fruit. Invite children to describe their favorite fruits.
2. Show the class the photographs of the different kinds of fruit. Pronounce the name of each fruit and show on the ***Inflatable Globe*** some countries where they are grown. (*bananas:* Uganda, India, Brazil, Ecuador; *kiwi fruit:* New Zealand, Spain, Japan; *mangos:* India, Mexico, Philippines; *papaya:* Brazil, Chile, India; *pineapple:* Mexico, Thailand, China)
3. As an alternative, bring in actual tropical fruits or fruit juice to share with the class. Before children sample fruits or fruit juice make sure that parents provide permission for sampling fruits in case any children are allergic to these fruits. Peel the fruit and have children help you slice some of the fruit to make a fruit salad that will be shared by the class.

MUSIC CONNECTION

LEARNING STYLE: AUDITORY/KINESTHETIC

Sing "Frère Jacques" ("Are You Sleeping?")

GROUP

15 TO 30 MINUTES

Objective: To learn a song sung by children and families around the world.

1. Tell children that they are going to sing a song in English and in French. Versions of this song are sung in different languages around the world. Teach the children the English, then the French versions of "Frère Jacques."
2. Have children act out the lyrics by closing their eyes and pretending to sleep while placing their hands on one side of their face, and by pulling on a bell rope.

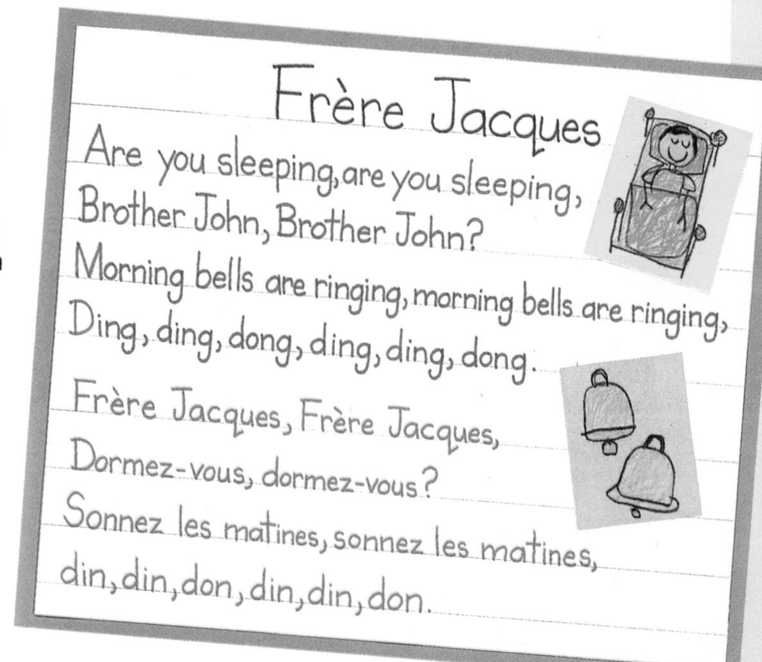

UNIT 2

LESSON 4

At Work

UNIT 2 THEME BIG BOOK, PAGES 12–13

LESSON OVERVIEW

Family members earn a living by working.

LESSON OBJECTIVES

- Identify different types of jobs and workplaces.
- Associate tools, uniforms, and vehicles with appropriate workers.

KEY CONCEPTS

job workers

RESOURCE REMINDER

Project Book
p. 18

Stickers Package
Sheet 7

Anthology
Parents Are People, pp. 30–31
If I Could Work, p. 52

GETTING READY

Make a Worker Puppet

ON YOUR OWN

15 TO 30 MINUTES

CURRICULUM CONNECTIONS Drama/Art

Objective: To introduce different types of workers.

Resource: ***Project Book*** p. 18

Materials: lunch bags (paper), paper-towel tubes, scissors, crayons, tape, glue, newspaper, drawing paper, yarn

1. Encourage volunteers to name each hat shown on ***Project Book*** p. 18, tell who might wear it and name where that person might work. Tell children that they will be using the hats to make worker puppets.
2. Have children color and cut out one of the hats. Then guide children to glue a hat to the bottom of a flattened lunch bag. Tell them to draw faces and hair or glue on yarn or paper for hair.
3. Stuff balls of newspaper into the bags. Then insert a paper-towel tube about halfway into the bag. Tie the bag at the neck with a piece of yarn.
4. Allow children to share and play with their worker puppets.

Project Book p. 18

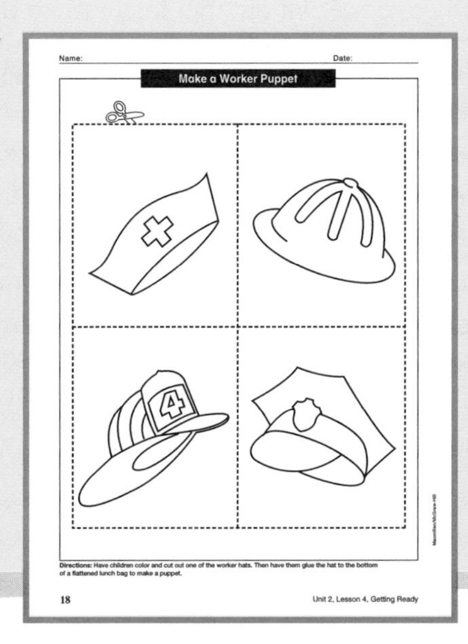
Name: Date:

Make a Worker Puppet

Directions: Have children color and cut out one of the worker hats. Then have them glue the hat to the bottom of a flattened lunch bag to make a puppet.

18 Unit 2, Lesson 4, Getting Ready

Macmillan/McGraw-Hill

1 Prepare

WARMING UP WITH THE READ ALOUD

Tell children that they will be learning about the jobs people work at to earn money. Read the poem in the Read Aloud to identify some jobs. Then reread the poem a line at a time and have children name the workers who perform the jobs.

- ***Which workers in the poem drive a special vehicle to do their job?*** *(firefighter, street sweeper)*
- ***Which workers make or fix things?*** *(shoemaker, baker, electrician)*

2 Teach

USING BIG BOOK PAGES 12–13

Point out to children that there are six workers in the photographs. Have children name the places in which the workers are working—for example, the bakers are in a bakery.

USE BIG BOOK STICKERS, SHEET 7

You can use the following ***Stickers*** in the lesson.

workers

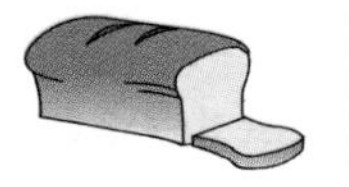

UNIT 2 THEME BIG BOOK

LESSON 4

At Work

12

Read Aloud

Workers

This worker feeds the lions at the zoo.
This worker drives an engine to the fire.
This worker makes a new sole for your shoe.
This worker mends a high electric wire.
This worker drives a sweeper through the streets.
This worker bakes a cookie or a bun.
This worker sells my parents food to eat,
And I'm very glad we've got them, every one!

Louise Binder Scott

Using the Anthology

Parents Are People, pages 30–31 Read the poem to children to explore jobs that some mothers and fathers do. Point out that fathers also do the jobs that the poem says mothers do and vice versa. Have volunteers identify people they know with similar occupations.

If I Could Work, page 52 Share the poem to identify jobs that children might find exciting. Have children recall the many kinds of "dream jobs" that the child would like to do if he or she were old enough to go to work. Have volunteers tell if anyone they know does similar jobs. Then have them tell of any dream job they would like to do if they were old enough to work and the reasons that they would want to do it.

13

Affix and then read the ***Sticker*** of the word *workers.* Have children identify the workers in the photographs and tell how they know what jobs they do.

Ask children what each of the workers might need to know to do his or her job. Explain that people work at jobs to earn money as well as because they like their work. Discuss the uniforms, tools, and vehicles the workers use. Focus children's attention on the photograph of Jim and his mother. Explain that some family members work at home to take care of children, do housekeeping, and shop so other family members can earn money outside of the home. Tell children that all kinds of work are very important. Have volunteers affix the ***Stickers*** of the phone, computer, envelope, bread, and groceries to the photographs of the workers who are associated with these items.

- ***Which workers shown make something that we can eat?*** *(The bakers make bread.)*

★**THINKING FURTHER:** ***Using Prior Knowledge*** ***Which workers help us to keep in touch with other people? How do you know?*** *(The lineswoman fixes phone lines, the postal worker delivers mail, and the office worker uses a computer to write letters; children may know about these workers from personal experience or the media.)*

3 Close

LESSON SUMMARY

Read the lesson question with children, pointing to each word as your read. Children may name the jobs shown in the Big Book, as well as others.

EVALUATE

Perform Puppet Skits Children can use the worker puppets they made in Getting Ready to play "Special Classroom Visitor." Put the puppets in a bag or box. Have each child blindly select a puppet, pretend to be that class visitor, and tell the class about the job that he or she does and the workplace in which the job is done.

CITIZENSHIP

Suggested Visitors Write a letter to parents or guardians inviting them to visit the class to speak about their jobs. Ask them to be prepared to tell about their job, any special training required for it, where they perform the job, and to identify any special tools or vehicles they use. Suggest that they bring in small tools and wear their uniform or any special clothing. Ask them to tell how their job helps others. Visitors might also share photographs of themselves at work.

Field Trip

Children will enjoy visiting local businesses to see parents of classmates at work. After each visit, have children help you to compose a thank-you note naming one or two things that they liked or observed.

LANGUAGE ARTS CONNECTION

LEARNING STYLE: VISUAL

Make a Worker's Alphabet Book

GROUP

15 TO 30 MINUTES

Objective: To represent different types of jobs and practice the alphabet.

Materials: drawing paper, crayons, marker, loose-leaf binder, hole puncher

1. Tell children that they will be making a class alphabet book that shows different workers. Direct each child to draw a picture of a worker doing a job. Ask children to think about where the worker might be working. Remind children to include tools, special clothing, or vehicles in their drawings.
2. Label children's drawings with the name of the occupation. Help each child to identify the first letter in the name of the worker's occupation and to write the letter at the top of the paper.
3. Punch holes in the pages and assemble them from A to Z in the binder. If time allows, children may draw workers to fill in any missing letters of the alphabet. Difficult pages such as Q, X, and Z provide a great opportunity for library use. With your help, children can look for photographs of workers such as a quiltmaker, an X-ray technician, or a zookeeper.

DRAMA CONNECTION

LEARNING STYLE: AUDITORY/ KINESTHETIC

Learning Center: Use Worker Play-Kits

GROUP

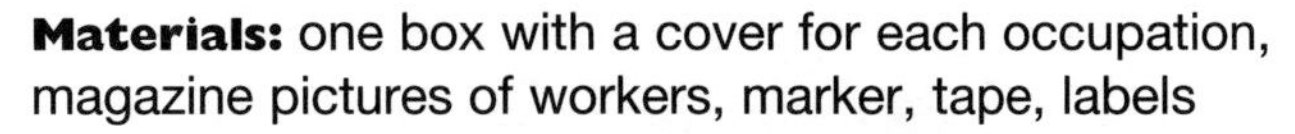

Objective: To role-play different occupations.

Materials: one box with a cover for each occupation, magazine pictures of workers, marker, tape, labels

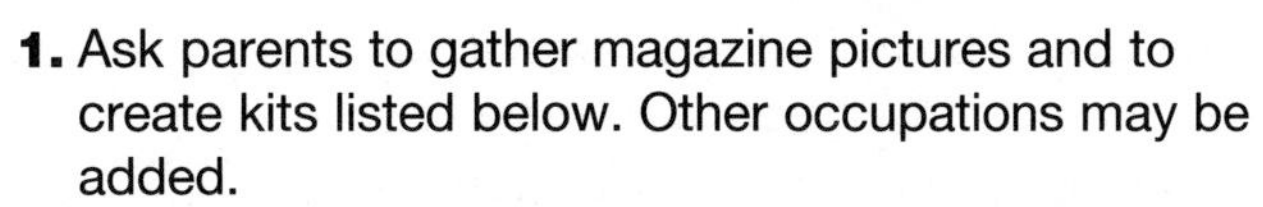
15 TO 30 MINUTES

1. Ask parents to gather magazine pictures and to create kits listed below. Other occupations may be added.

   Hairdresser/Barber: comb, brush, wigs, hand mirror, clips, clip-on curlers, apron, towel

   Police Officer: hat, badge, whistle

   Postal Worker: envelopes, stamps, mailbag

   Doctor/Nurse: bandages, stethoscope, mask, gloves, tongue depressors, doctor's bag, baby doll, flashlight

   Chef/Baker: bowls, spoons, apron, hat, pots, pans, whisk, rolling pin, measuring cups, plastic food, plastic plates

   Carpenter: hammer, measuring tape, tool belt or carpenter's apron, screwdriver, wrench, blueprint

   Supermarket Worker: food containers (cleaned), plastic food, play money, cash register, tags, grocery bags

   Waiter/Waitress: memo pads, plastic dishes and utensils, plastic food, aprons, placemats, play money
2. Label the boxes with the name of the worker or a picture of the worker.
3. Have small groups of children perform skits about workers in their workplaces in the Dramatic Play Learning Center. Have children return the contents to the appropriate kits when they are finished.

UNIT 2

LESSON 5

Needs and Wants

UNIT 2 THEME BIG BOOK, PAGES 14–15

LESSON OVERVIEW

Families provide for our needs and wants.

LESSON OBJECTIVES

- Identify food, clothing, shelter, and love as the four basic needs of families.
- Understand that families make and buy some of their needs.
- Recognize that wants are not necessary for people to live.
- Distinguish between needs and wants.

KEY CONCEPTS

needs	food	clothes	shelter
love	money	wants	

RESOURCE REMINDER

Project Book
p. 19

Stickers Package
Sheet 8

Anthology
A Chair for My Mother, pp. 14–16
The Toymaker, pp. 46–51

Technology Connection

VIDEODISC/VIDEO TAPE 1

Search Frame 16286, Play to 20640

GETTING READY

Make a Piggy Bank

ON YOUR OWN

30 MINUTES OR LONGER

CURRICULUM CONNECTION **Mathematics**

Objective: To identify, count, and sort play money.

Resource: *Project Book* p. 19

Materials: scissors, crayons, pencils, glue, construction paper (cut in half)

1. Ask children to guess what they might be making with the items on ***Project Book*** p. 19 (a piggy bank). Ask children to decorate the bank.
2. Then have them cut out the bank and glue only the sides and bottom edges to a half-sheet of construction paper, allowing for an opening at the top. Help children trim the edges around their banks.
3. Working with children, have them identify the coins and amounts on ***Project Book*** p. 19. Have children color the pennies with a brown crayon and the nickels and dimes with a gray crayon. Then have them cut out the coins.
4. The coins and amounts can be sorted into groups, matched, and counted. Then have children deposit the coins in their piggy banks. As you teach this lesson, be sure children understand that people use money to buy some needs and wants.

Project Book p. 19

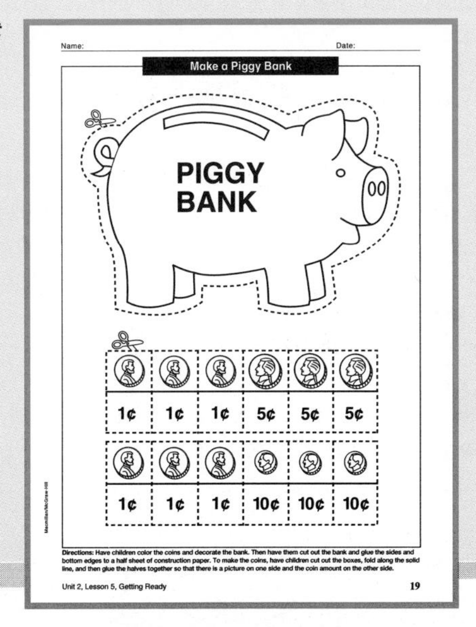
Name: Date:

Make a Piggy Bank

PIGGY BANK

1¢	1¢	1¢	5¢	5¢	5¢
1¢	1¢	1¢	10¢	10¢	10¢

Unit 2, Lesson 5, Getting Ready 19

WARMING UP WITH THE READ ALOUD

Tell children that today they will be talking about things that families make and buy. Share the poem in the Read Aloud to examine what one family needs to buy.

- ***What did the family need to buy? Why?*** *(The family needed to buy milk because they didn't have a cow.)*

★ **THINKING FURTHER:** ***Using Prior Knowledge*** ***What other things could you buy at the store? How do you know?*** *(Possible answers include other food, clothes, toys, and appliances. Children may say that they know this because of personal experience or the media.)*

USING BIG BOOK PAGES 14–15

Point out Jim's bulletin board in the Big Book. Tell children that the bulletin board shows things that we need and things that we may want.

USE BIG BOOK STICKERS, SHEET 8

You can use the following ***Stickers*** throughout the lesson.

Read Aloud

My Mother Said

We need some fruit,
We need some bread,
We need some milk,
My mother said.

Please pick the fruit,
I'll make the bread.
We have no cow,
My mother said.

To get the milk
Let's use our heads—
Off to the store!
My mother said.

Wendy Vierow

Using the Anthology

A Chair for My Mother, pages 14–16 After discussing the topic of wants, read the story to children. This story illustrates the concept of earning money and saving it to buy a special want. You may wish to make the connection between the jar that the family used and the piggy bank that children made in Getting Ready.

The Toymaker, pages 46–51 Read the play to share reasons that people do different kinds of work. This play also tells how families supplied their needs and wants long ago and how things changed over time. After reading, ask children to tell how the toymaker changed the way people worked long ago. Point out that by exchanging things made or grown, people could do the jobs they did well or liked to do. This way, families did not have to do everything for themselves.

Which are needs? Which are wants?

15

Tell children that the things on p. 14 are needs. Define the word as "things people must have to live." Explain that four basic needs are food, clothes, shelter, and love. Have volunteers affix the ***Stickers*** of the word *need* to the four photographs on p. 14. Point out that people may make or grow some of their needs, or they may use money to buy some of their needs. Point out that Jim's mother is making clothes and that Jim's father is buying food in a store.

Explain that the things on p. 15 show wants. Define *wants* as "things people would like but can live without." Have volunteers affix the ***Stickers*** of the word *want* to the five wants on the bulletin board. Explain that not all people want the same things.

- ***Why do people need shelter?*** *(Possible answers include to protect themselves and their possessions from the weather and to keep themselves safe.)*

★ **THINKING FURTHER: *Classifying*** ***What wants might people have?*** *(Possible answers include a vacation, furniture, a car, to spend more time with loved ones, and to see a movie.)*

Technology Connection

VIDEODISC/VIDEO TAPE 1

Enrich Lesson 5 with the video segment *Learning About Money.* Search Frame 16286.

See the bar code on p. 67.

3 Close

LESSON SUMMARY

Read the lesson question with children. Have volunteers identify the needs and wants on pp.14–15.

EVALUATE

Make a Minibook Have children make needs and wants minibooks. Provide each child with a minibook of two half-sheets of drawing paper folded in half and stapled along the fold. Provide labels that say *My Needs and Wants, food, clothes, shelter, love,* and *wants.* On the front of the minibooks, have children glue the label *My Needs and Wants.* On each inside page, have them glue one label and illustrate that page. Children can place their books in their portfolios.

Background Information

ABOUT TOPIC SENSITIVITY Make children aware of the various degrees of needs. For example, healthy food is a need yet items such as candy and cookies are not necessary for good health and could be considered wants by many. Likewise, unessential clothing such as sports uniforms and costumes could be considered wants. Children should also understand that place and environment affects people's needs for clothing, food, and shelter. For example, people living in warm climates need clothes to keep them cool such as shorts and T-shirts and do not need warm clothes like wool coats, hats, and mittens.

Because of varying family incomes, exercise care in discussing wants. Some children may have most of their wants supplied, while other children receive only their basic needs or even less.

ART CONNECTION

LEARNING STYLE: VISUAL

Make Cards that Hug

ON YOUR OWN

15 TO 30 MINUTES

Objective: To show that love and care are needs.

Materials: scissors, construction paper, markers, glitter glue; optional: yarn

Advance Preparation: Cut 6" circles from construction paper. Also cut 15 1/2" x 6" strips from different colors of construction paper. Make one circle and one strip for each child.

1. Tell children that they will be making a greeting card for someone they care about. Direct children to fold the strip of paper in half to find the center. Then have them glue the circle to the top of the strip at the center. Point out that they have just made their own head and arms.
2. Now have children trace their hands onto construction paper and cut them out. Then have them glue the hands to the end of each arm. Show them how to fold the arms toward the center so that the fingers overlap slightly, making a hug.
3. Have children draw their faces on the circle and decorate their arms using crayons or markers. Children might glue on yarn for hair.
4. Inside the card help them write a love and care message to a special person.

MATHEMATICS/DRAMA CONNECTION

LEARNING STYLE: AUDITORY/KINESTHETIC

Learning Center: Shop in Our General Store

GROUP

15 TO 30 MINUTES

Objective: To understand needs and wants through counting and role-playing.

Materials: food containers (cleaned), plastic food, small clothing items, small toys, masking tape, construction paper, markers, paper bags, cash register or money box, play money (or money from the Getting Ready activity, p. 67); optional: magazine cutouts of food, clothing, toys

1. Gather small classroom items or obtain from parents items to place in a classroom store. As an alternative, magazine cutouts of food, clothing, and other items could be used.
2. You may wish to write the prices of items on the construction paper and tape them to the items. Have children organize the items into a "store" in the Mathematics Learning Center.
3. Children can take turns being customers, storekeepers, cashiers, clerks, and delivery persons. As customers buy items, they should tell if the item is a *need* or a *want,* tell its price, and count out the appropriate coins.

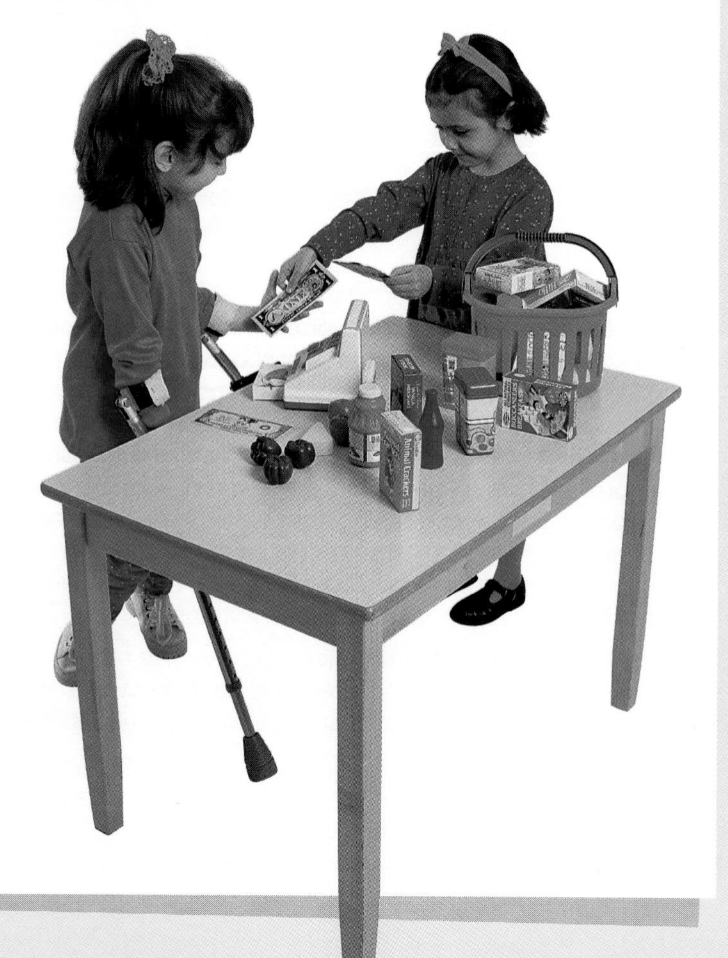

Finding Alike and Different

UNIT 2 THEME BIG BOOK PAGES 16–17

RESOURCE REMINDER

Project Book
p. 20

Stickers Package
Sheets 4, 8, 16

LESSON OVERVIEW

Comparing and contrasting is finding what is alike and different in things.

LESSON OBJECTIVES

- Compare and contrast the ways objects are alike and different.
- Compare and contrast the ways people are alike and different.

KEY CONCEPTS

alike different

GETTING READY

Create a Place Mat

ON YOUR OWN

15 TO 30 MINUTES

CURRICULUM CONNECTION Art

Objective: To recognize objects that are the same.

Resource: *Project Book* p. 20

Materials: crayons, pencils, scissors, construction paper, glue, glitter

1. Discuss with children the pictures on ***Project Book*** p. 20. Point out that there are two pictures of each object.
2. Have children color and cut out the pictures.
3. Children should glue pairs of same pictures together in a pattern of their choice onto a sheet of construction paper.
4. Encourage children to add decorations to the sheet. Finally children can glue their sheet of construction paper onto a second sheet of construction paper to make a place mat.

Project Book p. 20

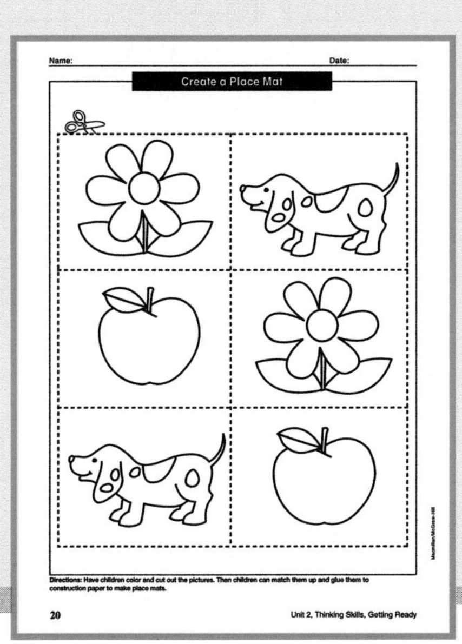

Name: Date:

Create a Place Mat

Directions: Have children color and cut out the pictures. Then children can match them up and glue them to construction paper to make place mats.

Macmillan/McGraw-Hill

20 Unit 2, Thinking Skills, Getting Ready

1 Prepare

WARMING UP WITH THE READ ALOUD

Tell children that they will be looking closely at things to find ways things are alike. Read the poem in the Read Aloud to identify how people can look alike. Explain that twins like Denny and Danny, who look alike, are called identical twins.

- ***Why do people confuse Denny and Danny?*** *(They look like each other.)*

> ★ **THINKING FURTHER: *Compare and Contrast In what other ways are Denny and Danny alike?*** *(Possible answers: They are boys, they are the same age, they have names that start with "D" and end in "Y," and they have the same parents.)*

2 Teach

USING BIG BOOK PAGES 16–17

Have children recognize that the boys in the pictures on p. 16 are alike in some ways.

> **USE BIG BOOK STICKERS, SHEETS 4, 8, 16**
>
> You can use the following ***Stickers*** throughout the lesson.
>
> 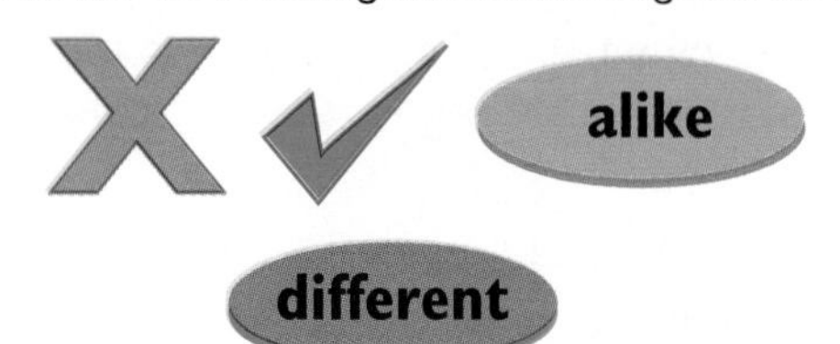
>

Affix the ***Sticker*** of the word *alike* and define the word as "being the same in some way." Model for children how to compare the photographs on p. 16 to find out how they are alike. For example, each one has a boy with a toy and both pictures were taken inside. The photographs on p. 17 are also alike because both pictures have one boy and two girls and both pictures were taken outside.

Affix the ***Sticker*** of the word *different* on the Big Book and define the word as "not the same." Have children suggest ways the photographs are different. For example, the boys in the pictures on p. 16 have different toys; one boy is wearing old-fashioned clothes, the other boy is wearing modern clothes. In the top photograph on p. 17 a boy holds a hockey stick, in the bottom photograph a girl is holding a hockey stick.

UNIT 2 THEME BIG BOOK

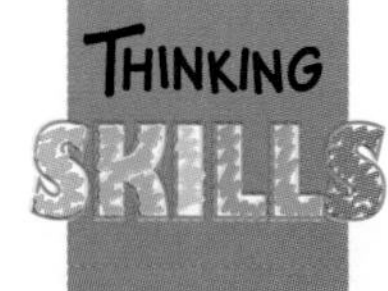

Finding Alike and Different

16

Read Aloud

The Twins

Denny and Danny
Are twins nearby.
Each of them looks
Like the other.

If we confuse them,
Then they sigh
And say, "No,
That's my brother!"

Jay Lee

How are these pictures alike and different 

17

Use these simple tips if children have difficulty comparing the objects.

HELPING YOURSELF

- Look at one thing.
- Choose a part of it.
- Look at another thing to see if the part you chose is on or in it.
- If it is, then the things are alike in one way.
- If it is not, then the things are different in one way.

- ***The photographs on p. 16 are alike because both boys are looking at the camera. In what other ways are they alike?*** *(Possible answers: Both boys are sitting, both are inside, both are sitting with a toy.)*

★**THINKING FURTHER:** ***Compare/Contrast*** ***How are the photos alike and different?*** *(Possible answers: Different: one boy on p. 16 is wearing old fashioned clothes, the other is wearing modern clothes. Alike: both boys are sitting on the floor. Different: the three children in one photo on p. 17 are standing on the sidewalk, the other children are standing on grass. Alike: both groups of children are standing in front of a house.)*

3 Close

LESSON SUMMARY

Read the lesson question with children, pointing to each word as you read. Have children explain why the items are alike and why they are different.

EVALUATE

Play the Alike Game Play a game with children to identify things that are alike. To begin the game, name an object in the classroom and ask a child to look for another item that is like it in any way. The game continues until an item cannot be named.

Curriculum Connection

Science Have children make fingerprints of their right and left index fingers by using an ink pad and white paper. Explain that there are three main types of fingerprints—arch, whorl, and loop. Arches look like hills, whorls start out as circles, and loops start out looking like the eye of a needle. Obtain pictures of these fingerprint types from source books to show children. Help children to identify the kind of fingerprint that they have. Ask children to find others who have fingerprints that are like theirs. Then have children look at their fingerprints more carefully to discover that no two are exactly alike. Tell children that people's fingerprints are alike in some ways, but different in other ways.

LANGUAGE ARTS CONNECTION

LEARNING STYLE: AUDITORY/KINESTHETIC

Find Alike and Different

GROUP

15 TO 30 MINUTES

Objective: To describe how objects are alike and how they are different

Materials: shoe box, several small items (Some items should be identical, such as a pair of mittens or a set of buttons. Other items should be similar, but not identical, such as shells, small rocks, or small plastic toys.)

1. Tell children that they will be playing an alike-and-different game. Have a volunteer select two items from the shoe box.
2. The volunteer tells how the two items are "alike" and/or how they are "different." Encourage the class also to comment on how the items are alike or different.

ART/LANGUAGE ARTS CONNECTION

LEARNING STYLE: AUDITORY/VISUAL

Learning Center: Paint Alike and Different

GROUP

15 TO 30 MINUTES

Objective: To compare the ways in which works of art are alike or different.

Materials: dinner-size paper plates (one for each child), red and blue tempera paint, paint brushes, hole puncher, string

1. Tell children that they will be making paintings in the Art Learning Center and then comparing how the paintings are alike and different. Have children make a painting on a paper plate using only red and blue paint. Suggest that each child paint a fun design.
2. Punch a hole at the top of the plate, thread with a piece of cut string, and hang it from a long string tacked along the chalkboard.
3. Ask children to take their paintings to the Language Arts Learning Center. Have them describe which paintings are alike, which are different, and how.

CLOSE WITH A POEM

LINKING SOCIAL STUDIES AND LITERATURE

Close Unit 2 with the poem "Four Generations" from pages 18–19 of the Big Book. The poem acts as a springboard to support these Social Studies concepts:

- Families can pass information down from one generation to the next.
- People in a family care about each other and share things with each other.

ABOUT THE POEM

A full instructional plan, along with the poem, appears on the following two pages.

In her poem "Four Generations," Mary Ann Hoberman uses rhymes and gentle humor to convey the concept of parents as the children of *their* parents.

ABOUT THE POET

Mary Ann Hoberman has written more than 20 books for children, among them the enormously popular "A House Is a House For Me." The mother of four grown children, she lives in Greenwich, Connecticut.

INTRODUCE

Using Prior Knowledge Work with children to list on a chart the three generations of family they know best: children, parents, and grandparents. Then help them recognize that the parents of their grandparents would be their great-grandparents, and add that generation to the list. You may wish to use drawings instead of words.

Generations

- *babies and children*
- *mother/father*
- *grandparents*
- *great-grandparents*

Previewing Share with children the title of the poem and the name of the poet. Point out that the boy and his father are two generations. Then ask volunteers to look at the picture and predict what they think this poem will be about. Remind them of the generations listings they made earlier.

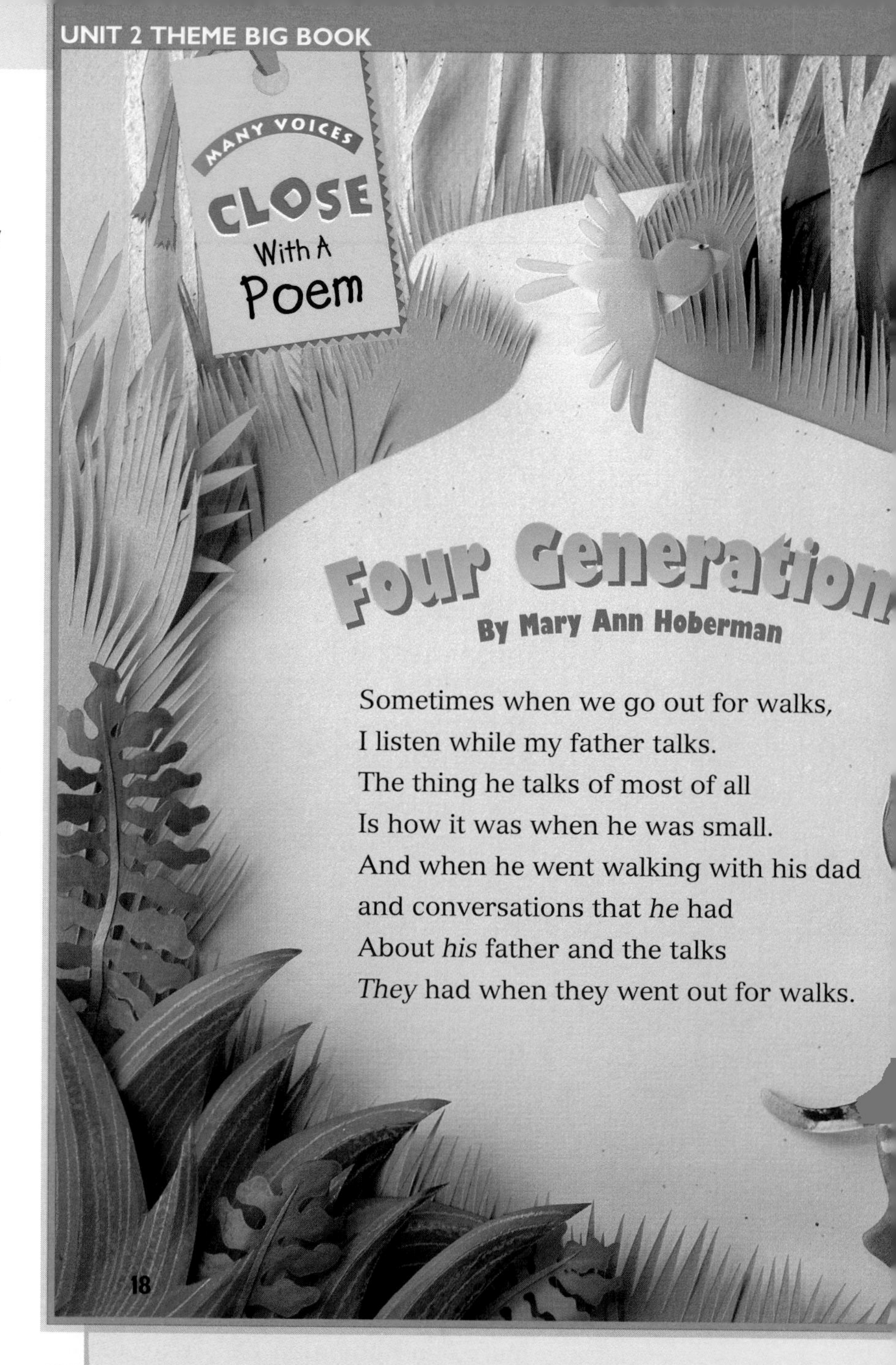

Curriculum Connection

Language Arts Point out to children that the poem includes several rhymes. Help them identify the pairs of rhyming words: *walks/talks, all/small, dad/had*. Write these on the chalkboard or on a chart.

- Ask children for words that rhyme with *-all* and *-ad*. Write these on the chalkboard or chart. (Possible answers: ball, call, fall, hall, mall, tall, wall; add, bad, fad, lad, mad, pad, sad)
- Invite children to choose any two rhyming words and draw a picture to illustrate them. Children can display their pictures in class and have classmates guess the words they illustrate.

READ

USING BIG BOOK PAGES 18–19

Read aloud the poem, emphasizing the words that refer to generations: *I, my father, his dad, his father*. Point to the words *generations* and *conversations.* Help children recognize that generations are children, parents, *their* parents, their parents' parents, and so on. Conversations are sharing of thoughts and memories.

SHARE

You can use these questions to prompt a discussion of the poem:

Who is telling this poem? *(the son)*

What does the father talk about? *(the same thing his father and grandfather talked about: their walks and talks with their fathers)*

Which four generations are talked about in this poem? *(son, father, grandfather, great-grandfather)*

Remind children that one of the important things family members do together is have conversations. Ask volunteers what they like to talk about with their own family members.

EXTENDING THE LITERATURE WITH ART/LANGUAGE ARTS

LEARNING STYLE: VISUAL

Make a Walking Partners Picture

ON YOUR OWN

15 TO 30 MINUTES

Objective: To make a family picture.

Resource: ***Project Book*** p. 21

Materials: markers, white construction paper, crayons, glue, scissors, fasteners

- Give each child a piece of construction paper. With markers, have them draw the background of a place they would enjoy going to take a walk and talk with a family member. The drawing could include such things as trees, grass, and mountains, or buildings and sidewalks.
- Give each child a copy of ***Project Book*** p. 21. Using crayons, have them color and then cut out the pieces. Help children attach the legs to the bodies with fasteners and glue the upper bodies to their drawings, leaving the legs free to "walk."
- Have children show their pictures, sharing who the family members are and the conversation they could be having.

Project Book p. 21

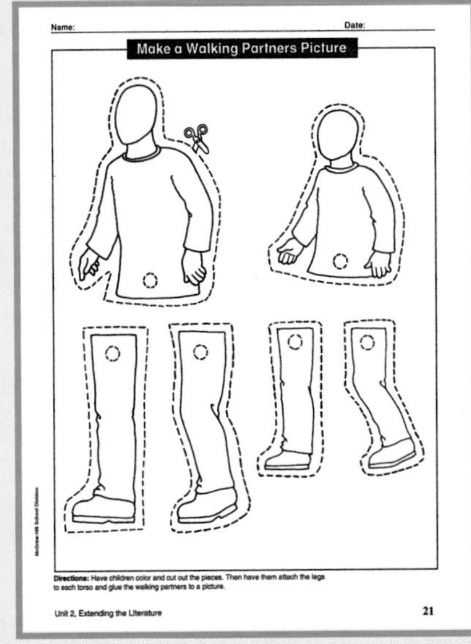
Name: Date:

Make a Walking Partners Picture

Directions: Have children color and cut out the pieces. Then have them attach the legs to each torso and glue the walking partners to a picture.

Unit 2, Extending the Literature 21

UNIT 2 ASSESSMENT

Assessment Opportunities

The CLOSE section of each lesson includes an EVALUATE activity. This page provides suggestions for using selected EVALUATE activities to integrate your assessment program with each day's lesson plan. The next page lists the main objectives of the unit and some of the activities that reinforce them. You may wish to make a copy of the checklist for each child.

EVALUATE Signs of Success

LESSON 1, Our Special Families

EVALUATE: *Make a Family Word Web, p. 49*

OBSERVATIONAL ASSESSMENT

- As children are illustrating their word webs, ask them to give examples of each word. Answers might include extended family members or other caregivers for *family members*. Record children's responses.

PORTFOLIO ASSESSMENT

The illustrated word webs can be part of children's portfolios.

- Children's illustrations should accurately define each word.
- Children's word webs should be set up according to your directions.

LESSON 3, Together as a Family

EVALUATE: *Perform Family Skits, p. 57*

OBSERVATIONAL ASSESSMENT

- Children should be able to perform skits about family members. You may want to use a tape recorder. You can also create a checklist including items such as understanding working together and the difference between work and play. You can take photographs as each group performs their skit.

PORTFOLIO ASSESSMENT

Tapes, checklists, and photographs can be part of children's portfolios.

- Children's skits should demonstrate an understanding of family activities, working together, and the difference between work and play.

AROUND THE WORLD, Families Are Everywhere

EVALUATE: *Draw Country Pictures, p. 61*

OBSERVATIONAL ASSESSMENT

- Children should display a clear understanding that families live in many countries around the world. As children are drawing, you may wish to ask them questions such as, "Do families live in other parts of the world or only in our country?" Record children's answers.

PORTFOLIO ASSESSMENT

The illustrations can be part of children's portfolios.

- Children's drawings should illustrate accurately something about another country from the lesson.
- Children should be able to name the country they are drawing.

UNIT 2 OBJECTIVES Checklist

1. Recognize that families vary.
2. Recognize that families live in different types of homes and neighborhoods.
3. Identify activities families do together.
4. Compare and contrast families and activities in other countries.
5. Identify jobs, workers, and workplaces.
6. Identify the four basic needs.
7. Distinguish needs from wants.
8. Distinguish alike from different.

Name ______________________________ Class ____________________

LESSON	ACTIVITY	PAGE	UNIT 2 OBJECTIVES	✓
LESSON 1	Draw a Special Group	47	1	
LESSON 1	Make Family Circles	50	1	
LESSON 1	Chart Family Sizes	50	1	
LESSON 2	Find Homes For Animals	51	2	
LESSON 2	Make Pocket Homes	54	2	
LESSON 2	Building Homes and Addresses	54	2	
LESSON 3	Make a Chart	55	3	
LESSON 3	Make Helping Handprints	58	3	
LESSON 3	Sing a Helping Song	58	3	
AROUND THE WORLD	Write a Postcard	59	3, 4	
AROUND THE WORLD	Try Fruit from Around the World	62	4	
AROUND THE WORLD	Sing “Frère Jacques”	62	4	
LESSON 4	Make a Worker Puppet	63	5	
LESSON 4	Make a Worker’s Alphabet Book	66	5	
LESSON 4	Use Worker Play-Kits	66	5	
LESSON 5	Make a Piggy Bank	67	7	
LESSON 5	Make Cards that Hug	70	6, 7	
LESSON 5	Shop in Our General Store	70	5, 7	
THINKING SKILL	Create a Place Mat	71	8	
THINKING SKILL	Find Alike and Different	74	8	
THINKING SKILL	Paint Alike and Different	74	8	

UNIT 3 Let's Explore
PLANNING GUIDE
Pupil Edition and Unit 3 Theme Big Book
Pages 80–119

INTRODUCTION
SUGGESTED PACING: 3 DAYS

Begin With The Literature Big Book, pages 83, 210–211

Using The Unit Opener
pp. 84–86

PROJECT IDEAS
- All Year Round! / ART
- Make a Location Collage / ART
- Enriching with Multimedia
- Seasons Booklets / SCIENCE
- Create the Seasons Around Us / ART

LESSON 1
SUGGESTED PACING: 1–2 DAYS

The Seasons Around Us
pp. 87–90

KEY CONCEPTS
year, seasons, winter, spring, summer, fall, weather

PROJECT IDEAS
- Make a Birthday Cake / ART
- Perform Seasons Fingerplays / DRAMA
- Make a Fish Kite / ART

RESOURCES
Project Book, p. 25 • Big Book Stickers Sheet 9 • Anthology, pp. 67–69, 72–75 • Word Cards

THINKING SKILLS
SUGGESTED PACING: 1–2 DAYS

Sort Things Into Groups
pp. 91–94

KEY CONCEPT
sort

PROJECT IDEAS
- Play The Matching Game / ART/MATHEMATICS
- Sort by Texture / SCIENCE
- Sort by Shape / MATHEMATICS

RESOURCES
Project Book, pp. 26–27 • Big Book Stickers Sheets 9, 10

LESSON 3
SUGGESTED PACING: 1–2 DAYS

On The Farm pp. 99–102

KEY CONCEPTS
farm, farmer, farmhouse, barn

PROJECT IDEAS
- Make Animal Puppets / ART/SCIENCE
- Grow a Garden from Seeds / SCIENCE
- Make a Farm Scene / ART

RESOURCES
Project Book, pp. 31–32 • Big Book Stickers Sheet 11 • Anthology, p. 66 • Anthology, pp. 10–13

LESSON 4
SUGGESTED PACING: 1–2 DAYS

Down By The Water
pp. 103–106

KEY CONCEPTS
water, ocean, beach

PROJECT IDEAS
- Explore the Water / ART/SCIENCE
- Make Egg-Carton Lobsters / ART/SCIENCE
- Paint Under-the-Sea Posters / ART

RESOURCES
Project Book, p. 33 • Big Book Stickers Sheet 12

CITIZENSHIP
SUGGESTED PACING: 1–2 DAYS

Making A Difference: Helping Animals pp. 107–110

KEY CONCEPTS
care, volunteer

PROJECT IDEAS
- Make an Animal Poster / ART
- Make Juice-Can Pencil Holders / ART/SCIENCE
- Make a Peanut-Butter Bird Feeder / SCIENCE

RESOURCES
Project Book, p. 34 • Desk Map

CLOSE WITH A POEM
SUGGESTED PACING: 1 DAY

When I Grow Up pp. 115–117

PROJECT IDEAS
- Find Ways to Travel / SCIENCE

RESOURCES
Project Book, pp. 36 • Anthology

UNIT ASSESSMENT
SUGGESTED PACING: 1 DAY

pp. 118–119

OBSERVATIONAL/PORTFOLIO ASSESSMENT, p. 118
- Make "Four Seasons" Books
- Make Sorting Cards
- Make "Down by the Water" Books

OBJECTIVES CHECKLIST, p. 119

McGRAW-HILL SCHOOL DIVISION'S HOME PAGE at http://www.mhschool.com contains on-line student activities related to this unit.

LESSON 2

SUGGESTED PACING: 1–2 DAYS

Around The City pp. 95–98

KEY CONCEPTS

city, transportation

PROJECT IDEAS

Make a Bus / MUSIC
Build a Floor-Map City / ART
Paint a City Mural / ART/LANGUAGE ARTS

RESOURCES

Project Book, pp. 28–30, 65–76 • Big Book Stickers Sheet 11 • Anthology, pp. 4–7 • Floor Map

LESSON 5

SUGGESTED PACING: 1–2 DAYS

In The Woods pp. 111–114

KEY CONCEPTS

woods, trees, ranger, camping

PROJECT IDEAS

Make a Turtle / ART/SCIENCE
Make Butterfly Mobiles / ART
Make a Class Forest / ART

RESOURCES

Project Book, p. 35 • Big Book Stickers Sheet 12 • Anthology, pp. 41–43

SHELTERED INSTRUCTION

Reading Strategies & Language Development

Contextualization, p. 84

Second-Language Support

Drama, p. 88
Using Dialog, p. 97
Using Props, p. 101

Meeting Individual Needs

McGraw-Hill Adventure Books

Assessment Opportunities

Ongoing Unit Project: Make a Location Collage, p. 85
Observational and Portfolio Assessment, p. 118
Objectives Checklist, p. 119
Evaluate, pp. 89, 93, 97, 101, 105, 109, 113

FOR FURTHER SUPPORT

- Language Support Handbook
- Social Studies Readiness

Unit Bibliography

MCGRAW-HILL ADVENTURE BOOKS Easy-to-Read Books

Daniels, Michele. ***A Playground.*** Fun playground objects such as a slide, swings, and a sandbox are pictured.

Lee, Mary. ***Old MacDonald Had A Farm.*** Old MacDonald has playful animals on his farm who make wonderful music together.

CLASSROOM LIBRARY

Cowen-Fletcher, Jane. ***Mama Zooms.*** New York: Scholastic Inc, 1993. A young boy sits in his mother's lap and imagines that her wheelchair is a zooming machine taking him from place to place.

READ ALOUD BOOKS

Cauley, Lorinda Bryan. ***The Town Mouse And The Country Mouse.*** New York: G.P. Putnam's Sons, 1984. A town mouse and a country mouse exchange visits and decide that they each prefer living in their own community.

Crews, Nina. ***One Hot Summer Day.*** New York: Greenwillow Books, 1995. A young girl enjoys summer activities in the city.

Dorros, Arthur. ***Abuela.*** New York: Dutton Children's Books, 1991. A young girl and her grandmother imagine they are flying over the city and seeing everything below.

Ehlert, Lois. ***Mole's Hill: A Woodland Tale.*** San Diego, CA: Harcourt Brace and Company, 1994. Mole has a plan to save her home when Fox tells her to move.

George, Lindsay Barrett. ***Around the Pond: Who's Been Here?*** New York: Greenwillow Books, 1996. A girl and boy follow a path in the woods and find clues that tell which animal has been there.

Gibbons, Gail. ***The Seasons of Arnold's Apple Tree.*** San Diego, CA: Harcourt Brace Jovanovich, 1984. A young boy has come to love a tree that is special in each season of the year.

Jackson, Ellen. ***Brown Cow, Green Grass, Yellow Mellow Sun.*** New York: Hyperion Books for Children, 1995. A young boy explores the colors that surround him at a farm.

Kimmel, Eric A., reteller. ***The Gingerbread Man.*** New York: Holiday House, 1993. A gingerbread man pops out of the oven, runs away, and meets many animals along the way.

■ Kuskin, Karla. ***City Dog.*** Boston, MA: Clarion Books, 1994. A city dog explores the unfamiliar sights of the countryside; told in lively rhyme.

Muller, Gerda. ***Circle of Seasons.*** New York: Dutton Children's Books, 1995. The traditions that come with each season are described and beautifully illustrated.

■ Tresselt, Alvin. ***The Mitten.*** New York: William Morrow & Co., 1989. Animals hide in a mitten when it snows until mitten bursts.

TEACHER BOOKS

Leslie, Clare Walker. ***Nature All Year Long.*** New York: Greenwillow Books, 1991. Ideas for activities for each season of the year are given, as well as facts that accompany each month's unique changes.

Time-Life for Children. ***Do Skyscrapers Touch the Sky?: First Questions and Answers About the City.*** Alexandria, VA: Time-Life, Inc., 1994. A simple question-and-answer format with detailed illustrations provide information on city life for classroom use.

TECHNOLOGY MULTIMEDIA

Let's Go to the Farm with Mac Parker. Video. Children learn about farm life through this refreshing presentation. Vermont Story Works. (800) 206-8383.

▯ ***Seasons.*** CD-ROM. No. T05774. Children can experience the changes that occur in each of the four seasons. National Geographic. (800) 368-2728.

FREE OR INEXPENSIVE MATERIALS

For a brochure on why leaves change color in the fall, write to: U.S. Department of Agriculture, Forest Service, P.O. Box 2417, Washington, DC 20013.

■ *Book excerpted in the Anthology*

▯ *National Geographic selection*

BEGIN WITH THE LITERATURE BIG BOOK

LINKING SOCIAL STUDIES AND LITERATURE

Introduce Unit 3 with the **Literature Big Book, *One Hot Summer Day.*** The story supports these Social Studies concepts:

- People find interesting and useful ways of adapting to seasonal weather.
- You can learn about your environment through exploration.

Literature Big Book

ABOUT THE STORY

A full instructional plan, along with the complete text of the story, appears on pages 210–211.

Nina Crew's lively photographs shows a little girl on her quiet city sidewalk and playground enjoying the sensations of a blistering hot morning that ends with a refreshing rain. Short descriptions make the reader feel hot: "Dogs pant. Hydrants are open. Women carry umbrellas for the shade. . . . Hot enough to fry an egg on the sidewalk."

ABOUT THE AUTHOR/ILLUSTRATOR

Nina Crews grew up in a household where picture books were created; her mother and father, Ann Jonas and Donald Crews, have written more than two dozen books for children. Nina, a graduate of Yale University, now lives in Brooklyn, New York. This is her first book.

USING THE Unit 3 Opener

USING BIG BOOK PAGES 2–3

Read aloud the unit title. Explain that when we explore, we search for something and look closely at it. Introduce Gloria and Jay. Tell children they will see Gloria again in other pages of the book. Children can preview the lessons as they look for Gloria.

DEVELOPING KEY CONCEPTS

In this unit, children explore the seasons, the weather, and places. Name each place and have volunteers share what they know.

city *A city is a place that is made up of many different neighborhoods.*

farm *A farm is land used to raise animals or to grow crops.*

beach *The beach is land along the edge of a body of water, usually covered with sand or pebbles.*

woods *Woods are places where trees grow closely together.*

USE BIG BOOK STICKERS, SHEET 9

Affix the ***Sticker*** labels for *beach* and *farm* near the location collages shown and place the other labels nearby. Read the words and tell children these words are names of places they will explore.

beach farm city woods

SHELTERED INSTRUCTION

Building context will help children grasp the concept of exploration. Use examples of your own explorations and those of the children and videotapes to clarify the concept. **[SDAIE STRATEGY: CONTEXTUALIZATION]**

BULLETIN BOARD

All Year Round!

Create a bulletin board that shows the months and the seasons of the year.

- Cover the bulletin board with plain paper. Cut out a large circle and label the months of the year around the circle like a clock. With a metal fastener, attach an arrow in the middle to point to the current month.
- Around the outside of the clock, label the four seasons near the appropriate months.
- Cut out pictures from magazines or have children make drawings showing things associated with each season. Have children place each picture around the edges of the clock, near the corresponding season.

ABOUT THE PHOTOGRAPH

Item 1 Point out that Gloria is holding a collage that shows the beach. Explain that a collage is made by gluing paper, cloth, and other things to paper to make a picture. Have children identify the things in Gloria's collage—such as the sun, clouds, sand, real shells, a cloth towel, a miniature umbrella, a starfish, a shovel and pail, and a fish.

Item 2 Tell children that Jay is holding a collage of a city neighborhood. Ask children to name things they see in his collage—such as a school, post office, car, plane, and people walking a dog.

Directions for making this Ongoing Unit Project can be found at the bottom of this page.

SCHOOL-TO-HOME

Nature Album

- Children will be exploring their surroundings in this unit. Help families work together to study the environment around their own homes by using a nature album.
- Give each child four pieces of colored construction paper, stapled together.
- Have children take their empty nature albums home. Encourage family members to help children find some samples from the environment to tape to each base, such as pebbles, leaves, or sticks.
- Children can then bring in their completed nature albums to share with the class.

ONGOING UNIT PROJECT

GROUP

Make a Location Collage

CURRICULUM CONNECTION Art

As part of Lessons 2–5, assign children to make one or all four location collages, including a city, a farm, the beach, and woods.

Advance Preparation: Gather shirt boxes, which will be used as the base of the collages. You might get sheets of birdcage liner paper or lightweight sandpaper to use in the beach collages.

1. After each lesson is completed, have children color and cut out the collage pieces from ***Project Book*** pp. 22–24. In addition, children can use items from ***Project Book*** pp. 31–33 for the farm and the beach collages, p. 66 for the woods collage, and pp. 67–76 for the city collage.
2. In a top or bottom of a shirt box, have children glue pieces of construction paper, the cutouts from the ***Project Book*** pages, and any additional items of their choice to make the collages. You might have children think about the weather and the seasons as they prepare their collages.

Assessment Suggestions

Signs of Success

- Children's collages should contain items that reflect the assigned location.
- As a class, children should be able to sort the completed collages according to location. Children will create an organized display by sorting.
- Children should be able to describe the items that make up their collages and tell what they are made of.
- Children should be able to identify elements of their collages that relate to weather and the seasons.

TECHNOLOGY CENTER

Enriching with Multimedia

RESOURCE: *National Geographic* Wonders of Learning

- Enrich Unit 3 with the Wonders of Learning CD-ROM *Our Earth*.

RESOURCE: *Videodisc/Video Tape 1*

- Enrich Unit 3 with the video segment *Climate.*

Search Frame 28905, Play to 32892

SCIENCE LEARNING CENTER

LEARNING STYLE: KINESTHETIC/VISUAL

Seasons Booklets

GROUP

30 MINUTES OR LONGER

Materials: construction paper, magazines, catalogs, scissors, tape, clothespins, crayons

1. Invite children to share any information they know about the seasons. Encourage them to talk about weather, animals, and plants they see during the year.
2. Then divide the class into four groups. Assign each group to a season. Have the groups look through magazines and catalogs to find pictures that represent their assigned seasons.
3. Then have children work in the Science Learning Center to create collages, or draw original pictures on construction paper to illustrate their seasons.
4. Have each group use clothespins to fasten the construction paper into booklets, so pages may be added easily.

TEACHER EXCHANGE

Thanks to Kayleen Pollard, Big Creek Elementary School, Cumming, Georgia

Create the Seasons Around Us

GROUP

30 MINUTES OR LONGER

Materials: brown construction paper, butcher paper, sponges, tissue paper, cotton balls, paint, glue, scissors, marker

1. Help each child trace his or her arm and hand on a sheet of brown construction paper. The traced arm and hand will become a "tree." Help children cut out the trees.
2. Then divide the class into four groups and assign each one a season. Each group goes to a "seasonal" work table.
3. The *Fall* table should have sponges and red, yellow, and orange paint. The *Winter* table should have glue and cotton balls. The *Spring* table should have glue and white and pink tissue paper for making blossoms. The *Summer* table should have green paint so children can make thumbprint leaves.
4. Encourage each group to decorate their trees with the materials at its table. You may wish to glue each picture to a large sheet of butcher paper to make a poster and label each season.

UNIT 3
LESSON 1

The Seasons Around Us

BIG BOOK PAGES 4–5

LESSON OVERVIEW

The four seasons of the year affect nature and people.

LESSON OBJECTIVES

- Identify the four seasons and describe the types of weather that usually characterize each of them.
- Recognize that seasons and weather change.
- Recognize that weather and seasons affect the way people, plants, and animals live.
- Identify the order of the four seasons.

KEY CONCEPTS

year	seasons	winter	spring
summer	fall	weather	

RESOURCE REMINDER

Project Book
p. 25

Stickers Package
Sheet 9

Anthology
The Mitten, pp. 67–69
Garden of Happiness, pp. 72–75

Word Cards

Technology Connection
VIDEODISC/VIDEO TAPE 2

Search Frame 28905, Play to 32892

GETTING READY

Make a Birthday Cake

ON YOUR OWN

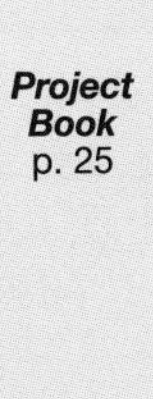
15 TO 30 MINUTES

CURRICULUM CONNECTION Art

Objective: To learn about the seasons of the year.

Resources: *Project Book* p. 25

Materials: oaktag, markers, pencils, crayons, scissors, tape

Advance Preparation: Create an oaktag poster for each of the four seasons. Write the name of the season at the top of the poster. Draw a birthday cake on each poster.

1. Discuss with children that everyone has a special day—a birthday.
2. Using *Project Book* p. 25, help each child to write his or her name on the line. Have children color and cut out the candle.
3. Help each child to discover what season his or her birthday is in. The seasons generally fall within these dates: Fall–September 21 to December 20; Winter–December 21 to March 20; Spring–March 21 to June 20; Summer–June 21 to September 20.
4. Have children tape their candles to the correct seasonal cake.

Project Book p. 25

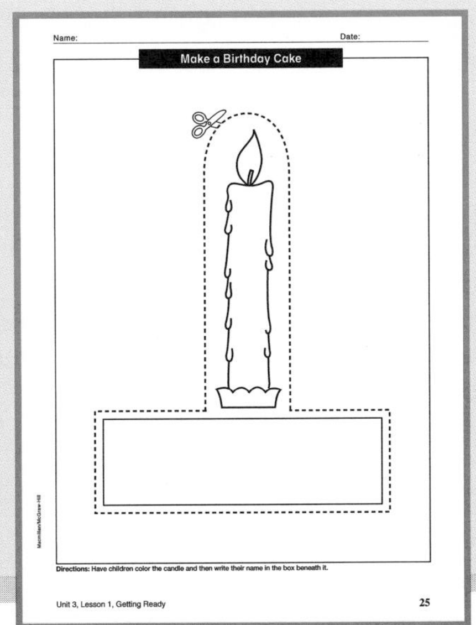
Name: Date:

Make a Birthday Cake

Directions: Have children color the candle and then write their name in the box beneath it.

Unit 3, Lesson 1, Getting Ready 25

1 Prepare

WARMING UP WITH THE READ ALOUD

Tell children that they will be learning about four special parts of a year called seasons. Elicit from children that the names of the seasons are winter, spring, summer, and fall. You may wish to introduce autumn as a synonym for fall. To introduce the seasons, share the poem in the Read Aloud.

- ***Which season is hot?*** *(summer)*
- ***Which season is snowy?*** *(winter)*

Tell children that weather changes as the seasons change. Explain that weather has to do with whether it is windy, sunny, foggy, cloudy, raining, hailing, snowing, warm, or cold. Point out that the words *hot* and *snowy* in the poem are weather-related words.

2 Teach

USING BIG BOOK PAGES 4–5

Point out that Gloria, whom children met in the Unit Opener on pp. 2–3, is displaying the posters of the four seasons. You may wish to point out that the posters show a home in Wisconsin.

Technology Connection

VIDEODISC/VIDEO TAPE 2
Enrich Lesson 1 with the video segment on *Climate.* Search Frame 28905.

See the bar code on p. 87.

UNIT 3 THEME BIG BOOK

LESSON 1

The Seasons Around Us

4

Read Aloud

Easy Seasons

Spring's all buttercups
and breezy.

Summer's hot and
bumblebees-y.

Autumn's bright with
colored trees-y.

Winter's snowy;
sniffly, sneezy.

Alan Benjamin

Using the Anthology

The Garden of Happiness, pages 72–75 A little girl plants a seed that becomes a beautiful flower. She is sad when the flower dies. Then, unexpectedly, its golden petals once again light up the street.

The Mitten, pages 67–69 Children will enjoy listening to this Ukranian folktale. In this retelling, eight woodland animals seek the shelter of a wool mitten on a cold winter's day.

Second-Language Support/Drama Review the four seasons of the year and ask children to say something about the kind of weather that occurs during each one. Then focus on key words and phrases that appear in the stories by dramatizing the words as they appear.

USE BIG BOOK STICKERS, SHEET 9

Use the following ***Stickers*** throughout the lesson.

Attach the ***Sticker*** *Fall* to the first poster. Discuss elements in the poster, including the fall clothing that Gloria is wearing. Continue with the other season posters, having volunteers attach the corresponding ***Stickers*** for *Winter*, *Spring*, and *Summer.* Discuss how plants, animals, and people change from season to season. Also discuss the order of the four seasons.

Use the ***Stickers*** of sun, rain, clouds, and snow to chart the weather throughout the week. Place the ***Stickers*** on the poster of the season that your area is experiencing.

- ***Which season comes before winter?*** *(fall)*

★ **THINKING FURTHER:** ***Compare and Contrast*** ***Which poster looks the most like the season we are in now? How do you know?*** *(Answers should reflect the season your area is currently experiencing.)*

You may wish to use the ***Word Cards*** of the seasons as you describe the effects of the seasons on your community.

3 Close

LESSON SUMMARY

Read the lesson question, pointing to each word as you read. Have children name the four seasons in order.

EVALUATE

Make "Four Seasons" Books Have children make "Four Seasons" books. It will be one in a collection of "Let's Explore" books prepared in the Evaluate sections of this Unit. Have each child assemble five sheets of paper horizontally and staple them along the top. Distribute labels that say *Four Seasons* for children to glue on their covers. Have children illustrate elements of each season. Provide labels saying *Fall, Winter, Spring,* and *Summer* for children to glue on the inside pages. For assessment suggestions, see p. 118.

Background Information

About the Seasons Seasons and weather conditions vary widely from region to region in the United States. Usual conditions for each part of the United States are described below.

- In the eastern parts of the United States, north of St. Louis, Missouri, and in much of the interior region, summer brings hot weather and winter brings snow. Occasionally snow or frost afflict the southeastern states into central Florida. Hurricanes often strike the East Coast during the fall.
- From the northern Pacific Coast inland to the Cascades, winter is the wet season, spring is normally green, and summer is often dry. Fog is prevalent along the northern Pacific Coast in summer.
- In Utah, New Mexico, Arizona, and southeast California and in sections of Nevada and southwest Texas, the climate is dry. Summers are hot and winters are mild.
- In the Rocky Mountain and Great Plains regions, the rainy seasons extend from late spring into summer.

DRAMA CONNECTION

LEARNING STYLE: AUDITORY/ KINESTHETIC

Perform Seasons Fingerplays

GROUP

15 TO 30 MINUTES

Objective: To identify the seasons of the year.

1. Divide the class into four groups. Tell children that each group will learn a fingerplay about a season of the year. When their season is called out, they will stand and perform their fingerplay.
2. Use this fingerplay for spring.

   "Raindrops"
   Rain is falling down, rain is falling down.
   (Raise arms, flutter fingers to ground, tapping floor, or tap palm of hand.)
   Pitter-patter, pitter-patter,
   Rain is falling down.
   Marion F. Grayson

3. Use this fingerplay for summer.

   "Sun"
   The sun is rising high, high in the sky.
   (With palms closed, slowly raise arms above head, spread arms wide and open fingers wide.)
   If I were a bird, I would fly, fly high,
   To the sun rising in the sky.
   Frances Ruffin

4. Use this fingerplay for fall.

   "Falling Leaves"
   Many leaves are falling down.
   (Flutter fingers from above head, down to floor several times.)
   Yellow, red and even brown.
   Falling on the frosty ground.
   Falling on the frosty ground.
   Marion F. Grayson

5. Use this fingerplay for winter.

   "Snowflakes"
   Snowflakes whirling all around, all around, all around.
   (Flutter fingers high above head, in the air, slowly falling to ground.)
   Snowflakes whirling all around
   Until they cover all the ground.
   Marion F. Grayson

ART CONNECTION

LEARNING STYLE: KINESTHETIC

Make a Fish Kite

ON YOUR OWN

30 MINUTES OR LONGER

Objective: To make the connection that wind is a part of weather found in many seasons.

Materials: drawing paper, scissors, tape, glue, crumpled paper, crepe-paper streamers, string

1. Tell children people fly kites in the wind. For each child, use two long sheets of drawing paper, about 24". Demonstrate how to draw a fish shape and invite children to draw the shape on both sheets of drawing paper to make a fish kite.
2. Help children cut out fish shapes. Help them to paint their fish with brightly colored paints.
3. When the paint is dry, have children place one fish shape, paint-side down, on the desk. Direct children to put 2–3 crumpled balls of paper on the fish shape. Then show children how to glue the two fish shapes together.
4. Children can glue on two or three crepe-paper streamers at the tail end.
5. Help children tape a length of string (about 22") just below the kites' noses so they can run with their kites behind them. When hung up, the fish kites will make an attractive display.

Sorting Things into Groups

UNIT 3 THEME BIG BOOK, PAGES 6–7

LESSON OVERVIEW

Sorting is a way of organizing objects.

LESSON OBJECTIVES

- Identify sorting as the process of organizing things into groups.
- Recognize the usefulness of sorting things into groups.
- Classify objects by sorting them into groups.

KEY CONCEPT

sort

GETTING READY

Play the Matching Game

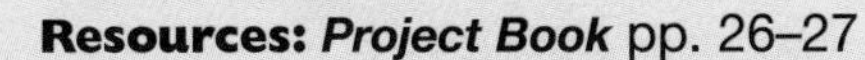

Objective: To introduce the concept of sorting through a matching game.

Resources: *Project Book* pp. 26–27

Materials: crayons, construction paper, glue, scissors

Advance Preparation: Cut out construction paper squares that are the size of the pictures on ***Project Book*** pp. 26–27 (eight per child).

1. Have children color and cut out each picture on ***Project Book*** pp. 26–27. Point out that there are two of each picture.
2. Then have children glue each picture to construction paper squares to make cards.
3. Children play the matching game by first placing their cards face down on a table or the floor. Then they turn over two cards at a time. When they make a match, they can put them in a pile. Two children can play together by using both decks of cards. The child with the most matches wins.

Project Book pp. 26–27

Name: Date:

Play the Matching Game

Directions: Have children color and cut out the pictures. Then have them glue the pictures to construction-paper squares to make playing cards.

Unit 3, Thinking Skills, Getting Ready 27

1 Prepare

WARMING UP WITH THE READ ALOUD

Have volunteers name different kinds of groups to which they belong. Point out that the groups they named are made up of people who are alike in some way. Tell children that they will be learning about how to place things that are alike into groups. Share the poem in the Read Aloud to identify a group of things that relate to winter.

- ***How are the clothes in the poem alike?*** *(They are clothes for winter.)*
- ***Why doesn't the poet need these winter clothes any more?*** *(Possible answers: It is spring, the weather is turning warmer, the clothes are too warm.)*

2 Teach

USING BIG BOOK PAGES 6–7

Tell children that Gloria needs help putting away her clothes. Suggest that one way is to stuff the clothes randomly into the dresser. Elicit from children that another way is to sort the clothes into groups and then put each group into its own drawer. Define *sorting* as "placing together things that are alike." Explain that we sort things to make things easier to find. Point out that when we place together things that are alike, we make a group.

USE BIG BOOK STICKERS, SHEETS 9–10

You can use the following ***Stickers*** throughout the lesson.

Read aloud the labels on the dresser. Explain that these labels are the names of groups, into which items that are alike will be placed. Have children use the ***Stickers*** of rings for summer and winter to identify clothing for those seasons. Then have children affix the ***Stickers*** of Gloria's winter and summer clothing to the appropriate drawers.

UNIT 3 THEME BIG BOOK

Read Aloud

It's Spring

No more snowsuits.
No more caps.
No more boots
or winter wraps.
No more, "Wear your
mittens, dear."
It's spring,
and barefoot time
is near!

Jane Belk Moncure

Into what groups can you sort these things?

7

- ***Into what two groups could you sort the clothes?*** *(summer and winter)*
- ***Which things would you place in the summer group?*** *(sandals, straw hat, bathing suit)*
- ***Which things would you place in the winter group?*** *(jacket, mittens, boots)*

★**THINKING FURTHER: *Classifying*** ***Into what other groups could you sort the clothes?*** *(Children might sort things into other groups by color, size, or subject.)*

Use these tips with children to help them sort the clothes into groups.

HELPING YOURSELF

- Select one thing.
- Look for others that are like it and place them together to make a group.
- Tell how they are alike by giving the group a name.

Have children name activities they do at home or at school that involve sorting, such as cleaning up toys or materials, placing recyclables in bins, organizing collections, or putting dishes away.

3 Close

LESSON SUMMARY

Read the lesson question with children, pointing to each word as you read. Children may say that they would sort the clothing into winter clothing and summer clothing, or other groups, such as by color, size, or subject.

EVALUATE

Make Sorting Cards Have pairs of children each make an envelope of sorting cards. Direct each pair to cut two groups of three related pictures from magazines and glue them onto index cards. You might suggest some groups such as clothes, transportation, workers, toys, animals, or food. Then have volunteers show how to sort the cards. For assessment suggestions, see p. 118.

Print Awareness

For functional reading purposes and to help children to sort and organize supplies and other classroom items, place handwritten labels on bins, boxes, envelopes, and shelves, as well as in closets. In addition to the labels, supplies might also be arranged in color-coded containers.

Curriculum Connection

Library Science Ask your school librarian to give children a tour of your school library, emphasizing how important it is to sort books into similar groups so that people can find what they are looking for easily. The librarian might discuss how books are first divided into two groups—make-believe stories (fiction) and books about real things (nonfiction). The nonfiction books are then further divided into many smaller groups, such as travel and history.

SCIENCE CONNECTION

LEARNING STYLE: KINESTHETIC

Sort by Texture

ON YOUR OWN

15 TO 30 MINUTES

Objective: To classify things as "rough" or "smooth" by using the sense of touch.

Materials: things with a texture that can be classified as being rough (sandpaper, slightly crumpled aluminum foil, burlap, dry cereal, rocks) or smooth (velvet, silk, cotton, uncrumpled aluminum foil), sheets of paper, glue

Advance Preparation: Mount the "rough" and "smooth" items on sheets of paper with glue and let them dry.

1. Invite children to touch each item. Then ask them to sort items according to the way they feel, "rough" or "smooth."
2. Have children place the rough-textured items in one pile, and those that feel smooth in another.

MATHEMATICS CONNECTION

LEARNING STYLE: KINESTHETIC

Learning Center: Sort by Shape

ON YOUR OWN

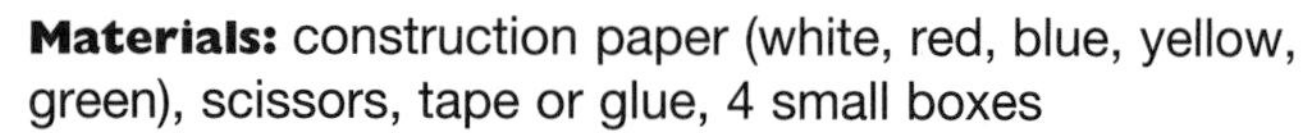

15 TO 30 MINUTES

Objective: To classify objects by sorting them into groups by shape.

Materials: construction paper (white, red, blue, yellow, green), scissors, tape or glue, 4 small boxes

Advance Preparation: First cut the following shapes: square, triangle, circle, and rectangle from the white construction paper. Tape or glue each shape onto a small box. Then cut each of the four shapes from the red, blue, yellow, and green construction paper so that there will be 16 cut in all. (Two sets can be made so that there can be greater participation.)

1. Place the boxes with their white patterns on a counter in the Mathematics Learning Center. Place the colored construction paper shapes on the counter in a random pattern.
2. Invite children to the Mathematics Learning Center to sort the pieces first by color and then by shape. Have them place the correct shapes into the correct boxes.

UNIT 3

LESSON 2

Around the City

UNIT 3 THEME BIG BOOK, PAGES 8–9

LESSON OVERVIEW

Cities are comprised of many neighborhoods with homes, buildings, many forms of transportation, and the people who live there.

LESSON OBJECTIVES

- Recognize that cities are made up of many different neighborhoods.
- Identify common forms of transportation, homes, buildings, and places of interest in cities.
- Recognize that people live, go to school, work, and have fun in cities.

KEY CONCEPTS

city transportation

RESOURCE REMINDER

Project Book
pp. 28–30, 65–76

Stickers Package
Sheet 11

Anthology
Maxie, pp. 4–7

Floor Map

GETTING READY

Make a Bus

ON YOUR OWN

15 TO 30 MINUTES

CURRICULUM CONNECTION Music

Objective: To learn about forms of transportation found in the city.

Resources: *Project Book* pp. 28–30

Materials: crayons, scissors, egg cartons cut in half (to make two sets of six), paint, paintbrushes, glue, tape

Advance Preparation: On chart paper, write the words of the "Wheels on the Bus" song or enlarge the song on *Project Book* p. 30.

1. Discuss with children different ways people get from place to place in a city.
2. Invite children to make a bus. Have them color and cut out the different parts of the bus on *Project Book* pp. 28–29.
3. Then each child can paint their egg-carton half and glue or tape their cutouts onto it to make a bus. Children can glue the windows to the sides and the wheels to the bottom.
4. After the children have completed their buses, have them sing the song "Wheels on the Bus," using their buses as props.

Project Book
pp. 28–30

Name: Date:

Make a Bus

"Wheels on the Bus"

The wheels on the bus
go round and round,
round and round,
round and round.
The wheels on the bus
go round and round,
all around the town.

The wipers on the bus
go swish, swish, swish,
swish, swish, swish,
swish, swish, swish.
The wipers on the bus
go swish, swish, swish,
all around the town.

The people on the bus
go up and down,
up and down,
up and down.
The people on the bus
go up and down,
all around the town.

The horn on the bus
goes "beep, beep, beep,"
"beep, beep, beep,"
"beep, beep, beep."
The horn on the bus
goes "beep, beep, beep,"
all around the town.

Directions: You may wish to enlarge a copy of this song to share with your class.

Macmillan/McGraw-Hill

30 Unit 3, Lesson 2, Getting Ready

1 Prepare

WARMING UP WITH THE READ ALOUD

Tell children that they will be learning about cities. Explain that a city is a place that is made up of many different neighborhoods where people live, go to school, work, and play. Share the poem in the Read Aloud to begin the discussion. Explain to children that the poem mentions a subway, which is a train that runs underground.

- ***What words in the poem describe sounds?*** (roars, rumbles, laughs, grumbles)
- ***What things in the city made these sounds?*** *(subways, people, machines)*

2 Teach

USING BIG BOOK PAGES 8–9

Focus on the word *city* in the lesson title. Tell children that the Big Book shows Gloria's scrapbook. Explain that the scrapbook shows things that are found in many big cities. You may wish to identify the cities shown in the photographs which include (from left to right) New York City, San Francisco, and San Diego.

USE BIG BOOK STICKERS, SHEET 11

Use the ***Stickers*** of workers, home, transportation, and places in a city throughout the lesson.

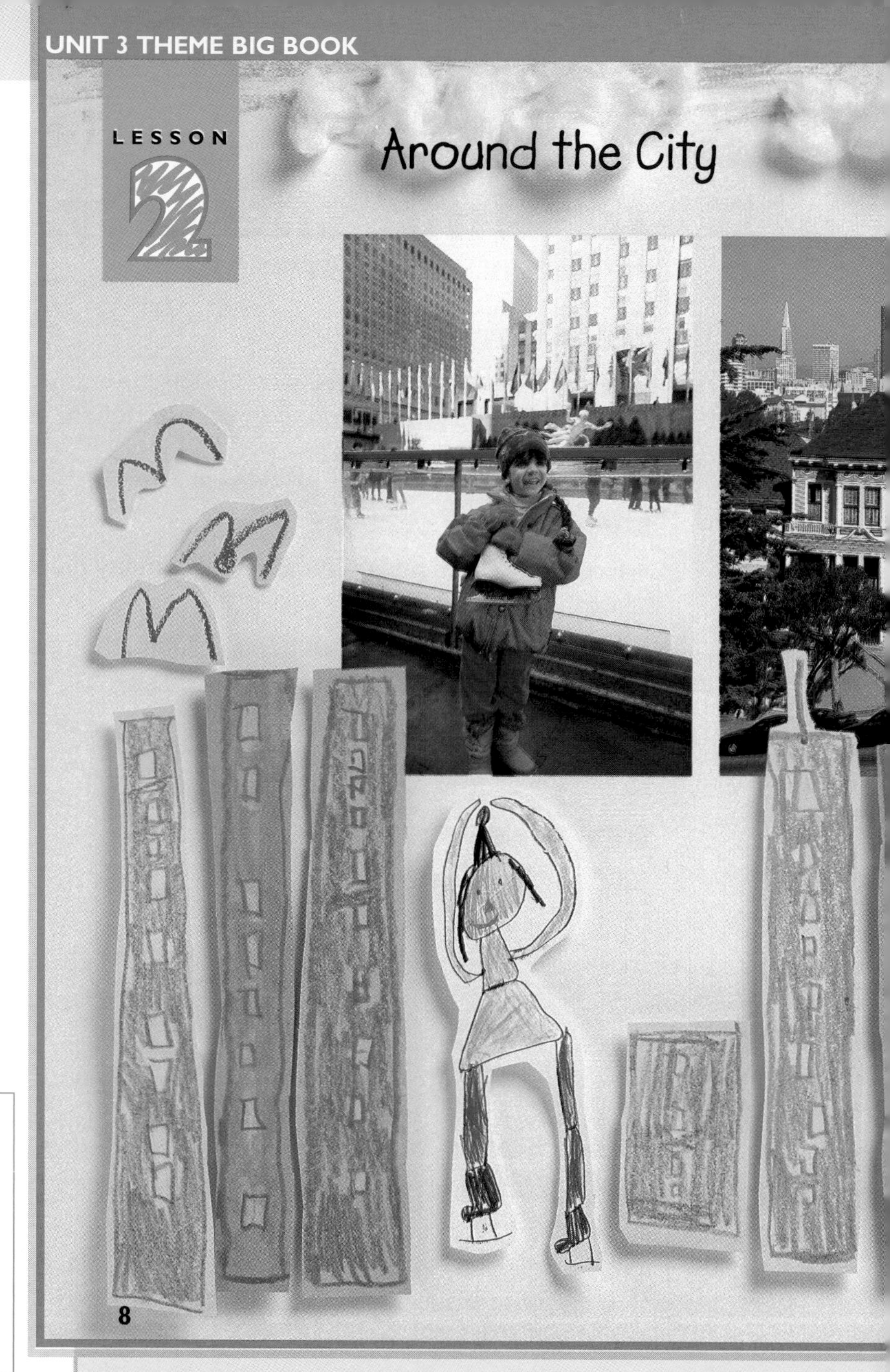

Read Aloud

Sing a Song of Cities

Sing a song of cities.
If you do,
Cities will sing back to you.

They'll sing in subway roars and rumbles.
People-laughs, machine-loud-grumbles.

Sing a song of cities.
If you do,
Cities will sing back to you.

Lee Bennett Hopkins

Using the Anthology

Maxie, pp. 4–7 You may wish to share the story as a way of introducing the topic of "cities." This story focuses on the daily routine of a woman in a city neighborhood and how her life affects the neighbors and workers in and around her brownstone. After reading, ask children to name the city workers in the story including the milk delivery person, the clerk at the grocery store, the superintendent, the mailman, the doctor, the bus driver, the nurse, and the restaurant worker. You might also discuss the city places named including the diner, the school, and the hospital as well as the kinds of transportation named such as the train and the school bus.

Have children place the ***Stickers*** into like groups near the photographs that pertain to them. Place the transportation ***Stickers*** of the plane and the bus near the photograph of the trolley and explain that these kinds of transportation can be found in city neighborhoods. Place the ***Stickers*** of the firefighter and police officer near the construction worker and ask children where they might find these workers in a city. Place the ***Stickers*** of the store and park near the ice skating rink and explain that these are places you might find in a city neighborhood. Finally, place the ***Sticker*** of the house near the attached houses and ask children what other housing they might find in a city neighborhood.

- ***What fun activity did Gloria do in the city and in what season did she do it?*** *(She went ice skating in the winter.)*

> ★ **THINKING FURTHER:** ***Making Conclusions*** ***Why might you guess that the tall buildings in some cities are called skyscrapers?*** *(They are so high they appear to touch or scrape the sky.)*

3 Close

LESSON SUMMARY

Point to each word as you read the lesson question. Have each child name something he or she might see in a city.

EVALUATE

Make "Around the City" Books Have children make "Around the City" books to add to their collection of "Let's Explore" books. Prepare labels that read *Around the City* and cut out skyscrapers from drawing paper. Each child will need at least four cutouts. Help them to staple the cutouts together along the top. Suggest that children decorate the front of their books and glue on the *Around the City* labels. Inside the books, children might illustrate places in a city, homes in a city, transportation in a city, and workers in a city. See the box at the left for second-language support for this activity.

Second-Language Support

Using Dialog Keep in mind the backgrounds and experiences of your second-language learners. If they live in a rural area or small town, they may not have acquired the language needed to talk about urban life. You may wish to build background about how a city is different. Foster this language development through an in-class activity. Invite children to look at the pictures in this unit and ask questions and volunteer information about what they think life is like in a big city. Confirm or correct the information they present, using simple sentences and pointing to related pictures in the book. Encourage children to repeat key words or sentences and point to related pictures in the book.

UNIT 3 Extending the Lesson

ART CONNECTION

LEARNING STYLE: KINESTHETIC

Learning Center: Build a Floor-Map City

GROUP

15 TO 30 MINUTES

Resources: ***K-1 Floor Map, Project Book*** pp. 65–76

Objective: To enhance map skills and to explore things found in a city neighborhood.

Materials: boxes and cartons (small, empty), scissors, crayons, glue

1. Make ***Project Book*** pp. 65–76 available in the Art Center.
2. Invite children to build a floor-map city neighborhood. Have them color and cut out the ***Project Book*** patterns. Then help them glue the patterns to boxes or cartons.
3. Encourage children to build a city on the ***Floor Map*** with the assembled patterns. As they work, ask children such questions as: "What kinds of buildings would you find in a neighborhood in the big city?" and "What other things might you see in a neighborhood in the big city?"

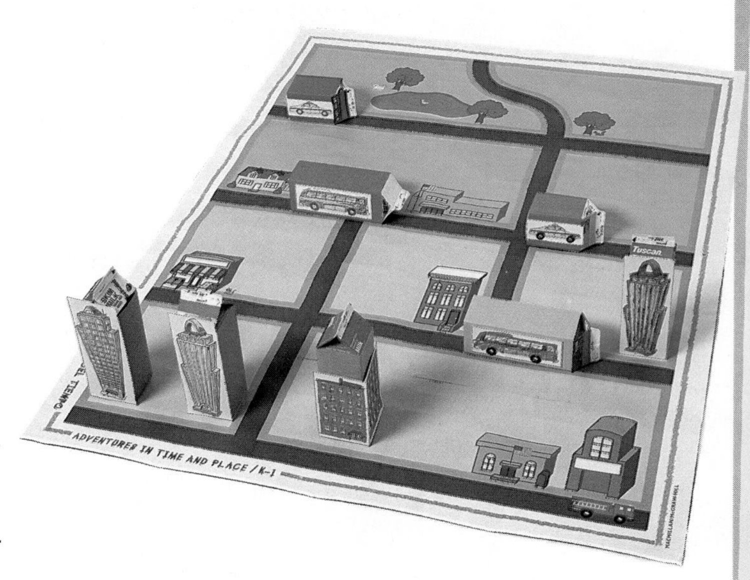

ART/LANGUAGE ARTS CONNECTION

LEARNING STYLE: AUDITORY/VISUAL

Paint a City Mural

GROUP

15 TO 30 MINUTES

Objective: To recognize the kinds of buildings and things found in a city neighborhood.

Materials: pictures of cityscapes and street scenes, cellophane tape, two lengths of brown wrapping paper (60" each), poster paints, paintbrushes

1. Explain to children that they will be making murals of city neighborhoods that show tall buildings, cars, people, parks, and other things. Encourage children to use the pictures for reference.
2. Tape the wrapping paper onto a chalkboard or wall. Divide the class into two groups, with each group working on one of the sheets of paper to create their own neighborhood. Each group will have brushes and paint.
3. When murals are complete, have children tell a short story about the portion of the mural that they painted.

UNIT 3

LESSON 3

On the Farm

UNIT 3 THEME BIG BOOK, PAGES 10–11

LESSON OVERVIEW

Farms are places that grow food or raise animals.

LESSON OBJECTIVES

- Identify common elements of farms including animals, crops, workers, buildings, and machines.
- Identify foods grown and animals raised on farms.
- Recognize that farms provide us with many of our needs.

KEY CONCEPTS

farm farmer farmhouse
barn

GETTING READY

Make Animal Puppets

15 TO 30 MINUTES

CURRICULUM CONNECTION Art/Science

Objective: To identify different farm animals and the sounds they make.

Resources: ***Project Book*** pp. 31–32

Materials: crayons, scissors, craft sticks, glue

1. Have children name each animal they see on ***Project Book*** pp. 31–32.
2. Children can then color and cut out each of the animals. Help each child glue the animals to craft sticks to make animal puppets.
3. Ask volunteers to make the sounds of each of the animals. Invite children to sing "Old McDonald Had a Farm," using their animal puppets as props.

Name: Date:

Make Animal Puppets

Directions: Have children color and cut out the animals. Then have them glue the animals to craft sticks to make animal puppets.

Unit 3, Lesson 3, Getting Ready 31

1 Prepare

WARMING UP WITH THE READ ALOUD

Tell children that they will be learning about farms. Define *farm* as "land used to raise animals or grow crops." Explain that farms are usually located away from big cities. Also explain that farmers are people who work and often live on farms. Share the poem in the Read Aloud to explore Jonathan's farm.

- ***What animals would Jonathan have on his farm?*** *(dog/terrier, cats, cows, pigs, birds)*
- ***Where would he keep his cows?*** *(barn)*

2 Teach

USING BIG BOOK PAGES 10–11

Read the title and focus on the word *farm*. Have children recall that Jonathan would raise animals and grow fruit on his farm. Explain that some farmers only raise food (such as fruit, grains, or vegetables) while others only raise animals (such as chickens, livestock, dairy cows, or fish). Discuss common farm animals and the needs they provide us with such as chicken's eggs and cow's milk. Discuss other needs grown on farms such as crops of vegetables, grains, and fruit.

UNIT 3 THEME BIG BOOK

Read Aloud

Jonathan's Farm

I'd like a little farm
with a house that's painted blue,
with a lively little terrier
and a pussy cat or two.

I'd build a little barn
to keep my gentle cows,
outside I'd build a pig-pen
for piglets and for sows;

I'd plant a little orchard
with apple and with plum
and all the birds would praise
their green kingdom.

Miriam Waddington

Using the Anthology

Hello, Farm, page 66 After discussing the Read Aloud poem, share this poem in the ***Anthology***. It further introduces the sights on a farm. If possible provide photographs or illustrations of the buildings, and other structures on a farm to reinforce the meaning of the words.

Hill of Fire, pages 10–13 After you have discussed the various foods that farmers typically grow on farms, treat children to this story about a rather unusual thing that grew in a cornfield in Mexico. The story tells about the eruption and formation of a volcano and is based on actual descriptions of an event that took place in 1943.

USE BIG BOOK STICKERS, SHEET 11

Use the ***Stickers*** of animals and food throughout the lesson.

Discuss the photographs with children. Point out the corn growing in the field. Explain that the corn provides food for people as well as animals such as chickens. Point out that the hay, which the farmers are baling in Iowa, is used by farm animals for food. Also point out the buildings in the photograph of a farm in Ohio, including the farmhouse, barns, and silo. Discuss other structures such as a coop, stable, shed, and pen. Identify common tools, machines, and vehicles. Have children place the ***Stickers*** of the farm animals near the photograph of the chick and the ***Stickers*** of the crops near the photograph of corn to make two groups—farm animals and foods.

- ***What animals do you see on this farm?*** *(lambs, a chick)*

★**THINKING FURTHER:** ***Using Prior Knowledge*** ***Why do farm animals have special homes? How do you know?*** *(Possible answers: To protect them from the weather, to keep them from running away, and to keep them from other animals; children may say that they know this from personal experience or from the media.)*

3 Close

LESSON SUMMARY

Read the lesson question with children, pointing to each word as you read. Encourage each child to name a farm item grown, an animal raised, a farm building, or a piece of farm machinery.

EVALUATE

Make "On the Farm" Books Have children make "On the Farm" books to add to their collection of "Let's Explore" books. Create labels that read *On the Farm* and cut sheets of drawing paper in the shape of a barn. Each child will need at least four cutouts. Help children to staple the cutouts together along the top. Children can draw a barn on the cover and glue on the title label. Inside the book, children can illustrate different animals, crops, buildings, farm tools, and machinery.

Background Information

Family Names for Farm Animals These names for common farm animal families might aid in your discussion.

Chicken: male—rooster; female—hen; young—chick; family group—flock. **Cattle:** male—bull; female—cow; young — calf; family group—herd. **Pig:** male—boar; female—sow; young—piglet; family group—herd. **Horse:** male—stallion; female—mare; newborn—foal; young male—colt; young female—filly; family group—herd or band. **Sheep:** male—ram; female—ewe; young—lamb; family group—flock.

Second-Language Support/Using Props You may wish to introduce the animals and tools found on a farm to begin the lesson with second-language learners. For example, teach "Old MacDonald Had a Farm" in the Getting Ready activity on p. 99 using farm photographs or pictures. You may wish to innovate the song by substituting pictures of farm tools and machines and introducing their functions instead of singing the sounds farm animals make.

SCIENCE CONNECTION

LEARNING STYLE: KINESTHETIC

Learning Center: Grow a Garden from Seeds

PARTNER

30 MINUTES OR LONGER

Objective: To show how some farm crops grow from seeds.

Materials (for each pair of children): 4 sunflower seeds, 4 bean seeds, marking pencil, 2 plastic cups (clear, tumbler-size), cellophane tape, spoon, potting soil, water, "Sunflowers" and "Beans" labels, blank labels, coffee stirrers, markers, pan of water

Advance Preparation: Soak bean seeds in a pan of water overnight.

1. Tell children that they will grow plants raised by some farmers.
2. Have pairs of children work together in the Science Learning Center. Help each child write his or her name on a plastic cup with a marking pencil or on labels attached to coffee stirrers.
3. Tell children to press their sunflower seeds and bean seeds onto two separate strips of tape. Then have children affix each tape strip inside a separate cup, 3" from the top.
4. Have children scoop enough of the soil into the cup to cover the seeds, being careful not to pack it too tightly. Help children to place their "Sunflowers" and "Beans" labels on the appropriate cups.
5. Tell children to add water to each cup so that the soil is dampened, but not flooded. Place the cups in a sunny place.
6. About the fifth day, the seeds should begin to sprout. Ask children to observe the plants as they grow.

ART CONNECTION

LEARNING STYLE: KINESTHETIC

Learning Center: Make a Farm Scene

GROUP

30 MINUTES OR LONGER

Objective: To recognize the kinds of buildings and animals found on a farm by making a barn and farm animals.

Materials: large grocery carton, 36" piece of cardboard (folded in the middle), scissors, glue, cellophane tape, cardboard tube from a roll of paper towels, aluminum foil, poster paint, paintbrushes, sheets of green construction paper, clay

Advance Preparation: To make the barn and silo, turn the carton upside down. Sketch an "I" shape in the middle of one side and cut along the sketch. Gently fold back the two flaps, which will serve as the barn door. To make a silo, cover a paper-towel tube with aluminum foil and tape or glue it to either end of the barn. Place barn in the Art Learning Center. Install the folded cardboard on top of the box to serve as a roof.

1. Tell children that they will make a farm with a large barn and several animals.
2. Have children paint the barn with red paint and the roof with black paint. When the paint is dry, children can place the barn on several sheets of green construction paper for grass.
3. Discuss the kinds of animals found on a farm. Then suggest some clay animals that the class might make for their farm—such as cows, pigs, horses, goats, and chickens.
4. Have children work in the Art Learning Center to make clay animals. They can paint the clay animals if they wish. They can place their animals around the barn.

UNIT 3

LESSON 4

Down by the Water

UNIT 3 THEME BIG BOOK, PAGES 12–13

LESSON OVERVIEW

People live, work, and play by the water.

LESSON OBJECTIVES

- Identify common sites and activities at the beach.
- Recognize that people live, work, and play near water.
- Recognize that plants, fish, and other creatures live in and near water.

KEY CONCEPTS

water   beach   ocean

RESOURCE REMINDER

Project Book
p. 33

Stickers Package
Sheet 12

Technology Connection
VIDEODISC

Search Frame 28901

GETTING READY

Explore the Water

GROUP

15 TO 30 MINUTES

CURRICULUM CONNECTION   **Art/Science**

Objective: To explore different aspects of water.

Resources: *Project Book* p. 33

Materials: sponges, basins or plastic pool, scissors, tape, crayons; optional: water toys

Advance Preparation: Fill a few basins or a plastic pool with water.

1. Ask children if they have ever gone swimming, been on a boat, or gone to the beach. Discuss their experiences.
2. Then have children color and cut out the fish and boat shapes on ***Project Book*** p. 33.
3. Help each child tape one of his or her pictures to a sponge, and then cut away the excess sponge along the picture. The children can then take off the picture and use their sponge shape in a water-filled basin or plastic pool to explore the water.

Project Book
p. 33

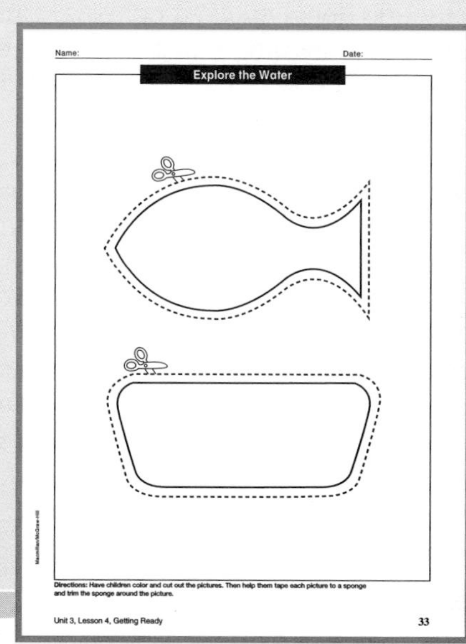

Name: Date:

Explore the Water

Directions: Have children color and cut out the pictures. Then help them tape each picture to a sponge and trim the sponge around the picture.

Unit 3, Lesson 4, Getting Ready 33

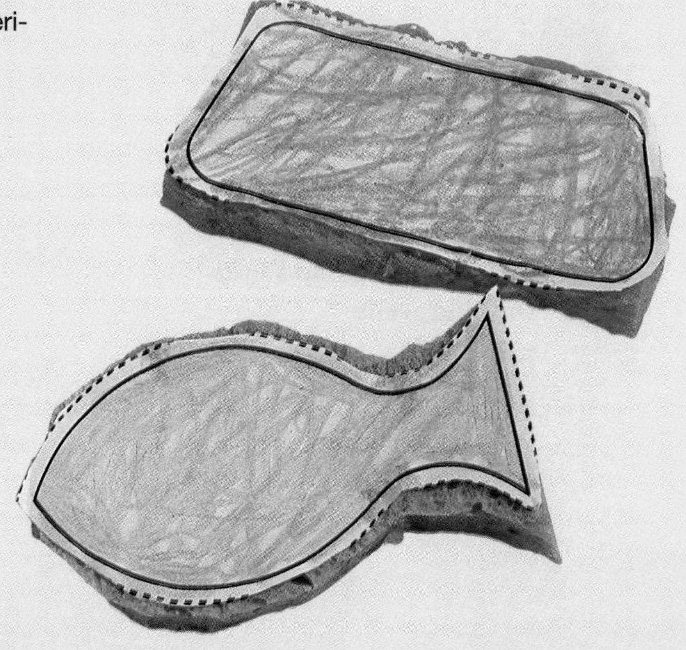

1 Prepare

WARMING UP WITH THE READ ALOUD

Tell children that they will be learning about people, places, and things by the water. Explain that "the land along the edge of the water is called a beach." Ask children to name different bodies of water that they may know such as ocean, lake, river, and stream. Before reading the poem in the Read Aloud, explain that *sea* is another word for ocean and that *shore* is another word for beach.

- ***What kind of land is at the seashore?*** *(Possible answers: sand and rocks)*
- ***What can you do at the seashore?*** *(Possible answers: swim, play, collect shells, dig, run, watch waves, and watch ships)*

2 Teach

USING BIG BOOK PAGES 12–13

Read the lesson title and focus on the word *water*. Tell children that all the photographs show things connected with water.

Technology Connection

VIDEODISC
Enrich Lesson 4 with the frame from the Glossary on *Ocean*, Search Frame 28901.

See the bar code on p. 103.

UNIT 3 THEME BIG BOOK

Down by the Water

Read Aloud

Shore

Play on the seashore
And gather up shells,
Kneel in the damp sands
Digging wells.

Run on the rocks
Where the seaweed slips,
Watch the waves
And the beautiful ships.

Mary Britton Miller

Curriculum Connection

Science Try these easy activities with your class.

- Test things to observe if they float or sink. Use a tub of water and items such as pebbles, rocks, sand, a cork, wood, a styrofoam cup, a polystyrene plate, a jar with a lid, a plastic bag, or an inflated balloon. Point out that the air in things helps them to float.
- Link the activity above to the environment. Add a tissue and baby oil to the tub of items to observe how dirty the water becomes. Stress that water with garbage is unsafe for living things.
- Observe a jar of tap water and a jar of water from a pond or other body of water to see how they are alike and different.
- Demonstrate how to make waves in a shallow pan of water by blowing across the top of the water. Point out that some waves on bodies of water are created in a similar way by the wind.
- Examine the properties of wet and dry sand.

CITIZENSHIP

Water Safety Water safety is an important issue for anyone who lives or vacations near bodies of water. In your discussion of water-related activities, stress the importance of wearing life jackets or other floation devices for nonswimmers. Help children to recognize words commonly posted on signs that may save lives such as *No Swimming, Lifeguard on Duty, Swim at Your Own Risk, Unprotected Beach, Keep off Rocks,* or *Danger.* You may wish to tell children that many beaches use green, yellow, and red flags much like traffic lights to indicate when people may swim.

Kids Care Include in your discussion the importance of keeping our shorelines and bodies of water clean and safe. Stress that garbage can be harmful to animals and plants as well as make our beaches and water unhealthy for people to use. Using waste and recycling containers is one big way children can help.

USE BIG BOOK STICKERS, SHEET 12

Use the following ***Stickers*** throughout the lesson.

Have children sort the ***Stickers*** into groups by affixing them near the photographs in the Big Book to which they correspond. For example, the ***Sticker*** of the lifeguard should go near the photographs of the fishermen to create a group of workers. Make children aware that people live and work near the water as well as vacation or play there. You may wish to point out that in the photograph, the beach houses are in New England, the fishermen are in Alaska, and the family is on Waikiki Beach in Oahu, Hawaii.

- ***What other activities can people do for fun at the water?*** *(Possible answers include swimming, building sand castles, boating, surfing, fishing, and collecting shells.)*

★ **THINKING FURTHER:** ***Classifying What things in the photographs are underwater? on the water? near the water?*** *(underwater—fish, plants; on the water—a boat; near the water—people, homes, birds)*

3 Close

LESSON SUMMARY

Read the lesson question with children, pointing to each word as you read. Have children take turns answering the question, naming workers, animals, and other things that they might see by the water.

EVALUATE

Make "Down by the Water" Books Have children make "Down by the Water" books to add to their collection of "Let's Explore" books. Each book can be made from at least four sheets of drawing paper, positioned horizontally and stapled together along the left side. Help children to draw waves along the top edge of their books. Provide labels that read *Down by the Water.* Children should glue these labels to the front of their books and illustrate the covers. Inside, children should illustrate people, animals, homes, and other items they might see by the water. For assessment suggestions, see p. 118.

ART/SCIENCE CONNECTION

LEARNING STYLE: KINESTHETIC

Make Egg-Carton Lobsters

Objective: To recognize some of the creatures that live underwater.

Materials: cardboard egg cartons, red poster paint, red construction paper, glue, tape, safety scissors, pipe cleaners, googley eyes; optional: markers

Advance Preparation: Ask parents to contribute used, but clean, cardboard egg cartons. Before the activity, cut egg cartons into four sections so that each section has three egg cups (in a straight row).

1. Tell children they will be making lobsters, which live in the ocean. Have children paint their egg-carton sections red.
2. Lobster claws can be made from red construction paper. Have children fold a sheet of construction paper in half. Demonstrate how to cut an oval shape from each half. Then, have children cut a small "v" from each claw.
3. Children can glue the claws onto the sides of the first egg cup.
4. For legs, have children glue or tape three pipe cleaners on the egg cartons so that they poke out at the sides.
5. Finally children can glue on googley eyes. As an alternative children can draw eyes.

ART CONNECTION

LEARNING STYLE: VISUAL

Paint Under-the-Sea Posters

15 TO 30
MINUTES

Objective: To recognize the different kinds of life underwater.

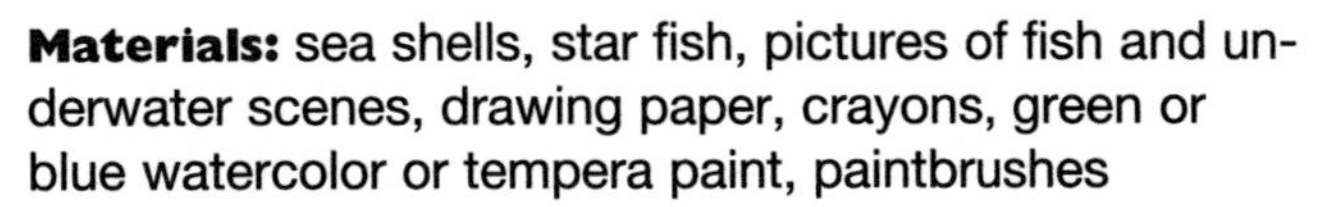

Materials: sea shells, star fish, pictures of fish and underwater scenes, drawing paper, crayons, green or blue watercolor or tempera paint, paintbrushes

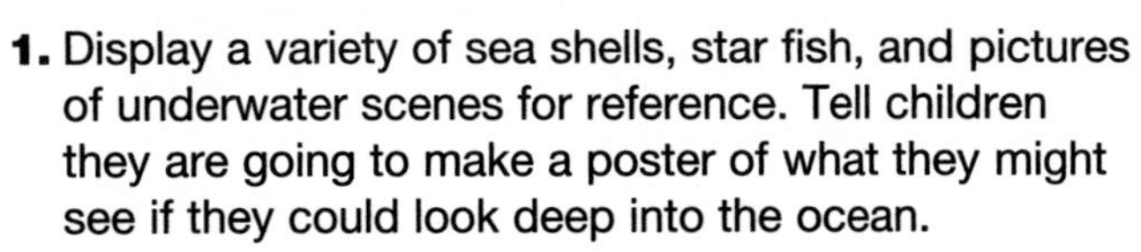

1. Display a variety of sea shells, star fish, and pictures of underwater scenes for reference. Tell children they are going to make a poster of what they might see if they could look deep into the ocean.
2. Have children make a crayon drawing of their "underwater" pictures, pressing *hard* on the crayons as they draw.
3. Next have children paint over their pictures with green or blue watercolor or tempera paint. Explain that the paint will resist the wax in different places and will give their picture an underwater look.
4. When posters have dried, hang them up end to end.

Helping Animals

UNIT 3 THEME BIG BOOK, PAGES 14–15

LESSON OVERVIEW

People can make a difference in the lives of sick, injured, and orphaned wild animals.

LESSON OBJECTIVES

- Recognize that all people can help and care for wildlife.
- Recognize that people can take responsibility and make a difference.

KEY CONCEPTS

care volunteer

RESOURCE REMINDER

Project Book
p. 34

Desk Map
United States

GETTING READY

Make an Animal Poster

ON YOUR OWN

15 TO 30 MINUTES

CURRICULUM CONNECTION Art

Objective: To learn about the idea of caring for animals.

Resources: *Project Book* p. 34

Materials: crayons, construction paper, glue

1. Ask children if any of them have a pet. Ask them about the responsibilities there are in owning a pet.
2. Have children draw a picture of their pet or favorite animal inside the frame on ***Project Book*** p. 34. Then have them glue the paper to a sheet of construction paper.
3. Invite volunteers to share their animal posters with the class.

Name: Date:

Make an Animal Poster

Directions: Have children draw a picture of their pet or favorite animal inside the frame. Then they can glue their picture and the frame to a piece of construction paper.

Macmillan/McGraw-Hill

34 Unit 3, Citizenship, Getting Ready

Project Book
p. 34

1 Prepare

WARMING UP WITH THE READ ALOUD

Share the rhyme in the Read Aloud. Afterwards, volunteers might dramatize the rhyme.

- ***What happened to the first frog?*** *(She stubbed her toe.)*
- ***How did the frogs try to make the first frog feel better?*** *(They shared a bug, sang a get-well song, and gave her a greeting card.)*

Tell children that sometimes animals in nature get hurt and need help. People can care for the animals to help them get well. Tell children that they will be learning about a child named Chris and how he and others helped to care for a dove that could not fly.

2 Teach

USING BIG BOOK PAGES 14–15

Read the lesson title. Explain that the photographs tell a story about helping an animal. Tell children that the photographs show a special place where animals can be helped in Fort Lauderdale, Florida. Explain that Fort Lauderdale is a city by the ocean.

Tell children that a boy named Chris found an injured dove. He decided to take responsibility for helping the dove. He needed to think about how to solve his problem.

Read Aloud

Five Little Frogs

The first little frog stubbed her toe.
The second little frog cried, "Oh, oh, oh!"
The third little frog said, "There, there,
Here is a bug that I will share."
The fourth little frog came along
And sang a special get-well song.
The fifth little frog looked so hard
To find a friendly greeting card.
The first little frog stubbed her toe.
But that was a long, long time ago.
She hops and hops with all her friends,
And that is all. Our story ends.

Louise Binder Scott

CITIZENSHIP

Helping Wildlife Share with children these tips from the Wildlife Care Center.

- Help preserve wildlife habitats. Avoid disturbing nesting areas during nesting seasons (March through September).
- Reduce litter's toll on wildlife. Dispose of all trash in animal-proof containers and pick up any litter you find. Cut open plastic 6-pack rings so that birds, fish, and other wildlife do not become trapped in the rings and become injured, starve, or die.
- Avoid handling or feeding wild animals.
- Help animals only if they need your help. If you find healthy young animals that seem to be alone, leave them alone. Many baby animals are not constantly watched by their parents. Place baby birds back in their nests if they have fallen out. Adult birds will still care for these birds after being touched by humans. Do not adopt wild baby birds or animals.

Point out that the first photograph shows a shoe box in which Chris placed an injured dove that he had found. Follow the bird tracks to the next two photographs. After reading the signs, you may want to define *wildlife* as "animals that live in nature," *treatment* as "ways to care for something," *rehabilitation* as "to make healthy again," and *facility* as a "special building." Point out that the other photograph shows Chris and his mother taking the dove to the Admissions Office of the Wildlife Care Center. Tell children that most people who work at the Wildlife Care Center are volunteers, or people who work without pay. They work together to help injured animals.

The next photograph shows a veterinarian at the Center examining the broken wing of the dove. Point out the X ray of the dove hanging in the background. The next photograph shows the veterinarian placing a bandage on the wing to set the bones in place. Tell children that once the dove was healthy again and able to fly, Chris and his mother went back to the Center to pick up the dove and take it back to the place where Chris found it. The last photograph shows Chris at that place releasing the dove to the wild. Children might use their ***Desk Maps*** to locate Florida in which the Wildlife Care Center is located.

- ***How did Chris and the people at the Wildlife Center make a difference?*** *(They helped save and care for an injured bird.)*

★**THINKING FURTHER:** ***Making Conclusions***
What other wildlife might the Center help? How do you know? *(Possible answers include a raccoon, a turtle, and other birds; children may draw this conclusion from the photograph, which has a sign that shows these animals.)*

Background Information

About the Wildlife Care Center The Wildlife Care Center is a private, non-profit hospital for sick, orphaned, or injured wildlife. The Center relies on donations from the public to fund its programs. Each year, the Center treats over 10,000 patients at its hospital. Beside small birds, raccoons, and turtles, the Center cares for other animals including herons, pelicans, owls, ducks, possums, rabbits, and skunks. The Center's main goal is to rescue, rehabilitate, and release animals to the wild. For those animals who cannot return to their natural habitat, the Center has an adoption program. Through the Adopt-a-Wildlife Friend program, donors provide support for the care and feeding of the wildlife that remains at the hospital. Another goal of the Center is to educate people to protect and preserve wildlife. The Wildlife Care Center is located at 3200 S.W. 4th Avenue, Fort Lauderdale, Florida 33315. It is open seven days a week. For more information, call (954) 524-4302.

3 Close

LESSON SUMMARY

Read the lesson question to children, pointing to each word as you read. Invite volunteers to share ways they have made a difference.

EVALUATE

Draw a Story Picture Have each child illustrate any part of the story. Then help children sort their pictures into groups that show the same parts of the story. Hang up children's pictures, in story order, around the classroom.

ART/SCIENCE CONNECTION

LEARNING STYLE: KINESTHETIC

Make Juice-Can Pencil Holders

ON YOUR OWN

15 TO 30 MINUTES

Objective: To demonstrate that recycling helps wildlife.

Materials: cardboard juice cans (clean, empty, with labels and tops neatly removed—one per child; parents might provide the cans), varying lengths of brightly colored yarn, glue or tape, construction paper; optional: magazine pictures of wildlife

1. Explain to children that recycling objects helps wildlife. Animals can hurt themselves on trash. Trash also takes up space and may destroy animals' homes. Explain to children that they can be responsible for helping wildlife. Tell children they will make something from a recycled object.
2. Have children take a length of yarn and tie or tape the yarn to the can. Then demonstrate how children can roll the yarn around the can to cover the can to make pencil or crayon holders.
3. Help children to line the inside of the can with construction paper, if they wish. They may also wish to tape or glue magazine pictures of wildlife to their cans.

SCIENCE CONNECTION

LEARNING STYLE: KINESTHETIC

Learning Center: Make a Peanut-Butter Bird Feeder

ON YOUR OWN

15 TO 30 MINUTES

Objective: To demonstrate how people can take responsibility for animals.

Materials: empty cardboard tubes (cut in halves or in thirds), plates or paper plates, peanut butter, birdseed, yarn or string

1. Explain that during winter in many parts of our country, the trees and ground are so covered with snow that birds cannot get enough food. People can help feed birds by putting up bird feeders.
2. Distribute cardboard tubes. With children in the Science Learning Center, working on their own or in small groups, gently roll the cardboard tubes across plates spread with peanut butter. Then have children roll the tubes across the plates with birdseed (make sure the peanut butter is covered with seed so that birds' beaks won't stick).
3. Have children run a length of yarn or string through the tubes. Help them make a knot so that the tubes hang about eight inches from the knot.
4. Tell children that they can have someone help them to hang their feeders from tree branches or from tall bushes near their home. Or you may choose to help children hang the birdfeeders near your school.

UNIT 3
LESSON 5

In the Woods

UNIT 3 THEME BIG BOOK, PAGES 16–17

LESSON OVERVIEW

Woods provide a home for wildlife as well as jobs, recreational activities, and products for people.

LESSON OBJECTIVES

- Recognize that woods are home to many kinds of plants and animals.
- Recognize that woods provide jobs and products.
- Identify recreational activities associated with woods.

KEY CONCEPTS

woods trees ranger
camping

RESOURCE REMINDER

Project Book
p. 35

Stickers Package
Sheet 12

Anthology
Wolf's Favor, pp. 41–43

GETTING READY

Make a Turtle

15 TO 30 MINUTES

CURRICULUM CONNECTION Art/Science

Objective: To identify different woodland animals.

Resources: *Project Book* p. 35

Materials: crayons, markers, scissors, empty halves of walnut shells or individual egg-carton sections, glue, construction paper

Advance Preparation: Using ***Project Book*** p. 35, cut out the turtle shapes. Prepare and distribute one turtle shape for each child.

1. Each child can make a turtle by coloring a turtle shape and then adding a shell (egg carton or walnut shell) at the center of it with glue. Or children may choose to draw the shell themselves.
2. Have children glue their turtles to construction paper.
3. Point out that some kinds of turtles live in the woods. Have children identify other woodland animals. You may choose to help children cut out, color, and glue the woodland animals on ***Project Book*** p. 24 around their turtles.

Project Book
p. 35

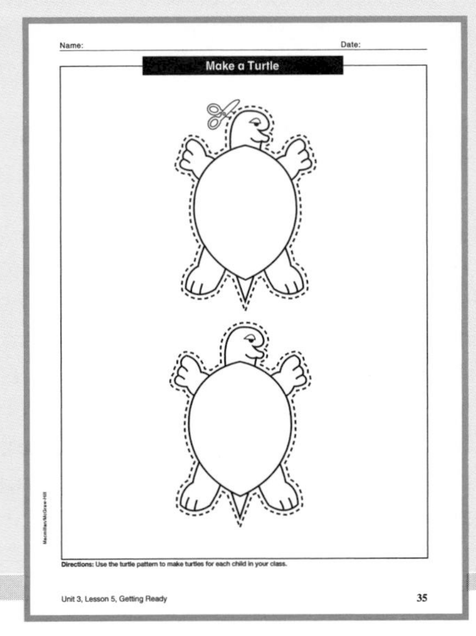

Name: Date:

Make a Turtle

Directions: Use the turtle pattern to make turtles for each child in your class.

Unit 3, Lesson 5, Getting Ready 35

1 Prepare

WARMING UP WITH THE READ ALOUD

Share the poem in the Read Aloud without revealing the title to children.

- ***What animal is the poem about?*** *(a squirrel)*
- ***What might be found in the shell?*** *(a nut)*

Tell children that they will be learning about a place where squirrels and other things in nature live.

2 Teach

USING BIG BOOK PAGES 16–17

Read the lesson title and focus on the word woods. Define the word as "a place where many trees grow closely together." Tell children that some woods are made up largely of pine trees while others are made up of several different types of trees. Explain that very large woods are often called forests. Invite children to share their knowledge about woods and forests.

USE BIG BOOK STICKERS, SHEET 12

Use the ***Stickers*** of animals, plants, workers, and the house in the woods throughout the lesson.

UNIT 3 THEME BIG BOOK

Read Aloud

The Squirrel

Whisky, frisky, hippity-hop,
Up he goes, to the treetop;
Whirly, twirly, round and round,
Down he scampers to the ground!
Furley, curly, what a tail!
Tall as a feather, broad as a sail!
Where's his supper? In a shell,
Snap, crackity, out it fell.

Anonymous

Using the Anthology

Wolf's Favor, pages 41–43 This fable, set in a forest, tells about the good deeds of a porcupine, a wolf, a cow, a squirrel, a fox, a chicken, a snake, and a lamb. After reading, ask children to name the two animals typically found on farms and not in forests.

Background Information

Family Names for Woodland Animals These family names may be helpful in your discussion. **Deer:** male—buck; female—doe; young—fawn. **Fox:** male—fox; female—vixen; young—kit. **Opossum:** male and female—opossum; young—baby. **Rabbit:** male—buck; female—doe; young—baby. **Raccoon:** male—buck; female—raccoon; young—cub. **Skunk:** male and female—skunk; young—kitten. **Squirrel:** male and female—squirrel; young—baby.

17

Point out that Gloria is hiking through the woods and collecting items she finds on her hike. As you discuss the photographs, have children sort the ***Stickers*** in groups near the photograph to which the ***Sticker*** best corresponds. For example, ***Stickers*** of forest workers should be placed near the photograph of the park ranger showing the children the slug in the park. You may wish to tell children that the photographs show a forest in South Carolina, people camping in Oregon, and a ranger in Washington.

- ***In what season did Gloria hike through the woods? Tell how you know.*** *(Fall; she is collecting colored leaves and is dressed for cool weather.)*

★**THINKING FURTHER:** ***Making Predictions***
What do you think will happen to the acorns dropped from trees? Why do you think this might happen? *(Possible answers: People might collect the acorns; the acorns might become food for squirrels and other animals; they might grow into new trees; children may predict these answers because of prior knowledge they have about the subject.)*

3 Close

LESSON SUMMARY

Read the lesson question with children, pointing to each word as you read. Encourage each child to provide answers, naming people, places, homes, or animals and plants that they might see in the woods.

EVALUATE

Make "In the Woods" Books Have children make "In the Woods" books to add to their collection of "Let's Explore" books. In advance, prepare title labels that read *In the Woods* and cut pine tree shapes from drawing paper. Each child will need at least four trees. Help children to staple the trees together along the top. Invite children to decorate the covers and to glue on the title labels. Inside, children can illustrate people, places, animals, and plants that can be found in the woods.

Field Trip

Take a field trip to a wooded section of a local park to observe wildlife. Use the buddy system to keep children from separating from the group. Before you go, have children suggest items for a checklist of things you might see in the woods such as trees, plants, animals, and animal homes. As children observe these things, they can complete the checklist. New items observed can be added to the checklists.

CITIZENSHIP

On their field trip, make children aware of signs throughout the park and environmental issues such as the importance of using recycling and trash receptacles, the negative impact of disturbing natural habitats, and issues dealing with fire safety. Remind children to only collect samples of nonliving things such as fallen leaves or bark, sticks, or pine cones.

ART CONNECTION

LEARNING STYLE: KINESTHETIC

Make Butterfly Mobiles

Objective: To recognize that some butterflies live in the woods.

Materials: sheets of tissue paper (in a variety of colors), scissors, pipe cleaners, tape, metal or plastic clothes hangers, nylon string

Advance Preparation: Fold sheets of tissue paper into thirds vertically and horizontally so that there are nine squares of tissue paper per sheet. Cut out the squares and stack them by color.

1. Invite children to select squares of two different colors of tissue paper.
2. Have children place the two squares one on top of the other. Then demonstrate how to scrunch the sheets in the middle so that there are two "wings" of a butterfly. Help children to secure the middle with tape.
3. Distribute two pipe cleaners to each child. Have children fold one pipe cleaner in half, then wrap another pipe cleaner around it to form "antennae." Then demonstrate how to wrap the first pipe cleaner around the butterfly's middle.
4. The two ends of the second pipe cleaner should point out at each side as "antennae." Show children how to fluff up the butterfly wings.
5. Have children slip a 6" piece of nylon string through the pipe cleaner middle and tie the butterfly onto a hanger decorated with pipe cleaners.
6. Groups of children can work together to assemble the mobiles. Each hanger mobile can hold four to five butterflies.

ART CONNECTION

LEARNING STYLE: VISUAL

Make a Class Forest

Objective: To show that many trees make a forest.

Materials: sheets of 8 1/2" x 11" construction paper (brown, black, green), scissors, glue; optional: red, orange, and yellow construction paper, crayons

Advance Preparation: Make tree trunks from brown construction paper by folding the sheet horizontally then cutting to yield six strips.

1. Tell children that each of them will make a tree and that all of their trees, when put together, will make a forest. Children should choose to make one of two kinds of trees: evergreens (such as pines and firs), or broad-leafed trees (such as oaks and maples).
2. Give each child one of the tree trunks that you made.
3. Help children to cut a tree top by folding a sheet of green construction paper in half. To make a broad-leafed tree, have children cut a half-circle and open it out into a full circle. To make an evergreen tree, have children cut tiered triangles, or one triangle to open into a larger triangle. Then have them glue the top to the tree trunk.
4. Have children write their names along the trunk in crayon or a marker.
5. Optional: Have children use crayons to color "pine cones" on their trees, or glue on "pine cones" made from colored construction paper. Children may also wish to color acorns to show an oak tree.

CLOSE WITH A POEM

LINKING SOCIAL STUDIES AND LITERATURE

Bring Unit 3 to a close with the poem "When I Grow Up" from pages 18–19 of the Big Book. The poem acts as a spring board to support these Social Studies concepts:

- Earth is made up of many different environments.
- Forms of transportation move people and things from place to place.

ABOUT THE POEM

A full instructional plan, along with the poem, appears on the following two pages.

Alan Benjamin's poem "When I Grow Up" explores the pleasures of a trip to the shore as well as the joys of imagining a journey to the stars.

ABOUT THE POET

Alan Benjamin never forgot the wonders of childhood. He has written over 25 books for children, including *One Thousand Monsters, Rat-a-tat, Pitterpat,* and *Little Rainbow Library.* He has also taught classes on writing and illustrating children's books and has worked as an editor and art director in children's publishing for over 30 years.

INTRODUCE

Using Prior Knowledge Review with children what they have learned about a beach environment. You may wish to record key words in a web such as the following:

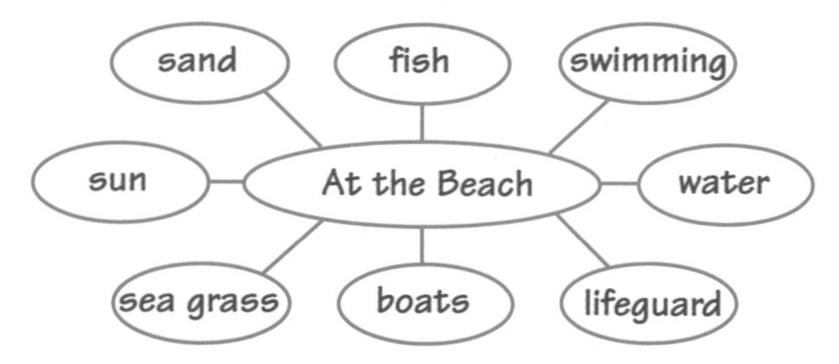

Previewing Read aloud the title of the poem and the name of the poet. Then encourage children to look at the picture and speculate on what the girl in the picture might want to do when she grows up. Record responses on the chalkboard and review them after reading the poem.

Second-Language Support

Using Visuals Before reading the poem with children, preview the vocabulary by making a list of the nouns mentioned in the poem and inviting children to collaborate on a mural illustrating all of them. Include these words: *car, shore, motorboat, ocean, land, sea, boat, rocket ship*, and *star*. Start by guiding a child as he or she draws the background including the *ocean* and the *land*. Point out the *shore* where these two meet. Next explain that *sea* is another word for *ocean*. Invite another child to add some *stars* in the sky. Invite other children to add a *boat (motorboat)*, a *car* and a *rocket*. Then point to the picture and ask children to repeat the names of the items. Invite volunteers to locate each item in the picture on pages 18 and 19.

CITIZENSHIP

Protecting the Environment Point out to children that beaches are special places that must be cared for and looked after so that they can remain beautiful places for everyone to enjoy.

- Invite children to work in teams. Encourage teams to think of two or three rules that people should follow in order to protect our beaches—for example: don't litter, don't bother the animals, and don't pick wild flowers or plants.
- Have team members dictate their rules to you.
- Write each team's rules on chart paper. Then read aloud the rules in class and have children vote on the three rules that they think are most important.

READ

USING BIG BOOK PAGES 18–19

Read aloud the poem, emphasizing the rhyming words. Invite children to clap out the beat of the poem as you read it once more.

At this time, you may wish to play the poem on the ***Anthology Cassette***.

SHARE

Use these questions to prompt discussion of the poem:

- ***In what three things does the girl in the poem dream of traveling?*** *(car, motorboat, rocket ship)*
- ***Which thing would she use in the water? on land? in the air?*** *(motorboat; car; rocket ship)*
- ***Besides the beach, what are some places you would like to travel to when you grow up? Why?*** *(Accept all reasonable answers.)*

Help children understand that besides traveling to places in cars, boats, and rockets, people can also travel to new places in their imagination. Encourage children to tell about places that they have visited in their own imagination.

EXTENDING THE LITERATURE WITH SCIENCE

LEARNING STYLE: VISUAL

Find Ways to Travel

ON YOUR OWN

30 MINUTES OR LONGER

Objective: To sort vehicles.

Resource: ***Project Book*** p. 36

Materials: crayons, scissors, glue or tape

- Remind children that the girl in the poem talked about traveling on land, on sea, and in the sky.
- Give each child a copy of ***Project Book*** p. 36. Read aloud the directions. Point out that the big picture shows the land, the sea, and the sky. Invite children to identify the vehicles in the small pictures at the bottom of the page.
- Ask children to color and cut out the pictures of the vehicles. Have them glue or tape each vehicle on the big picture, placing it where it is used: on land, on water, or in the air.

Project Book p. 36

Name: Date:

Find Ways to Travel

Directions: Have children color the large picture and the vehicles. Then have them cut out the vehicles and tape or glue them to the large picture to show where the vehicles are used.

36 Unit 3, Extending the Literature

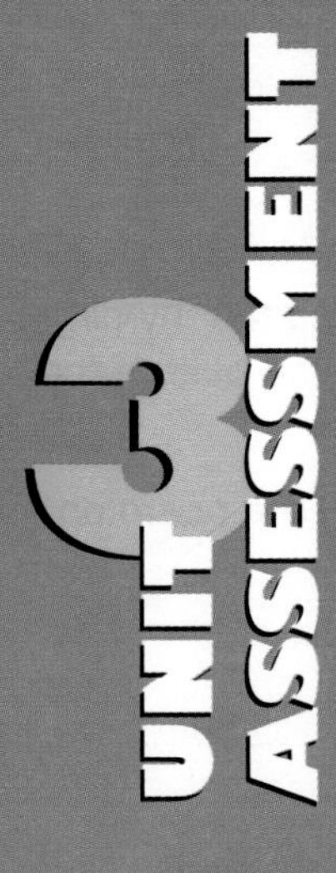

Assessment Opportunities

The CLOSE section of each lesson includes an EVALUATE activity. This page provides suggestions for using selected EVALUATE activities to integrate your assessment program with each day's lesson plan. The next page lists the main objectives of the unit and some of the activities that reinforce them. You may wish to make a copy of the checklist for each child.

EVALUATE Signs of Success

LESSON 1, The Seasons Around Us

EVALUATE: Make "Four Seasons" Books, p. 89

OBSERVATIONAL ASSESSMENT

- Ask questions such as, "In what season would you find snow and ice?" Record children's answers.

PORTFOLIO ASSESSMENT

The four seasons books can be part of children's portfolios.

- Children's illustrations should accurately reflect characteristics of each season.
- Children's illustrations should be properly labeled.

STUDY SKILLS, Sorting Things into Groups

EVALUATE: Make Sorting Cards, p. 93

OBSERVATIONAL ASSESSMENT

- Using a tape recorder, record children's conversations. Listen for an understanding of common group characteristics and what it means to group things together.

PORTFOLIO ASSESSMENT

The sorting cards can be part of children's portfolios.

- Children's pictures should relate to one another.
- Children should be able to sort their cards into groups.

LESSON 4, Down by the Water

EVALUATE: Make "Down by the Water" Books, p. 105

OBSERVATIONAL ASSESSMENT

- Create a checklist including animals, people, and homes relating to the lesson. Children's books should include at least two items from the list.

PORTFOLIO ASSESSMENT

The "Down by the Water" books can be part of children's portfolios.

- Children's books should be assembled according to your directions.

UNIT 3 OBJECTIVES Checklist

1. Identify the four seasons.
2. Recognize and understand the effects of weather and of the seasons.
3. Develop sorting skills.
4. Recognize different characteristics of a city.
5. Identify forms of transportation.
6. Identify different characteristics of a farm.
7. Recognize attributes of the shore and of water.
8. Recognize that people can take responsibility to care for wildlife.
9. Identify common jobs, plants, animals, and activities associated with woods.

Name ______________________ Class ______________

LESSON	ACTIVITY	PAGE	UNIT 3 OBJECTIVES	✔
LESSON 1	Make a Birthday Cake	87	1	
LESSON 1	Perform Seasons Fingerplays	90	1, 2	
LESSON 1	Make a Fish Kite	90	2	
THINKING SKILL	Play the Matching Game	91	3	
THINKING SKILL	Sort by Texture	94	3	
THINKING SKILL	Sort by Shape	94	3	
LESSON 2	Make a Bus	95	4, 5	
LESSON 2	Build a Floor-Map City	98	4	
LESSON 2	Paint a City Mural	98	4	
LESSON 3	Make Animal Puppets	99	6	
LESSON 3	Grow a Garden from Seeds	102	6	
LESSON 3	Make a Farm Scene	102	6	
LESSON 4	Explore the Water	103	5, 7	
LESSON 4	Make Egg-Carton Lobsters	106	7	
LESSON 4	Paint Under-the-Sea Posters	106	7	
CITIZENSHIP	Make an Animal Poster	107	8	
CITIZENSHIP	Make Juice-Can Pencil Holders	110	8	
CITIZENSHIP	Make a Peanut-Butter Bird Feeder	110	8	
LESSON 5	Make a Turtle	111	9	
LESSON 5	Make Butterfly Mobiles	114	9	
LESSON 5	Make a Class Forest	114	9	

Let's Explore

PLANNING GUIDE

Pupil Edition and Unit 4 Theme Big Book Pages 120–155

INTRODUCTION

SUGGESTED PACING: 3 DAYS

Begin With The Literature Big Book, pages 123, 212–213

Using The Unit Opener pp. 123–126

PROJECT IDEAS
- Red, White, and Blue! / ART
- Make a Globe / ART
- Enriching with Multimedia
- Symbols Banner / ART
- Hold an Earth-Friendly Picnic/ SCIENCE

LESSON 1

SUGGESTED PACING: 1–2 DAYS

This Is Our Country pp. 127–130

KEY CONCEPTS
United States of America, American, state

PROJECT IDEAS
- Make a Map of the U.S. / ART
- Make a State Symbol / ART
- Make a State Map / ART

RESOURCES
Project Book, pp. 41–42 • Big Book Stickers Sheets 13–14 • Desk Map • Geo Big Book, pp. R2–R3 • TECHNOLOGY Videodisc/ Video Tape 1

LESSON 2

SUGGESTED PACING: 1–2 DAYS

This Is Our Flag pp. 131–134

KEY CONCEPTS
American flag, symbol, Pledge of Allegiance

PROJECT IDEAS
- Make Flag and Star Stickers / ART
- Make a Class Flag / ART
- Parade to Songs About Our Flag / MUSIC

RESOURCES
Project Book, p. 43 • Big Book Stickers Sheet 14 • Anthology, pp. 123–125 • Floor Map

LESSON 3

SUGGESTED PACING: 1–2 DAYS

Looking At Land And Water pp. 139–142

KEY CONCEPTS
Earth, land, globe

PROJECT IDEAS
- Make a Land-and-Water Chart / ART
- Sail Around the World / ART
- Make Clay Models of Land and Water / ART

RESOURCES
Project Book, pp. 45–46 • Big Book Stickers Sheet 15 • Anthology, p. 81–82 • Geo Big Book, pp. R5c–R5f, R6–R7 • Inflatable Globe • TECHNOLOGY Videodisc/Video Tape 2

AROUND THE WORLD

SUGGESTED PACING: 1–2 DAYS

Our Great Big World pp. 143–146

KEY CONCEPTS
continent

PROJECT IDEAS
- Make a Map of Earth / ART
- Display Animals of the World / ART
- Play "Cat and Lynx" / PHYSICAL EDUCATION

RESOURCES
Project Book, pp. 37–40, 47 • Big Book Stickers Sheets 15, 16 • Geo Big Book, pp. R4–R5, R5g–R5h • Inflatable Globe

LESSON 4

SUGGESTED PACING: 1–2 DAYS

Caring For Earth pp. 147–150

KEY CONCEPTS
recycle, litter

PROJECT IDEAS
- Make a Paper Keeper / ART
- Perform a Clean Water Test / SCIENCE
- Make Bird Feeders / SCIENCE/ART

RESOURCES
Project Book, p. 48 • Big Book Stickers Sheet 15 • Anthology, pp. 77–80

UNIT ASSESSMENT

SUGGESTED PACING: 1 DAY

pp. 154–155

OBSERVATIONAL/PORTFOLIO ASSESSMENT, p. 154
- Make Flag-Flying Pictures
- Recite a Simple Task
- Draw Earth and a Globe

OBJECTIVES CHECKLIST, p. 155

McGRAW-HILL SCHOOL DIVISION'S HOME PAGE at http://www.mhschool.com contains on-line student activities related to this unit.

THINKING SKILLS

SUGGESTED PACING: 1–2 DAYS

Putting Things In Order

pp. 135–138

KEY CONCEPTS

order, time, first, next, last

PROJECT IDEAS

Connect the Dots / MATHEMATICS
Make "Ants on a Log" / HOME ECONOMICS
Make a Class Schedule / ART/MATHEMATICS

RESOURCES

Project Book, p. 44 • Big Book Stickers Sheet 14 • Word Cards

CLOSE WITH A SONG

SUGGESTED PACING: 1 DAY

One Light, One Sun

pp. 151–153

PROJECT IDEAS

Make a Flag / ART

RESOURCES

Project Book, p. 49

SHELTERED INSTRUCTION

Reading Strategies & Language Development

Schema Building, p. 124

Second-Language Support

Using Props, p. 129
Using Visuals, p. 145
Drama, p. 149

Meeting Individual Needs

McGraw-Hill Adventure Books

Assessment Opportunities

Ongoing Unit Project: Make a Globe, p. 125
Observational and Portfolio Assessment, p. 154
Objectives Checklist, p. 155
Evaluate, pp. 129, 133, 137, 141, 145, 149

FOR FURTHER SUPPORT

- Language Support Handbook
- Social Studies Readiness

Unit 4 Bibliography and Resources

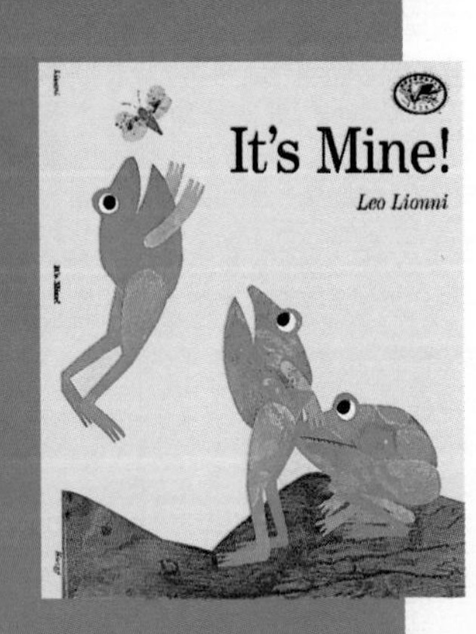

MCGRAW-HILL ADVENTURE BOOKS Easy-to-Read Books

Evans, Kay. ***Hello.*** A girl and boy take an imaginary trip to visit animals in the wild.

Jo, Amy. ***Planting Seeds.*** A brother and sister plant vegetable seeds to create a beautiful garden.

CLASSROOM LIBRARY

Baer, Edith. ***This Is the Way We Eat Our Lunch: A Book About Children Around the World.*** New York: Scholastic Inc., 1995. The different ways in which children eat their lunch around the world are described in rhyming couplets.

READ ALOUD BOOKS

Alexander, Martha. ***Where Does the Sky End, Grandpa?*** San Diego, CA: Harcourt Brace and Company, 1992. A grandchild and grandfather admire nature around them as they take a walk outdoors.

Asch, Frank. ***Water***. San Diego, CA: Harcourt Brace & Company, 1995. A colorful presentation describes how water is all around us, and important to all on Earth.

Bates, Katharine Lee. ***America the Beautiful.*** New York: Atheneum, 1993. An attractively illustrated, picture-book version of the song "America the Beautiful."

Benson, Laura Lee. ***This Is Our Earth.*** Watertown, MA: Charlesbridge Publishing, 1994. This book, written in rhyme with full-page illustrations, instills respect for Earth.

Halpern, Shari. ***My River.*** New York: Macmillan Publishing Co., 1992. Frogs, fish, and all the other animals that live in and near the river remind us how important the river is to each of us.

Hobson, Sally. ***Chicken Little.*** New York: Simon & Schuster Books for Young Readers, 1994. A chicken spreads the rumor that the sky is falling after an acorn falls on his head.

Kalan, Robert. ***Moving Day.*** New York: Greenwillow Books, 1996. A hermit crab is in search of a new home and tries many shells before finding the right one.

■ Lionni, Leo. ***It's Mine!*** New York: Alfred A. Knopf, 1985. Three selfish frogs learn a valuable lesson about sharing the land, air, and water around them.

Ryder, Joanne. ***Earthdance.*** New York: Henry Holt & Company, 1996. Colorful illustrations combine with text inviting children to imagine they are Earth, home to all living things.

TEACHER BOOKS

Bell, Neill. ***The Book of Where or How to Be Naturally Geographic.*** Boston, MA: Little, Brown & Co., 1982. This helpful resource contains suggestions for activities based on geographic concepts.

Milord, Susan. ***Hands Around the World: 365 Creative Ways to Build Cultural Awareness and Global Respect.*** Charlotte, VT: Williamson Publishing, 1992. A variety of games and activities are provided to help make children aware of various cultures around the world.

TECHNOLOGY MULTIMEDIA

Dash McTrash and the Pollution Solution. 5 sound filmstrips. SSAC-2020. Dash McTrash and friends intend to clean up the city. Society For Visual Education. (800) 829-1900.

▯ ***Our Earth.*** CD-ROM. Children can learn about beginning map concepts as they explore planet Earth. National Geographic. (800) 368-2728.

FREE OR INEXPENSIVE MATERIALS

For a copy of "It's Their World, Too!"—a list of tips and activities about how we can clean up the environment—write to: Humane Services, Inc., Educational Coordinator, 2 Mark Bird Lane, Elverson, PA 19520.

■ *Book excerpted in the Anthology*

▯ *National Geographic selection*

BEGIN WITH THE LITERATURE BIG BOOK

LINKING SOCIAL STUDIES AND LITERATURE

Introduce Unit 4 with the **Literature Big Book, *The Earth and I.*** The story acts as a spring-board to support these Social Studies concepts:

- Our country is part of a larger world.
- People must appreciate and protect the world in which they live.

Literature Big Book

ABOUT THE STORY

A full instructional plan, along with the complete text of the story, appears on pages 212–213.

Children learn about Earth as if it were a friend instead of just a planet. With wonderful illustrations and simple language, the reader is shown that, just like friends, we take care of Earth and Earth takes care of us.

ABOUT THE AUTHOR/ILLUSTRATOR

Frank Asch is both the author and illustrator of this book and many other popular children's books. He spoke with students around the country and asked them to complete the phrase "The Earth and I . . ." When the responses repeatedly came back saying "The Earth and I are friends," Mr. Asch was inspired to write this book. The author lives in a small town in Vermont with his wife and son.

USING THE
Unit 4 Opener

USING BIG BOOK PAGES 2–3

Read aloud the unit title, then ask children to name our country. Introduce the kindergartners from left to right as Paul, Laura, and Sam. Invite children to preview the unit as they look for Sam in the lessons.

DEVELOPING KEY CONCEPTS

Children will learn about the United States, its flag, Earth's land and water, ways to care for Earth, and sequence pictures. Read aloud the terms. Ask children to share what they know about them.

country *A country is the land and the people who live there.*

Earth *Earth is the planet on which we live.*

globe *A globe is a model of Earth.*

USE BIG BOOK STICKERS, SHEETS 14–15

Affix the ***Sticker*** labels *first, next,* and *last* near the appropriate steps for making a globe. Then affix the remaining labels near the completed model of Earth.

first next last

Sheltered Instruction

Helping children connect different curriculum areas can be achieved with graphic organizers and story mapping. In this unit, geography, ecology, sociology, and health can be linked. **[SDAIE STRATEGY: SCHEMA BUILDING]**

BULLETIN BOARD

Red, White, and Blue!

Turn your bulletin board into a giant American flag created by your class.

- Cover the bulletin board with white paper. Create a large blue rectangle to cover the upper left corner, where the stars of the flag will go. Trace 50 stars on white paper. Help your class cut out the stars.
- To form stripes, help children link together loops of construction paper into seven red and six white chains.
- Assemble the flag on the bulletin board using a stapler. As you do so, use the opportunity to discuss the origin and meaning of the United States flag.

ABOUT THE PHOTOGRAPH

Tell children that the photograph shows how Paul, Laura, and Sam worked together carefully to make a globe, which is a model of Earth. Define *Earth* for children. Point to the ***Sticker*** labels as you discuss each item.

Item 1 Point out that Paul is holding a large balloon. Explain that blowing up a balloon is the *first* thing the children did to make the globe.

Item 2 Point out that Laura is holding another balloon, which has strips of newspaper glued all over it and is now being painted blue. Explain that this is what the children did *next* to make a globe.

Item 3 Point out that Sam is showing them a completed globe. Share that the globe was painted and then cutouts of land were glued onto it. Explain that this is what the children did *last.* Compare the completed project with the Inflatable Globe.

Directions for this Ongoing Unit Project can be found at the bottom of this page.

SCHOOL-TO-HOME

Our Country and Our World

- Children will be introduced to the United States, the world, and the globe in this unit. Families can help explore these concepts at home using a map of the United States or ***Project Book*** pp. 41–42 and a globe if they have one.
- Encourage families to use the map of the United States to identify states in which they or relatives live, or have traveled, or states in the news. Families can also compare the maps with weather maps shown on television.
- Families can use a globe to identify other countries where many food items come from.

ONGOING UNIT PROJECT

GROUP

Make a Globe

CURRICULUM CONNECTION **Art**

Children will work in small groups to make a papier-mâché globe.

Advance Preparation: Cut newspaper into 2-inch- or 3-inch-wide strips. Inflate one balloon for each group.

Make a pint of glue for each group. For one pint, combine 1 cup whole-wheat flour and 1 1/4 cups water in a large bowl until a soupy consistency is achieved. Pour the glue into an aluminum baking tin.

1. Demonstrate how to pull a strip of newspaper through the glue. Run the strip between your fingers to remove the excess glue. Apply the sticky strip to a balloon. Direct children to repeat the process until they have covered their balloons.
2. Allow the papier-mâché to dry completely before children paint the globes blue.
3. Have children color and cut out the continents on ***Project Book*** pp. 37–40. Suggest that they use any color except blue. Assist children in using the ***Inflatable Globe*** to glue the continents to their globes.

Assessment Suggestions

Signs of Success

- Children should be able to prepare the continents and glue them on their papier-mâché globes.
- Children should refer to their projects as globes.
- Children should be able to identify land and water on their globes.

TECHNOLOGY CENTER

Enriching with Multimedia

RESOURCE: *National Geographic* Wonders of Learning

- Enrich Unit 4 with the Wonders of Learning CD-ROM *Our Earth.*

RESOURCE: *Videodisc/Video Tape 2*

- Enrich Unit 4 with the video segment *Looking at Earth.*

Search Frame 23972, Play to 28878

ART LEARNING CENTER

LEARNING STYLE: VISUAL

Symbols Banner

GROUP

30 MINUTES OR LONGER

Materials: mural paper; paint; paintbrushes; red, white, and blue ribbon

1. Begin a discussion about the symbols of our country that children recognize—such as the American flag, an eagle, and the Statue of Liberty. Create a list of these symbols on the chalkboard.
2. Tell children that they are going to create banners of United States symbols. Let them know that they will be working on the banners in groups.
3. Have children use the materials in the Art Learning Center to paint their favorite symbols on mural paper. Also encourage them to create their own symbols for the United States.
4. When all children have completed their banners, attach lengths of ribbon to the top and sides and hang the banners in a central area.

TEACHER EXCHANGE

Thanks to Denise Graham, Travis Heights Elementary, Austin, Texas

Hold an Earth-Friendly Picnic

GROUP

30 MINUTES OR LONGER

Materials: reusable picnic supplies, picnic basket, variety of food

1. Have children brainstorm ideas for an "Earth-friendly" picnic, in which all the trash left over can be reused in some way.
2. Children should realize that they can use washable plates, silverware, and cups. They may choose cloth napkins and a cloth tablecloth or blanket that can be washed and used again. The children will need to choose foods that can be stored in reusable sealable bags (sandwiches, fruit, and so on). Leftover breadcrumbs can be fed to birds and fruit seeds can be planted.
3. After the picnic, have children discuss ways that they were able to be Earth-friendly.

UNIT 4

LESSON

1

This Is Our Country

UNIT 4 THEME BIG BOOK, PAGES 4–5

LESSON OVERVIEW

The United States of America is made up of 50 states. Together they make up the country in which we live.

LESSON OBJECTIVES

- Recognize the name and shape of the United States of America.
- Recognize the name and shape of one's own state.
- Identify the United States of America as the country in which we live.
- Identify the people who live in the United States as Americans.

KEY CONCEPTS

United States of America   American   state

RESOURCE REMINDER

Project Book
pp. 41–42

Stickers Package
Sheets 13–14

Desk Map
United States

Geo Big Book
pp. R2–R3

Technology Connection
VIDEODISC/VIDEO TAPE 1

Search Frame 5438, Play to 10527

GETTING READY

Make a Map of the United States

ON YOUR OWN

15 TO 30 MINUTES

CURRICULUM CONNECTION **Art**

Objective: To make a map to learn about the United States of America as a country.

Resource: *Project Book* pp. 41–42

Materials: scissors, crayons, glue, blue construction paper

1. Help children cut out the map pieces on ***Project Book*** pp. 41–42.
2. Demonstrate how to make a map by gluing the two larger pieces onto the center of the construction paper to form the contiguous portion of the United States. Then have children glue the box with Alaska onto the upper left corner of their papers and the box with Hawaii onto the bottom left corner.
3. Throughout the lesson, children will label, color, and identify parts of the map.

Project Book
pp.
41–42

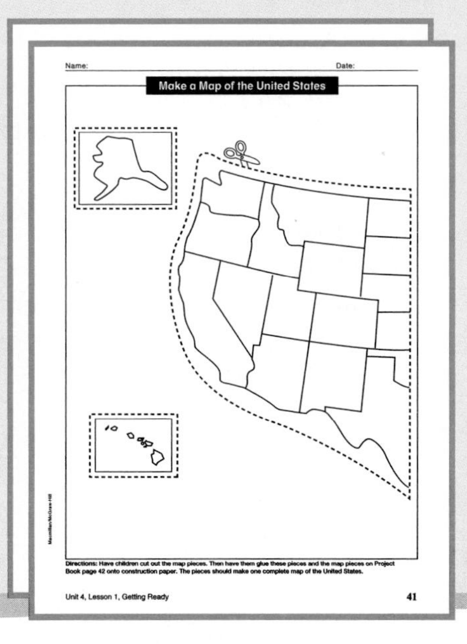

Name: Date:

Make a Map of the United States

Directions: Have children cut out the map pieces. Then have them glue these pieces and the map pieces on Project Book page 42 onto construction paper. The pieces should make one complete map of the United States.

Macmillan/McGraw-Hill

Unit 4, Lesson 1, Getting Ready 41

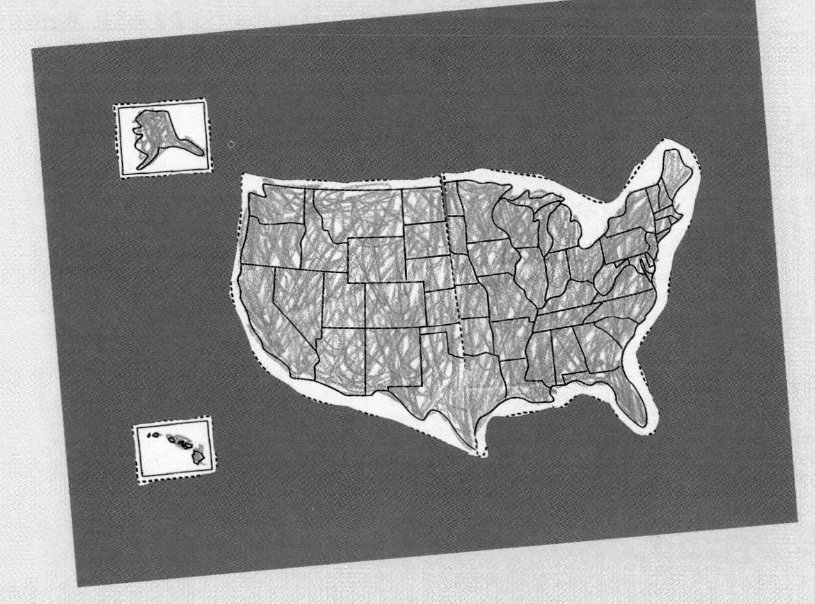

1 Prepare

WARMING UP WITH THE READ ALOUD

Tell children that they will be learning about the United States of America. Explain that the United States is also called America or the United States for short. People who live in the United States call themselves Americans. Using the United States ***Desk Maps*** or the maps children made in Getting Ready, have children trace the outline of our country. Explain that the land they traced is the United States of America. Invite children to listen to the Read Aloud poem.

- ***What kinds of transportation does the poem name?*** *(planes, rafts, boats, tugs, ships, trains)*

Technology Connection

VIDEODISC/VIDEO TAPE 1
Enrich Lesson 1 with the video segment *Living in the United States*, Search Frame 5438.

See the bar code on p. 127.

2 Teach

USING BIG BOOK PAGES 4–5

Point out that the boy who is holding the sign in the picture is Sam from the Unit Opener. Have children compare their maps from Getting Ready or the United States ***Desk Maps*** to the one on the Big

LESSON

This Is Our Country

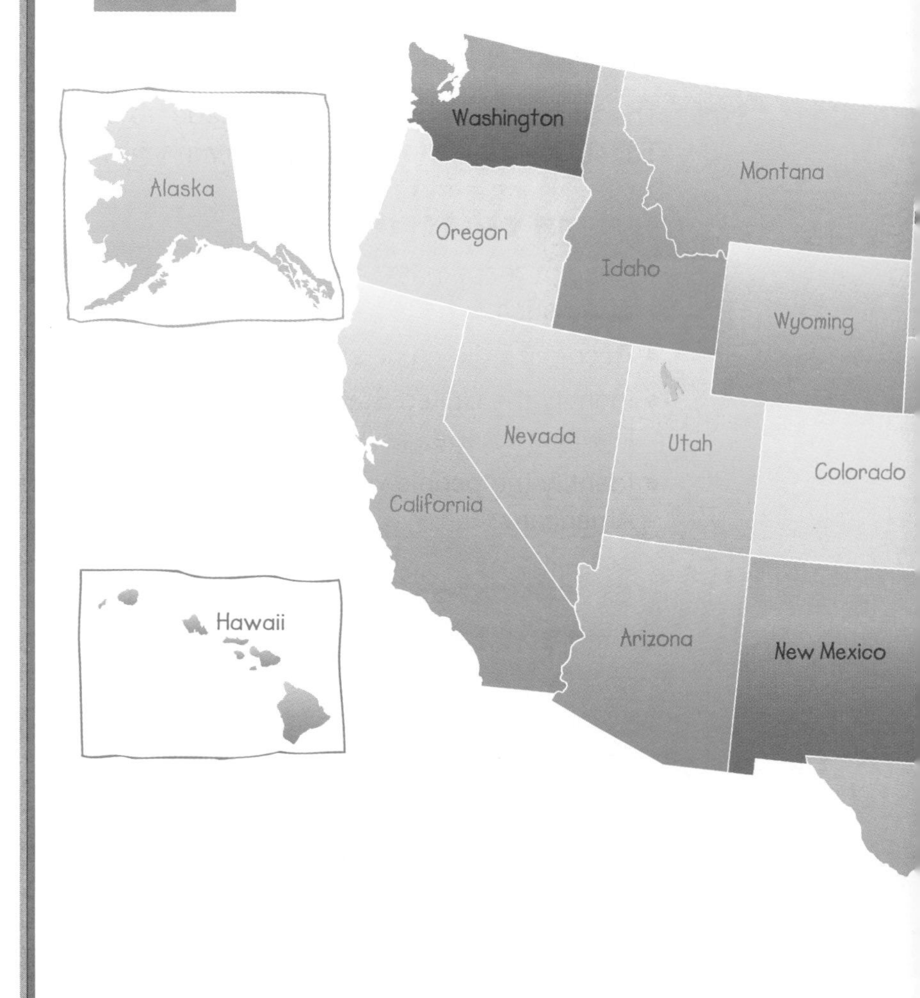

4

Read Aloud

I Love America

I love America:
Her lakes and rolling seas,
Her wooded mountainsides,
Her giant redwood trees!

I love America:
Her fields of yellow grain,
Her villages and farms
That stretch across the plains.

I love America:
Her mountains bleak and grand,
Her highways smooth and wide
That circle all the land.

I love America:
Her factories and planes,
Her rafts and boats and tugs,
Her ships and streamlined trains.

I love America:
From East to shining West,
For all she means to me;
I love my country best!

Nona Keen Duffy

USE BIG BOOK STICKERS, SHEETS 13–14

Use these ***Stickers*** throughout the lesson.

Book pages to see that both show our country. Read the lesson title and define *country* as "a land shared by the people who live there." Tell children the United States is the country in which they live; people who are born in the United States are called Americans. Tell children many people also move here to become Americans. Explain that people from other countries also live in our country.

Tell children that the United States is made up of fifty parts called states. Point out that the states are different sizes and shapes. Name your state and use the ***Sticker*** arrow to identify its location. Children can color and label their state on their maps. Use the other ***Sticker*** arrows to identify states children may have visited or lived in. If you live in Washington, D.C., affix that ***Sticker*** on the map.

- ***What does the map show?*** *(our country, the United States of America)*

★ **THINKING FURTHER: *Compare and Contrast Which is bigger, our state or our country? How can you tell?*** *(Our country is bigger; it is made up of fifty states.)*

You may wish to reinforce the lesson with the ***Geo Big Book*** by using *The United States* map on pp. R2–R3.

CITIZENSHIP

American Songs Invite children to listen to songs such as "America," "America, the Beautiful," and "This Land Is Your Land." As children listen to "America, the Beautiful," you may wish to display pictures of things named in the song such as fields, mountains, plains, and oceans. As they listen to "This Land Is Your Land," use the map on the Big Book to point out the states named. Explain to children that these songs are special to Americans because they are about our country. More suggestions for listening to patriotic songs can be found on p. 134.

Second-Language Support/Using Props Play a recording of one song. Ask children to tell you some of the words they heard and what they think the song is about. Accept all reasonable responses. Then ask children to repeat one line at a time after you. Answer any questions they may have as you go along. Use pantomime, maps, and photographs to clarify unfamiliar terms. Then invite children to sing along with the recording.

3 Close

LESSON SUMMARY

Read the lesson question with children, pointing to each word as you read. Their responses may include the United States, America, or the United States of America.

EVALUATE

Label Maps On the chalkboard, write the words *country* and *state*. Provide labels for children to label their ***Desk Maps*** or maps from Getting Ready. Have them draw lines from the labels to the parts of the map to show their location.

ART CONNECTION

LEARNING STYLE: VISUAL

Make a State Symbol

ON YOUR OWN

15 TO 30 MINUTES

Objective: To learn about your state's symbols.

Materials: samples of your state's symbols, drawing paper, crayons, pencils

Advance Preparation: Gather and display samples or pictures of your state's symbols, such as the state flag, bird, tree, flower, and animal.

1. Tell children that they will be making a bulletin board of state symbols. Discuss each state symbol and write the name of each symbol on the chalkboard. You may want to remind children that a symbol can be a picture or thing that stands for something. Invite children to choose one state symbol to illustrate.
2. Encourage children to come forward and share their work with the class. Afterwards, all of the symbols can be displayed on a bulletin board titled: "Our State Symbols." The bulletin board in the photograph shows the state symbols of Florida.

ART CONNECTION

LEARNING STYLE: VISUAL

Make a State Map

ON YOUR OWN

15 TO 30 MINUTES

Objective: To make a state map and become familiar with the shape of one's state.

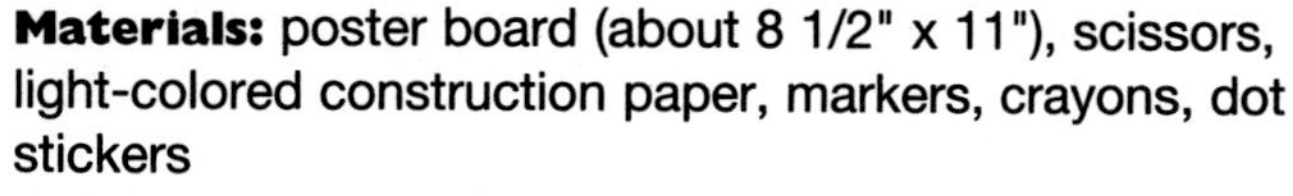

Materials: poster board (about 8 1/2" x 11"), scissors, light-colored construction paper, markers, crayons, dot stickers

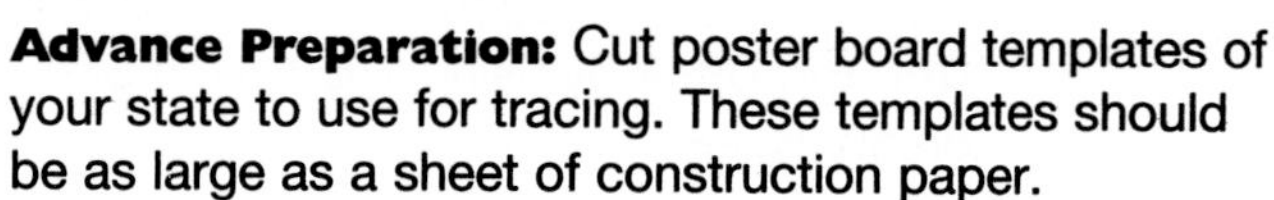

Advance Preparation: Cut poster board templates of your state to use for tracing. These templates should be as large as a sheet of construction paper.

1. Tell children that they will be making a state map. Have children use pencils to trace the state templates onto construction paper. Then have them outline the state with a dark marker or crayon.
2. Help children write your state name onto the construction paper.
3. Provide children with dot stickers. Ask children to name their community. Write the name of your community on the chalkboard. Show the approximate location of your community on their maps. Then have children place a dot sticker on their maps.
4. Suggest that children draw a picture of themselves near the dot sticker. Children may then wish to color their state.

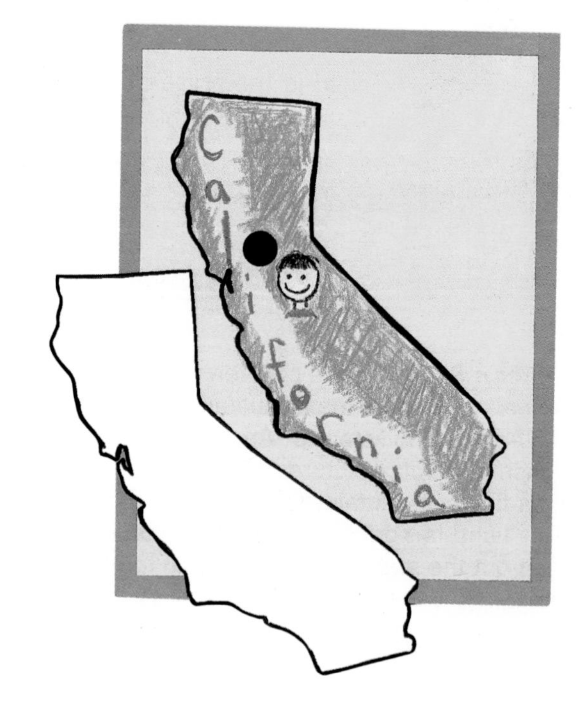

UNIT 4

LESSON 2

This Is Our Flag

UNIT 4 THEME BIG BOOK, PAGES 6–7

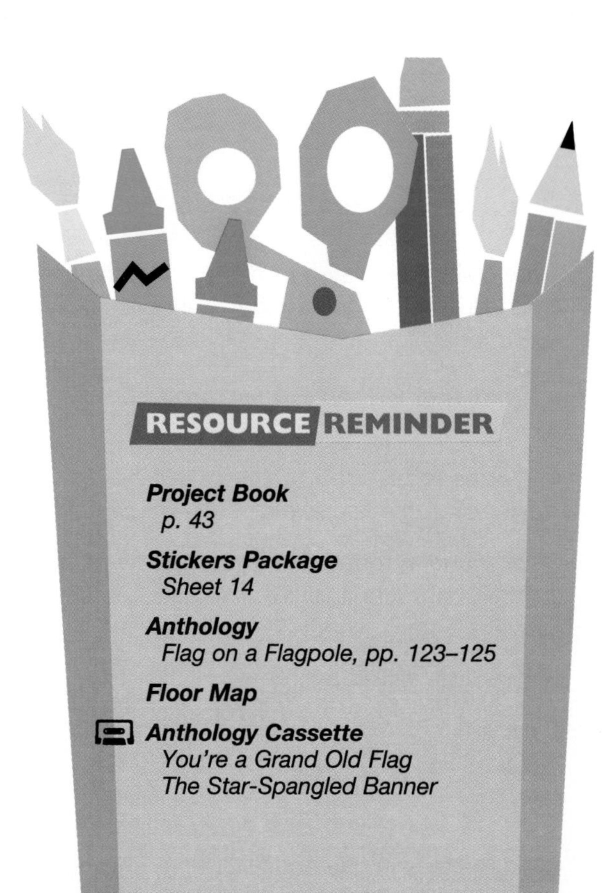

RESOURCE REMINDER

Project Book
p. 43

Stickers Package
Sheet 14

Anthology
Flag on a Flagpole, pp. 123–125

Floor Map

Anthology Cassette
You're a Grand Old Flag
The Star-Spangled Banner

LESSON OVERVIEW

The American flag is one of the most important symbols of the United States of America.

LESSON OBJECTIVES

- Recognize the American flag as the flag of the United States of America.
- Identify and say the Pledge of Allegiance.
- Recognize the American flag as a symbol of the United States of America.

KEY CONCEPTS

American flag
symbol
Pledge of Allegiance

GETTING READY

Make Flag and Star Stickers

ON YOUR OWN

15 TO 30 MINUTES

CURRICULUM CONNECTION Art

Objective: To learn about the American flag.

Resource: *Project Book* p. 43

Materials: red and blue crayons, scissors, glue; optional: clear contact paper

1. Using ***Project Book*** p. 43, have children color every second stripe of their flag red, beginning with the top stripe. Then have them use a blue crayon to color the background behind the stars. Children can decorate the large stars as they choose.
2. Help children cut out their flags and stars.
3. Have children glue their flags and stars to folders. Or children can position slightly larger pieces of clear contact paper over the cutouts to make the stickers removable. Suggest that children use these stickers to decorate folders, binders, or other belongings.
4. Have children refer to their flag stickers as you introduce and discuss the American flag in this lesson.

Project Book
p. 43

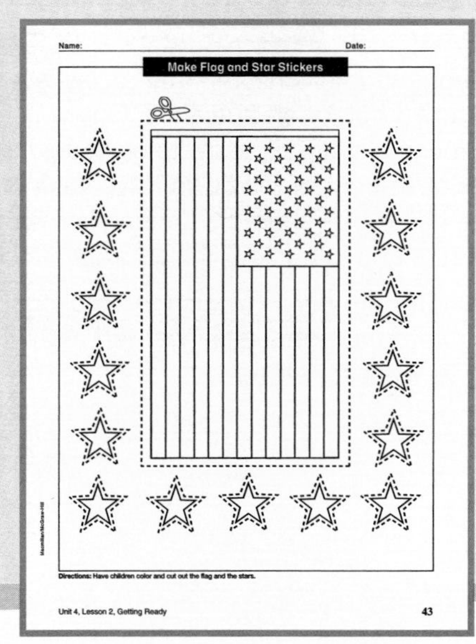
Name: Date:

Make Flag and Star Stickers

Directions: Have children color and cut out the flag and the stars.

Unit 4, Lesson 2, Getting Ready 43

1 Prepare

WARMING UP WITH THE READ ALOUD

Invite children to listen to the poem in the Read Aloud to identify the flag they will be learning about today.

- ***What flag will we be learning about?*** *(the American flag)*
- ***Where is the flag in the poem being flown?*** *(on a flagpole)*

Display and introduce the American flag and have children compare it with the flag sticker they made in Getting Ready.

2 Teach

USING BIG BOOK PAGES 6–7

Read the lesson title and elicit from children the name of our country and the name of the flag shown. Tell children that the American flag is a symbol of our country. Remind them that a symbol is a drawing, color, or object that stands for something else.

USE BIG BOOK STICKERS, SHEET 14

Use these ***Stickers*** throughout the lesson.

LESSON 2

This Is Our Flag

6

Read Aloud

Honoring Our Flag

Unfold the flag
Then send it high
Atop the flagpole to the sky.
We see your colors—
Red, white, and blue
The American flag
Oh we love you!
A pledge we make
And say it aloud
To tell everyone
That we're very proud.

Catherine M. Tamblyn

Using the Anthology

Flag on a Flagpole, pages 123–125 Children will enjoy listening to this play. By hearing this play, children will learn that a group can work together to achieve a desired goal.

Before you read, tell children that a play is a story that can be acted out for an audience. One way to help children follow the dialog is to invite eight volunteers to stand or sit in front of the class. Give each of these children the name of a character in the play. As you read each part, stand in back of the appropriate character.

After reading the play, discuss the reasons that the children voted for what they wanted and why it is important to work together.

Affix the ***Sticker*** of the American flag on the Big Book and then affix the ***Stickers*** of the stars and stripes to identify the parts of the flag. Explain that each star on the American flag stands for a state in our country and that the stripes stand for the first thirteen states that formed our country long ago.

Identify Sam and his friend in the Big Book and point out that they are honoring our flag and our country by saying the Pledge of Allegiance. Tell children that to *pledge allegiance* means to "promise to be loyal or true to our country." Recite the Pledge of Allegiance with children. Have volunteers identify the words *flag* and *United States of America* in the pledge.

You may wish to define difficult words in the pledge, such as *liberty* meaning "freedom," *justice* as meaning "fairness," and *republic* meaning "our government, or the way our country is run." Finally, you may wish to invite a Boy or Girl Scout troop to share a flag-folding ceremony with your class.

- ***What do the stars on the American flag stand for?*** *(states)*

★ **THINKING FURTHER:** ***Using Prior Knowledge*** ***If each star on our flag stands for a state, how many stars are on the flag? How do you know?*** *(50; students may say that they learned there are 50 states in the previous lesson.)*

3 Close

LESSON SUMMARY

Read the lesson question with children, pointing to each word as you read. Children should say that the flag is red, white, and blue.

EVALUATE

Make Flag-Flying Pictures Have each child draw two places, one of which is in your community, where they have seen the American flag flying. Create a master list of the places children have drawn and identify those that are in your community. You may wish to invite children to use the ***Floor Map*** to build places in the community where flags are flown. For assessment information, see p. 154.

Background Information

ABOUT THE AMERICAN FLAG

- The American flag was adopted on June 14, 1777.
- Although some people attribute the creation of the first American flag to the seamstress Betsy Ross, many scholars believe it was designed by Francis Hopkinson, a delegate to the Continental Congress.
- The first flag had thirteen stripes of red and white and thirteen white stars on a blue background.
- Nicknames for the flag include "The Stars and Stripes," "Freedom's Banner," and "Old Glory."
- The American flag should be displayed in a dignified manner. People should never wear a real flag, burn it, or let it touch the ground.
- When the American flag is carried in a procession in the United States, it should be either carried to the right or in front of all other flags.
- For more information about the flag and Flag Day, see p. 228.

ART CONNECTION

LEARNING STYLE: VISUAL

Learning Center: Make a Class Flag

GROUP

30 MINUTES OR LONGER

Objective: To explore symbolism by making class flags.

Materials: (per group) large sheet of construction paper or similar size pieces of cloth, dowel or stick; colored markers, crayons, scraps of construction paper, glue, paint, brushes, glitter glue, staples

1. Review with children that the American flag is a symbol of our country. Tell children that they will be making class flags. Divide the class into small groups. Ask each group to generate an idea for a flag that shows something special about the class. For example, if your class has a class pet, children may wish to create a flag showing the pet. Explain that the flags can have a design, words, or both. Offer to help children with any words they might want to write.
2. Make available construction paper or cloth in the Art Learning Center. Then allow each group to choose the materials they wish to use for creating the design of the flag.
3. The flags can be completed by stapling the sheet of construction paper or cloth to dowels or sticks.
4. Encourage each group to tell about their flag before displaying the flags.

MUSIC CONNECTION

LEARNING STYLE: AUDITORY/ KINESTHETIC

Parade to Songs About Our Flag

GROUP

30 MINUTES OR LONGER

Objective: To exhibit pride in our country by listening to patriotic songs about our nation's flag and by participating in a parade.

Resources: ***Project Book*** p. 43, ***Anthology Cassette***

Materials: tape player, one paper tube per child, crayons, glue

1. Tell children that one way we can honor the American flag is to sing songs about it. Teach children the words to two patriotic songs by playing a tape of "You're a Grand Old Flag" and "The Star-Spangled Banner" on the ***Anthology Cassette***. After playing the tape and having children sing along, have them describe how listening to the songs made them feel.
2. Suggest that the class might enjoy marching in a classroom parade. To make handheld flags for the parade, children can cut out the flag on ***Project Book*** p. 43, color it, and glue it onto a paper tube. You may wish to make paper hats for children to wear.
3. You might also share with the class a recording of "The Stars and Stripes Forever."

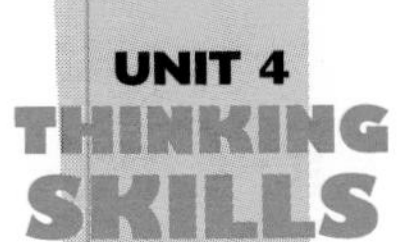

Putting Things in Order

UNIT 4 THEME BIG BOOK, PAGES 8–9

LESSON OVERVIEW

Placing things in order helps to organize information.

LESSON OBJECTIVES

- Use number order.
- Identify the order of pictures to show a sequence.
- Use the words *first, next,* and *last* to put pictures in order.
- Identify and read hourly times.

KEY CONCEPTS

order time first next last

RESOURCE REMINDER

Project Book
p. 44

Stickers Package
Sheet 14

Word Cards

GETTING READY

Connect the Dots

ON YOUR OWN

15 TO 30 MINUTES

CURRICULUM CONNECTION **Mathematics**

Objective: To understand the order and sequence of numbers.

Resource: ***Project Book*** p. 44

Materials: pencils, crayons

1. Read the numbers on ***Project Book*** p. 44 aloud randomly and have children locate them.
2. Help children to complete the picture by connecting the dots in order from 1–15. Ask children to tell what they think the completed picture will show.
3. Have children color their pictures. You may wish to identify the eagle at the top of the mast as an important symbol of our country.

Project Book
p. 44

Name: Date:
Connect the Dots
Directions: Have children complete the picture by connecting the dots. Then have them color the picture.
44 Unit 4, Thinking Skills, Getting Ready

1 Prepare

WARMING UP WITH THE READ ALOUD

Remind children that they connected the dots in order by number in the picture in Getting Ready. Elicit from children what would have happened if they did not connect the dots in order. Tell children that they will be learning more about placing things in order.

Obtain a small American flag and invite a volunteer to act out the poem in the Read Aloud. Pause after reading each action to separate them.

- ***What does the poem say to do before you wave the flag?*** *(Take the flag.)*
- ***What does the poem say to do after you wave the flag?*** *(Possible answers include hold it high and see its colors.)*

2 Teach

USING BIG BOOK PAGES 8–9

Read the lesson title with children. Elicit from them things they put in order such as letters in alphabetical order, books in order by size on a shelf, or numbers. Tell children that pictures can be placed in order by time to tell a story. Invite children to study the photographs. Tell children that these photographs are in order by time.

USE BIG BOOK STICKERS, SHEET 14

Use the following ***Stickers*** throughout the lesson.

first next last

1 2 3 8:00 9:00 10:00

As you ask the suggested questions containing the words first, next, and last, affix the ***Stickers*** of these words with the appropriate pictures in the Big Book.

You may also wish to use the ***Word Cards*** for *first, next,* and *last* as you teach the lesson.

UNIT 4 THEME BIG BOOK

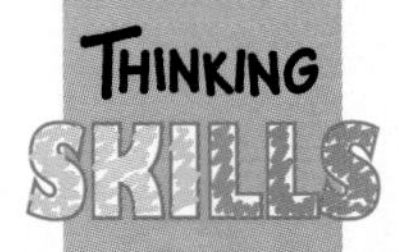

Putting Things in Order

8

Read Aloud

Waving the Flag

Take the flag and wave it.
Hold it high above,
See its colors, red, white, and blue,
Our American flag we love.

Rebecca Boynton

- ***Which picture shows what Sam did first? What did he do?*** *(The first picture; he ate breakfast.)*
- ***Which picture shows what Sam did next? What did he do?*** *(The middle picture; he made a flag.)*
- ***Which picture shows what Sam did last? What did he do?*** *(The picture on the right; he showed his teacher the flag he made.)*

★**THINKING FURTHER:** ***Making Conclusions*** ***How do you know that the last thing Sam did was to show his teacher the flag?*** *(He had to make the flag before he could show it to her; some children may respond that the time on the clock is later than in the other pictures.)*

Use these steps with children who appear to be having difficulty sequencing.

HELPING YOURSELF

- Look at each picture or thing.
- Choose the kind of order in which to put the pictures or things—such as by time or by size.
- Find the picture or thing that comes first and then next.
- Continue until all the pictures or things are placed in order.

You may wish to also affix the ***Stickers*** showing digital-time clocks near the clocks in the photographs to reinforce time skills.

3 Close

LESSON SUMMARY

Read the lesson question with children, pointing to each word as you read. Have children affix the ***Stickers*** of the numbers 1–3 to show that the pictures are in order by time. You may also wish to have children switch sticker 3 with sticker 2 to order the pictures by size.

EVALUATE

Recite a Simple Task Have children think of a simple task that they do at home or at school. Invite children to tell the class about the task using the words *first, next,* and *last.* Possible tasks include making a sandwich or making a bed. Invite children to hold up the appropriate ***Word Cards*** as they describe their tasks. For assessment information, see p. 154.

Curriculum Connection

Mathematics Relate this sequencing skill to reading hourly times on clocks. Depending on the ability of children to tell time, you may wish to review, in order, the numbers on the face of a demonstration analog clock, as well as identify the hour hand and minute hand and tell what each does. Invite volunteers to read the time shown on each clock in the photographs on the Big Book pages.

Tell children that the clocks could have helped them to put the pictures in order because they tell the time when Sam did each activity. On a demonstration clock, show the three times beginning with 8:00. You may also wish to show time on a digital clock. Questions you might ask children include: "At what time did Sam show his teacher his flag? Which time is later, 9:00 or 10:00? Which time is earlier, 10:00 or 8:00?" and "What time of day do the three pictures show?"

HOME ECONOMICS CONNECTION

LEARNING STYLE: KINESTHETIC

Learning Center: Make "Ants on a Log"

GROUP

30 MINUTES OR LONGER

Objective: To use a set of directions in order to make a snack.

Materials: markers, crayons, large index cards, labels, cutting board, plastic knives, small paper plates or napkins, washed celery, peanut butter, raisins or chocolate chips

Advance Preparation: Obtain permission from parents and guardians for children to eat celery, peanut butter, raisins, or chocolate chips, in case of allergies. Then using three large index cards and crayons or markers, prepare cards with illustrations for making this snack. On the first card, show a plain stalk of celery broken or cut into two pieces. On the second card, show the pieces of celery with some peanut butter. On the third card, show the celery with peanut butter topped with raisins or chocolate chips. Also prepare labels of the words *first, next,* and *last to* affix to the cards in step 1.

1. Tell children that they will make a snack by following in order illustrated directions on cards. Display and review the cards with children. Have children suggest how to place the directions in order by using the words *first, next,* and *last.* Affix the labels to the cards.
2. Next place the cards, snack ingredients, and utensils in the Home Economics Learning Center. Invite small groups to arrange the cards in the proper order and then follow the ordered directions to prepare their snack.
3. As the children eat their snack, suggest that they teach someone at home to make "Ants on a Log."

ART and MATHEMATICS CONNECTIONS

LEARNING STYLE: AUDITORY/VISUAL

Make a Class Schedule

GROUP

30 MINUTES OR LONGER

Objective: To understand the order of a daily schedule in a classroom.

Materials: drawing paper, crayons and markers; optional: small manipulative clocks, labels

1. Tell children that they will be making a class schedule together. Tell them that a schedule is a way of putting something in order by time. Have children help you generate a list of activities the class does on a daily basis, such as music time, circle time, playground time, snack time, and sharing time.
2. Give each child a subject or an activity. Have the children draw a picture or a symbol to represent the activity they were given.
3. When children finish, invite them to tell about their drawings. Then help them to display the pictures in time order according to your class schedule today. You may wish to add labels to their pictures describing the activities.
4. Each day, children can help you to display a new schedule with the drawings. If small manipulative clocks are available, set them with the appropriate times and display them along with the pictures.

UNIT 4

LESSON 3

Looking at Land and Water

UNIT 4 THEME BIG BOOK, PAGES 10–11

LESSON OVERVIEW

Earth is made up of land and water. A globe is a model of Earth.

LESSON OBJECTIVES

- Recognize that Earth is a planet in space.
- Recognize that Earth is made up of land and water.
- Determine that a globe is a model of Earth.
- Identify land and water on a globe.

KEY CONCEPTS

Earth land globe

RESOURCE REMINDER

Project Book
pp. 45–46

Stickers Package
Sheet 15

Anthology
It's Mine!, pp. 81–82

Inflatable Globe

Geo Big Book,
pp. R5c–R5f; R6–R7

Technology Connection
VIDEODISC/VIDEO TAPE 2

Search Frame 23972, Play to 28878

GETTING READY

Make a Land-and-Water Chart

CURRICULUM CONNECTION Art

Objective: To match people, activities, and things to land and water environments.

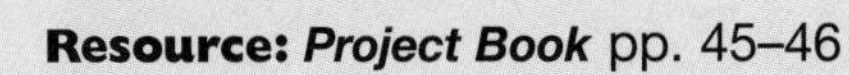

Resource: ***Project Book*** pp. 45–46

Materials: scissors, glue, crayons, construction paper

1. Elicit from children that the illustrations on ***Project Book*** p. 45 show a forest and a beach. Have them identify the picture that shows water by coloring the water blue.
2. Then have children identify the pictures on ***Project Book*** p. 46. Point out that each of these things or people can be found in one of the places shown on ***Project Book*** p. 45.
3. Invite children to color and cut out the pictures on p. 46 and glue them next to the place where the things are found on p. 45.
4. Children can now color the rest of page 45 and glue it to a piece of construction paper.

Project Book
pp. 45–46

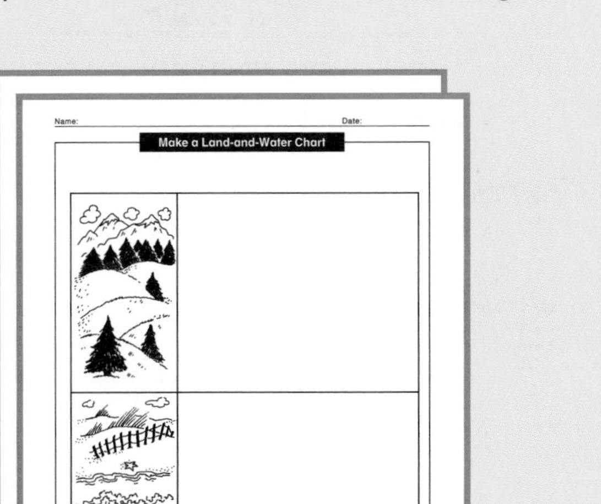

1 Prepare

WARMING UP WITH THE READ ALOUD

Tell children that they will be learning about a place called Earth. Point out that *Earth* is the name of our world. Elicit from children what they already know about Earth. Explain that Earth is really a planet in space that is shaped like a ball and is made out of land and water. Share the Read Aloud poem to begin the discussion.

- ***How does the poet describe the size of the world?*** *(great and wide)*
- ***How does the poet think the world looks?*** *(beautiful, wonderful)*

Technology Connection

VIDEODISC/VIDEO TAPE 2
Enrich Lesson 3 with the video segment *Looking at Earth*, Search Frame 23972.

See the bar code on p. 139.

2 Teach

USING BIG BOOK PAGES 10–11

Read the lesson title.

USE BIG BOOK STICKERS, SHEET 15

Use the Earth, globe, land, and water ***Stickers*** throughout the lesson.

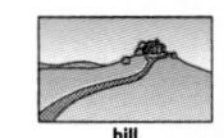

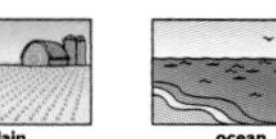

Affix the ***Sticker*** of Earth near the photograph of Earth. Explain that this is how Earth looks to astronauts in space. Remind children that Earth is a planet in space. Explain that this photograph of Earth was taken from space.

Ask volunteers to identify both land and water in the photograph. Ask children to describe land and water, such as hills, mountains, lakes, rivers, and oceans. Have volunteers place the ***Stickers*** of different kinds of land and water near the photograph of Earth. Discuss with children the types of land and water shown on the ***Stickers***.

Read Aloud

The World

Great, wide, beautiful,
wonderful World,
With the wonderful water
round you curled,
And the wonderful grass
upon your breast,
World, you are beautifully drest.

William Brighty Rands

How is a globe like Earth?

11

Direct children's attention to the globe. Affix the ***Sticker*** of the globe near the photograph. Tell children that a globe is a model of Earth. You may wish to have children examine your classroom globe and the ***Inflatable Globe***. Point out that the globe is round like Earth and that a globe shows the land and water on Earth. Have volunteers identify land and water on the ***Inflatable Globe***. Then have children identify land and water on your classroom globe. Elicit from children the name of our country and then point out its location on the globe and on the photograph of Earth. Also identify on a globe the location of your state.

- ***What is Earth made of?*** *(land and water)*

> ★**THINKING FURTHER:** ***Compare and Contrast*** ***How is a globe different from Earth?*** *(Possible answers: A globe is a model, it has a stand, it is smaller, people do not live on it, it has labels.)*

To reinforce the lesson, you may wish to use the following pages in the ***Geo Big Book***: The United States Landforms, pp. R5c–R5d; Globe, p. R5e; Satellite Photograph of Earth, p. R5f. You may also wish to review different kinds of land and water shown in the ***Geo Big Book*** in the Dictionary of Geographic Words on pp. R6–R7.

3 Close

LESSON SUMMARY

Read the lesson question with children, pointing to each word as you read. Children might respond that a globe and Earth are both round and they both show land and water.

EVALUATE

Draw Earth and a Globe Have children draw a picture of Earth and of a globe. If time allows, children can dictate sentences to you using the words *Earth* and *globe*. For assessment information, see p. 154.

Using the Anthology

It's Mine!, pages 81–82 This fable tells about three selfish frogs who learn to share their island home and the water and air around it. Before reading, show children a picture of an island or draw one on the chalkboard using green and blue chalk. Point out that an island is land with water all around it.

Curriculum Connection

Science You may wish to explore Earth as part of the solar system and include these simple facts in your discussion:

- Earth is third in order from the sun.
- Earth is the only planet known to have human, animal, and plant life.
- Earth is the only planet known to have oceans.

ART CONNECTION

LEARNING STYLE: KINESTHETIC

Sail Around the World

PARTNER

30 MINUTES OR LONGER

Objective: To identify water and land on a globe by "sailing" around the world.

Resource: ***Inflatable Globe***

Materials: (per child) half a walnut shell; modeling clay, toothpicks, white scrap paper, scissors, tape; optional: drawing paper

1. Tell children they will be making boats to "sail" around the world. Have children make a model of a boat by filling half a walnut shell with modeling clay.
2. Then have children make a sail and mast by cutting a small triangle from scrap paper and taping or pasting it onto a toothpick. Have them place the mast upright in the clay-filled boat. (Optional: Children can make boats out of folded drawing paper.)
3. Invite pairs of children to take turns "sailing their boats around the world" without touching land using the ***Inflatable Globe***. Suggest that they begin their voyage at the United States.
4. You might ask the pairs of children to stand on opposite sides of the globe and have one child sail his or her boat toward the partner. Have the partner respond when he or she can see the boat, and also tell when it disappears from view.

ART CONNECTION

LEARNING STYLE: KINESTHETIC

Learning Center: Make Clay Models of Land and Water

GROUP

15 TO 30 MINUTES

Objective: To examine different landforms and bodies of water.

Materials: (per group) one box lid or cardboard base; modeling clay of different colors; pictures of mountains, hills, plains, rivers and lakes; optional: drawing paper, scissors, crayons, craft sticks, tape

1. Tell children they will be making models of land and water out of clay. Tell children that Earth is made of different types of land and water. Hold up pictures of land and water, one at a time, and ask children to describe the types of land and water displayed. On the chalkboard, write the names of the kinds of land and water shown.
2. Provide each group with modeling clay, and a box lid or cardboard base in which to make the models.
3. In the Art Learning Center, allow groups to make plains, hills, mountains, rivers, and lakes on their own, or instruct them to make the following:
   - Make plains by pressing the clay flat.
   - Make hills by adding small rounded mounds of clay.
   - Make mountains by stacking many pieces of clay together and making the tops pointed (peaked).
   - Make rivers by rolling clay into long strips.
   - Make lakes by flattening small balls of clay.
4. Afterwards you might ask questions such as, "What is flat land called? What might flat land be good for? Which land is the highest? Which land is not as high as mountains, but not as flat as plains?"
5. Optional: To extend this activity, children can add labels or small drawings of the landforms taped to craft sticks to their models.

Our Great Big World

UNIT 4 THEME BIG BOOK, PAGES 12–13

LESSON OVERVIEW

Earth is home to people, plants, and animals.

LESSON OBJECTIVES

- Recognize that people, plants, and animals live on Earth.
- Recognize that the world is made up of continents and oceans.
- Identify North America as the continent on which we live.

KEY CONCEPT

continent

RESOURCE REMINDER

Project Book
pp. 37–40, 47

Stickers Package
Sheets 15–16

Inflatable Globe

Geo Big Book
pp. R4–R5, R5g–R5h

GETTING READY

Make a Map of Earth

ON YOUR OWN

15 TO 30 MINUTES

CURRICULUM CONNECTION Art

Objective: To practice identifying land and water on a globe.

Resources: ***Project Book*** p. 47; ***Inflatable Globe***

Materials: scissors; glue; blue, green, and red crayons

1. Elicit from children that ***Project Book*** p. 47 shows a map of part of Earth. Read the labels on the page.
2. Have children tell what color they think of when they hear the word *land.* Direct them to color the box next to that word green. Ask children what color they think of when they hear the word water. Direct them to color the box next to that word blue. Then have children color the land and water on the map using the appropriate colors.
3. Have children identify the land with the dark outline as the United States. Have them trace the outline with a red crayon.
4. Direct children to cut out the labels at the bottom of the page. Have them glue the label *Earth* in the box next to the map and the label *United States of America* on the United States.
5. Have children compare their maps to the ***Inflatable Globe*** to see that their maps only show part of Earth.

Project Book
p. 47

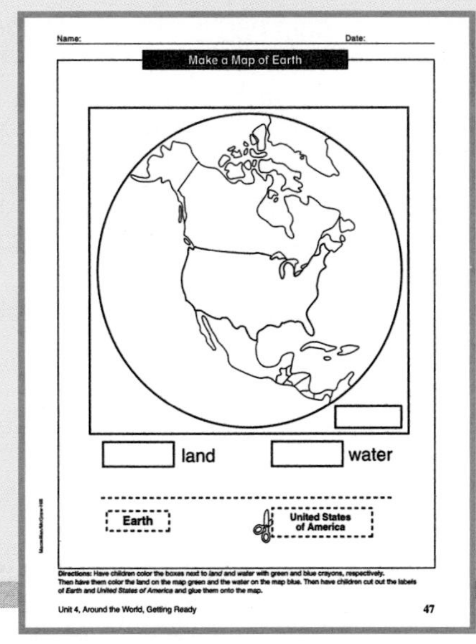

1 Prepare

WARMING UP WITH THE READ ALOUD

Share the poem in the Read Aloud and then have children perform the actions indicated to find out what they will be learning about today.

- ***How does the poet describe the world's size and shape?*** *(big and round)*

> ★**THINKING FURTHER:** ***Classifying*** ***What two things in the poem are seen in the sky?*** *(birds, sun)*

2 Teach

USING BIG BOOK PAGES 12–13

Read the lesson title and then tell children that the map on the Big Book shows land and water that make up the world. Explain that the world is made of seven large pieces of land called continents.

USE BIG BOOK STICKERS, SHEETS 15–16

Use the following ***Stickers*** throughout the lesson.

Europe | North America | South America

Asia | Africa | Australia | Antarctica

X X X X X X X X

Our Great Big World

12

Read Aloud

Here Is Our World

Here is our world, our big, round world.
  (Spread arms.)
Here are the mountains high.
  (Stretch arms up.)
Here is a fish that swims in the sea.
  (Move hand back and forth.)
Here are the birds that fly.
  (Motion of flying.)
Here is the sun, the bright, warm sun.
  (Make circle of arms.)
Here are the leaves that fall.
  (Let raised hands fall gently.)
Here is our world, our big, round world,
To be enjoyed by all.
  (Spread arms.)

Fingerplay by
Louise Binder Scott

Background Information

About the Illustrations The following are the names of the birds, mammals, fish, and plants shown on the map on the Big Book.

- North America: bald eagle, black bear, lobster, black spruce, scarlet macaw, snowy owl
- South America: llama, mackerel, banana tree
- Europe: white stork, herring, reindeer
- Africa: fish eagle, lion, coelacanth (fish) [sē´ lə kanth´], date palm, humpback whale
- Asia: whooper swan, yak, pufferfish, coconut palm, eastern fir
- Australia: kookaburra, kangaroo, eucalyptus tree
- Antarctica: penguin, seal, blue whale

Point out that each continent is shown in a different color on this map. You may also wish to point to the continents on a globe in the ***Geo Big Book*** on pp. R4–R5 in a world map and on pp. R5g–R5h in a satellite photograph. As you name each continent, affix the ***Stickers*** with the continents' names.

Introduce North America as the continent in which the children live. Point out the photographs of the children from different countries and explain that these children live on the different continents of the world.

Next explain that the world's large bodies of water surrounding the continents are oceans. You may wish to point out the four oceans in the ***Geo Big Book*** on the world map on pp. R4–R5.

Use the Background Information on p. 144 to help you name and identify the different animals and plants on the continents and oceans. Explain that the map shows just some of the things in nature found on each continent. You may wish to point out that Antarctica is so cold and dry that no trees grow there. Have children use the *X* ***Stickers*** to sort the things on the map into groups. For example, they might put one set of colored *X*s on all the plants, another on the birds, another on land animals, and another on water animals.

- ***What things in nature do you see in North America?*** *(Children should point to or generally name the bald eagle, black bear, lobster, and spruce tree. They may also point to the scarlet macaw in Central America and the snowy owl in Greenland.)*

> ★**THINKING FURTHER:** ***Compare and Contrast* Is the United States bigger or smaller than North America? Tell why.** *(Our country is smaller; it is only part of the continent of North America.)*

3 Close

LESSON SUMMARY

Point to each word as you read the lesson question with children. Encourage children to name plants and animals.

EVALUATE

Label Maps Write on the chalkboard *North America, continent,* and *ocean.* Prepare labels of these words and have children use the words to label the maps they made in the Getting Ready.

Print Awareness

Write on the chalkboard, in alphabetical order, the names of the seven continents. Say the names of the continents with children. Elicit from children that the first four continents begin with a capital *A* and end with a lowercase *a.* Children might also identify that the continents South America and North America end in a lowercase *a* and have the word *America* in common.

Second-Language Support/Using Visuals Have available the ***Inflatable Globe***, the world map from the Big Book or the ***Geo Big Book*** on pp. R4-R5. Point to the names of the continents and ask children to repeat them after you. Encourage children to point out and name the continent where they or their family originally came from. Encourage children to demonstrate how the continents' names are alike by pointing to the letters. For example, you might say, "Please find all the capital A's," or "Please circle the continents whose names have two words in them.

ART CONNECTION

LEARNING STYLE: AUDITORY/ KINESTHETIC/VISUAL

Display Animals of the World

GROUP

30 MINUTES OR LONGER

Objective: To make a display of animals from around the world.

Resources: ***Inflatable Globe***; optional: ***Project Book*** pp. 37–40

Materials: mural paper, markers, tempera paint, brushes, scissors, source books about animals, children's own stuffed or plastic animals from home, magazines with animal pictures

Advance Preparation: Invite children to bring from home a plastic or stuffed animal. Draw and label rough outlines of each continent on seven large sheets of mural paper. (You may wish to enlarge the continent shapes from the ***Project Book*** to assist you in drawing the outlines.)

1. Tell children they will be making a display of animals from around the world. Show the seven continents on the ***Inflatable Globe***. Write the name of each continent on the chalkboard.
2. Divide your class into seven groups. Assign each group a continent to paint.
3. Have children cut out a picture of an animal from a magazine or take out their stuffed animals. Then invite children to take turns telling the class about their animals. Use source books to identify the continents on which the animals live.
4. Have children place their animals or magazine cutouts on or near the appropriate continents.

PHYSICAL EDUCATION CONNECTION

LEARNING STYLE: KINESTHETIC

Play "Cat and Lynx"

GROUP

15 TO 30 MINUTES

Objective: To play a game that originated in southern Africa.

Materials: 12 boxes or cartons

1. Tell children that they will be playing a game that is played in southern Africa. Stagger the boxes in a playing area among bushes or other natural obstacles, or place them in an obstacle course.
2. Divide your class into two teams and give the teams the names "Cat" and "Lynx." Tell children these animals live in Africa. Have each team stand in line on opposite sides of the playing area, at least 20 feet apart.
3. Have a Cat and a Lynx greet each other in the center of the playing area. Their greetings should include characteristics about themselves. For example, the Lynx might say, "I'm so fast, I know I'll catch you for dinner!" The Cat might reply, "You may be bigger, but you won't catch me!" Any dialog can be used but as soon as the Cat says "Catch me," the chase is on.
4. The two players must run around the obstacles but cannot jump over them, nor can one player reach over an obstacle to tag the other. Once the chase begins, the teammates clap and count to 20. If the Cat has not been caught within that time, the two players go back to their teams and the next two teammates play. If the Cat is tagged, he or she joins the Lynx team, and so on.
5. If all Cats are caught, the Lynx team wins, but if every Lynx has had a turn, and more than half of the Cats remain, the Cat team wins.

UNIT 4

LESSON 4

Caring for Earth

UNIT 4 THEME BIG BOOK, PAGES 14–15

LESSON OVERVIEW

Children will discover and appreciate their responsibility in taking care of the environment.

LESSON OBJECTIVES

- Develop a responsible role in taking care of Earth.
- Distinguish between things in nature and things made by people.
- Identify recyclable items and carry out a recycling project.
- Define and identify litter.

KEY CONCEPTS

recycle   litter

RESOURCE REMINDER

Project Book
p. 48

Stickers Package
Sheet 15

Anthology
Miss Rumphius, pp. 77–80

GETTING READY

Make a Paper Keeper

ON YOUR OWN

15 TO 30 MINUTES

CURRICULUM CONNECTION Art

Objective: To learn about recycling in the classroom.

Resource: ***Project Book*** p. 48

Materials: one paper lunch bag per child, ribbon or yarn, crayons, markers, glitter, scissors, glue, hole puncher

1. Read the labels and discuss the items on ***Project Book*** p. 48. Have children color and cut out the pictures.
2. Tell children they will be making paper keepers that can hold scrap paper, which can be used again in other projects. Explain that by saving scrap paper, they are acting responsibly to cut down on trash. They also save trees, which give us paper.
3. Have children glue their pictures on one side of the lunch bag. Invite children to further decorate their bags with markers and glitter.
4. Punch a hole on each side of the back of the lunch bag and attach yarn for hanging. Children can hang their paper keepers from the backs of their chairs.
5. When the children's bags are full, they can empty their paper keepers into a large bin or cardboard box to use later on.

Project Book
p. 48

Name: Date:

Make a Paper Keeper

Earth is in my hands.

I care to do my share.

PAPER KEEPER

Directions: Have children color and cut out the pictures. Then have them glue the pictures to a paper bag.

48 Unit 4, Lesson 4, Getting Ready

WARMING UP WITH THE READ ALOUD

Tell children that they will be learning about things they can do to care for Earth such as saving scrap paper. Explain that when we care for something, we show we like it by giving it extra attention. Share the Read Aloud with children.

- ***Why is a green Earth good?*** *(Possible answers: A green Earth is healthy, a green Earth is covered with living plants and trees.)*
- ***What can people do to help keep Earth green?*** *(Possible answers: Plant a seed, save paper, and adopt plants.)*

USE BIG BOOK PAGES 14–15

Read the lesson title, pointing out the word *caring*. Review with children how Chris and others cared for the dove in Unit 3, Making a Difference, pp. 14–15. Elicit from children that Sam and the animals are being responsible by caring for Earth.

USE BIG BOOK STICKERS, SHEET 15

Use this ***Sticker*** during the lesson.

Caring for Earth

14

Thinking Green

If you look green, you're probably not feeling very well. But if the Earth is green, it's a healthy planet.

A green Earth means that plants are growing. It means that the soil is good, there's plenty of water, the air is clean, animals have places to live and things to eat.

And some wonderful news: Anyone can help keep the Earth green. It's so easy. You can plant a seed, give it some water, and watch it grow. You can save paper so that fewer trees will be cut down. You can "adopt" plants that are already growing and help them enjoy life. . . .

We need lots of greenery in our world. Let's start planting!

The Earthworks Group

Using the Anthology

Miss Rumphius, pages 77–80 Read this story to show how one person made the world a more beautiful place. After reading the first page, have children suggest possible things Alice could do to make the world more beautiful. At the conclusion of the story, ask volunteers to name things they would do to make the world more beautiful. Show children a lupine or a photograph of one to give meaning to the word.

Curriculum Connection

Science Allow children to grow lupines or other flowers to make the world more beautiful. Plant seeds in small plastic cups or in divided portions of egg cartons filled with a light potting mixture. Place in a sunny location. Use a spray bottle to keep moist.

Have children identify the things found in nature and the things made by people. Point out that newpapers, bottles, and cans are things that people recycle or use again. Display the ***Sticker*** that shows the symbol for recycling and ask children where they have seen it before. Explain that the recycle symbol is found on things that can be recycled. Have children affix the ***Sticker*** on the recycling bin in the Big Book. Explain that some people are responsible and care for Earth by recycling, cleaning up trash, planting trees, and more.

Ask children what litter is and then define the word as "trash that is scattered about." Explain that litter makes Earth unattractive.

- ***How has the tire been recycled?*** *(It was made into a swing.)*
- ***What is the elephant doing to care for Earth?*** *(watering a plant)*
- ***What is the flamingo doing to help out?*** *(recycling a can)*

> ★ **THINKING FURTHER:** ***Putting Things in Order*** ***What had to be done with the newspapers before the birds could tie them up for recycling?*** *(Possible answer: They needed to be collected or stacked in a pile.)* ***What will happen next?*** *(Possible answer: They will be taken to a recycling center or put into recycling containers or bins.)*

3 Close

LESSON SUMMARY

Read the lesson question with children, pointing to each word as you read. Children should name different ways people care for Earth. Record children's answers on sentence strips. Children can use the sentence strips in the activity suggested in Evaluate.

EVALUATE

Make a Class Collage Invite children to contribute items to a class collage that identifies ways they and others care for Earth. Children can contribute their own illustrations or photographs from discarded magazines or newspapers. Children might also add small recyclable items and the sentence strips from above to the collage. Working in small groups, children should glue their contributions on a large sheet of mural paper.

Field Trip

Taking an Awareness Walk Take a walk through a park, the schoolyard, or the school neighborhood to observe ways people in the community are caring for the environment. You might identify signs, trash and recycling containers, bird houses or feeders, or any curbside recycling efforts underway. Have children identify community helpers caring for Earth.

Visiting Your Community's Recycling Center Arrange for a tour of your community's recycling facility. Find out and discuss the rules associated with recycling, such as how people in the community should bundle, sort, and dispose of items. Children might learn where the items go after your community collects them.

Second-Language Support/Dramatization As you tour the neighborhood and find people caring for the environment, explain in several different ways what people are doing. Point to and act out as you tell children what the people are doing.

SCIENCE CONNECTION

LEARNING STYLE: KINESTHETIC

Learning Center: Perform a Clean Water Test

GROUP

30 MINUTES OR LONGER

Objective: To discover differences in water samples.

Materials: containers with lids, adhesive labels, coffee filters, strainer, bowl, magnifying glasses

Advance Preparation: Set up a lab in the Science Learning Center. Collect different samples of water in labeled containers with lids. These samples may include tap water, rain water, water from melted snow or ice, or water from a puddle or a body of water.

1. Tell children that it is everyone's responsibility to keep our water clean. Explain to them that they will be looking at different water samples.
2. Place coffee filters in the Science Learning Center. Demonstrate how to pour some of the contents of one container *slowly* through a filter into a bowl. Then pour the water back into the container.
3. Explain that children can use a different filter for each container. Then they should use a magnifying glass to examine the particles on each filter.
4. As they work, ask children questions such as "Which water looks the dirtiest? Which looks the cleanest? Why are they so different? Do some filters look dirty even though the water looks clean?"

ART and SCIENCE CONNECTIONS

LEARNING STYLE: KINESTHETIC

Make Bird Feeders

ON YOUR OWN

30 MINUTES OR LONGER

Objective: To practice recycling half-gallon milk and juice cartons by making them into bird feeders.

Materials: stapler, utility knife, hole puncher, contact paper (with flowers or another design), scissors, bird seed; (per child) one half-gallon milk or juice cantainer, one 6" dowel, 16" length of string or strong yarn

1. Tell children they will be responsibly caring for Earth by recycling milk or juice cartons to make bird feeders. Have children bring to school empty and clean half-gallon milk or juice containers.
2. Show children how to fold in the spouts to their containers, and how to staple the spout closed. Help them punch a hole through the top of each container and demonstrate how to attach the length of string for hanging.
3. Make an opening by cutting out a circle, 2" in diameter, on one side of the container. Add a perch by poking a hole below the opening with a utility knife. Show children how to feed a dowel through the hole until it pokes through the back of the container.
4. Have children cut leaves and flowers or other designs from contact paper to decorate their feeders.
5. Finally, children should add the bird seed to the bottom of the container and hang them outside on a sturdy tree branch.

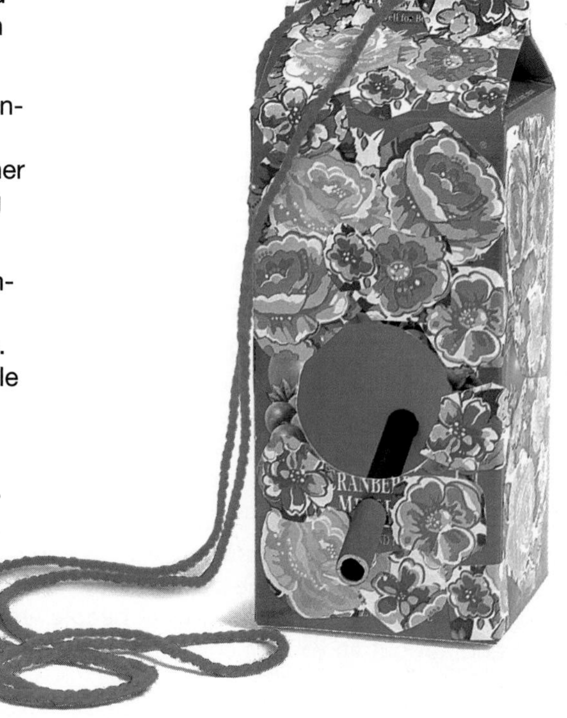

CLOSE WITH A SONG

LINKING SOCIAL STUDIES AND LITERATURE

Close Unit 4 with the song "One Light, One Sun" from pages 16–17 of the Big Book. The song acts as a springboard to support these Social Studies concepts:

- We are all part of one world.
- It is important to love and care for each other, and for Earth, our home.

ABOUT THE SONG

A full instructional plan, along with the song, appears on the following two pages.

In his song "One Light, One Sun," composer Raffi expresses a love for Earth and the people on it, who share hopes, dreams, and joy.

As children join in singing "One Light, One Sun," they can begin to recognize that people all over the world love and appreciate Earth.

ABOUT THE COMPOSER

Raffi is one of the most beloved of children's singers/songwriters. For two decades he has created songs children love to sing, from the rousing "Baby Beluga" to gentle lullabies. At his concert appearances all over the world, parents and children join together to sing about the wonders of Earth.

INTRODUCE

Using Prior Knowledge Review with children what they have learned about Earth. You may wish to create a web to record important features of Earth.

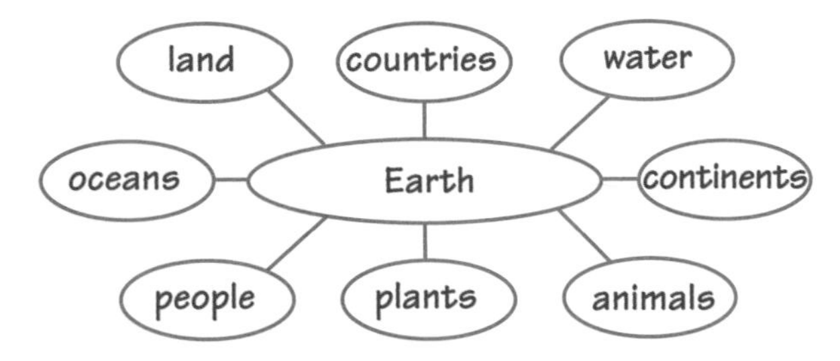

Previewing Read aloud the title of the song. Point out that the globe in the illustration shows that all living things are like a family because they share the planet. Help children recognize that Earth turns around the sun, which sheds light everywhere at different times.

CITIZENSHIP

Sharing with Others Invite children to share their musical talents with others.

- When children are familiar with the song "One Light, One Sun" arrange to have them sing it to a special audience, such as a senior citizen group, a preschool class, or another kindergarten class.
- Practice the song as a group before it is presented to the audience.
- If you wish, work with children to create a mural that depicts the beauties of our Earth. The mural can be displayed as a backdrop for your musical presentation.

READ

USING BIG BOOK PAGES 16–17

Present the song by reading it aloud or singing it. Then invite children to sing the song with you as they follow the words in the Big Book.

SHARE

Use questions such as the following to spark a discussion of the song:

- ***What things do we share with other people of the world?*** *(Possible answers include water, air, and land.)*
- ***Why is it important to take care of Earth?*** *(Possible answer: Just as our family members need care to stay healthy, so do the land, air, water, plants, and animals around us.)*
- ***How can people all over the world share one love?*** *(Possible answers: Be kind to each other, share what you have with others, take care of Earth, give someone you love a hug.)*
- ***What can our class do to share our love with others in the world?*** *(Possible answers: Send a group letter to someone who is sick, make a happy card or picture for a child in another country, help clean up the neighborhood, plant a tree.)*

EXTENDING THE LITERATURE WITH ART

LEARNING STYLE: VISUAL

Make a Flag

ON YOUR OWN

15 TO 30 MINUTES

Objective: To create a flag showing different people, places, and animals from around the world.

Resource: *Project Book* p. 49

Materials: crayons, scissors

- Display the flag of the United States. Remind children that each star on the United States flag stands for a state.
- Using ***Project Book*** p. 49, have children color the large blank flag to design a flag showing different people, places, and animals that all share Earth. Children can cut out the flags and post them on a classroom wall.

Project Book
p. 49

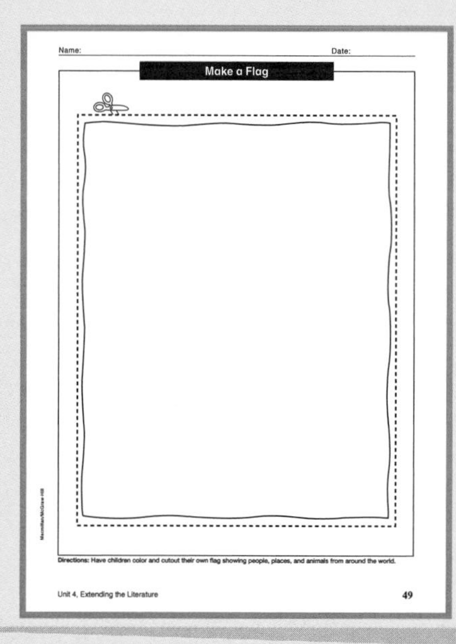
Name: Date:

Make a Flag

Directions: Have children color and cutout their own flag showing people, places, and animals from around the world.

Unit 4, Extending the Literature 49

UNIT 4 ASSESSMENT

Assessment Opportunities

The CLOSE section of each lesson includes an EVALUATE activity. This page provides suggestions for using selected EVALUATE activities to integrate your assessment program with each day's lesson plan. The next page lists the main objectives of the unit and some of the activities that reinforce them. You may wish to make a copy of the checklist for each child.

EVALUATE Signs of Success

LESSON 2, This is Our Flag

EVALUATE: Make Flag-Flying Pictures, p. 133

OBSERVATIONAL ASSESSMENT

- Ask questions such as, "Where was the flag placed?" Children should be able to describe the location of the flag. Record children's answers.

PORTFOLIO ASSSESSMENT

The flag-flying pictures can be part of children's portfolios.

- Children's illustrations should show accurately two places where one could find the American flag.
- Children's drawings should show places in your community.

STUDY SKILLS, Putting Things in Order

EVALUATE: Recite a Simple Task, p. 137

OBSERVATIONAL ASSESSMENT

- Children should be able to tell the class how they performed a task at home or at school.
- Using a tape recorder, record tasks which children tell the class.

PORTFOLIO ASSESSMENT

The tapes can be part of children's portfolios.

- Children should be able to describe their task in order using *first, next,* and *last.*

LESSON 3, Looking at Land and Water

EVALUATE: Draw Earth and a Globe, p. 141

OBSERVATIONAL ASSESSMENT

- Ask questions such as "What is a globe?" as children draw their pictures.

PORTFOLIO ASSESSMENT

The pictures can be part of children's portfolios.

- Children should draw both Earth and a globe.

UNIT 4 OBJECTIVES Checklist

1. Identify the United States of America.
2. Recognize one's state.
3. Recognize the American flag.
4. Identify the order of things.
5. Distinguish between land and water.
6. Recognize what a globe is.
7. Recognize that the world is made up of continents and oceans.
8. Recognize some of the people, plants, and animals that live on Earth.
9. Recognize one's responsibility of caring for Earth and the things that live on it.

Name ______________________ Class ______________________

LESSON	ACTIVITY	PAGE	UNIT 4 OBJECTIVES	✓
LESSON 1	Make a Map of the United States	127	1	
LESSON 1	Make a State Symbol	130	2	
LESSON 1	Make a State Map	130	2	
LESSON 2	Make Flag and Star Stickers	131	3	
LESSON 2	Parade to Songs About Our Flag	134	3	
THINKING SKILL	Connect the Dots	135	3, 4	
THINKING SKILL	Make "Ants on a Log"	138	4	
THINKING SKILL	Make a Class Schedule	138	4	
LESSON 3	Make a Land-and-Water Chart	139	5	
LESSON 3	Sail Around the World	142	5, 6	
LESSON 3	Make Clay Models of Land and Water	142	5	
AROUND THE WORLD	Make a Map of Earth	143	5	
AROUND THE WORLD	Display Animals of the World	146	7, 8	
AROUND THE WORLD	Play "Cat and Lynx"	146	8	
LESSON 4	Make a Paper Keeper	147	9	
LESSON 4	Perform a Clean Water Test	150	9	
LESSON 4	Make Bird Houses or Feeders	150	9	

Hooray For Special Days!

PLANNING GUIDE

Pupil Edition and Unit 5 Theme Big Book
Pages 156–199

INTRODUCTION

SUGGESTED PACING: 3 DAYS

Begin With The Literature Big Book, pages 159, 214–215

Using The Unit Opener

pp. 160–162

PROJECT IDEAS
- Make a Holiday Quilt/ ART
- Holidays Book / LANGUAGE ARTS/ART
- Enriching with Multimedia
- Make Parade Pom-Poms/ ART

LESSON 1

SUGGESTED PACING: 1–2 DAYS

Columbus Day pp. 163–166

KEY CONCEPTS
Christopher Columbus, Columbus Day, holiday

PROJECT IDEAS
- Make a Three-Ship Collage / ART
- Make Soap Ships / ART
- Make Taino Pottery / ART

RESOURCES
Project Book, p. 55 • Big Book Stickers Sheet 17 • Anthology, p. 88 • Inflatable Globe

LESSON 2

SUGGESTED PACING: 1–2 DAYS

A Day Of Thanks pp. 167–170

KEY CONCEPTS
Pilgrims, Wampanoag, feast, Thanksgiving Day

PROJECT IDEAS
- Write a Thank-You Note / LANGUAGE ARTS
- Make a Turkey Cup / ART
- Make Thanksgiving-Day Placemats / ART

RESOURCES
Project Book, p. 56 • Big Book Stickers Sheet 17 • Anthology, pp. 91–93 • Inflatable Globe • TECHNOLOGY Videodisc/Video Tape 3

LESSON 3

SUGGESTED PACING: 1–2 DAYS

Martin Luther King, Jr., Day pp. 175–178

KEY CONCEPTS
Martin Luther King, Jr., freedom, Martin Luther King, Jr., Day, peace

PROJECT IDEAS
- Make Memory Medals / ART
- Make Peace Doves / ART
- Make a Friendship Wreath / ART

RESOURCES
Project Book, p. 59 • Big Book Stickers Sheet 17 • Anthology, pp. 118–122

LESSON 4

SUGGESTED PACING: 1–2 DAYS

Presidents' Day pp. 179–182

KEY CONCEPTS
George Washington, Abraham Lincoln, President, Presidents' Day

PROJECT IDEAS
- Make "Special American" Cards / LANGUAGE ARTS/ART
- Make a Tricorn Hat / ART/MUSIC
- Make a Stovepipe Hat / ART

RESOURCES
Project Book, p. 60 • Big Book Stickers Sheet 17 • Anthology, pp. 102–110 • • Anthology, pp. 117

THINKING SKILLS

SUGGESTED PACING: 1–2 DAYS

Making Predictions

pp. 183–186

KEY CONCEPT
prediction

PROJECT IDEAS
- Make a Book / MATHEMATICS/ART
- Predict the Ending of a Story / ART/LANGUAGE ARTS
- Make a Prediction About Balls / PHYSICAL EDUCATION/ART

RESOURCES
Project Book, p. 61 • Big Book Stickers Sheet 18

LESSON 5

SUGGESTED PACING: 1–2 DAYS

Happy Birthday, U.S.A.!

pp. 191–194

KEY CONCEPTS
Fourth of July
Independence Day

PROJECT IDEAS
- Make Lemonade / ART
- Make a Fourth-of-July Sash / ART
- Paint Firework Designs / ART

RESOURCES
Project Book, p. 63 • Big Book Stickers Sheet 19 • Desk Map • Inflatable Globe • TECHNOLOGY Videodisc/Video Tape 3

CLOSE WITH A SONG

SUGGESTED PACING: 1 DAY

Over The River And Through The Wood

pp. 195–197

PROJECT IDEAS
- Make a Song Scene / ART

RESOURCES
Project Book, p. 64
• Anthology

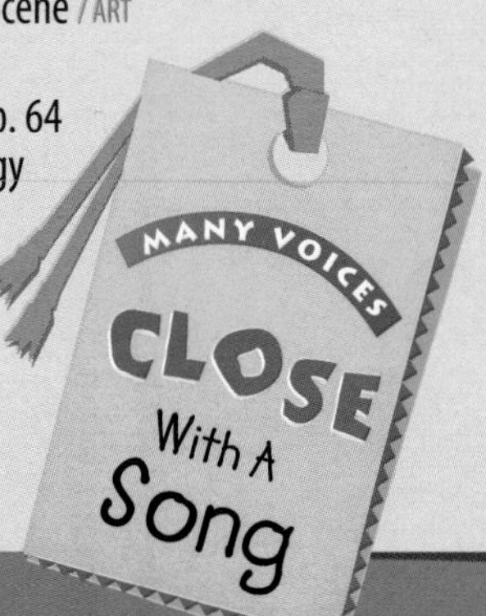

UNIT ASSESSMENT

SUGGESTED PACING: 1 DAY

pp. 198–199

OBSERVATIONAL/PORTFOLIO ASSESSMENT, p. 198
- Perform Columbus-Day Skits
- Make Giving-Thanks Pictures
- Identify Birthdays

OBJECTIVES CHECKLIST, p. 199

McGRAW-HILL SCHOOL DIVISION'S HOME PAGE at http://www.mhschool.com contains on-line student activities related to this unit.

STUDY SKILLS

SUGGESTED PACING: 1–2 DAYS

Looking At Calendars

pp. 171–174

KEY CONCEPT
calendar

PROJECT IDEAS
Sequence Calendar Cutouts / MATHEMATICS
Learning Center: Make Weather Calendars / SCIENCE
Make a Calendar Birthday Train / MATHEMATICS

RESOURCES
Project Book, pp. 57–58 • Big Book Stickers Sheets 17, 18 • Floor Map • Word Cards

AROUND THE WORLD

SUGGESTED PACING: 1–2 DAYS

Birthdays Near and Far

pp. 187–190

KEY CONCEPT
birthday

PROJECT IDEAS
Make Balloon Badges / ART
Play a Party Game / PHYSICAL EDUCATION
Make Birthday Piñatas / ART

RESOURCES
Project Book, p. 62 • Big Book Stickers Sheet 19 • Anthology, pp. 126–127 • Inflatable Globe

SHELTERED INSTRUCTION

Reading Strategies & Language Development

Bridging, p. 160

Second-Language Support

Using Dialog, p. 168
Making Connections, p. 173
Using Props, p. 188

Meeting Individual Needs

McGraw-Hill Adventure Books

Assessment Opportunities

Ongoing Unit Project: Make a Holiday Quilt, p. 161
Observational and Portfolio Assessment, p. 198
Objectives Checklist, p. 199
Evaluate, pp. 165, 169, 173, 177, 181, 185, 189, 193

FOR FURTHER SUPPORT
- Language Support Handbook
- Social Studies Readiness

UNIT 5 ORGANIZER

Unit 5 Bibliography and Resources

MCGRAW-HILL ADVENTURE BOOKS Easy-to-Read Books

Miranda, Anne. ***A Party.*** A table, a chair, a cup, and a toy kitten and bear are part of a girl's tea party.

Nayer, Judy, ***Happy Birthday, America!.*** Past and present ways of celebrating the Fourth of July, our country's birthday, are compared.

CLASSROOM LIBRARY

Brown, Janet Mitsui. ***Thanksgiving at Obaachan's.*** Chicago: Polychrome Publishing Corp., 1994. A Japanese American girl describes Thanksgiving at her grandmother's house.

READ ALOUD BOOKS

Ballard, Robin. ***Carnival!*** New York: Greenwillow Books, 1995. This presentation of a carnival is lively, colorful, and celebratory.

Brenner, Martha. ***Abe Lincoln's Hat.*** New York: Random House, 1994. A story about Abraham Lincoln that will amuse young children while they learn some facts about our sixteenth President.

Chocolate, Debbie. ***Kente Colors.*** New York: Walker & Company, 1996. A colorful description of the significance of the Kente cloth costumes of Ghana.

Chocolate, Debbie. ***My First Kwanzaa Book.*** New York: Scholastic Inc., 1992. A young boy celebrates the holiday of Kwanzaa with his family and learns about his heritage.

Dragonwagon, Crescent. ***Alligators and Others All Year Long.*** New York: Macmillan Publishing Company, 1993. A group of animals celebrate each month of the year in lively poetry.

Feldman, Eve B. ***Birthdays! Celebrating Life Around the World.*** Mahwah, NJ: Bridgewater Books, 1996. Children from around the world describe how they celebrate their birthdays.

Marzollo, Jean. ***In 1492.*** New York: Scholastic Inc., 1991. This description of Columbus's first voyage is told in rhyme and attractively illustrated.

Mora, Pat. ***A Birthday Basket for Tía.*** New York: Macmillan Publishing Company, 1992. A young girl is eager to plan a special surprise party for her aunt's ninetieth birthday.

Schlank, Carol Hilgartner, and Barbara Metzger. ***Martin Luther King, Jr.: A Biography for Young Children.*** Mt. Rainier, MD: Gryphon House, 1990. A biography of Dr. Martin Luther King, Jr., written especially for the primary-grade child.

Yolen, Jane. ***The Three Bears Holiday Rhyme Book.*** San Diego, CA: Harcourt Brace & Company, 1995. Holidays, as celebrated by three bears, are described in rhyme with appealing, colorful illustrations.

TEACHER BOOKS

Marzollo, Jean. ***My First Book of Biographies.*** New York: Scholastic Inc., 1994. The stories of famous people from different times in history are collected and presented in brief and simple style.

Warren, Jean, and Elizabeth McKinnon. ***Small World Celebrations: Around the World Holidays to Celebrate with Young Children.*** Everett, WA: Warren Publishing House, Inc., 1988. Children can learn about various cultures through a variety of songs, poems, and art activities.

TECHNOLOGY MULTIMEDIA

Holiday Songs Around the World. Video. Children can learn about songs from the United States and other countries around the globe. Educational Activities. (800) 645-3739.

People Behind the Holidays. CD-ROM. Children can explore the lives of the famous people we pay tribute to on certain holidays. National Geographic. (800) 368-2728.

FREE OR INEXPENSIVE MATERIALS

For an introductory guide to Arbor Day with activities and program ideas, write to: International Society of Arboriculture, Robin Kopp, P.O. Box GG, Savoy, IL 61874.

National Geographic selection

BEGIN WITH THE LITERATURE BIG BOOK

LINKING SOCIAL STUDIES AND LITERATURE

Introduce Unit 5 with the **Literature Big Book, *Light the Candle! Bang the Drum!*** The story supports these Social Studies concepts:

- People celebrate different holidays all over the world to remember important people and events.
- Traditional food, music, activities, and symbols make holidays special.

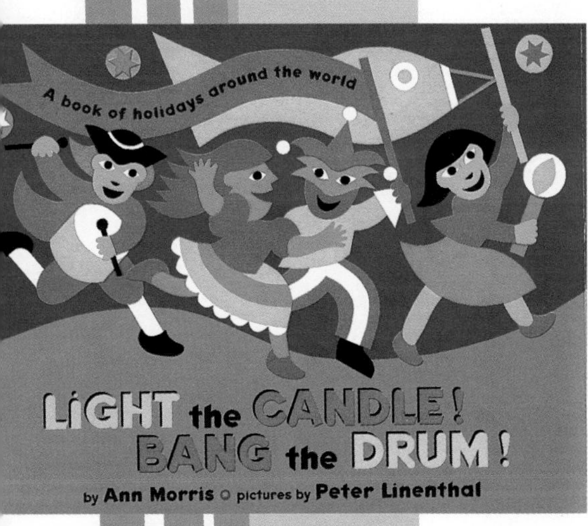

Literature Big Book

A full instructional plan, along with the complete text of the story, appears on pages 214–215.

ABOUT THE STORY

Simple descriptions and brilliant cut-paper illustrations introduce children to 24 holidays around the world. Children will recognize Easter bunnies and Thanksgiving turkeys, but may be meeting St. Lucia's crown of seven candles and the bright powder paintings of *Diwali* for the first time.

This book will help children learn the universality of holiday moods—joy, reverence, fun—and the singularity of each culture's festivities. Background information on each holiday is given at the end of the book.

ABOUT THE AUTHOR

Ann Morris has written many books for children with an emphasis on multicultural activities and arts. She lives in New York City.

ABOUT THE ILLUSTRATOR

Peter Linenthal has taught art in elementary schools for twenty years; he is also a painter and sculptor. Mr. Linenthal lives in San Francisco, California.

USING THE
Unit 5 Opener

USING BIG BOOK PAGES 2–3

Read aloud the unit title and ask children what a special day is. Explain that *hooray* is a cheer people shout when they are happy or excited. Introduce Matt and Lily. Tell children they will be seeing Lily again in other pages. Children may preview the unit while looking for Lily in the lessons.

DEVELOPING KEY CONCEPTS

Children learn these concepts in addition to individual holidays. Read the words aloud and ask volunteers to define them. Have children name holidays they know.

holiday *A special day when we remember important people and events that happened in the past.*

birthday *A special day that honors the day a person was born.*

USE BIG BOOK STICKERS, SHEET 17

Read the ***Sticker*** labels aloud. Discuss the holiday quilt, affix the labels near the appropriate patches.

holiday birthday

Sheltered Instruction

Finding children's personal links to the unit concepts will help them understand the new material. Brainstorm with children to create a web reflecting their experience of special occasions. Also identify literature that focuses on the concepts of holidays and birthdays.
[SDAIE STRATEGY: BRIDGING]

UNIT 5 THEME BIG BOOK

BULLETIN BOARD

Holiday Calendar

Turn your bulletin board into a holiday calendar.

- Cover the bulletin board with twelve large squares. Label one for each month of the year. Cut out simple shapes and pictures representing different holidays. Put all of the cutouts in a bag.
- Ask children to name different holidays. As they do, give them the item representing that holiday.
- Have children glue or tape each item to the appropriate month. Use the activity as an opportunity to discuss different holidays.

ABOUT THE PHOTOGRAPH

Point out that Lily is holding a holiday quilt. Her class worked together to create the paper patches. Then they stitched the patches together. Explain that real quilts are made of layers of cloth that are sewn together. As you point to each patch, have children name the picture symbol they see. Have them share which patch reminds them of a special day and why. On this holiday quilt, the cake stands for birthdays; the Earth stands for Earth Day; the stovepipe hat stands for Lincoln's Birthday or Presidents' Day; the trees stand for Earth Day or Arbor Day; the dove stands for Martin Luther King, Jr., Day; the heart stands for Valentine's Day; the three ships stand for Columbus Day; the shamrock stands for St. Patrick's Day; the bowl of fruit is for Kwanzaa; and the turkey stands for Thanksgiving Day.

Directions for this Ongoing Unit Project can be found at the bottom of this page.

SCHOOL-TO-HOME

Our Special Days

- In this unit, children will be learning about many of the major holidays celebrated in our country. Point out that families celebrate their own special days as well. For each child, bind together twelve blank calendar forms from ***Project Book*** p. 57.
- Suggest that children work with their families to record the names of the months and the days of each month on the calendars.
- Ask families to display the calendar and to add their own special days to it—such as anniversaries, birthdays, and other family events.

ONGOING UNIT PROJECT

Make a Holiday Quilt

CURRICULUM CONNECTION **Art**

During this unit, children can make patches for a holiday quilt. Patches can be made for the six special days in this unit as well as the eleven holidays featured in the **Holiday Section** beginning on p. 217. Add any other holidays your class celebrates.

Advance Preparation: Make patches for the quilt by cutting 8 1/2" x 8 1/2" squares from construction paper of various colors. Punch six holes at even increments along the top and bottom of each patch and four more holes along the sides.

1. After each lesson or holiday, invite children to design picture symbols to represent the holiday. Children may wish to use the symbols for Valentine's Day; Martin Luther King, Jr., Day; Thanksgiving Day; Earth Day; and Presidents' Day found on ***Project Book*** pp. 50–54. Children can color and cut out the symbols or use them as templates.
2. Have children cut out their symbols from construction paper and glue them on patches.
3. Have children take turns sewing the patches together using thick yarn and a child's needle.

Assessment Suggestions

Signs of Success

- Children should be able to describe their symbols and tell how they relate to the holiday.
- Children should be able to identify the majority of symbols for the various holidays on the completed holiday quilt.

TECHNOLOGY CENTER

Enriching with Multimedia

RESOURCE: *National Geographic* Wonders of Learning

- Enrich Unit 5 with the Wonders of Learning CD-ROM *People Behind the Holidays.*

RESOURCE: *Videodisc/Video Tape 3*

- Enrich Unit 5 with the video segment *Celebrate and Remember.*

Search Frame 50671, Play to 53200

LANGUAGE ARTS AND ART LEARNING CENTER

LEARNING STYLE: VISUAL

Holidays Book

ON YOUR OWN

30 MINUTES OR LONGER

Materials: chart paper, marker, construction paper, drawing paper, crayons, hole puncher, yarn

1. Begin a discussion about holidays children are familiar with and enjoy celebrating. Tell children that they will be making a Holidays book.
2. Post a list of the holidays and other information in the Language Arts Learning Center.
3. Have children visit the Art Learning Center and create drawings about their favorite holidays. Help children to write labels for their drawings. Have children make book covers.
4. Help children punch holes in the left edges of their drawings and fasten the pages with yarn. Then display the books in the Language Arts Learning Center.

TEACHER EXCHANGE

Thanks to: Helen Horton, Rosecrans School, Compton, California

Make Parade Pom-Poms

ON YOUR OWN

15 TO 30 MINUTES

Materials: red, white, and blue construction paper; paper-towel tubes; glue; scissors, sparkles

1. Help each child cut strips of red, blue, and white construction paper.
2. Then have children glue these strips onto a paper towel tube to make a pom-pom.
3. Children can use these pom-poms in their patriotic class celebrations and Fourth of July parades.

UNIT 5

LESSON

1

Columbus Day

UNIT 5 THEME BIG BOOK, PAGES 4–5

RESOURCE REMINDER

Project Book *p. 55*

Stickers Package *Sheet 17*

Anthology *Columbus, p. 88*

Inflatable Globe

LESSON OVERVIEW

Columbus Day recognizes the explorer Christopher Columbus, who reached the Americas while searching for an all-water route to Asia.

LESSON OBJECTIVES

- Recogize that on Columbus Day people remember Christopher Columbus and his voyage to the Americas.
- Define *holiday* as "a special day."
- Identify the Taino as Native Americans who were living in the place where Columbus landed.
- Recognize that the arrival of Columbus in the Americas changed the way of life for many people.

KEY CONCEPTS

Christopher Columbus Columbus Day holiday

GETTING READY

Make a Three-Ship Collage

ON YOUR OWN

30 MINUTES OR LONGER

CURRICULUM CONNECTION **Art**

Objective: To become familiar with Columbus Day.

Resource: *Project Book* p. 55

Materials: construction paper (dark blue, light blue, brown, yellow, white), glue, scissors

1. Ask children what kind of transportation is shown on *Project Book* p. 55 and where ships are found. Children might name parts of the ships such as sails, masts, flags, hulls, crow's nests, and the rigging.
2. Have children color the fish and ships. You might suggest that they color the hulls brown and the crosses on the flags red, keeping the sails white.
3. Have children construct the sea by cutting waves from the dark-blue paper. Have them cut out a yellow sun, white clouds, and a small piece of brown paper for land.
4. Direct children to glue the sea at the bottom of the sheet of light-blue paper and to glue the land in the left corner over the sea. Then have them glue the ships, fish, sun, and clouds where they belong.
5. Children can refer to their collages as the Read Aloud poem on p. 164 is explored. At that time, identify Columbus on the largest ship, the *Santa María*.

Project Book p. 55

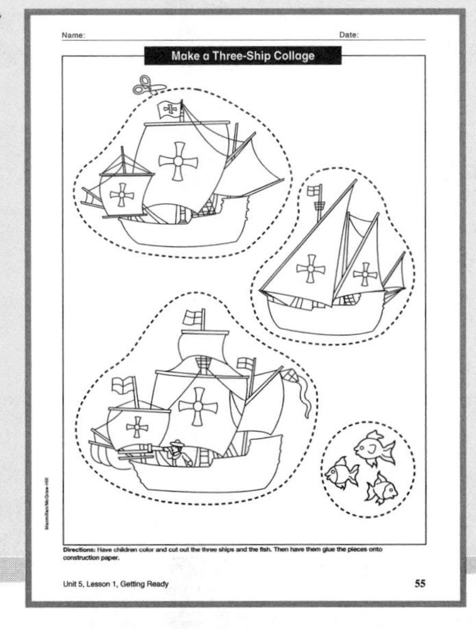

Name: Date:

Make a Three-Ship Collage

Directions: Have children color and cut out the three ships and the fish. Then have them glue the pieces onto construction paper.

Unit 5, Lesson 1, Getting Ready 55

1 Prepare

WARMING UP WITH THE READ ALOUD

Share the poem in the Read Aloud. Identify Columbus as Christopher Columbus and his three ships as the *Niña,* the *Pinta,* and the *Santa María.* On the ***Inflatable Globe***, trace Columbus's route from Spain to the Bahamas. Tell children that Columbus and his sailors made this voyage long ago. Point out that the voyage took more than two months at sea. Explain that it took courage to explore areas unknown to these sailors.

- ***How many ships did Columbus have?*** *(three)*

★**THINKING FURTHER:** ***Making Conclusions*** ***Why do you think Columbus sailed night and day through all kinds of weather?*** *(Possible answers: He may have worried that the food and water would run out; there was no place to stop the ships.)*

2 Teach

USING BIG BOOK PAGES 4–5

Read the lesson title. Explain that Columbus Day is a holiday.

USE BIG BOOK STICKERS, SHEET 17

Use these ***Stickers*** throughout the lesson.

holiday 

LESSON

Columbus Day

The Granger Collection

4

Read Aloud

from *In 1492*

In fourteen hundred ninety-two
Columbus sailed the ocean blue.
He had three ships and left from Spain;
He sailed through sunshine, wind and rain.
He sailed by night; he sailed by day;
He used the stars to find his way.
A compass also helped him know
How to find the way to go.

Jean Marzollo

Using the Anthology

Columbus, page 88 Read the words to this song and have children chime in on the last two verses. Mention that sailors often used the stars to help them stay on course at night. Write the year of the voyage on the chalkboard. Explain that the word *lad* refers to young boys.

Curriculum Connection

Science Prior to Columbus Day, have children study how the wind can move things like leaves, a balloon, your school flag, or bubbles. Make note of changes in wind direction over several days. On a very windy day, have pairs of children take turns holding a sheet like a sail to feel the strength of the wind and to find that it can physically move them. Explain that wind power helped to bring Columbus's ships to the Americas.

Who do we remember on Columbus Day?

Place the ***Sticker*** *holiday* near the words *Columbus Day* and define *holiday* as "a special day." Explain that some holidays remember important people or things from our country's past. Tell children that on Columbus Day, we remember Christopher Columbus and his voyage to the Americas. Explain that the word *Americas* has an *s* on the end because Columbus explored places belonging to two different American continents; South America and North America.

Point to the picture of Columbus landing in the Americas. Place the ***Sticker*** of Columbus near Columbus. Identify his sailors and the Taino. Explain that the Taino were Native Americans living in the place where Columbus landed. Explain that after Columbus returned to Spain and told others what he had seen, more people came to the Americas.

Point to the other photo and explain that some people remember Columbus on Columbus Day with parades. Explain that Lily and her friends have made soap ships of the *Niña,* the *Pinta,* and the *Santa María.* See p. 166 if you wish to make these ships with your class. Tell children that Columbus Day falls on the second Monday in October. Although many people remember Columbus for his voyage, others do not celebrate Columbus Day because most Native Americans were mistreated after Columbus arrived in the Americas.

- ***How are Lily and her friend remembering Columbus on Columbus Day?*** *(They made soap ships and are sailing them.)*
- ***What do their soap ships stand for?*** *(Columbus's ships—the* Niña, *the* Pinta, *and the* Santa María*)*

3 Close

LESSON SUMMARY

Read the lesson question, pointing to each word as you read. Children may say that we remember Christopher Columbus and the Taino on Columbus Day.

EVALUATE

Perform Columbus-Day Skits Have children dramatize the meeting of Columbus and his sailors with the Taino. Encourage them to think about what the Taino might have thought about strangers coming to their home and what the sailors might have thought about being in an unfamiliar place. Afterwards, ask children how their lives would have been different if they lived with the Taino during Columbus's time. For assessment suggestions, see p. 198.

Background Information

About Christopher Columbus's Voyage You may wish to supply children with additional information about the topic.

- Christopher Columbus was born in Italy, in 1451.
- In 1492 Columbus convinced King Ferdinand and Queen Isabella of Spain to finance his expedition to find an all-water route westward that would bring him to China and India, where he could trade for gold, silk, tea, and spices.
- When Columbus reached the Americas on October 12, 1492, he thought he had arrived in the East Indies. Therefore, he named the Taino "Indians."
- Columbus made three additional voyages to the Americas. He died in 1506, unaware of the continent he had reached.
- Columbus's voyage changed life on many continents. For example, the potato was brought from South America to Europe, the horse was brought from Europe to North America, and diseases were carried to the Americas, which killed many Native Americans. Europeans conquered the Americas and introduced their way of life.

ART CONNECTION

LEARNING STYLE: KINESTHETIC

Make Soap Ships

Objective: To become familiar with Columbus's voyage by sailing ships in a tub of water.

Materials: floatable soap (one bar per child), wooden skewers or pencils, pencil sharpener or art knife, white construction paper, scissors, glue, crayons, toothpicks, tub of water

Advance Preparation: Have children bring from home a new bar of floatable soap. (It can be returned later for reuse). Sharpen skewers or pencils with an art knife or pencil sharpener.

1. Have children cut two "sails" from large squares of white construction paper. Have children draw a cross as used by Columbus on his ships (as shown). The pencils or skewers will serve as "masts." Caution children to be careful with the sharpened skewers and pencils. Children should then glue the sails, wrong sides together, to the masts.
2. Have children make two smaller, rectangular sails out of red construction paper to add above the large sails. Help children to carefully push the point of the mast into the soap.
3. Children can add to their ships with small cutouts of Columbus and sailors glued to toothpicks. Invite children to launch their ships in a tub of water.

ART CONNECTION

LEARNING STYLE: KINESTHETIC

Make Taino Pottery

Objective: To learn that the Taino used pottery for carrying water or for cooking.

Materials: plastic quart bottles (well-rinsed bleach bottles, for example), scissors, strips of newspaper, water-diluted glue, poster paint (tan, brown, or red), paint brushes.

Advance Preparation: Cut the quart bottles one-third of the way from the bottom. Soak newspaper strips in diluted glue.

1. Explain to children that the actual pottery used by the Taino was made from clay. Show children how to cover the bottles with strips of glue-soaked newspaper strips. Make sure the newspaper strips overlap and cover the interior of the opening.
2. Allow the bottles covered with newspaper strips to dry.
3. Have children paint their "pottery" with tan, brown, or red poster paint.

UNIT 5

LESSON 2

A Day of Thanks

UNIT 5 THEME BIG BOOK, PAGES 6–7

LESSON OVERVIEW

Thanksgiving Day is a holiday on which Americans give thanks for what we have, as well as remember the feast shared by the Pilgrims and the Wampanoag.

LESSON OBJECTIVES

- Identify Thanksgiving Day as a holiday on which Americans give thanks.
- Identify the Wampanoag who helped the Pilgrims and shared the feast of Thanksgiving with them.
- Compare Thanksgiving long ago with present-day celebrations.

KEY CONCEPTS

Pilgrims | Wampanoag
feast | Thanksgiving Day

RESOURCE REMINDER

Project Book
p. 56

Stickers Package
Sheet 17

Anthology
. . . If You Sailed on the Mayflower*,*
pp. 91–93

Inflatable Globe

Technology Connection
VIDEODISC/VIDEO TAPE 3

Search Frame 42326, Play to 50627

GETTING READY

Write a Thank-You Note

ON YOUR OWN

15 TO 30 MINUTES

CURRICULUM CONNECTION Language Arts

Objective: To be introduced to Thanksgiving Day.

Resource: ***Project Book*** p. 56

Materials: crayons, pencils, scissors

1. Ask children what they say when someone helps them. Then have volunteers name other reasons for saying "thank you."
2. Tell children that ***Project Book*** p. 56 shows a thank-you note.
3. Suggest to children they think of someone to whom they can give the thank-you note. Have children draw a picture for the person they are thanking. Have each child sign the note by writing his or her name on the space provided.
4. Invite children to color in the letters on the page and to give their notes to the person they wish to thank.

Project Book p. 56

WARMING UP WITH THE READ ALOUD

Tell children that they will be learning about a holiday on which we give thanks and the reasons that we celebrate it. Read the poem in the Read Aloud to begin discussion.

- ***What is the poet thankful for?*** *(noses)*
- ***What kinds of foods and spice are mentioned in the poem?*** *(apple pie, turkey, cranberry, onion, cinnamon)*

USING BIG BOOK PAGES 6–7

Read the lesson title.

USE BIG BOOK STICKERS, SHEET 17

Use these ***Stickers*** throughout the lesson.

Place the ***Stickers*** of the Pilgrims and the Wampanoag on the picture of the painting. Explain that long ago the Pilgrims came to America on a ship called the *Mayflower.* On the ***Inflatable Globe*** show their route from England to North America. Explain that the Wampanoag lived in the place where the Pilgrims landed. Explain that other Native American groups lived in other parts of North America.

A Day of Thanks

6

Read Aloud

A Thanksgiving Thought

The day I give thanks for having a nose
Is Thanksgiving Day, for do you suppose
That Thanksgiving dinner would taste as good
If you couldn't smell it? I don't think it would.
Could apple pies baking—turkey that's basting
Not be for smelling? Just be for tasting?
It's a cranberry-cinnamon-onion bouquet!
Be thankful for noses on Thanksgiving Day.

Bobbi Katz

Using the Anthology

. . . If You Sailed on the *Mayflower*, pages 91–93 This excerpted selection will provide you and your class with some interesting facts regarding the Pilgrims, the *Mayflower,* schooling, clothing, Plymouth, Squanto, children's jobs, and how the Pilgrims felt when they saw the shore of America and why they settled where they did.

Second-Language Support/Using Dialog Invite children to describe a thanksgiving festival from their country of origin and answer questions other children may have about it.

How do we give thanks on Thanksgiving Day?

7

Tell children that life for the Pilgrims was hard. There was not enough food and many Pilgrims became sick or died. The Wampanoag helped the Pilgrims to survive by teaching them how to hunt, fish, and plant. Explain that the first Thanksgiving was a large meal called a feast held by the Pilgrims to give thanks to God for all they had. The picture on p. 168 was painted by the 20th century American artist, Jerome Brownscombe.

Point to the photograph. Tell children that many Americans today celebrate a day of thanks similar to the one shared by the Pilgrims and the Wampanoag. Place the ***Sticker*** of Thanksgiving Day on the photograph. Explain that on this holiday, friends and family gather for a meal and give thanks. Point to the turkey cups Lily made. If you wish to make these with your students, see p. 170. Tell children that some people also attend religious services, and watch parades or football games. Thanksgiving is celebrated on the fourth Thursday in November.

- ***For what were the Pilgrims thankful?*** *(Possible answers include food, new homes, and friends.)*

★**THINKING FURTHER: *Compare and Contrast* *How is Lily's Thanksgiving celebration like the one shared by the Pilgrims and the Wampanoag?*** *(In both, families and friends are gathered together and they are sharing a feast.)*

Technology Connection

VIDEODISC/VIDEO TAPE 3
Enrich Lesson 2 with the video segment on *Plymouth*, Search Frame 42326.

See the bar code on p. 167.

Background Information

About the Pilgrims and their Voyage You may wish to supply children with the following information.

- The Pilgrims left England because they wanted religious freedom. Aboard the *Mayflower* were 102 passengers, 34 of these were children, and a crew of about 26 men.
- The Pilgrims began their voyage on September 6, 1620. They were to join the settlers in Jamestown, Virginia. Storms blew the *Mayflower* off course, and they reached the coast of what is now Cape Cod, Massachusetts, on November 11.
- Half of the Pilgrims died from illness the first winter.
- The three-day celebration of thanks included feasting, games, and prayer. Fifty Pilgrims and about ninety Wampanoag attended. Turkey, corn bread, boiled carrots, turnips, and pumpkins were among the foods served.

3 Close

LESSON SUMMARY

Read the lesson question to children, pointing to each word as you read. Children should explain how people give thanks on Thanksgiving Day.

EVALUATE

Make Giving-Thanks Pictures On one-half of a sheet of paper have children draw something for which the Pilgrims were thankful. On the other half, have them draw something for which they are thankful. Help children label the pictures *Pilgrims* and *Me* and the overall picture, *Giving Thanks.* Ask children how the two halves are alike and different. For assessment suggestions, see p. 198.

ART CONNECTION

LEARNING STYLE: KINESTHETIC

Make a Turkey Cup

Objective: To observe Thanksgiving by making a turkey cup.

Materials: oaktag, pencils, scissors, sheets of autumn-colored construction paper (brown, red, orange, yellow, purple, and green), glue, small party-favor cups (one per child), red and yellow crayons, googley eyes.

Advance Preparation: Use oaktag to make several turkey-head templates (as shown). Also use oaktag to make feather templates (one per child).

1. Have children place the turkey-head templates onto brown construction paper and trace the shape with a pencil. Help children to cut out the turkey head, and use a red crayon to color the wattle and a yellow crayon to color the beak. Then have children glue the turkey head onto the party-favor cup.
2. Have children use their turkey-feather template to trace seven feathers onto construction paper. (Suggest using different colors.) Five feathers will serve as tail feathers and two will be used for wings.
3. Show children how to glue the five tail feathers in a fan-like design on the party-favor cup. Then have them glue two feathers on the sides for wings.
4. Have children draw eyes or glue googley eyes onto each side of the turkey head.

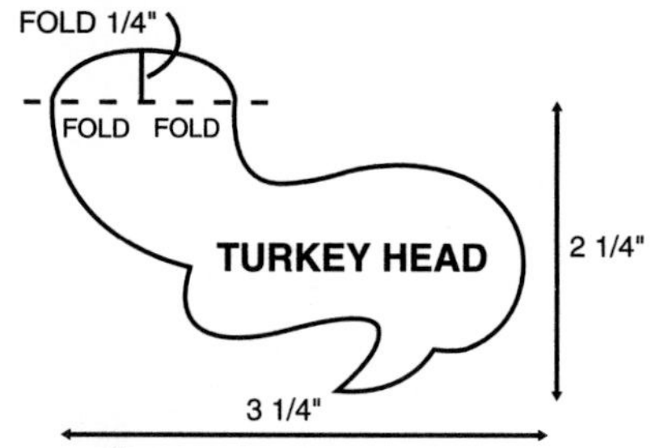

ART CONNECTION

LEARNING STYLE: KINESTHETIC

Make Thanksgiving-Day Placemats

Objective: To create placemats to be used at Thanksgiving-Day celebrations.

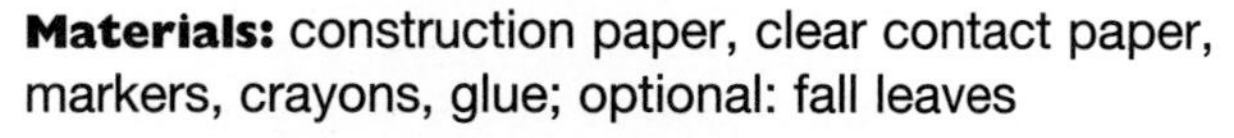

Materials: construction paper, clear contact paper, markers, crayons, glue; optional: fall leaves

1. Have children either collect leaves from outside or draw leaves on colored construction paper and cut them out.
2. Children can arrange their leaves on a piece of construction paper and then glue them down.
3. Help children place a clear piece of contact paper over the leaves and construction paper to create a placemat.

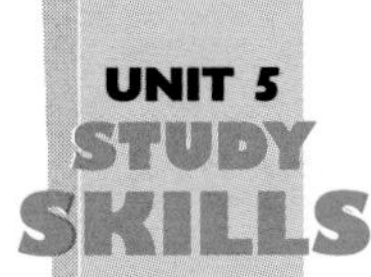

Looking at Calendars

UNIT 5 THEME BIG BOOK, PAGES 8–9

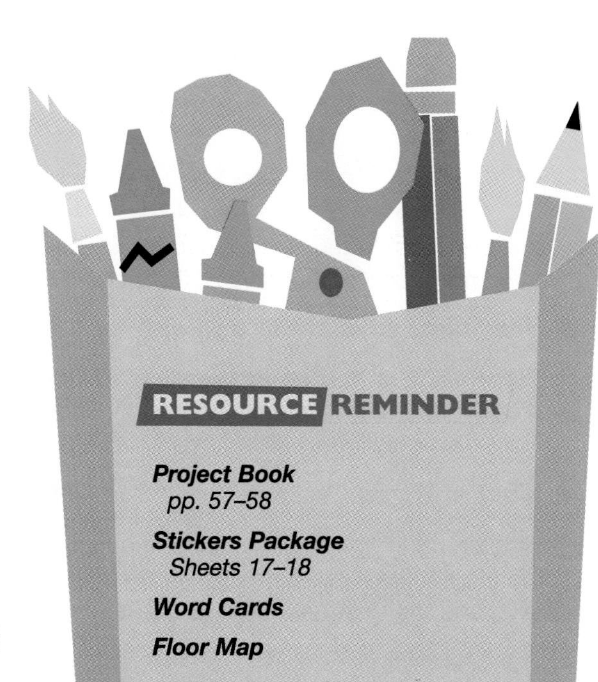

RESOURCE REMINDER

Project Book
pp. 57–58

Stickers Package
Sheets 17–18

Word Cards

Floor Map

LESSON OVERVIEW

Calendars are charts that show the days, weeks, and months of the year.

LESSON OBJECTIVES

- Determine the use of a calendar.
- Recognize how calendars are organized.
- Identify that calendars can be used to record special days and activities.

KEY CONCEPT

calendar

GETTING READY

Sequence Calendar Cutouts

ON YOUR OWN

30 MINUTES OR LONGER

CURRICULUM CONNECTION Mathematics

Objective: To be introduced to calendar skills

Resource: ***Project Book*** pp. 57–58

Materials: one file folder per child, scissors, crayons, construction paper

Advance Preparation: Color and cut out the labels for the months on ***Project Book*** p. 58. Glue them in correct order onto a piece of construction paper.

1. Have children cut out the calendar form on ***Project Book*** p. 57 and color and cut out the labels for months and holiday symbols on ***Project Book*** p. 58.
2. Have each child store the calendar form and holiday symbols in a file folder for later use.
3. Display the months of the year you prepared. Together with children first count each month 1–12, then read the name of each month out loud.
4. On a flat surface or table, have children place their own labels for the months in correct order using your display as a guide.
5. Ask children to find and name the first and last month, the current month, and their birthday month.
6. Store the labels for the months with the symbols and calendar form in the file folders for later use.

Project Book
pp. 57–58

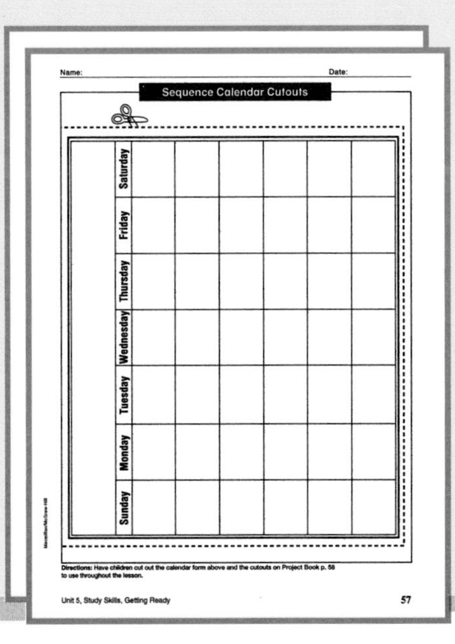

Name: Date:

Sequence Calendar Cutouts

Sunday | Monday | Tuesday | Wednesday | Thursday | Friday | Saturday

Directions: Have children cut out the calendar form above and the cutouts on Project Book p. 58 to use throughout the lesson.

Unit 5, Study Skills, Getting Ready 57

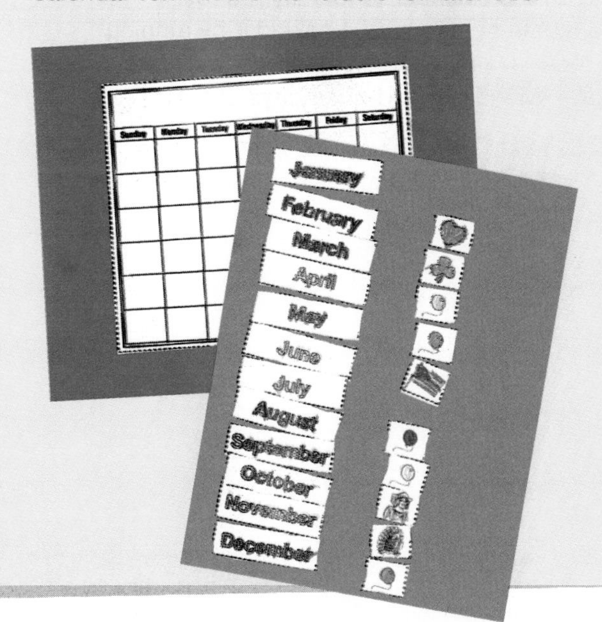

1 Prepare

WARMING UP WITH THE READ ALOUD

Share the poem in the Read Aloud to assess children's knowledge of the days of the week.

- ***How many days are in a week?*** *(seven)*
- ***What are the names of the days of the week?*** *(Sunday, Monday, Tuesday, Wednesday, Thursday, Friday, Saturday)*
- ***What is March?*** *(a month; the third month)*

Tell children that they will be learning about something in the classroom that shows days, weeks, and months. Ask them to guess what it is.

2 Teach

USING BIG BOOK PAGES 8–9

Read the lesson title and then point to the calendar. Explain that a *calendar* is a chart that shows the days in a month.

USE BIG BOOK STICKERS, SHEETS 17–18

Use these ***Stickers*** throughout the lesson.

Share with children the organization of a calendar. Invite a volunteer to read the name of the month. Then point to and read aloud the names of the days of the week in order. Share that each block on the calendar is a day and that each day has a number. Together count the number of days in the month. Run your finger across seven blocks on the calendar to identify a week. Demonstrate how to read a calendar by running your finger down each column to show all the Sundays, Mondays, and other days of the week.

UNIT 5 THEME BIG BOOK

Read Aloud

Seven Kites in March

Here's a kite for Monday,
And one for Tuesday, too.
Here's a kite for Wednesday
(All day I think of you.)
Here's a kite for Thursday.
And Friday—see me throw it!
Here's a kite for Saturday.
(I like you and you know it.)
Here's a kite for Sunday.
(I like to hear you speak.)
I flew all seven kites today,
For each day in the week!

Louise Binder Scott

Tell children that Thanksgiving is the fourth Thursday in November. Have a volunteer affix the ***Sticker*** of Thanksgiving on the correct date. Ask if any children have a birthday in November. If so, have them use the ***Stickers*** of the birthday cakes to find their birthdays on the calendar.

Explain that Election Day occurs on either the first or second Tuesday in November. On the Big Book calendar, it is November 5. Tell children that on this day, Americans vote for people whom they choose to be their leaders. To help children understand voting, ask them if they have ever voted for someone to be the leader in a game. Have a volunteer place the ***Sticker*** of the VOTE! button on the correct date.

Point out that November 11 is Veterans Day. Tell children that on Veterans Day, we honor all the people who have fought in wars for our country. Have a volunteer place the ***Sticker*** of the American flag on the correct date.

Use a bound calendar to show children that months have different numbers of days. Point out that twelve calendar pages together show all the days, weeks, and months in a year.

- ***What month does this calendar show?*** *(November)*
- ***How many days are in this month?*** *(30)*

★ **THINKING FURTHER:** ***Classifying*** ***In what season is the month of November?*** *(fall)*

You may wish to use the ***Floor Map*** to have children plan parade routes for special holidays on the calendar, such as Thanksgiving.

3 Close

LESSON SUMMARY

Read the lesson question, pointing to each word as you read. Children might suggest that calendars help us to know the days on which certain dates fall and that people can use a calendar to record special days or activities they need to do.

EVALUATE

Make a Calendar Using a calendar form or ***Project Book*** pp. 57–58, assist children in making a calendar for the current month. As an alternative, you might have children make calendars for their birthday months.

Print Awareness

List the names of the days of the week in order on the chalkboard or write the days on cards and place them in a pocket chart to encourage student accessibility. Point out that each word begins with a capital letter. Have children identify the two days that begin with the letter *S* and then the two days that begin with *T*. Help children to identify the word *day* as being the same in all words. You may wish to use the ***Word Cards*** showing the days and months.

Second-Language Support/Making Connections
Write the days of the week on the chalkboard and teach children a simple chant to familiarize them with their names. (For example, *Sunday, Monday, Tuesday, fun. Wednesday, Thursday, Friday, run. On Saturday our work is done.*) Invite children to clap out the rhythm as they chant the words. Then ask children to look at the words as you ask questions such as, "Which word has a capital *S*?" or "Which word has a small *o*?" Ask the children to point to the letters you mention.

SCIENCE CONNECTION

LEARNING STYLE: VISUAL

Learning Center: Make Weather Calendars

Objective: To observe the weather and to record observations on a calendar.

Resource: *Project Book* pp. 57–58

Materials: glue, construction paper, crayons

1. To make a weather calendar, children can use the calendar on ***Project Book*** p. 57 and the calendar labels for months from ***Project Book*** p. 58 prepared in Getting Ready. Have children glue the labels of the name of the current month at the top of the calendar. Then have them glue the calendars onto a sheet of construction paper.
2. Help children to number the days on their calendars. Suggest that they write the numbers small so that they can add drawings.
3. As a collaborative effort, have children suggest symbols that can stand for different kinds of weather—such as a sun, a cloud, a sun with clouds, a raindrop, and a snowflake.
4. In the Science Learning Center, have children draw the appropriate weather symbol on their calendars each day for a week or month.
5. Using the completed weather calendars, you can make a tally chart, a picture graph, or a bar graph that shows the total number of rainy, cloudy, sunny, and snowy days during the week or month.

MATHEMATICS CONNECTION

LEARNING STYLE: VISUAL

Make a Calendar Birthday Train

Objective: To practice using calendars by making a "birthday train" of calendars, which show class birthdays and other special days.

Resource: *Project Book* pp. 57–58

Materials: scissors, glue, construction paper, crayons, markers

Advance Preparation: Cut 26 train wheels and twelve 2"x 1/2" car connectors from black construction paper (as shown). You may wish to have children use their folders from Getting Ready.

1. Have the class form twelve groups and assign each one a month of the year. Help each group to prepare for its assigned month by using the calendar from ***Project Book*** p. 57 and the labels for months and holiday symbols from ***Project Book*** p. 58. Have children glue the names of the months on the calendar. Help children to write the dates of the month onto the calendar and glue the appropriate holiday symbols on their calendars.
2. Have groups glue their calendars onto a sheet of construction paper to make a "calendar train car." Help children to glue two wheels on at the bottom of the cars.
3. Use the connectors to join the calendar cars together to make a "train." Have children write their names on their birth date.

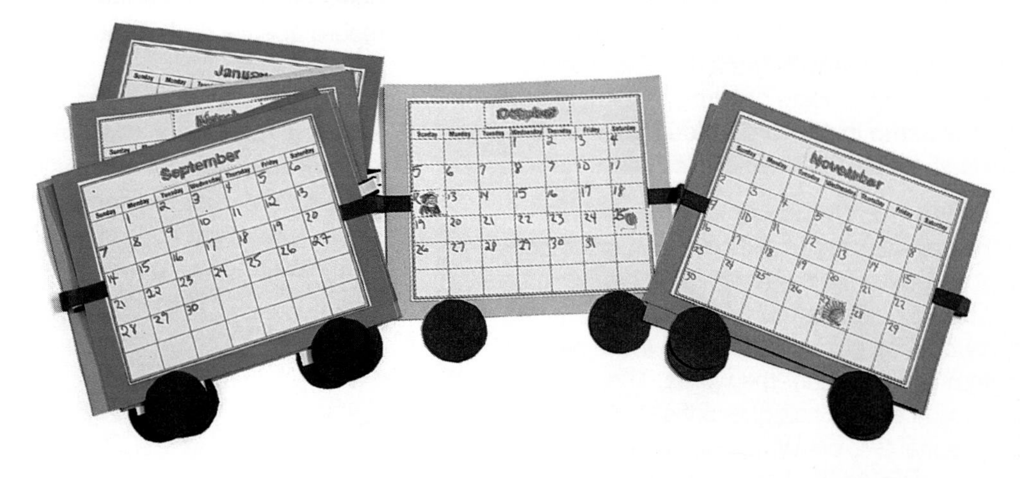

UNIT 5

LESSON

3

Martin Luther King, Jr., Day

UNIT 5 THEME BIG BOOK, PAGES 10–11

LESSON OVERVIEW

Martin Luther King, Jr., Day is a holiday on which we honor Martin Luther King, Jr.

LESSON OBJECTIVES

- Recognize that we honor Martin Luther King, Jr., on the holiday, Martin Luther King, Jr., Day.
- Recognize that Martin Luther King, Jr., worked to make rules and laws more fair for all Americans.
- Locate Martin Luther King, Jr., Day on a calendar.

KEY CONCEPTS

Martin Luther King, Jr.	freedom
Martin Luther King, Jr., Day	peace

RESOURCE REMINDER

Project Book
p. 59

Stickers Package
Sheet 17

Anthology
Martin Luther King Day, pp. 118–122

GETTING READY

Make Memory Medals

ON YOUR OWN

30 MINUTES OR LONGER

CURRICULUM CONNECTION Art

Objective: To learn about Martin Luther King, Jr., Day.

Resource: ***Project Book*** p. 59

Materials: scissors, glue, hole puncher, yarn, markers, crayons

1. Explain to children that they will be making a memory medal. Discuss what remembering someone means. Have children cut out the pieces on ***Project Book*** p. 59.
2. Have children glue the pieces back to back. Then help children punch a hole as indicated on the medal.
3. Help children attach yarn to the medal so it can be worn in memory of Martin Luther King, Jr.
4. As children learn about Martin Luther King, Jr., in this lesson, have them color the portrait as well as draw a dream for a better world in the space on the back.

Project Book p. 59

Name: Date:

Make Memory Medals

Martin Luther King, Jr.

Directions: Have children cutout and assemble the pieces to make a memory medal. Then have them color the portrait and draw a dream for a better world in the cloud outline.

Unit 5, Lesson 3, Getting Ready 59

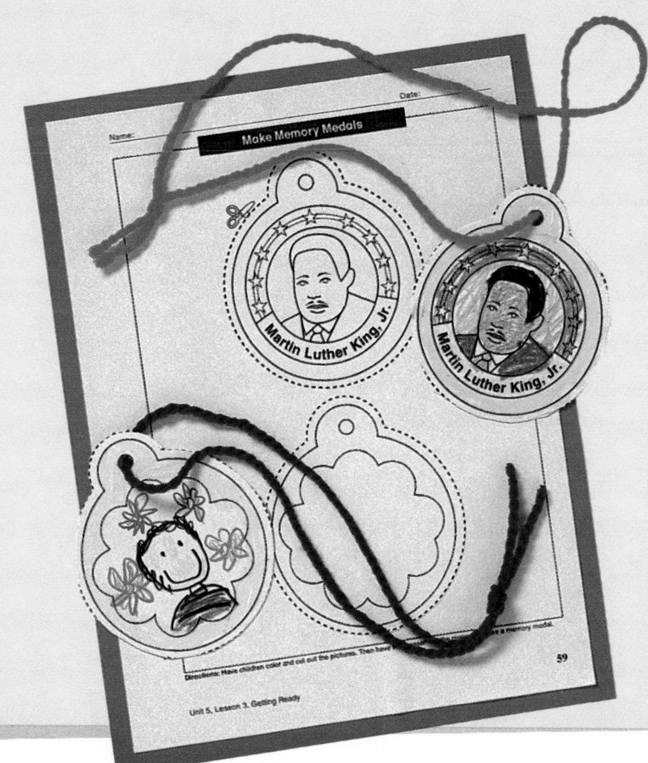

1 Prepare

WARMING UP WITH THE READ ALOUD

Tell children that they will be learning about a special American named Martin Luther King, Jr., and about a holiday that Americans celebrate to remember him. After sharing the poem in the Read Aloud, clarify that Dr. King was a minister who had a degree called a Ph.D.—the highest degree a person can earn in college. Make sure that children understand he was not a medical doctor. Explain to children that the dream that Dr. King has in the poem is not the kind of dream you have at night. It was his wish for something special.

- ***When do some dreamers have dreams?*** *(Possible answers: at night, through the day)*
- ***What was Dr. King's dream, or wish?*** *(He dreamed of the day that freedom was near.)*

To clarify the dream named in the poem, tell children that when Martin Luther King, Jr., had a dream to make things better, some rules or laws in our country treated African Americans unfairly. These rules kept African Americans from doing the same things and going to the same places as white people. Explain that when Martin Luther King, Jr., spoke of a day of freedom, he meant that one day, all Americans would be treated fairly and would be free to do the same things.

UNIT 5 THEME BIG BOOK

LESSON 3

Martin Luther King, Jr., Day

10

Read Aloud

A Dream

What is a dream?
Does it only come at night—
When you're fast asleep
And the covers are tight?
Some dreamers have dreams
Wide awake, through the day.
When they share their dreams,
People listen to what they say.
Dr. King had a dream
That was wonderful to hear.
He dreamed that the great day
Of freedom was near—
And he told his dream
To the world—*loud and clear!*

Dee Lillegard

Using the Anthology

Martin Luther King Day, pages 118–122 You may wish to read excerpts from this biography. This engaging story provides many interesting details about Martin Luther King, Jr.'s youth, family, rules at home, values, career choices, and his work as a civil rights leader. Topics of segregation are presented in a simple fashion. The biography opens with the excitement of the first celebration of Martin Luther King, Jr., Day and concludes with traditions Americans follow on this holiday.

2 Teach

USING BIG BOOK PAGES 10–11

Read the lesson title and identify Martin Luther King, Jr., in the photograph as the man we honor on this holiday. Tell children that the photo shows him speaking to a large crowd in Washington, D.C., about fairness for all people.

USE BIG BOOK STICKERS, SHEET 17
Affix the ***Sticker*** near Martin Luther King, Jr.

Share that Martin Luther King, Jr., Day is celebrated on the third Monday in January. Have a volunteer identify the holiday on a calendar. Share that Martin Luther King, Jr., gave many speeches about peaceful ways to get along and work together. Define peace as "not fighting." Explain that on Martin Luther King, Jr., Day, we remember the man who worked peacefully to change rules and laws to make things more fair for all Americans. On this holiday, people attend parades and speeches, and they visit memorials that honor him. Point out that Lily and her friends have made peace doves to celebrate the holiday. To make these doves with children, see the instructions on page 178.

- ***Why are the children making doves to celebrate Martin Luther King, Jr., Day?*** *(the doves are symbols for peace)*

★**THINKING FURTHER: *Using Prior Knowledge* *How can you be fair to others? How do you know about being fair?*** *(Possible answers may include by sharing or by treating others as one wants to be treated oneself; children may say that they know about fairness from personal experience or the media.)*

3 Close

LESSON SUMMARY

Read the lesson question, pointing to each word as you read. Children should explain that we remember Martin Luther King, Jr., because he tried to make things fair for all people.

EVALUATE

Perform Fairness Skits Have children perform skits that focus on fairness. Provide children with ideas for scenarios, such as a child not letting others have a turn on a swing.

Background Information

About Martin Luther King, Jr. You may wish to share with children some additional information about this topic.

- Martin Luther King, Jr., was born on January 15, 1929 in Atlanta, Georgia.
- He was ordained a minister in 1947.
- In 1963 Martin Luther King, Jr., led the March on Washington and delivered his "I Have a Dream" speech from the steps of the Lincoln Memorial.
- During the 1950s and 1960s, segregation laws in many parts of the South and elsewhere in the United States prohibited African Americans from attending white schools; using the same restaurants, public restrooms, pools, hotels, drinking fountains as white people; and riding in the front of buses with white people.
- Martin Luther King, Jr., was assassinated on April 4, 1968, in Memphis, Tennessee.
- In 1983 Martin Luther King, Jr., Day was declared an annual federal holiday by the United States Congress.

ART CONNECTION

LEARNING STYLE: KINESTHETIC

Make Peace Doves

ON YOUR OWN

30 MINUTES OR LONGER

Objective: To remember Martin Luther King, Jr., as a man of peace by making peace doves.

Materials: oaktag, pencils, white or gray construction paper, scissors, 12" length of yarn (per child), rulers, stapler, glue, tape, orange and black crayons, hole puncher

Advance Preparation: Make oaktag templates of doves. Doves should be about 10" wide and 3" deep. Cut construction paper into 6" x 7" pieces.

1. Help children to trace the dove template onto a full sheet of construction paper and cut it out.
2. Help children to pleat the construction paper. Help them to fold the pleated strip in half. Cut a V-shaped notch in the unfolded ends of the pleated strip.
3. Help children cut a slit halfway down the back of the dove. Help them insert the pleated strip into the slit. Reinforce with glue or tape.
4. Have children punch a hole on the back of the dove and attach yarn for hanging. Children can draw eyes and color in a beak.

ART CONNECTION

LEARNING STYLE: VISUAL

Make a Friendship Wreath

PARTNER

30 MINUTES OR LONGER

Objective: To honor the dream of Martin Luther King, Jr., for friendship among people.

Materials: construction paper (many colors including brown, tan, pink, and white to represent different skin tones), pencils, glue, scraps of construction paper, markers, crayons

1. Divide children into four groups, giving each group construction paper in one of the 4 colors (brown, tan, pink, white) to represent a different skin tone.
2. Have children, working in pairs, trace each other's hands and wrists onto construction paper.
3. Have each pair cut out two shirt cuffs from different color construction paper and then glue them onto the wrists of their hand cutouts.
4. Help children use markers to write their names on the shirt cuffs and if desired, a friendship word on the hand cutouts. Then have them glue their cutouts side-by-side with thumbs overlapping.
5. Help children to assemble the wreath by "joining" their hands with other classmates' hands.

UNIT 5

LESSON 4

Presidents' Day

UNIT 5 THEME BIG BOOK, PAGES 12–13

LESSON OVERVIEW

Presidents' Day is a holiday in which Americans jointly honor Presidents George Washington and Abraham Lincoln.

LESSON OBJECTIVES

- Recognize Presidents' Day as a holiday that honors both George Washington and Abraham Lincoln.
- Identify George Washington and Abraham Lincoln as two of our country's Presidents.
- Locate Presidents' Day on a calendar.

KEY CONCEPTS

George Washington
President
Abraham Lincoln
Presidents' Day

RESOURCE REMINDER

Project Book
p. 60

Stickers Package
Sheet 17

Anthology
George Washington's Breakfast, pp. 102–110
Young Abe Lincoln, p. 117

GETTING READY

Make "Special American" Cards

ON YOUR OWN

30 MINUTES OR LONGER

CURRICULUM CONNECTION **Language Arts/Art**

Objective: To learn about Presidents' Day

Resource: ***Project Book*** p. 60

Materials: pennies and quarters, masking tape, crayons, markers or pencils, scissors

1. Without revealing the Presidents' names, ask children if they know who the special Americans on ***Project Book*** p. 60 are and where they may have seen these faces before.
2. Distribute quarters and pennies. Have children name the coins and compare the likenesses on the coins with the silhouettes on ***Project Book*** p. 60. Then have them make coin rubbings in the space next to the appropriate silhouette. Children can tape the coins under the page and make the rubbing with a dark crayon.
3. Have children color the silhouettes black and the curtain bunting red or blue.
4. Have children cut out the page and fold it to make a card.
5. As the Presidents are introduced in the lesson, children can draw pictures and you can help them write sentences about the Presidents or Presidents' Day.

Project Book
p. 60

Name: Date:

Make "Special American" Cards

Directions: Have children color the pictures and cut out the whole page. Then have them make coin rubbings next to the appropriate silhouettes. Finally, have the children fold the page vertically to make a card.

60 Unit 5, Lesson 4, Getting Ready

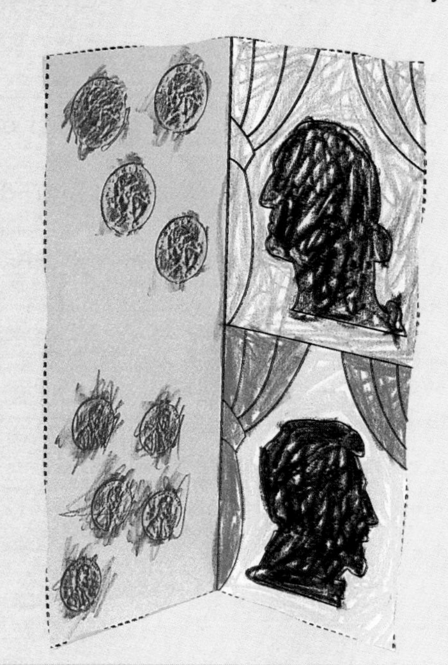

1 Prepare

WARMING UP WITH THE READ ALOUD

Tell children that they will be learning about two special Americans and the holiday we celebrate to remember them. Share the poem in the Read Aloud. Explain that George Washington and Abraham Lincoln were both Presidents of the United States of America and that the President is the leader of our country. Tell children that Washington was our first President and that Lincoln was our sixteenth President.

- ***In what month were both men born?*** *(February)*
- ***Why are George Washington and Abraham Lincoln special?*** *(They were leaders or Presidents.)*

2 Teach

USING BIG BOOK PAGES 12–13

Read the lesson title. Tell children that Presidents' Day is the holiday on which Americans remember George Washington and Abraham Lincoln and what they did to help our country.

USE BIG BOOK STICKERS, SHEET 17

Use these ***Stickers*** throughout the lesson.

George Washington

Abraham Lincoln

Presidents' Day

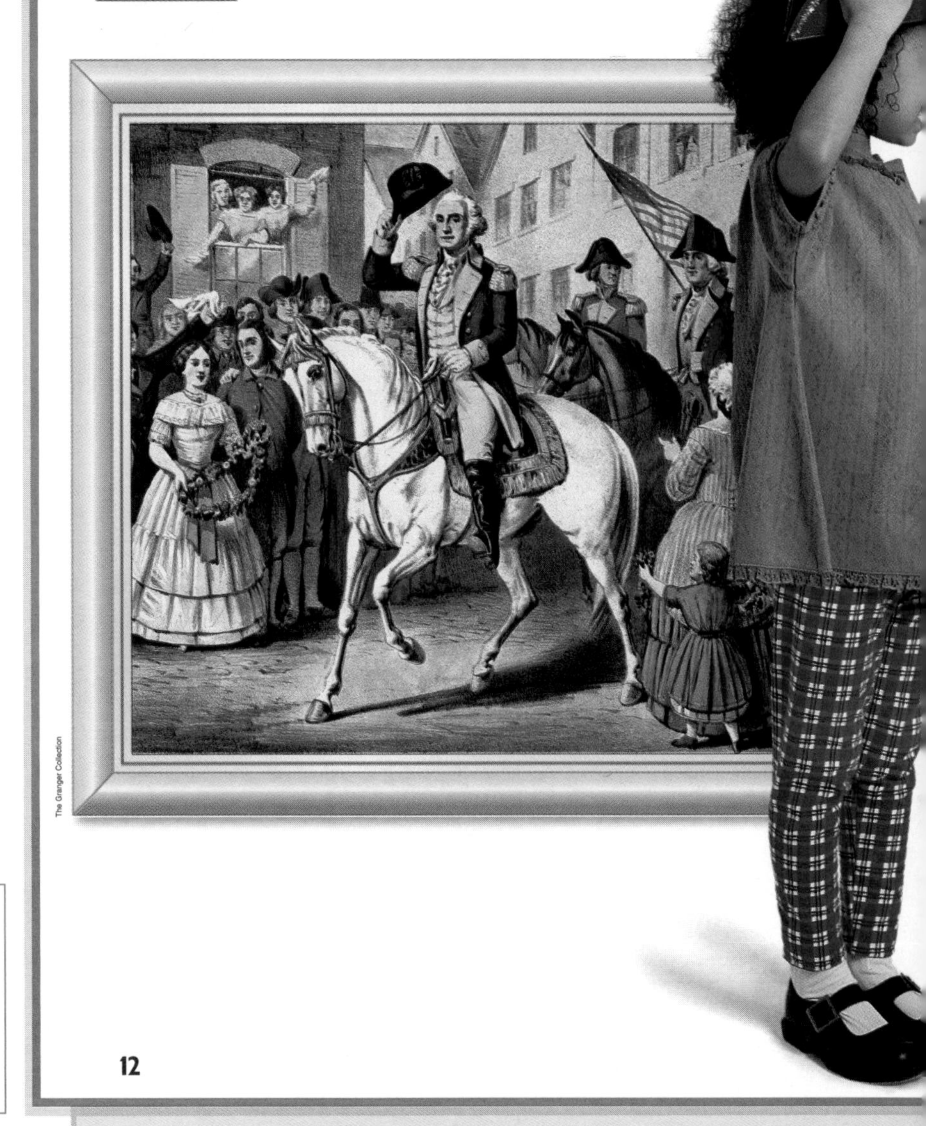

The Granger Collection

12

Read Aloud

Two Presidents

George Washington helped start our
wonderful land.
Abe Lincoln made sure that united we'd
stand.
Each was born on a February day
Each was there to lead the way.

Two special men to remember
Who made our country great,
Our first and sixteenth Presidents
What a good reason to celebrate!

—Sheila Dori

Using the Anthology

George Washington's Breakfast, pages 102–110
This story will provide your class with some interesting and factual details about the life of our first President as a boy named George investigates what this famous American liked to eat for breakfast. In addition to discovering what George Washington ate for breakfast, children will learn the names of his dogs and horses, his shoe size, and things he liked to do, such as count things. This selection also names reference materials and sources the boy used to obtain information.

Young Abe Lincoln, page 117 Invite children to sing or just listen to the words of this song, which provides the listener with some details about the life of Abraham Lincoln as well as highlights his character, such as his willingness to work hard, his honesty, and how he served our country.

Place the ***Sticker*** of George Washington near the picture of him in New York in the Big Book. Place the ***Sticker*** of Abraham Lincoln near the picture of him in Springfield, Illinois. Point out to children that both men are riding horses to travel. Ask children how their lives might be different if they had to travel by horse.

Tell children that George Washington helped to start our country long ago and that he was our first President. Share that George Washington is remembered for being an honest leader who cared about our country. Tell children that Abraham Lincoln helped to keep our country together and he helped change some of our country's laws to end slavery. Explain that slavery is when people are forced to work for others without pay.

Point out that Lily and her friend are celebrating Presidents' Day by wearing hats like those worn by Washington and Lincoln long ago. To make these hats with your class, see the instructions on page 182. Tell children that Presidents' Day is the third Monday in February. Have children locate the holiday on a calendar. Explain that Washington and Lincoln's birthdays were once celebrated separately, but were combined into Presidents' Day.

- ***In what month is Presidents' Day?*** *(February)*

> ★**THINKING FURTHER:** ***Making Conclusions*** ***Why do you think Presidents' Day is celebrated in February?*** *(February is the month in which Washington and Lincoln were born.)*

You may also wish to discuss and show children a photograph of our current President.

LESSON SUMMARY

Read the lesson question, pointing to each word as you read. Children may say that we remember both George Washington and Abraham Lincoln on Presidents' Day.

EVALUATE

Complete Sentences Have children complete sentences such as "We remember George Washington because ____. We remember Abraham Lincoln because ____." and "Presidents' Day is in the month of ____."

Background Information

About George Washington and Abraham Lincoln
You may wish to provide children with some additional information.

- George Washington was born in Virginia on February 22, 1732.
- In 1775 Washington was chosen to lead the American army against the British in the American Revolution.
- Washington became our nation's first President in 1789.
- Washington died at Mount Vernon, in Virginia, in 1799.
- Abraham Lincoln was born in Kentucky on February 12, 1809. He grew up in Indiana and also lived in Illinois.
- Lincoln began to practice law in 1836.
- In 1861 Lincoln became the sixteenth President. That year the Civil War began.
- In 1863 Lincoln issued the Emancipation Proclamation, freeing enslaved people in the Confederacy.
- In 1865 Lincoln was shot at Ford's Theater in Washington, D.C., and died soon after.

ART and MUSIC CONNECTIONS

LEARNING STYLE: AUDITORY/KINESTHETIC

Make a Tricorn Hat

ON YOUR OWN

30 MINUTES OR LONGER

Objective: To celebrate Presidents' Day by making a tricorn hat such as one worn by George Washington.

Materials: oaktag, pencils, scissors, stapler or glue, gold ribbon, blue or black construction paper

Advance Preparation: Make several hat templates (as shown).

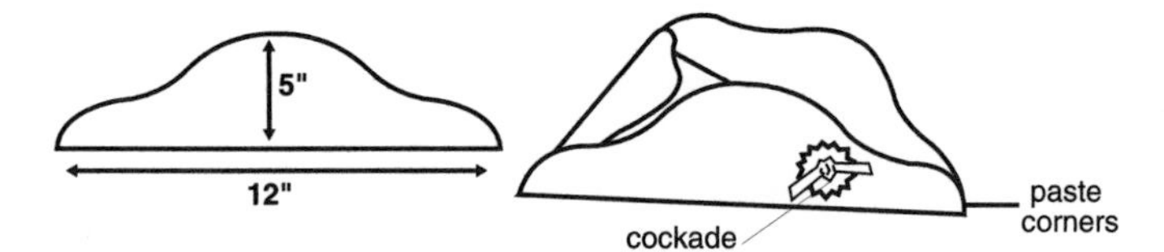

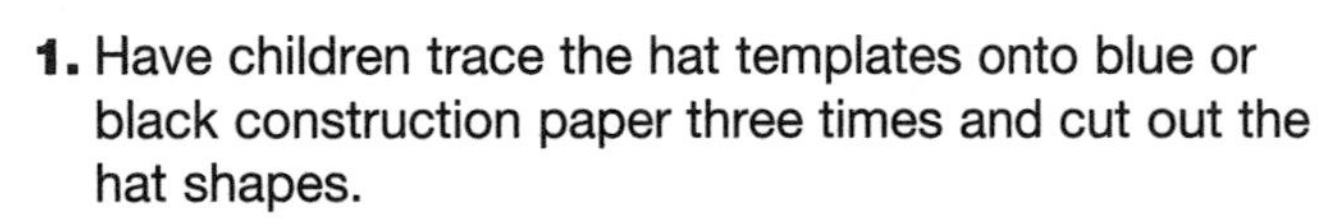

1. Have children trace the hat templates onto blue or black construction paper three times and cut out the hat shapes.
2. Help children to assemble the hat by stapling or gluing the three corners of the hat shapes together.
3. Children may wish to glue ribbons or decorations to their hats.
4. Children can wear their hats while singing and marching to the high-spirited tune "Yankee Doodle." This song was popular in the Continental Army during the American Revolution.

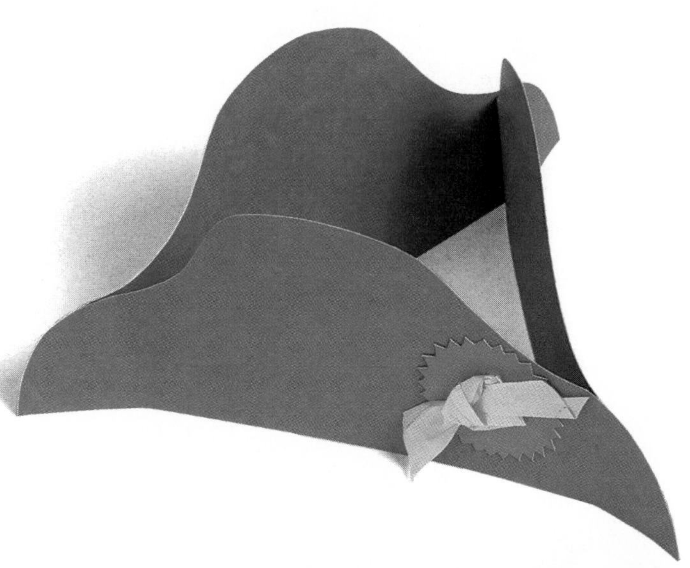

ART CONNECTION

LEARNING STYLE: KINESTHETIC

Make a Stovepipe Hat

ON YOUR OWN

30 MINUTES OR LONGER

Objective: To celebrate Presidents' Day by making a stovepipe hat such as one worn by Abraham Lincoln.

Materials: black construction paper, masking tape, stapler, chalk or light crayon, scissors, ruler, glue

Advance Preparation: Tape two sheets of black construction paper together horizontally.

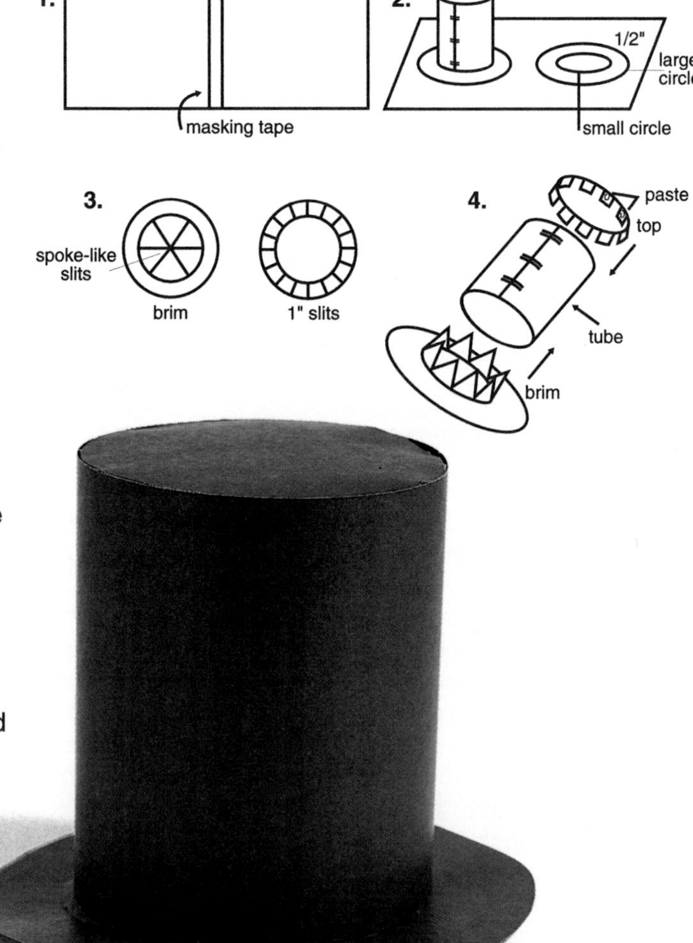

1. Roll the prepared construction paper into a tube around a child's head for fit and staple the ends together.
2. Place the tube upright on black construction paper. Then using chalk or a light crayon, trace around the tube to make two small circles. Then draw a circle, approximately 1/2" larger, around both. Have children cut around the large circles.
3. Have children cut about ten 1" slits from the outside of the larger circle to the inside of the small circle. Then have children fold the tabs down and glue them to the top inside of the tube.
4. To make the brim, have children poke a hole in the center of the remaining circle and cut about seven spoke-like slits to the small circle. Have children fold these tabs up, and glue the tabs to the inside of the tube.

Making Predictions

UNIT 5 THEME BIG BOOK, PAGES 14–15

LESSON OVERVIEW

Making a prediction is telling what will happen next.

LESSON OBJECTIVES

- Predict possible outcomes of story pictures.
- Predict possible outcomes of a narrated story.

KEY CONCEPTS

prediction

RESOURCE REMINDER

Project Book
p. 61

Stickers Package
Sheet 18

GETTING READY

Make a Book

ON YOUR OWN

15 TO 30 MINUTES

CURRICULUM CONNECTIONS **Mathematics/Art**

Objective: To prepare for making predictions by reviewing the sequencing skill.

Resources: ***Project Book*** p. 61

Materials: scissors, marker, stapler, crayons

1. Direct children to cut out the four sections on ***Project Book*** p. 61 and to place the blank section aside.
2. Have children place the three pictures in order to tell a story. Then have volunteers use the words *first, next* and *last* to tell what each picture shows. You might suggest children number the pictures.
3. Have children make a book by stapling together the pictures in order, with the blank section or cover on top.
4. Invite children to color the illustrations and to draw a cover for their book.

Project Book p. 61

Name: Date:
Make a Book

Directions: Have children color and cut out the pictures. Then have them assemble the pictures in the correct order to make a book.
Unit 5, Thinking Skills, Getting Ready 61

1 Prepare

WARMING UP WITH THE READ ALOUD

Share the poem in the Read Aloud.

- ***How many of you have ever felt this way about a book?*** *(Ask children to raise their hands.)*
- ***What stories have you heard? What were they about? What did you imagine would happen later?*** *(Children should name the stories, tell what they were about, and share their thoughts regarding the outcomes.)*

2 Teach

USING BIG BOOK PAGES 14–15

Tell children that when they share what they think will happen in a story, they are making a prediction. Read aloud the lesson title. Direct children to look at the pictures and listen for clues about what might happen as you read the story below. Explain to children that the famous story they are about to hear probably is not true. You may wish to share with children the *Background Information* at this time.

George Washington and the Cherry Tree

George Washington's father had a favorite cherry tree. When George was six years old, he was given a hatchet to chop wood.

- ***What is a hatchet?*** *(a tool; a small ax with a short handle)*

> ★**THINKING FURTHER:** ***Making Predictions***
> ***What do you think will happen next in the story? Name a clue that helps you to make your prediction.*** *(Possible answers: George chops the cherry tree down, he chops pieces from the tree, he makes cut marks in the tree's bark, and he knocks down all the cherries with his hatchet; a clue that helps to make these predictions is that George is swinging his hatchet at the tree.)*

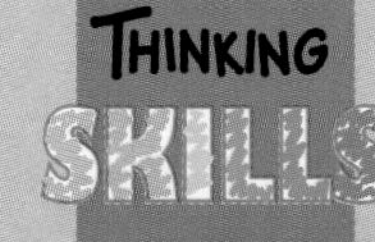

Making Predictions

14

Read Aloud

After the End

After a book is finished,
don't you wish you knew
everything that happened
AFTER it was through?

—Aileen Fisher

USE BIG BOOK STICKERS, SHEET 18

Use this ***Sticker*** to show the ending of the pictures in the Big Book.

Place the ***Sticker*** of George and the felled cherry tree on the Big Book and continue with the story.

George decided to use his new hatchet on the cherry tree. George's father saw the tree and he was angry. He asked, "Do you know who cut down my cherry tree?"

Have children make a prediction about what happened next and then continue the story.

George answered, "I cannot tell a lie! I did cut it with my hatchet." George's father did not punish him because he was happy that George had told the truth.

Use these steps with children who are having difficulty making predictions.

HELPING YOURSELF

- First, look at the pictures and listen for clues in the story.
- Next, think about what you already know and what you might do.
- Then, make a good guess about what might happen.

Background Information

About the Cherry Tree Story You may wish to supply children with some of the history behind this story.

- Most people believe that the story about George Washington and the cherry tree never really happened.
- For almost 200 years, Americans have passed this story down from generation to generation because it is about an important value, honesty.
- The story was originally created just after Washington died by an early biographer named Parson Mason L. Weems. The purpose of the story was to show the honesty George Washington displayed as a boy and carried with him through adulthood.
- Because of this story, Americans continue to associate cherries and hatchets with George Washington as well as eating cherry pies and cherry tarts on Presidents' Day and on Washington's Birthday.

3 Close

LESSON SUMMARY

Read the question, pointing to each word as you read. Review with children that all predictions are acceptable. Children should review possible endings to the story, which include George chopping down part or all of the tree, making marks in the tree, and knocking down the cherries.

EVALUATE

Make Predictions Read stories, such as *George Washington's Breakfast* on pp. 102–110 of the ***Anthology***. Have children predict the endings. Compare their predictions with the actual endings.

ART and LANGUAGE ARTS CONNECTIONS

LEARNING STYLE: AUDITORY/VISUAL

Predict the Ending of a Story

ON YOUR OWN

30 MINUTES OR LONGER

Objective: To practice making predictions.

Materials: drawing paper, crayons

1. Share the following story about young Abraham Lincoln with children.

   When Abe Lincoln was a young man, he loved to read. He enjoyed reading so much that he read his own books and letters over and over again. Wherever he went, he asked people if they had any new books or newspapers that he could read. One day, a man named Pitcher said that he would lend Abe a book that he had at home. In order to borrow it, however, Abe would have to walk a very long way to get it.

2. Have children predict the ending of the story by drawing a picture. When they finish, have children share their predictions with the class and tell why their predictions may have happened. (The true ending to this story is that Abe walked 20 miles to Pitcher's home just to borrow the book.)

PHYSICAL EDUCATION CONNECTION

LEARNING STYLE: KINESTHETIC/VISUAL

Make a Prediction About Balls

GROUP

30 MINUTES OR LONGER

Objective: To practice making predictions by making an old-fashioned style ball, comparing it with a contemporary ball, and predicting its ability to bounce, roll, and be thrown.

Materials: stone, yarn, felt, glue or tape; (for the teacher: thread, sewing needle)

1. Tell children that if they lived at the times when Washington or Lincoln lived, they would not have played with balls like the ones today. Explain that long ago, children made their own balls by wrapping yarn or pieces of cloth around a little stone and then covering it with a kind of leather called buckskin.
2. Ask for a few volunteers to help make a ball like those made by children long ago. To begin, have children tape the end of the yarn to a stone and then wrap the yarn around it until the stone is completely covered. In place of buckskin, children can cover the ball with a small piece of felt. Stitch the felt closed or glue or tape the felt down securely to make the ball round.
3. Find a ball approximately the same size as the ball the children made. Allow all children to handle both balls.
4. Have children predict which ball will bounce higher, which will roll farther, and which might be thrown farther. Suggest that children give reasons for supporting their predictions. Record the predictions in the form of a tally.
5. Test children's predictions, explaining that all predictions are valid whether or not they are true.
6. To close, you may wish children to sit in a circle on the floor and pass the balls, using a rhythmic pattern.

Birthdays Near and Far

UNIT 5 THEME BIG BOOK, PAGES 16–17

RESOURCE REMINDER

Project Book
p. 62

Stickers Package
Sheet 19

Anthology
La Piñata, pp. 126–127

Inflatable Globe

LESSON OVERVIEW

People around the world celebrate birthdays.

LESSON OBJECTIVES

- Name the date of one's own birthday.
- Identify some traditions associated with birthdays.
- Recognize that birthday traditions vary among families around the world.

KEY CONCEPT

birthday

GETTING READY

Make Balloon Badges

ON YOUR OWN

15 TO 30 MINUTES

CURRICULUM CONNECTION Art

Objective: To create badges for birthday celebrations.

Resource: *Project Book* p. 62

Materials: scissors, glue, crayons, masking tape, one safety pin and a 7" length of curling ribbon per child; optional: folder or shoe box

1. Point out that ***Project Book*** p. 62 shows pieces of a balloon badge that children can wear on their next birthday. Explain that the badge will tell others that it is their special day.
2. Read the sayings on the cutouts with children. Have children cut out the saying of their choice and glue it on the balloon.
3. Have children color the balloons and then cut them out. Help them cut slits at the base of the balloon as indicated. Gather the slits together and tie them with ribbon.
4. Help children to attach a safety pin to the backs of the balloons with masking tape. Save the balloon badges in a folder or shoe box for children to wear on their birthdays.

Project Book p. 62

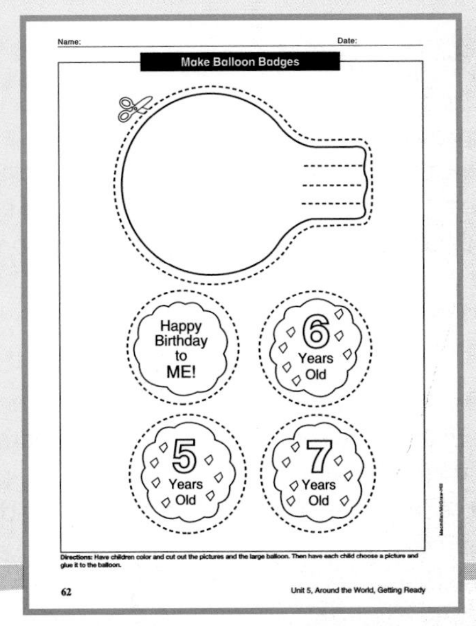

Name: Date:

Make Balloon Badges

Happy Birthday to ME!

6 Years Old

5 Years Old

7 Years Old

Directions: Have children color and cut out the pictures and the large balloon. Then have each child choose a picture and glue it to the balloon.

62 Unit 5, Around the World, Getting Ready

1 Prepare

WARMING UP WITH THE READ ALOUD

Share the poem in the Read Aloud without revealing the title and the word birthday in the last line.

- ***What is the poem about?*** *(a party table)*
- ***What kind of party might it be? What words helped you to know?*** *(a birthday party; words such as cake, favors, balloons)*

> ★ **THINKING FURTHER:** ***Classifying What four things on the party table are alike? Tell how.*** *(Possible answers: The tablecloth, plates, cups, and hats are alike; they are made of paper; the plates, cups, forks, and spoons are alike; they are used to eat.)*

Explain that a birthday is a special day, once a year, that honors the day a person was born.

2 Teach

USING BIG BOOK PAGES 16–17

Read the lesson title and then focus children's attention on the center photograph.

> **USE BIG BOOK STICKERS, SHEET 19**
> Use these ***Stickers*** throughout the lesson.
>
> 
>
> 
>
> 
>
> 
>
> 
>

UNIT 5 THEME BIG BOOK

Birthdays Near and Far

16

Read Aloud

Party Table

We have a paper tablecloth
with dogs and dancing cats
and paper plates/and paper cups
and matching paper hats
and forks for eating up the cake
and poppers/and white spoons
and whistles for the favors
and a bunch of pink balloons,
a plate with wrapped-up candy
a dish with bubble gum
and now the table's ready
for my birthday guests to come!

—Myra Cohn Livingston

Using the Anthology

La Piñata (The Piñata), pages 126–127 As you discuss the birthday celebration in Mexico, share this traditional Mexican birthday song with children.

Background Information

About Piñatas A clay or papier-mâché piñata—filled with candy, toys and good-luck charms—is hung by a rope. Players are blindfolded and are spun around. Each is given several chances to break the piñata with a stick while someone moves the piñata up and down. Once the piñata is broken, everyone can scramble for its contents.

Second-Language Support/Using Props You might wish to have on hand an actual piñata to demonstrate what it is and how it is used. Invite children to share how or if they celebrate birthdays in their homes.

How do these children celebrate birthdays?

17

Explain that Lily's birthday is taking place in the United States. Identify the countries in the Big Book by placing the ***Stickers*** as follows:

- pp. 16–17, center, U.S.A.,
- p. 16, top, England,
- p. 16, bottom, Ghana,
- p. 17, top, Abu Dhabi,
- p. 17, bottom, Mexico.

Locate these countries on the ***Inflatable Globe***. Discuss the party activities in the photographs. You may wish to share the Background Information about birthdays in these countries.

- ***How old do you think Lily and the boy in England are? How do you know?*** *(Possible answers: They are six because there are six candles on both of their cakes; they are five because there are five candles on the cake and an extra one to grow on.)*
- ***What things might people do to celebrate a birthday?*** *(Possible answers: Have a cake with candles for the number of years and one to grow on, make wishes while blowing candles out, give and receive cards, sing the birthday song, and play party games.)*

★**THINKING FURTHER:** ***Making Predictions***
What is the boy in Mexico doing at his birthday party? Make a prediction about what he might do next. How can you tell? *(He is swinging at a piñata; he may hit or break the piñata next; children may say that they base their predictions on the fact that he is swinging at the piñata.)*

You may wish to make a birthday chart showing each month and listing the children with birthdays for that month under the appropriate months.

3 Close

LESSON SUMMARY

Read the lesson question, pointing to each word as you read. Children might point to the pictures as they name ways of celebrating.

EVALUATE

Identify Birthdays Have children name their birthdays and identify them on a calendar. Children might share birthday traditions that they know of or practice themselves. For assessment suggestions, see p. 198.

Background Information

ABOUT BIRTHDAYS

- When American children sing the birthday song and share birthday cake, they are following an old German custom.
- In England, birthdays are celebrated much like they are in the United States.
- In Ghana, the mother carries her baby out of the house for the first time at a ceremony called the *outdooring.* Family and friends greet the baby and give presents. Ghanaian babies are given several names—one of which tells the day of the week on which the baby was born.
- Abu Dhabi is one of the seven independent Arab states on the Arabian peninsula that make up the federation called the United Arab Emirates (UAE). The official language is Arabic. Each of the seven states of UAE is ruled by a prince called an *emir*. The photograph in the Big Book shows the emir's son celebrating his birthday.
- In Mexico, many children are named according to the saint's day on which they are born. Mexican children may also have a piñata at their parties.

PHYSICAL EDUCATION CONNECTION

LEARNING STYLE: AUDITORY/KINESTHETIC

Play a Party Game

GROUP

15 TO 30 MINUTES

Objective: To become familiar with another culture by playing a traditional game that originated in England.

Materials: a knotted handkerchief, chart paper, markers, a map or globe

Resource: ***Inflatable Globe***

A-Tisket, A-Tasket This game is for five or more players and uses a knotted handkerchief. A player is declared "It" and he or she holds the handkerchief. The other players join hands and form a circle with "It" on the outside. "It" skips around the circle singing the rhyme below. On the last words, "It" drops the handkerchief behind a player and continues to skip around the circle. The other player must pick up the handkerchief and skip around the circle the other way in order to get back to his or her place. The player who arrives at the empty place first joins the circle. The other must be "It" for the next round.

1. Explain to children that they will be learning to play a game from England. Point to England on the ***Inflatable Globe***.
2. Write the words *A-Tisket, A-Tasket* on chart paper as shown and teach the words to the class.
3. Expain to children how to play the game.

ART CONNECTION

LEARNING STYLE: KINESTHETIC

Learning Center: Make Birthday Piñatas

GROUP

30 MINUTES OR LONGER

Objective: To become familiar with another culture by making Mexican piñatas.

Materials: grocery bags (large, brown, paper), stapler, hole puncher, 10-foot cord or strong yarn, piñata presents (items such as balloons, wrapped candies, pennies, stickers, erasers, new pencils), tempera paint, brushes, scissors, construction paper, glue, crepe paper, markers, crayons, blindfold, plastic baseball bat

1. Divide the class into ten groups and assign each group a different month of the school year. Children can assemble the piñata for their month in the Art Learning Center.
2. To make a piñata, direct children to put one paper bag inside another. Then have children fill their bags with presents (the contents might vary according to the month). Have children fold the tops of the bags over twice and staple them. Help children to punch two holes on either side of the fold. Attach a cord through the holes.
3. Have groups write the names of their month on the pinata. Allow children to decorate their piñata using materials of their choice. You might suggest that they decorate piñatas with pictures or designs that relate to special days in their month.
4. Collectively celebrate children's birthdays each month with a piñata party. Hang the piñata in the gym or from a tree. Blindfold a birthday child and spin him or her around. Have the child try to break open the piñata with a baseball bat with other children at a safe distance away. After several attempts, another birthday child can have a turn. When the piñata breaks, all children can collect the goodies!

UNIT 5

LESSON 5

Happy Birthday, U.S.A.!

UNIT 5 THEME BIG BOOK, PAGES 18–19

LESSON OVERVIEW

Independence Day is a holiday Americans celebrate to honor our country's birth.

LESSON OBJECTIVES

- Recognize that Independence Day is our country's birthday.
- Recognize that the term "Fourth of July" is another name for Independence Day.
- Identify ways Americans celebrate Independence Day.
- Locate the Fourth of July on a calendar.

KEY CONCEPTS

Fourth of July   Independence Day

RESOURCE REMINDER

Project Book
p. 63

Stickers Package
Sheet 19

Inflatable Globe

Desk Map
United States

Technology Connection
VIDEODISC/VIDEO TAPE 3

Search Frame 50671, Play to 53200

GETTING READY

Make Lemonade

GROUP

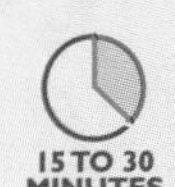
15 TO 30 MINUTES

CURRICULUM CONNECTION Art

Objective: To learn how to follow a recipe for a holiday celebration.

Resource: *Project Book* p. 63

Materials: glue, scissors, crayons

Utensils: measuring cup, measuring spoon, pitcher, wooden spoon, fruit juicer

Ingredients: 6–10 lemons, water, sugar, ice cubes, maraschino cherry juice

1. Tell children that many people like to drink lemonade on the Fourth of July and on hot summer days. Read the recipe card for lemonade with children. Tell children that the pictures at the bottom of ***Project Book*** p. 63 show some ingredients in the recipe.
2. Direct children to cut out the recipe card and the pictures. Help children to glue the pictures next to the appropriate lines of directions on the recipe card. Invite children to color the pictures.
3. Have small groups of children follow the recipe cards to make pitchers of lemonade. Children can take the recipe cards home to make their own lemonade for summer holiday celebrations.

Project Book p. 63

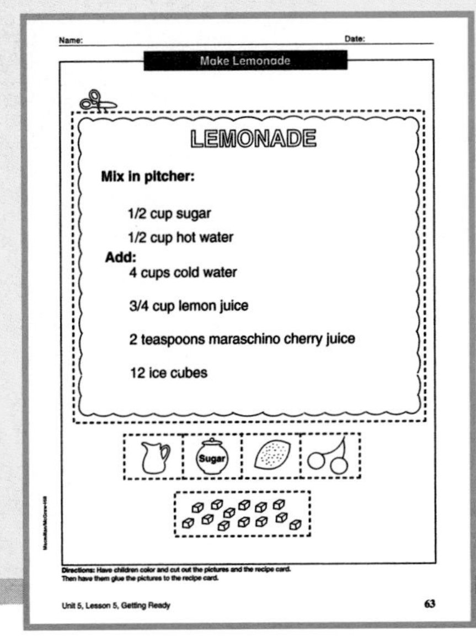

Name: Date:

Make Lemonade

LEMONADE

Mix in pitcher:

1/2 cup sugar
1/2 cup hot water

Add:
4 cups cold water
3/4 cup lemon juice
2 teaspoons maraschino cherry juice
12 ice cubes

Directions: Have children color and cut out the pictures and the recipe card. Then have them glue the pictures to the recipe card.

Unit 5, Lesson 5, Getting Ready 63

1 Prepare

WARMING UP WITH THE READ ALOUD

Tell children that the poem they will hear is about a holiday Americans celebrate called the Fourth of July. Share the poem in the Read Aloud.

- ***Why is everyone excited?*** *(It is the Fourth of July.)*
- ***What things does the poem say people do on the Fourth of July?*** *(People watch bands in parades, they eat apple pie at picnics, and they watch rockets, or fireworks.)*

Have a child locate the Fourth of July on a calendar.

Technology Connection

VIDEODISC/VIDEO TAPE 3
Enrich Lesson 5 with the video segment *Celebrate and Remember,* Search Frame 50671.

See the bar code on p. 191.

2 Teach

USING BIG BOOK PAGES 18–19

Read the lesson title and tell children that *U.S.A.* stands for the words "United States of America."

Use the ***Desk Maps*** to review our country's shape. Explain that our country's birthday is the Fourth of July. Share that another name for this holiday is Independence Day.

LESSON 5

Happy Birthday, U.S.A.!

18

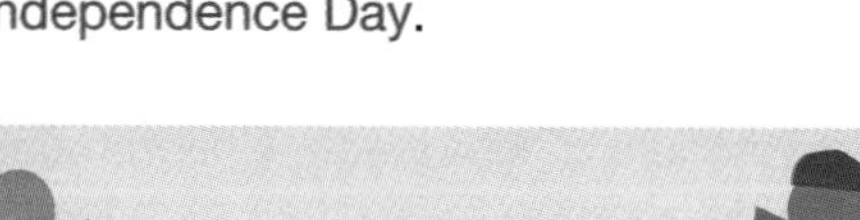

Read Aloud

Fourth of July

Everyone's excited
  on the 4th of July.
We stand along the sidewalk
  when the band goes by.
And then we have a picnic;
  we have apple pie.
And at night we watch the rockets,
  throwing stars across the sky.

Aileen Fisher

Print Awareness

On the chalkboard, show the connection visually between the abbreviation *U.S.A.* and the words that it stands for. Write the capital letters and have children name them. Then write the words *United, States,* and *America* next to the appropriate letters. Have volunteers trace the capital letter and its matching capital letter in the word.

CITIZENSHIP

Invite volunteers to describe in their own words what being proud means. Afterwards tell children that Independence Day is a holiday on which many Americans do things to show how proud we are to live in our country. We sing and listen to music about our country, its land, and its flag; we display an important symbol of our country—the American flag; and we wear clothing that is red, white, and blue.

19

Background Information

About Independence Day You may wish to supply children with some additional information about this topic.

- Thomas Jefferson was the author of the Declaration of Independence.
- On July 4, 1776, the members of the Continental Congress approved the Declaration of Independence and the thirteen colonies became the United States of America.
- The first Independence Day was celebrated on July 4, 1777, in Philadelphia. In honor of the celebration, warships fired their cannons, bells rang, and fireworks lit up the sky. Festivities also included games, sports, balls, and bonfires. Since that day, our country has celebrated its independence each year on the Fourth of July.
- In addition to fireworks and parades, celebrations today in many parts of the United States also include outside parties, picnics, community events, and air shows.

Place the ***Stickers*** *Fourth of July* and *Independence Day* near the title and read them aloud.

USE BIG BOOK STICKERS, SHEET 19

Use the ***Stickers*** throughout the lesson.

Point out the picture of the signing of the Declaration of Independence. Tell children that long ago, America followed the laws of England. Locate England on the ***Inflatable Globe***. Explain that most Americans did not like England's laws. They wanted to be free, or independent. On July 4, 1776, American leaders signed a Declaration of Independence. This paper told the king of England that America was to be a new, free country called the United States of America. The king did not like this idea and he sent troops to fight the Americans. After a long fight, the Americans won the war. Many Americans celebrated the birth of their new country with parades and fireworks.

Tell children that today, we celebrate our country's birthday in the same way. Point out the sashes that Lily and her friends have made for the holiday. To make the sashes with your own class, see page 194 for instructions.

Ask children to compare the parades on pp. 18–19. Ask children to consider how it might have been to be in a parade in Washington's time.

- ***How are Lily and her friends celebrating the Fourth of July?*** *(Possible answers: They have decorated the bike and wagon, are waving flags, and are wearing red, white, and blue.)*

★**THINKING FURTHER:** ***Using Prior Knowledge*** ***What decorations might you see on this holiday? How do you know?*** *(American flags, streamers, balloons, and other items in red, white, and blue; children may say that they know from personal knowledge or the media.)*

3 Close

LESSON SUMMARY

Read the lesson question, pointing to each word as you read. Children should list different ways that people celebrate the holiday—such as with picnics, parades, and fireworks.

EVALUATE

Draw Fourth-of-July Pictures Have children draw Independence-Day celebrations.

ART CONNECTION

LEARNING STYLE: KINESTHETIC

Make a Fourth-of-July Sash

ON YOUR OWN

30 MINUTES OR LONGER

Objective: To understand the significance of the Fourth of July by making and wearing patriotic sashes.

Materials: plastic shelf liner (white, nonstick), scissors, markers or crayons (red, white, and blue), glitter, flag stickers, stapler

Advance Preparation: Cut shelf liner into strips (4" wide by 36" long).

1. Tell children that they will be making sashes to wear for the Fourth of July. Distribute shelf-liner strips. Show children how to fold a strip in half and cut a V-shaped notch at the ends.
2. Have children make a Fourth-of-July design on one side of a strip using markers or crayons, glitter, and/or flag stickers.
3. When children have completed their designs on the strips, help them to staple the ends together about three inches from the ends to create a sash. Demonstrate to children how to wear the sash across their chest.

ART CONNECTION

LEARNING STYLE: KINESTHETIC

Paint Firework Designs

ON YOUR OWN

15 TO 30 MINUTES

Objective: To help children understand the significance and symbols of the Fourth of July by making fireworks designs.

Materials: muffin tin, tempera paints, marbles, black construction paper, scissors, sturdy paper or plastic dinner plates, plastic spoons, silver and gold glitter, hole puncher, 12" lengths of yarn

Advance Preparation: Cut circles from construction paper and glue them inside the paper plates. Fill a muffin tin with different color tempera paints and drop a marble in each color.

1. Have children roll a marble around in the paint until it is well coated. Then have them use a spoon to transfer the marble onto the paper-lined plate.
2. Show children how to swirl the marble gently around until the paint wears off and then return the marble to the same color of paint in the tin. Have children repeat the procedure with other colors.
3. When children finish, have them sprinkle glitter over the wet paint.
4. Punch a hole in the paper plates and attach yarn for hanging.

CLOSE WITH A SONG

LINKING SOCIAL STUDIES AND LITERATURE

Bring Unit 5 to a close with the song, "Over the River and Through the Wood." This song, which can be found on pages 20–21 of the Big Book, may be used as a springboard to support these Social Studies concepts:

- The twelve months of the year include special days we call holidays.
- Families gather to celebrate Thanksgiving with a special meal.

ABOUT THE SONG

A full instructional plan, along with the song, appears on the following two pages.

This festive song recalls the pleasure of an old-fashioned sleigh ride. Set to a traditional melody, with words by Lydia Maria Child, it has been popular for over a century.

As they sing this song together, children will enjoy its "galloping" rhythm and vivid images of frosty countryside.

ABOUT THE POET

Lydia Maria Child was an American writer and abolitionist from Medford, Massachusetts. The words in the song "Over the River and Through the Wood" are based on an original poem written by her in 1844 titled "A Boy's Thanksgiving Day." After the Civil War she wrote much on behalf of the freedmen and Indian rights.

INTRODUCE

Using Prior Knowledge Display a calendar for the present year. Invite children to name their favorite holidays and list them on the chalkboard. Then help children point to the months in which they occur. Guide children to remind them that Thanksgiving is in November.

Previewing Tell children they are going to sing a song about a family going to grandmother's house for Thanksgiving. Read aloud the title. Then have volunteers look at the illustration and tell what they see. What season is it? How do they know? Remind them that Thanksgiving comes in the late fall, when the weather in some areas can be very cold, even snowy.

UNIT 5 THEME BIG BOOK

Curriculum Connection

Mathematics After sharing the song, invite children to recall other special holiday foods, such as Easter eggs, birthday cake, and Fourth of July hot dogs.

- Make a chart on the chalkboard. Across the top, write "Holidays" and "Food." Ask volunteers to name holidays and the foods that go with them, and list them on the chart. You may want to use holiday symbols or designs in place of words.
- Then have the children vote for their favorite holidays. Count the votes, making a stroke for each one. Ask children which are the most popular and least popular holidays.

READ

USING BIG BOOK PAGES 20–21

Read aloud the words to the song. Explain that "dapple" means spotted, and that a strong wind can blow snow into piles called "drifts." Help children learn the song by repeating each phrase. When they are familiar with the words and music, invite them to sing the song together. The *long*-short-short rhythm of the song can be counted *one*-two-three. Ask children to join in counting and clapping to this rhythm.

SHARE

How is Thanksgiving like other holidays? How is it different? *(Answers may include: Alike: We celebrate with our family and have a special meal at Christmas; it is an American holiday, like the Fourth of July; it is in the fall, like Columbus Day. Different: We remember the Wampanaug and the Pilgrims; we do not exchange presents.)*

EXTENDING THE LITERATURE WITH ART

LEARNING STYLE: VISUAL

Make a Song Scene

ON YOUR OWN

Objective: To connect song images with Thanksgiving

Resource: ***Project Book*** p. 64

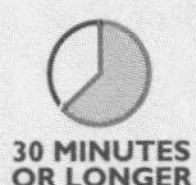
30 MINUTES OR LONGER

Materials: crayons, scissors, glue, construction paper

- Remind children that the song contained special images—the sleigh, the horse, the snow-covered trees, and grandmother's house.
- Give each child a copy of ***Project Book***, p. 64, and point out the images.
- Invite children to color and cut them out. Then have them make a song scene by gluing the cutouts to a sheet of construction paper.
- Display the pictures in the classroom.

Project Book p. 64

Assessment Opportunities

The CLOSE section of each lesson includes an EVALUATE activity. This page provides suggestions for using selected EVALUATE activities to integrate your assessment program with each day's lesson plan. The next page lists the main objectives of the unit and some of the activities that reinforce them. You may wish to make a copy of the checklist for each child.

EVALUATE Signs of Success

LESSON 1, Columbus Day

EVALUATE: *Perform Columbus-Day Skits, p.165*

OBSERVATIONAL ASSESSMENT

- Children should be able to dramatize the meeting of Columbus and the Taino.
- You may use a tape recorder to record each child's skit. You may also wish to take photographs of the children performing.

PORTFOLIO ASSESSMENT

The tapes and photographs can be part of children's portfolios.

- The tapes should reflect an understanding of the thoughts of the Taino, the sailors, and Columbus.

LESSON 2, A Day of Thanks

EVALUATE: *Make Giving-Thanks Pictures, p.169*

OBSERVATIONAL ASSESSMENT

- Ask questions such as, "Why were the Pilgrims celebrating?" Record each child's answer.

PORTFOLIO ASSESSMENT

The giving-thanks pictures can be part of children's portfolios.

- One picture should illustrate something the Pilgrims were thankful for.
- The other picture should illustrate something children are thankful for.

AROUND THE WORLD, Birthdays Near and Far

EVALUATE: *Identify Birthdays, p.189*

OBSERVATIONAL ASSESSMENT

- Children should be able to share birthday traditions with the class.
- You may wish to tape-record children sharing traditions.

PORTFOLIO ASSESSMENT

The recited birthday dates and tapes can be part of children's portfolios.

- Children should be able to identify their birthdays. You can record the month, date, and year each child recites to you.

UNIT 5 OBJECTIVES Checklist

1. Recognize the meaning of Columbus Day.
2. Recognize the meaning of Thanksgiving Day.
3. Identify a calendar and its function.
4. Recognize the meaning of Martin Luther King, Jr., Day.
5. Recognize the meaning of Presidents' Day.
6. Recognize how to make predictions.
7. Recognize that birthdays are celebrated around the world.
8. Recognize the meaning of the Fourth of July.

Name ______________________ Class ______________________

LESSON	ACTIVITY	PAGES	UNIT 5 OBJECTIVES	✔
LESSON 1	Make a Three-Ship Collage	163	1	
LESSON 1	Make Soap Ships	166	1	
LESSON 1	Make Taino Pottery	166	1	
LESSON 2	Write a Thank-You Note	167	2	
LESSON 2	Make a Turkey Cup	170	2	
LESSON 2	Make Thanksgiving-Day Placemats	170	2	
STUDY SKILL	Sequence Calendar Cutouts	171	3	
STUDY SKILL	Make Weather Calendars	174	3	
STUDY SKILL	Make a Calendar Birthday Train	174	3	
LESSON 3	Make Memory Medals	175	4	
LESSON 3	Make Peace Doves	178	4	
LESSON 3	Make a Friendship Wreath	178	4	
LESSON 4	Make "Special American" Cards	179	5	
LESSON 4	Make a Tricorn Hat	182	5	
LESSON 4	Make a Stovepipe Hat	182	5	
THINKING SKILL	Make a Book	183	6	
THINKING SKILL	Predict the Ending of a Story	186	5, 6	
THINKING SKILL	Make a Prediction About Balls	186	6	
AROUND THE WORLD	Make Balloon Badges	187	7	
AROUND THE WORLD	Play a Party Game	190	7	
AROUND THE WORLD	Make Birthday Piñatas	190	7	
LESSON 5	Make Lemonade	191	8	
LESSON 5	Make a Fourth-of-July Sash	194	8	
LESSON 5	Paint Firework Designs	194	8	

index

UNIT PROJECTS

LEARNING CENTER IDEAS

READ ALOUDS

LITERATURE BIG BOOKS

CLOSE WITH A POEM/SONG

CREDITS

COVER: Pentagram

ILLUSTRATIONS: Andrea Maginnis: pp. 8, 44, 84, 124, 160

PHOTOGRAPHS: All photographs are by Macmillan/McGraw-Hill School Division and David Mager for MMSD.

ACKNOWLEDGMENTS: The publisher gratefully acknowledges permission to reprint the following copyrighted material:

Unit 1

"First Day of School" from **I Wonder How, I Wonder Why** by Aileen Fisher. Copyright 1962 by Aileen Fisher. Reprinted by permission of Abelard-Schuman, Ltd.

From **I'm Busy, Too** by Norma Simon. Copyright 1980 by Norma Simon. Reprinted by permission from General Publishing, Limited, Toronto.

"Point to the Right" from **Let's Do Fingerplays** by Marion Grayson. Copyright 1962 by Marion F. Grayson. Reprinted by permission of Robert B. Luce, Inc., Washington.

"Ten Little Firemen" from **Let's Do Fingerplays** by Marion Grayson. Copyright 1962 by Marion F. Grayson. Reprinted by permission of Robert B. Luce, Inc., Washington.

Unit 2

"My Day" by Rebecca Boynton from **Finger Frolics**, revised. Copyright 1976, 1983 by Partner Press, Livonia, Michigan. Reprinted by permission from the publisher.

"The Twins" by Jay Lee from **All Together.** Copyright 1925 by Dorothy Aldis. Reprinted by permission of G.P. Putnam's Sons.

"What is a Family?" from **Fathers, Mothers, Sisters, Brothers** by Mary Ann Hoberman. Copyright 1991 by Mary Ann Hoberman. Reprinted by permission of Little, Brown and Company, Inc.

"Workers" from **Rhymes for Learning Times** by Louise Binder Scott. Copyright 1983 by T. S. Denison & Co., Inc. Reprinted by permission of the publisher.

Unit 3

"Easy Seasons" from **A Nickel Buys a Rhyme** by Alan Benjamin. Copyright 1993 by Alan Benjamin. Reprinted by permission of William Morrow and Company, Inc., New York.

"Falling Leaves," "Raindrops," and "Snowflakes" from **Let's Do Fingerplays** by Marion Grayson. Copyright 1962 by Marion F. Grayson. Reprinted by permission of Robert B. Luce, Inc., Washington.

"Five Little Frogs" from **Rhymes for Learning Times** by Louise Binder Scott. Copyright 1983 by T. S. Denison & Co., Inc. Reprinted by permission from the publisher.

"It's Spring" from **In Spring** by Jane Belk Moncure. Copyright 1985 by Abdo Consulting Group, Inc. Reprinted by permission of the publisher.

"Jonathan's Farm" from **Collected Poems** by Miriam Waddington. Copyright 1986 by Miriam Waddington. Reprinted by permission of Oxford University Press.

"Shore" from **Menagerie** by Mary Britton Miller. Reprinted by permission of the author.

"Sing a Song of Cities" from **Good Rhymes, Good Times** by Lee Bennett Hopkins. Copyright 1972 by Lee Bennett Hopkins. Reprinted by permission of Curtis Brown, Ltd.

Unit 4

"Here Is Our World," fingerplay by Louise Binder Scott from **Rhymes for Learning Times**. Copyright 1983 by T. S. Dension & Co., Inc. Reprinted by permission of the publisher.

"I Love America" by Nona Keen Duffy from **Poetry Place Anthology**. Copyright 1983 by Scholastic, Inc. Reprinted by permission of Scholastic, Inc.

"Thinking Green" from **50 Simple Things Kids Can Do to Save the Earth** by The Earthworks Group. Copyright 1989 by John Javna, The Earthworks Group. Reprinted by permission of Andrews and McMeel Publishers.

"Waving the Flag" by Rebecca Boynton from **Finger Frolics**, revised. Copyright 1976, 1983 by Partner Press, Livonia, Michigan. Reprinted by permission of the publisher.

"The World" by William Brighty Rands from **Childcraft—The How and Why Library**. Reprinted by permission of Dodd, Mead & Company.

Unit 5

"After the End" from **Always Wondering** by Aileen Fisher. Copyright 1991 by Aileen Fisher. Reprinted by permission from HarperCollins.

"A Dream" from **My First Martin Luther King Book** by Dee Lillegard. Copyright 1987 by Regensteiner Publishing Enterprises, Inc. Reprinted by permission of The Child's World.

"Fourth of July" from **In Summer** by Aileen Fisher. Copyright 1985 by The Child's World, Inc. Reprinted by permission of The Child's World.

From **In 1492** by Jean Marzollo. Copyright 1991 by Jean Marzollo. Reprinted by permission of Scholastic, Inc.

"Party Table" from **Birthday Poems** by Myra Cohn Livingston. Copyright 1989 by Myra Cohn Livingston. Reprinted by permission of Holiday House, New York.

"Seven Kites in March" from **Rhymes for Learning Times** by Louise Binder Scott. Copyright 1983 by T. S. Denison & Co., Inc. Reprinted by permission of the publisher.

"A Thanksgiving Thought" by Bobbi Katz. Copyright 1978 by Bobbi Katz. Reprinted by permission of the author.

BIG BOOKS

"Someone Special, Just Like You" by Tricia Brown. Text copyright © 1982, 1984 by Tricia Brown and Fran Ortiz. Reprinted by permission of Holt, Rinehart and Winston.

"I Go with My Family to Grandma's" by Riki Levinson. Text copyright © 1986 by Riki Levinson. Reprinted by permission of Dutton Child Books.

"One Hot Summer Day" by Nina Crew. Text copyright © 1995 by Nina Crew. Reprinted by permission of Greenwillow Books, a division of William Morrow & Company, Inc.

"The Earth And I" by Frank Asch. Copyright 1994 by Frank Asch. Reprinted by permission of Harcourt Brace & Company.

"Light the Candle! Bang the Drum!" by Ann Morris. Text copyright © 1997 by Ann Morris. Illustrations copyright © 1997 by Peter Linenthal. Reprinted by permission of Dutton Children's Books, a division of Penguin Books USA Inc.

HOLIDAY SECTION

"The Best Valentine" by Margaret Hillert. Copyright by Margaret Hillert. Reprinted by permission of the author.

"For Father's Day" by Sandra Liatsos. Copyright by Sandra Liatsos. Reprinted by permission of the author.

"Happy New Year" from **Rhymes for Learning Times** by Louise Binder Scott. Copyright 1983 by T. S. Denison & Co., Inc. Reprinted by permission of the publisher.

"Kwanzaa's Here" from **Small World Celebrations** by Jean Warren and Elizabeth McKinnon. Copyright 1988 by Warren Publishing House, Inc. Reprinted by permission of Warren Publishing House, Inc.

"On Mother's Day" from **Skip Around the Year** by Aileen Fisher. Copyright 1967 by Aileen Fisher. Reprinted by permission of HarperCollins.

"St. Patrick's Day" from **Rhymes for Learning Times** by Louise Binder Scott. Copyright 1983 by T. S. Denison & Co., Inc. Reprinted by permission the publisher.

"Santa's Reindeer" from **Rhymes for Learning Times** by Louise Binder Scott. Copyright 1983 by T. S. Denison & Co., Inc. Reprinted by permission of the publisher.

"Song" from **Summer Green** by Elizabeth Coatsworth. Copyright 1948 by The Macmillan Company. Reprinted by permission of The Macmillan Company.

INSTRUCTIONAL PLANS
LITERATURE
BIG BOOKS

UNIT 1

THE LITERATURE BIG BOOK INSTRUCTIONAL PLAN

SOMEONE SPECIAL, JUST LIKE YOU

The following lesson plan provides support to help you link the Literature Big Book to the Social Studies concepts in Unit 1.

- Each of us is special.
- People are alike and different in their interests, feelings and abilities.
- School is a place where children learn.

INTRODUCE

Using Prior Knowledge Invite children to help you make a list of activities they like to do. You might make three different lists with the headings: *home, school,* and *community.* Make a tally next to each item to see which activities are the favorite among members of your class.

GETTING READY

Invite children to pair up with another classmate that they don't know very well. Ask them to find out things about each other such as their favorite color, ice cream flavor, animal, sport, hobby and so on. Afterwards point out that people do not always like or do the same things as each other. Discuss that these differences do not make one person better than another and that accepting and appreciating each other's differences is important.

Previewing Display the cover of the Literature Big Book and read aloud the title, as well as the names of the author and the photographer. Encourage children to look carefully at the cover and think about the name of the book, and then guess what the book might be about. You may wish to record predictions on a chart or on the chalkboard and return to them after you read the Literature Big Book aloud.

READ

The complete text of the story is provided on the next page.

USING THE STORY

Tell children that the author wrote this book to help her son and other people learn about children who cannot hear, speak, see, walk or do things in the same ways as most children. She hoped that by reading her book and looking at the photographs we would become more comfortable with people's differences and also learn that we are all alike in many ways. Point out that everyone wants to feel important, be loved, learn, play, do well, and to be liked by others.

Read and discuss pp. 6–11. Share that "special," means being you in your very own way. On p. 9, suggest how the walker helps the girl get around at school. Tell children that the boy on p. 10 cannot hear. Explain that the word meaning "cannot hear" is *deaf.* Share that he can learn about sound by feeling the beat of the tambourine rather than hearing the sound it makes. Point out that the boy on p. 11 cannot see. Explain that the word meaning "cannot see" is *blind.* Ask children if they can think of other ways the blind boy can learn about the tunnel without seeing it. ***Drawing Conclusions/Using Prior Knowledge***

As you read pp. 12–33, compare and contrast the things the children in the book like to do with the activities already listed on the chalkboard. Point out those that are the same and those that are different. ***Compare and Contrast***

Complete the story. On p. 46 point out that the teacher is telling the sleepytime story using American Sign Language. Explain that by moving her hands in different ways she makes *signs* that mean different things. The *signs* are words for deaf children. ***Extend Concepts***

SHARE

Encourage children to share their ideas and responses to the story. Clarify any parts that children do not understand.

- ***What things can a blind person do?*** *(Answers will vary but may include brushing teeth, petting a rabbit, walking on a balance beam.)*
- ***What things can a deaf person do?*** *(Answers will vary but may include playing the piano, talking on the phone, listening to stories told in sign language.)*

★ **THINKING FURTHER:** ***Making Conclusions*** ***What are some things that make us all special?*** *(Answer may include our smile, sweet kisses, and hugs.)*

TEXT OF
SOMEONE SPECIAL, JUST LIKE YOU

Meet someone special,
someone just like you.
Someone who may not walk the same way you do,
or hear the same sounds,
or see the same things.
But just like you...
she likes to blow bubbles,
eat ice cream,
and smell pretty flowers.
And, like you, she likes to have fun—
and go down slides,
play with toys,
and go swimming.
He likes to go to school,
and do art,
and learn from his teacher how to talk with his hands if he can't hear,
and read with her fingers if she can't see.
He likes school trips—
especially to a science museum
or to the aquarium!
Then, she likes to go home,
eat lunch,
wash up,
and have quiet time.
Sometimes, he is lonely—
like times when he is waiting for his dad.
And sometimes he cries when it hurts.
Whenever he falls down, just like you, he gets himself right up again.
For even without seeing the same things you do,
he can brush his teeth,
pet a rabbit,
and walk a balance beam.
Even without hearing the same sounds you do, he can
play the piano,
talk on the telephone,
and listen to sleepytime stories. Even without walking the same way
you do, she can do all the same things that you like to do:
dance,
swing,
and best of all, help a friend.
What makes someone special are the same things that make you special, too!
A beautiful smile,
sweet kisses,
and lots of hugs.

EXTENDING THE LITERATURE WITH LANGUAGE

USING SIGN LANGUAGE

Remind children that people who cannot hear are deaf. Tell children that some deaf people make words with their fingers and hands to help them communicate to others. Explain that the words they form with their fingers and hands are called *signs*. Invite children to share if they have ever seen a person using sign language. Teach children how to fingerspell their names using the Manual Alphabet for the Deaf. Point out that the hand alphabet is one language used throughout the world. Then teach children signs for words such as "I," "me," "you," and "school" or simple sentences such as "I love you." Children might also enjoy learning the numbers 1–10. They might be surprised that they already know the first five number signs!

USING THE LITERATURE BIG BOOK

UNIT 2

THE LITERATURE BIG BOOK INSTRUCTIONAL PLAN

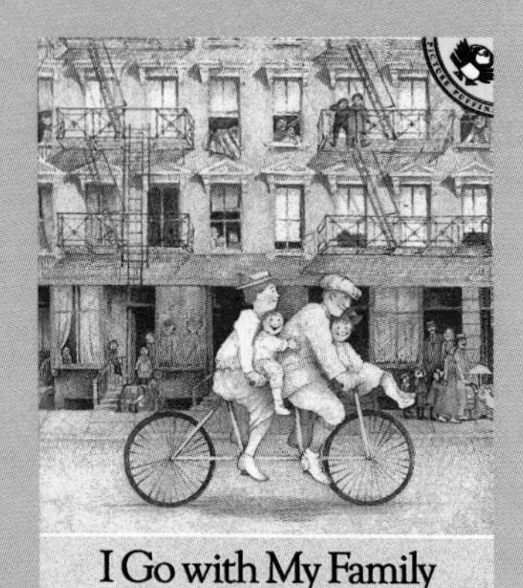

I GO WITH MY FAMILY TO GRANDMA'S

The following lesson plan provides support to help you link the Literature Big Book to the Social Studies concepts in Unit 2.

- Every family is unique.
- Family members love and care for each other.
- Recognize how families lived long ago.

INTRODUCE

Using Prior Knowledge Invite children to talk about who lives in families. Ask them to tell the names we use for family members, such as mother, father, sister, brother, and so on. Encourage children to describe what members of a family do and say to show they love and care for others in the family. Record their responses in a list on the chalkboard. You can begin the discussion by talking about what people in your family do to show they love and care for each other.

GETTING READY

Have children recognize that everyone, everywhere, has a family, and that families can be small or big. Remind them that animals are part of families, too. Ask children to choose a partner and take turns describing their families to each other.

Previewing Display the cover of the Literature Big Book and read aloud the title and the names of the author and the illustrator. Point out the old-fashioned clothes and bicycle-built-for-two, and ask if this story takes place now or many years ago. Ask the children why they think this family is going to Grandma's house. Record their responses on the chalkboard and refer to them during the reading.

READ

The complete text of the story is provided on the next page.

USING THE STORY

The book begins with Millie, in Manhattan, getting ready to go with her mother, father, and little brother to Grandma's by bicycle. Then Bella, in Brooklyn, describes her family and their way of getting to Grandma's. Three other girls and their families also show how they travel to Grandma's. Encourage the children to notice how many children are in each family, and how each family is like and unlike the others.

Read aloud until all five families arrive at Grandma's. Ask the children to point out some of the activities going on in the back yard. Invite them to predict what may happen now that everyone is together. ***Noting Details; Making Predictons***

As you complete the reading of the book, encourage children to notice that every single person in the family is included in the family photograph. Ask children how they think the family members feel about each other. Point out that the pictures show many different interactions: playing, teasing, hugging, scolding, and so on. ***Identifying characters' behavior***

SHARE

Encourage children to share their ideas and responses to the book. Remind them that all the people in a family care for each other.

- ***Families have a special responsibility to take care of children. How do the adults in this big family take care of their children?*** *(Possible answers: Grown-ups give them food, keep them warm, dress them carefully, play with them, give them hugs and kisses.)*
- ***Why was it important for all the families to go to Grandma's house?*** *(Possible answers: to have their picture taken; to visit with each other; to share news; to celebrate)*

★ **THINKING FURTHER:** ***Making Inferences*** ***What do you think family members ought to do to get along with each other?*** *(Possible answers: share; be polite; offer to help; be kind)*

TEXT OF

I GO WITH MY FAMILY TO GRANDMA'S

My name is Millie and I live in Manhattan.

I go with my family on a red and yellow bicycle

to Grandma's.

My name is Bella and I live in Brooklyn.

I go with my family on a golden yellow trolley

to Grandma's.

My name is Carrie and I live in Queens.

I go with my family in Papa's white wagon

to Grandma's.

My name is Beatie and I live in the Bronx.

I go with my family on a dark blue train and a dark green train

to Grandma's.

My name is Stella and I live in Staten Island.

I go with my family in Papa's big car on a red and white ferry

across the water, to the city

to Grandma's.

EXTENDING THE LITERATURE WITH ART

"FUTURE FAMILY REUNION" PICTURES

Invite children to imagine the kind of party they would like to have with their family and friends. Where would they have it? How would people get there? What would they eat? What games would they play?

Provide children with crayons and paper. Ask them to draw a picture of their imaginary party.

UNIT 3

THE LITERATURE BIG BOOK INSTRUCTIONAL PLAN

ONE HOT SUMMER DAY

The following lesson plan provides support to help you link the Literature Big Book to the Social Studies concepts in Unit 3.

- People find interesting and useful ways of adapting to seasonal weather.
- You can learn about your environment through exploration.

INTRODUCE

Using Prior Knowledge Invite children to talk about things that they might do in hot weather. Would they rather be indoors or out? What would they choose to wear? What kinds of food and drink would they enjoy? Record their responses in a list on the chalkboard. You can begin the discussion by talking about your own favorite hot-weather activities.

GETTING READY

Encourage children to discuss different kinds of weather. Ask children to choose a partner and act out a fun activity that takes place in heat, in rain, or in snow. Remind them of special items they may need: pail and shovel; ball; marbles; umbrella. Ask if they enjoy activities by themselves or if they like to have a friend along.

Previewing Display the cover of the Literature Big Book and read aloud the title and the name of the author/illustrator. Encourage children to think about the cover illustration and book title and to notice the little girl's environment. Clues such as blue skies and green leaves, brick buildings, bright colors and light clothing suggest a city in summer. Invite children to predict what the little girl could do there on a hot day. Record predictions on the chalkboard and return to them during the reading so that children can confirm or revise them.

READ

The complete text of the story is provided on the next page.

USING THE STORY

Point out that the little girl in the story is experiencing her neighborhood in a special way because of the hot weather. Although her mother suggests she play inside games, she prefers to be outside because there are different things to do and see in the neighborhood when it is very hot. Encourage children to look carefully at the photographs. Point out that some are collages made up of several photos pasted together.

Read aloud the first part of the story, up to and including the part where the sky gets dark and cloudy. Ask the children to recount the fun things the little girl has done in the heat: teased her shadow, made drawings in the shade, eaten two grape Popsicles. Then ask the children what may happen next, now that the clouds have come. ***Sequence***

Continue reading the story through to the end. Ask the children how they feel when a rainstorm comes to break the heat. Would they enjoy dancing in the rain? As you complete the reading of the story, point out that the story starts with "it's hot" and ends with "It's nice and cool," and that almost every line says something about the weather. ***Main idea***

Then point out that the little girl had a wonderful time in both the heat and the rain, enjoying different activities in her neighborhood as the weather changed. ***Recognizing characteristics of the environment***

SHARE

Encourage children to share their ideas and responses to the story. Clarify any parts that children do not understand. For instance: "hot enough to fry an egg on the sidewalk" is a figure of speech. Remind the children that a sidewalk could not really get as hot as a stove, but the language makes us feel the heat in a strong way.

- ***What special things did the little girl do because it was hot?*** *(She teased her shadow; she stayed in the shade to draw pictures; she ate two Popsicles in a row.)*

★ **THINKING FURTHER: *Cause and effect What happens when the clouds pile up in the sky?*** *(Rain, thunder, and lightning may follow; next the weather may cool.)*

- ***When it's very hot in your neighborhood, what do you like to do?*** *(Accept all answers.)*

To spark discussion of this question, turn to the page where the little girl teases her shadow. Encourage children to describe games they make up to play by themselves.

TEXT OF
ONE HOT SUMMER DAY

It's summer, and it's hot.

Dogs pant. Hydrants are open. Women carry umbrellas for the shade.

Hot enough to fry an egg on the sidewalk. Well, maybe not.

My mother tells me to play inside games. She has the fan on high.

Instead, I stand outside and tease my shadow.

Then I run into the shade and draw pictures.

It's too hot to play on the swings or in the sandbox.

I eat two grape Popsicles in a row.

I look at the sky. It's getting dark and cloudy.

Thunder comes, and then big drops.

I dance in the rain. I sing in the rain.

I splash in the rain. The rain stops.

It's nice and cool. I run to the playground, and I swing high.

EXTENDING THE LITERATURE WITH ART

DRAW A CHANGE IN THE WEATHER

Invite children to think about a playground with a playhouse, swings, a place to climb, and a slide. Now ask them to draw themselves at this playground two times: first on a very hot day and then on a cool, windy day. Before they make their drawings, encourage children to decide what they would be doing and what they would be wearing.

UNIT 4

THE LITERATURE BIG BOOK INSTRUCTIONAL PLAN

THE EARTH AND I

The following lesson plan provides support to help you link the Literature Big Book to the Social Studies concepts in Unit 4.

- Our country is part of a larger world.
- People must appreciate and protect the world in which they live.

INTRODUCE

Using Prior Knowledge Invite children to talk about things that they like to do outdoors. Encourage children to describe the things that they like to look at in nature. You can begin the discussion by talking about your favorite outdoor activities and what you appreciate in nature.

GETTING READY

Tell children that you will be reading to them a story about a boy who considers Earth to be his friend. Then have groups of children brainstorm what it means to be a friend. What do friends do? How do friends treat each other? Children can dictate their ideas to you or draw pictures of what it means to be a friend.

Previewing Display the cover of the Literature Big Book and read aloud the title, as well as the name of the author/illustrator. Encourage children to look at the cover illustration and think about the title of the book. Then invite them to guess what will happen in the story. Record predictions on a chart on the chalkboard and return to them during the reading so that children can confirm or revise them.

READ

The complete text of the story is provided on the next page.

USING THE STORY

Before reading the story, point out that the boy in the story has a very special relationship with Earth. Show children a globe and tell them that this globe shows planet Earth. Point out that we must all try to have a special relationship with our planet so that we can protect it.

Read aloud the first part of the story, up to and including the part where Earth helps the boy to grow. Invite children to discuss the things the boy does with Earth and the things that Earth does for the boy. ***Noting Details/Sequence***

Continue reading the story through to the end. Invite children to repeat along with you the final sentence, "The Earth and I are friends." Talk with children about the boy's friendship with Earth. ***Repetitive Language/Main Idea***

As you complete the reading of the story, point out that the boy in the story is very aware of what Earth provides him with, and that he knows he must take care of Earth like a friend. ***Recognizing responsibility for protecting the environment.***

SHARE

Encourage children to share their ideas and responses to the story. Clarify any parts that children do not understand.

- ***What made Earth and the boy sad?*** *(They were sad when people littered and did not take care of Earth.)*

★ **THINKING FURTHER:** ***Cause and Effect*** ***What did the boy do when he saw that Earth was sad?*** *(He cleaned up the litter so that Earth would be happy again.)*

TEXT OF
THE EARTH AND I

The Earth and I are friends.

Sometimes we go for long walks together.

I tell her what's on my mind.

She listens to every word.

Then I listen to her.

The Earth and I are friends.

We play together in my backyard.

I help her to grow.

She helps me to grow.

I sing for her.

She sings for me.

I dance for her.

She dances for me.

When she's sad,

I'm sad.

When she's happy,

I'm happy.

The Earth and I are friends.

EXTENDING THE LITERATURE WITH ART

EARTH SOUNDS

Begin a discussion with children about the sounds in nature that they are familiar with—for example, the patter of the rain on the window or sidewalk, thunder, the croak of a frog, or chirping of a bird. Encourage children to mimic some of these sounds.

Then invite children to make drawings of things in nature that make noise such as animals, types of weather, or waves. When finished, collect all the drawings.

Holding up one drawing at a time, ask children to mimic the sound belonging to that thing in nature. You may choose to write the sound on each drawing.

Assist children in making a "Sounds of Nature" bulletin board display of their drawings.

UNIT 5

THE LITERATURE BIG BOOK INSTRUCTIONAL PLAN

LIGHT THE CANDLE! BANG THE DRUM!

The following lesson plan provides support to help you link the Literature Big Book to the Social Studies concepts in Unit 5.

- People celebrate different holidays all over the world to remember important people and events.
- Traditional food, music, activities, and symbols make holidays special.

INTRODUCE

Using Prior Knowledge Invite children to talk about holidays they remember. Ask them for details. What special foods or costumes or traditions go with the holiday? Which family members participate? You can begin the discussion by talking about holidays you have enjoyed.

GETTING READY

Elicit from children that many holidays are celebrated over the course of a year. Ask them to recall which ones occur in winter, spring, summer, and fall. Invite them to choose a partner and take turns naming holidays.

Previewing Display the cover of the Literature Big Book and read aloud the title, as well as the names of the author and the illustrator. Encourage children to look at the cover illustration and think about the title of the book, including the subtitle, "A book of holidays around the world." Then invite them to name all the holidays they can think of. Record these on the chalkboard and return to them during the reading so children can confirm them.

READ

The complete text of the story is provided on the next page.

USING THE STORY

Before reading the story, point out that holidays are observed all over the world and families everywhere celebrate them. Remind children that people in different countries around the world speak different languages. Ask them to listen for the names of holidays they have never heard before. ***Understand the rich, complex nature of a given culture***

Read aloud the names of the first six holidays of the year, through Carnival. Remind the children that the first holiday of the year is New Year's Day in the winter. Invite children to predict whether holidays occur in all seasons. You may want them to name the other three seasons. ***Understand the meaning of time and chronology***

As you read the book, encourage children to notice that some holidays celebrate seasonal changes while others celebrate important people and ideas. Talk with children about why we need special days to remember people and events. ***Develop a keen sense of historical empathy***

SHARE

Encourage children to share their ideas and responses to the book. Ask them if some holidays were hard to understand. Clarify the purpose and activities associated with them.

- ***What holiday that is new for you would you like to celebrate?*** *(Help children recall the celebrations and make choices. Accept all answers.)*
- ***What activities take place on the Fourth of July?*** *(watching fireworks, waving flags, picnicking)*

★ **THINKING FURTHER:** ***Making Predictions*** ***What is the next holiday we celebrate? How will we celebrate it?*** *(Answer will vary with the calendar. Remind children of the reasons for the celebration.)*

TEXT OF

LIGHT THE CANDLE! BANG THE DRUM!

A BOOK OF HOLIDAYS AROUND THE WORLD

[NOTE: Background on each holiday is given on the book's final page.]

NEW YEAR'S DAY Goodbye, old year! At midnight, a new year begins. Horns blow. People throw confetti. Everyone shouts: "Happy New Year!"

MARTIN LUTHER KING, JR., DAY Martin Luther King, Jr., wanted people of all races to love and respect one another. We celebrate his life and dreams for a better world.

LUNAR NEW YEAR A new moon signals the new year. Red candles burn, and children get good-luck gifts in red paper. Firecrackers scare away the bad spirits.

VALENTINE'S DAY Make a card with hearts and flowers and give it to the one you love. *Will you be my valentine?*

PRESIDENTS' DAY Two great American leaders—George Washington and Abraham Lincoln—were born in February. We honor them and all they did for our country.

CARNIVAL Everyone is in masks and costumes. There is singing and dancing and lots of noise in the street. Come join the parade!

SAINT PATRICK'S DAY Shamrocks are everywhere! The whole town turns green and dances a jig to celebrate with the Irish!

EASTER The Easter bunny brings brightly colored eggs that we hunt for in the grass. Put them in your basket and celebrate the arrival of spring.

MAY DAY Spring is here at last. To celebrate, people gather flowers. In the town square, they dance around the maypole with ribbons in their hands.

CHILDREN'S DAY Kites in the shape of fish wave over rooftops. They are meant to show strength and courage. Elders wish the children health and happiness.

GREEN CORN FESTIVAL The corn is ripe. Native Americans give thanks at a big feast. There is eating, singing, and dancing throughout the day.

EID AL-FITR Prayers and fasting are over. Families dress in new clothes and visit friends, bringing sweets, flowers, and presents.

FOURTH OF JULY Parades, waving flags, fireworks! It's Independence Day in the United States—the day when freedom first rang in our land.

HALLOWEEN Children dressed as witches, goblins, and spooky ghosts yell, "Trick or Treat!" Pumpkins are carved to look like scary faces. *Boo!*

DIWALI *Diwali* means "row of lights." Floors are painted with bright-colored powders. Twinkling lights everywhere mark the new year.

DAY OF THE DEAD Rattle, rattle! Skeletons shake their bones and bang their drums. We remember relatives and friends who have died, and we celebrate life.

LOY KRATHONG Little boats, each with a candle and a wish, float down the river. Overhead, fireworks light their way under the full moon.

THANKSGIVING We help ourselves to all we can eat. We give thanks for what we have and we think of the Pilgrims and the Native Americans of long ago.

HANUKKAH Light the menorah! Spin the dreidel! Families come together to sing, laugh, eat latkes—and remember the flame that burned for eight nights.

ST. LUCIA'S DAY The daughter of the house wears a crown with seven candles. She brings sweet buns and light in the early morning.

POSADAS Children dressed as Joseph and Mary go from house to house. At last they find a place to stay. Then the piñata is broken, and out pours the candy.

RUSSIAN WINTER FESTIVAL Brrrr! Snow is falling. Skiers fly by. *Clop clop* go the three horses pulling the sled. Sleigh bells ring to welcome Grandfather Frost and the New Year.

CHRISTMAS Merry Christmas! It's time to trim the tree and make cookies and sweets. People sing carols and exchange presents at this joyful time.

KWANZAA For seven days, African-Americans celebrate their history and customs. Families gather and rejoice in the seven symbols of the holiday.

EXTENDING THE LITERATURE WITH ART

A CARD FOR TODAY

Invite children to choose a person, an event, or a special good feeling to celebrate. Ask them to think about an activity, food, or special clothing for their celebration. Who would they like to celebrate with? What would they call their holiday? Ask them to draw a picture of the celebration.

Holiday Section – Contents

Background information, read alouds, and activities for Columbus Day, Thanksgiving Day, Presidents' Day, the Fourth of July, and birthdays can be found in Unit 5.

Bibliography

READ ALOUD BOOKS

Anaya, Rudolph. ***The Farolitos of Christmas.*** New York: Hyperion Books for Children, 1995.

Aliki. ***Christmas Tree Memories.*** New York: HarperCollins, 1991.

Bauer, Caroline Feller, ed. ***Thanksgiving Stories and Poems.*** New York: HarperCollins, 1994.

Bunting, Eve. ***Night Tree.*** San Diego, CA: Harcourt Brace and Company, 1991.

Drucker, Malka. ***Grandma's Latkes.*** San Diego, CA: Harcourt Brace and Company, 1992.

Gibbons, Gail. ***St. Patrick's Day.*** New York: Holiday House, 1994.

Hopkins, Lee Bennett, ed. ***Ring Out, Wild Bells: Poems About Holidays and Seasons.*** San Diego, CA: Harcourt Brace and Company, 1992.

Livingston, Myra Cohn, sel. ***Poems for Fathers.*** New York: Holiday House, 1989.

Low, Alice, sel. ***The Family Read-Aloud Holiday Treasury.*** Boston, MA: Little, Brown & Co., 1991.

Marzollo, Jean. ***Happy Birthday, Martin Luther King.*** New York: Scholastic Inc., 1993.

Mills, Claudia. ***Phoebe's Parade.*** New York: Macmillan Publishing Company, 1994.

Most, Bernard. ***Happy Holidaysaurus!*** San Diego, CA: Harcourt Brace and Company, 1992.

Pinkney, Andrea Davis. ***Seven Candles for Kwanzaa.*** New York: Dial Books for Young Readers © 1993.

Waters, Kate, and Slovenz-Low, Madeline. ***Lion Dancer: Ernie Wan's Chinese New Year.*** New York: Scholastic Inc., 1990.

TEACHER BOOKS

Penner, Lucille. ***Celebration: The Story of American Holidays.*** New York: Macmillan Children's Group, 1994.

Silverthorne, Elizabeth. ***Fiesta! Mexico's Great Celebrations.*** Brookfield, CT: The Millbrook Press, 1992.

Walter, Mildred Pitts. ***Kwanzaa: A Family Affair.*** New York: Lothrop, Lee & Shepard Books, 1995.

TECHNOLOGY MULTIMEDIA

Holidays and Calendar Skills. CD-ROM. Orange Cherry New Media, Distributed by Educational Software. (800) 955-5570.

Holiday Magic. Software. McCarthy-McCormack, Distributed by Educational Software. (800) 955-5570.

Holiday Songs Around the World. Video. Educational Activities. (800) 645-3739.

□ ***People Behind the Holidays.*** CD-ROM, National Geographic. (800) 368-2728.

Holiday Facts & Fun Video Series. (11 programs) No. RB8148. Rainbow Educational Media. (800) 331-4047.

FREE OR INEXPENSIVE MATERIALS

For a leaflet about flags in early American history, and information about the flag of today, write to: Dettra Flag Company, Inc., Publication Manager, P.O. Box 408, 120 Montgomery Avenue, Oaks, PA 19456-0408.

□ *National Geographic selection*

Hanukkah

Use with Unit 5

Background Information

ABOUT HANUKKAH

- Hanukkah, the Jewish Festival of Lights, is celebrated in the Hebrew month of Kislev, usually in December. It is an eight-day holiday celebrating religious freedom for Jews.
- The holiday dates back to 165 B.C. when Jews won a three-year war against Syrian rulers. Jewish leader Judah Maccabee led the Jews to victory, enabling them to worship freely once again.
- The Jews wanted to rededicate the Temple of Jerusalem, a holy place of prayer, by lighting candles. They had oil to light the candles for only one day but miraculously the oil lasted eight days.
- Jews celebrate Hanukkah by lighting a candelabra called a menorah, which contains eight candles representing the eight days the oil burned and a ninth to light the others. They exchange small gifts, play games, and eat traditional dishes such as latkes (potato pancakes).

Read Aloud

Candles of Hanukkah

Burn little candles, burn, burn, burn.
Hanukkah is here.
Burn little candles, burn, burn, burn.
Burn so bright and clear.
Eight little candles in a row,
Hanukkah is here.
Eight little candles in a row,
Burn so bright and clear.
Dance little candles, dance, dance, dance.
Hanukkah is here.
Dance little candles, dance, dance, dance.
Hanukkah is here.

Hebrew Folk Song

Make a Finger Menorah

ON YOUR OWN

15 TO 30 MINUTES

CURRICULUM CONNECTION Art

Objective: To recognize that a menorah is part of a Hanukkah celebration.

Materials: scissors, blue and yellow construction paper, markers, ruler, glue, glitter glue

1. Discuss the meaning of the menorah as explained in the Background Information. Then have children fold a blue sheet of construction paper in half.
2. Have children draw a line with a ruler approximately 1" from the bottom of the page. Ask children to place their left hands on the paper on the left side of the fold so that their wrists are on top of the ruler line. Have them spread their fingers apart and trace around them with the exception of the thumb. Repeat the procedure with the right hand on the right side of the fold.
3. Have children draw a big middle candle along the fold.
4. Have children glue on flames made from yellow construction paper. They can use glitter glue to decorate their menorahs.

Background Information

ABOUT CHRISTMAS

- Christmas celebrates the birth of Jesus in Bethlehem about 2,000 years ago. This is a legal holiday in the United States and is observed by many Christians around the world on December 25.
- Traditionally in the United States, families celebrate Christmas by attending church services, singing carols, and decorating their homes with lights and symbols such as crèches and Christmas trees.
- The exchanging of gifts during Christmas represents the gifts that were taken to Bethlehem by the Three Kings and symbolizes the spirit of loving and giving.
- The following are ways of saying "Merry Christmas" in other languages: *God Jul,* Swedish and Norwegian; *Joyeux Noël,* French; *Feliz Navidad,* Spanish.
- Traditionally, Santa's eight reindeer are named Dasher, Dancer, Prancer, Vixen, Comet, Cupid, Donner, and Blitzen.

Read Aloud

Santa's Reindeer

One, two, three, four, five little reindeer.
(Point to one finger at a time.)
Stood by the North Pole gate.
"Hurry, Santa," called the reindeer,
"Or we will all be late!"
One, two, three, four, five little reindeer
(Point to fingers again.)
Santa said, "Please wait!
Wait for three more little reindeer,
Then we will have eight."
(Hold up three fingers on the other hand.)

Louise Binder Scott

Make Reindeer Pockets

ON YOUR OWN

30 MINUTES OR LONGER

CURRICULUM CONNECTION Art

Objective: To create reindeer pockets for Christmas and holiday mail.

Materials: construction paper, scissors, glue, hole puncher, 20" length of red or green ribbon or yarn per child; optional: glitter

1. Tell children they will make reindeer pockets to hold their holiday mail. Have children place a sheet of brown construction paper on their desk horizontally. Then help them fold two triangles along a diagonal line from each corner at the top of the paper to the bottom of the paper. Have children glue one triangle over the other and turn the paper faceup.
2. Next children can cut out a large circle from red construction paper for a nose and two smaller circles from black construction paper for eyes. Glitter can be added to the nose. Have children glue on the nose and eyes. Have children cut two petal-shaped ears from construction paper and glue them on the top outer points.
3. Then have children make a pair of antlers by tracing their hands onto construction paper. Have them cut out the antlers and glue them on.
4. Punch a hole through each ear and secure a length of ribbon or yarn for hanging.

Folding Instructions

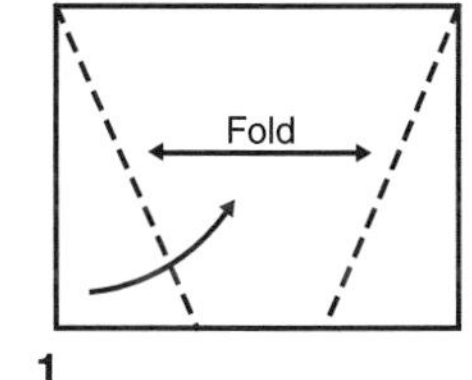

1

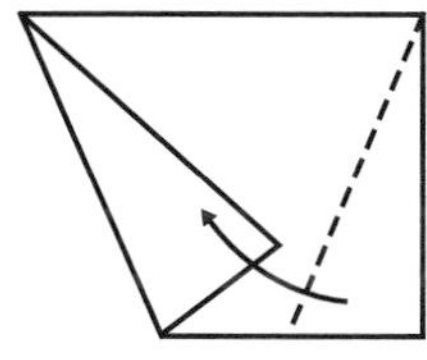
2

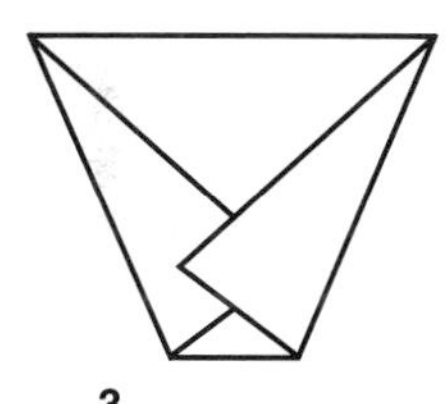
3

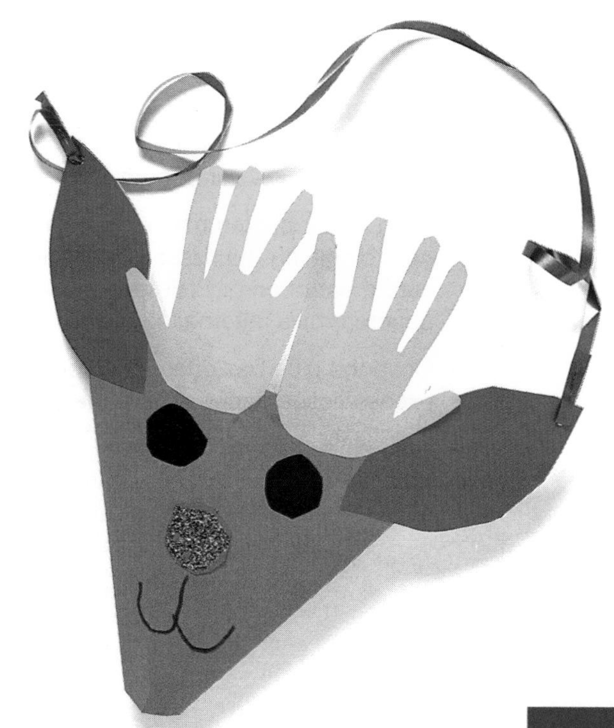

Kwanzaa

Use with Unit 5

Background Information

ABOUT KWANZAA

- Kwanzaa honors African American heritage, family life, and the richness and diversity of African culture.
- This holiday was founded by Dr. Maulana Karenga in 1966. The holiday customs come from different African harvest celebrations.
- Kwanzaa is celebrated from Dec. 26 through Jan. 1. Each day, families light black candles called *mishumaa saba*. Other Kwanzaa symbols include a unity cup called *kikombe cha umoja*, one ear of corn or *muhindi* for each child in the family, fresh fruits and vegetables called *mazao*, a seven-branched candle holder or *kinara*, and a straw mat or *mkeka* on which the other symbols are placed. The colors red, green, and black represent the blood, hope, and color of the peoples of Africa.
- There are seven principles of Kwanzaa—unity, self-determination, collective work and responsibility, cooperative economics, purpose, creativity, and faith. Families celebrate one principle each day.

Kwanzaa's Here

(sung to the tune of *Three Blind Mice*)

Red, green, black,
Red, green, black.
Kwanzaa's here,
Kwanzaa's here.
The decorations are quite a sight,
We light a candle every night,
The holiday is filled with light.
Kwanzaa's here.

Jean Warren

Create Corn Necklaces

ON YOUR OWN

15 TO 30 MINUTES

CURRICULUM CONNECTION Art

Objective: To become familiar with Kwanzaa by making corn necklaces.

Materials: oaktag, tissue paper (red, green, black), scissors, glue, hole puncher, yarn

Advance Preparation: Create a pattern of an ear of corn for children to trace onto oaktag. Cut tissue paper into small-sized squares to be used as kernels by the children.

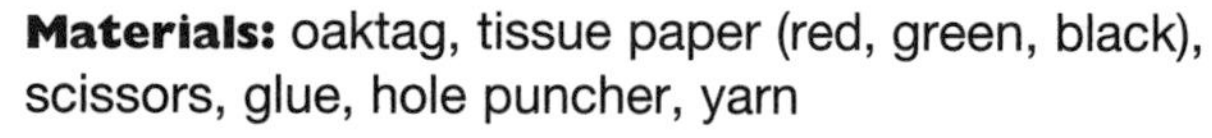

1. Tell children that they will be making corn necklaces. Provide each child with one piece of oaktag and have them trace the corn pattern onto it and then cut out the ear of corn.
2. Then have children make the kernels for their ear of corn by gluing the tissue paper squares to their cutout ear of corn. Children can glue their tissue paper in rows, alternating colors as they go.
3. Once the glue has dried, children can trim off the excess tissue paper around the edges.
4. Help children punch a hole at the top of the corn and then string a length of yarn through it. Children can tie the ear of corn around their necks and wear it as they learn about Kwanzaa.

New Year's Day

Use with Unit 5

Background Information

ABOUT NEW YEAR'S DAY

- New Year's Day is a legal holiday throughout the United States, celebrated on the first day of the new calendar year.
- This holiday dates back to ancient times when the new year was observed at harvest time. In 46 B.C. the Roman ruler, Julius Caesar, established a new calendar and declared January 1 New Year's Day.
- Traditionally at midnight, noisemakers are sounded, a custom that was based on the belief that one needs to drive out the old year before the arrival of the new one.
- New Year's Day is often celebrated with parades, fireworks, the making of New Year's resolutions, and reunions of families and friends.

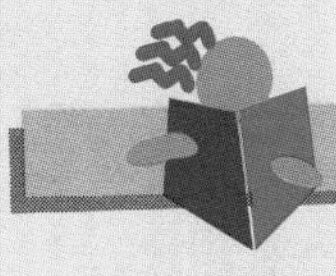

Read Aloud

Happy New Year

On New Year's Day, on New Year's Day,
This is what I always say:
"Happy New Year, Daddy,
(Hold up pointer finger.)
Happy New Year, Mother,
(Hold up ring finger.)
Happy New Year, Sister,
(Hold up small finger.)
Happy New Year, Brother."
(Hold up thumb.)
On New Year's Day, On New Year's Day,
This is what I always say:
"HAPPY NEW YEAR!"

Louise Binder Scott

Make Noisemaker Shakers

ON YOUR OWN

15 TO 30 MINUTES

CURRICULUM CONNECTION Art

Objective: To create noisemakers to celebrate New Year's.

Materials: two small paper plates and three small jingle bells (per child), ruler, hole puncher, curling ribbon in different colors, markers, glitter glue, stickers, paint, paint brushes

1. Tell children that they will be making noisemakers. Explain that some people use noisemakers to bring in the New Year. First, have children hold their two plates face to face as you punch six holes around each rim, making sure that the holes on the two plates remain aligned.
2. Then have children thread three 5" lengths of ribbon through three of the holes and through the jingle bells. Help children fasten the bells in place. Paper chains or colorful ribbon streamers can be attached to the other holes.
3. Children can decorate their noisemakers with markers, glitter glue, stickers, or paint.

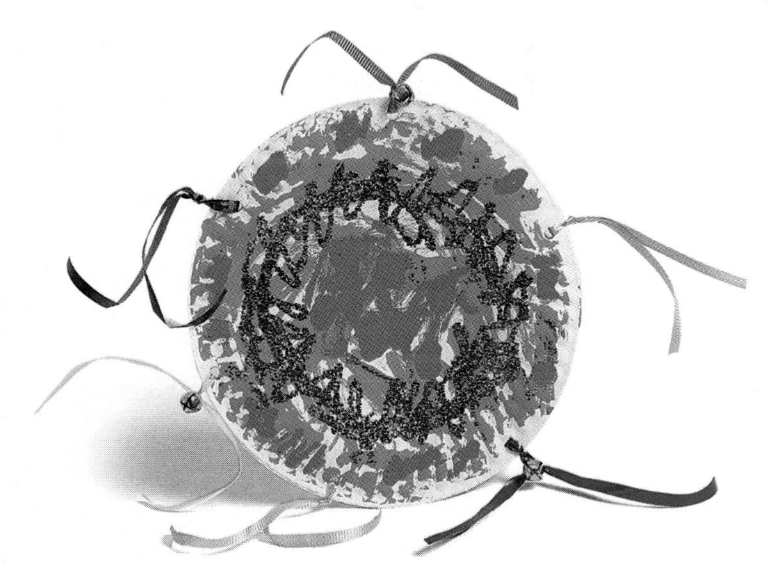

Three Kings Day

Use with Unit 5

Background Information

ABOUT THREE KINGS DAY

- Three Kings Day—also called the Epiphany, Little Christmas, the Feast of the Three Kings, and Twelfth Night—is celebrated by Christians on January 6. It honors the Three Kings who traveled to Bethlehem to deliver gifts to the baby Jesus as tokens of love, esteem, and respect.
- Some children of Spanish heritage place their shoes near a door, on a window sill, or by a manger scene, on the night of January 5. The Three Kings are supposed to fill their shoes with gifts. Often the children leave water for the camels of the Three Kings.
- Other traditions of this holiday include holding parties and eating a crown-shaped cake which contains a trinket such as a tiny doll or a bean. The finder of the trinket gets to be king for the day.

January Sixth

Call it the Epiphany
Or Three Kings Day.
Call it Little Christmas
Or Holy Kings Day.
On January sixth,
We remember the day
Three kings brought presents
From far away.

Bergen Katz

Wear a Crown

ON YOUR OWN

15 TO 30 MINUTES

CURRICULUM CONNECTION Art

Objective: To become familiar with Three Kings Day by making crowns.

Materials: oaktag, markers or crayons, scissors, pencils, tape, glitter glue

Advance Preparation: Make crown templates for children to trace.

1. Invite children to make a king's crown. First, help children to trace their crown templates two times onto a piece of oaktag.
2. Then, have children cut out the two pieces and decorate them with markers, crayons, or glitter.
3. Finally, cut a strip of oaktag for each child long enough to fit around his or her head. Tape the two crown pieces to it (one in front and one in back). Secure the crown by taping it inside the strip.

Valentine's Day

Use with Unit 5

Background Information

ABOUT VALENTINE'S DAY

- On February 14, many people in the United States celebrate Valentine's Day. It is a day when people celebrate their love and affection for each other.
- Traditionally, candy and flowers are exchanged on this holiday.
- Red, white, and pink are the common colors of the holiday, and roses, hearts, love birds, and Cupids with bows and arrows can be found as decorations. Cupid was the Roman god of love.
- One of the many legends that surrounds Valentine's Day is that birds choose their mates on February 14.

Read Aloud

The Best Valentine

Some valentines are paper,
Shaped like hearts of pink and gold.
Some valentines are flowers
In a soft green tissue fold.
Some valentines are candy,
But the one I got instead
Was a furry little puppy
With a collar that was red.

Margaret Hillert

Make Heart-Filled Mobiles

ON YOUR OWN

15 TO 30 MINUTES

CURRICULUM CONNECTION Art

Objective: To celebrate Valentine's Day by making mobiles.

Materials: oaktag, tissue paper, glitter glue, crayons, markers, scissors, string, hangers, pipecleaners, red construction paper, hole punchers

Advance Preparation: Create heart patterns out of oaktag of varying sizes.

1. Discuss with children what the heart represents—love, friendship, and caring. Then tell them they will be making heart-filled mobiles.
2. Have each child trace at least three heart patterns onto red construction paper. Then have them cut out the hearts.
3. Invite children to decorate their hearts with glitter, crayons, markers, and tissue paper. Then help each child punch a hole at the top of each heart and tie a piece of string or pipecleaner through it.
4. Help children wrap pipecleaners around the wire hangers and then tie their hearts to it.

St. Patrick's Day

Use with Unit 5

Background Information

ABOUT ST. PATRICK'S DAY

- On March 17, the patron saint of Ireland, Saint Patrick, is honored by Irish Americans throughout the United States as well as people of Irish heritage throughout the world.
- Many Irish celebrate the day as a religious holiday, attending church and family gatherings. Many Irish Americans also celebrate with parades, dancing, and enjoying traditional Irish meals of corned beef, cabbage, and Irish soda bread.
- The tradition of wearing green on St. Patrick's Day stems from an old Irish custom. Hundreds of years ago the Irish burned green leaves and boughs and spread the ashes over their fields believing it would enrich the soil.
- Harps, leprechauns, and shamrocks are the symbols of this holiday.

Read Aloud

St. Patrick's Day

St. Patrick's Day is here, you see.
We'll pick some shamrocks, one, two, three.
(Hold up three fingers.)
We'll count the leaves and look them over,
And maybe find a four-leafed clover.
(Hold up four fingers.)
I'll sew green buttons for my vest.
(Point to chest.)
Green for St. Patrick is the best.
I'll wear a green hat, very high,
(Measure height.)
And dance a jig—at least I'll try.
(Shuffle feet.)

Louise Binder Scott

Make St. Patrick's Day Hats

ON YOUR OWN

15 TO 30 MINUTES

CURRICULUM CONNECTION **Art**

Objective: To make hats for St. Patrick's Day.

Materials: oaktag, scissors, construction paper (green, black), glue, glitter, green ribbon, stapler

Advance Preparation: Create oaktag templates for a St. Patrick's Day hat, hatband, and shamrock. Also cut for each child two 1 1/2" x 12" headbands from black construction paper.

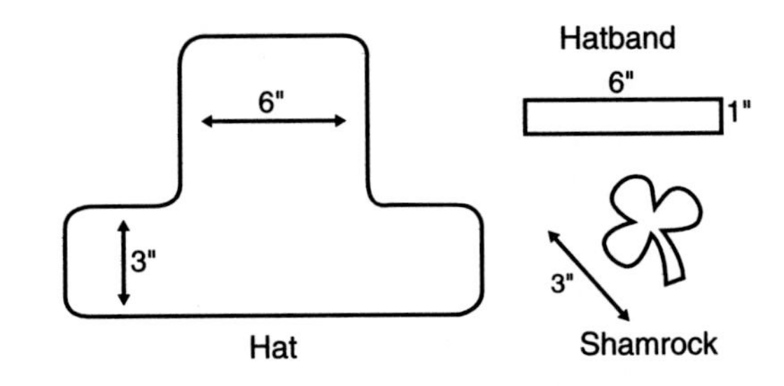

1. Tell children that they will be making hats for St. Patrick's day. Help children trace the hat and shamrock patterns onto green construction paper and cut them out. Then have them trace the hatband onto black construction paper and cut it out.
2. Have children glue the hatband just above the brim. Then have them glue a length of ribbon and the shamrock onto the hatband. Glitter can be added to the hat for decoration. Children may also wish to decorate their hats with markers.
3. Staple one end of the two headbands together. Fit the headband around the child's head and then staple the band to the brim of the hat.

Arbor Day

Use with Units 4 & 5

Background Information

ABOUT ARBOR DAY

- Arbor Day is a special day that is set aside for planting trees. It is celebrated at different times throughout the United States. Southern states and Hawaii celebrate Arbor Day at various times from December to March. Northern states usually celebrate it between April and May.
- Arbor Day began in Nebraska, when Julius Sterling Morton, a newspaper publisher, realized the many benefits of planting trees, including enriching the soil and conserving its moisture. Through his efforts, the first Arbor Day was celebrated in 1872.

Read Aloud

Song

Elms are proud
and cedars dark,
poplars have silver
leaf-shadowed bark,
aspens whisper,
willows weep,
and all the tree-toads
have gone to sleep.

Elizabeth Coatsworth

Make Terrific Terrariums

CURRICULUM CONNECTION **Science**

Objective: To celebrate Arbor Day by planting seeds.

Materials: marigold or zinnia seeds, plastic cups (transparent), potting soil, tape, water

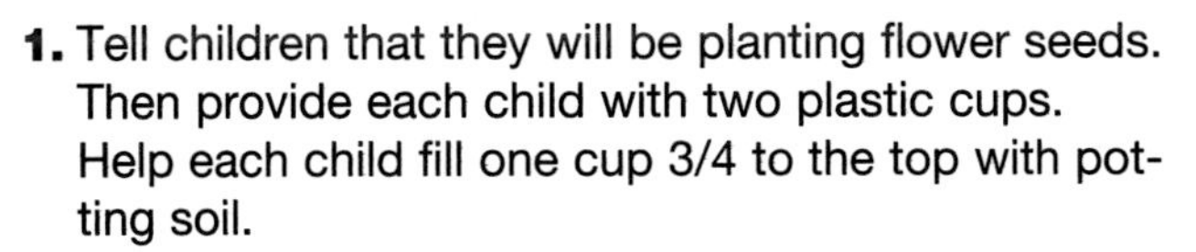

1. Tell children that they will be planting flower seeds. Then provide each child with two plastic cups. Help each child fill one cup 3/4 to the top with potting soil.
2. Children can use their finger to dig small holes in the soil where they can then place seeds in the hole and cover them with soil.
3. Next children can spray water into the second cup and place it over the seed cup. Help children tape the cups together.
4. Place the terrariums on a counter where they will receive a lot of sunlight. Once the seedlings have sprouted, the children can take them home, or transplant them into a window box for the room. Children should remove the cover cup as the seedling grows.

Mother's Day

Use with Unit 5

Background Information

ABOUT MOTHER'S DAY

- On Mother's Day, children honor their mother or caregiver by giving her cards, gifts, and flowers. Mother's Day is celebrated on the second Sunday in May.
- The first known suggestion for celebrating Mother's Day in the United States was made by Julia Ward Howe in 1872. The day was celebrated in various places around the country for a number of years.
- Anna Jarvis is considered the founder of Mother's Day. Starting in 1907, she worked to make the day a nationally recognized holiday. Finally in 1914 a national resolution recognizing Mother's Day was signed by Woodrow Wilson.
- Anna Jarvis also began the tradition of wearing carnations on Mother's Day. She chose this flower because it was her mother's favorite.

Read Aloud

On Mother's Day

On Mother's Day we got up first,
so full of plans we almost burst.

We started breakfast right away
as our surprise for Mother's Day.

We picked some flowers, then hurried back
to make the coffee—rather black.

We wrapped our gifts and wrote a card
and boiled the eggs—a little hard.

And then we sang a serenade,
which burned the toast, I am afraid.

But Mother said, amidst our cheers,
"Oh, what a big surprise, my dears.
I've not had such a treat in years."
And she was smiling to her ears!

Aileen Fisher

Make Salt-Dough Necklaces

GROUP

30 MINUTES OR LONGER

CURRICULUM CONNECTION Art

Objective: To make necklaces to give to someone special on Mother's Day.

Materials: measuring cup, tablespoon, bowl, flour, salt, water, toothpicks, paint, markers, plastic sewing needle, yarn

1. Tell children they will be making necklaces out of dough. With the children's help, mix two cups of flour, one cup of salt, and one-half cup of water. (If more dough is needed, add ingredients in these proportions). Add the water slowly so that when mixed the dough is stiff but not crumbly.
2. Once the dough has stiffened, have children make medium-sized balls. Children can use toothpicks to poke a hole through the balls wide enough to pull yarn through.
3. Set the balls on a counter to dry. (Drying may take two days.) Once they are dry, give each child an equal number of balls to string and decorate. Help children first to string the balls using a plastic needle and yarn and then to decorate them with paints and markers.
4. When the paint is dry, the balls will look like beads. Children can either wear or give their necklaces to someone special on Mother's Day.

Father's Day

Use with Unit 5

Background Information

ABOUT FATHER'S DAY

- On Father's Day, children honor their father or caregiver by giving cards and gifts. Father's Day is celebrated on the third Sunday in June.
- In 1909, after hearing a sermon on Mother's Day, Sonora Louise Smart Dodd drew up a petition to make Father's Day a national holiday. Through her efforts, the first Father's Day was celebrated in 1910 in Spokane, Washington.
- Many resolutions to make Father's Day a national holiday have been proposed over the years, but it was not until 1972 that a resolution was signed by President Richard M. Nixon.

Read Aloud

For Father's Day

I found a seashell
for my dad,
just right for Father's Day.
I polished it
until it shone.
I hid it deep away.

When I gave it
to my dad
he held it to his ear
and told me I
had given him
the whole, wide sea to hear.

Sandra Liatsos

Make Window Ornaments

CURRICULUM CONNECTION Art

Objective: To make window ornaments to give to someone special on Father's Day.

Materials: colored tissue paper, paper doilies, glitter, glue, hole puncher, yarn or ribbon

1. Tell children they will be making a special window ornament for Father's Day. First, have children help you tear pieces of tissue paper.
2. Then set out glue and doilies.
3. Have children glue pieces of tissue paper onto a doily. Children may want to add glitter to their ornament.
4. Help children punch a hole at the top of the ornament and thread a length of yarn through it. Tie the ends together and encourage children to give their ornament to someone special on Father's Day.

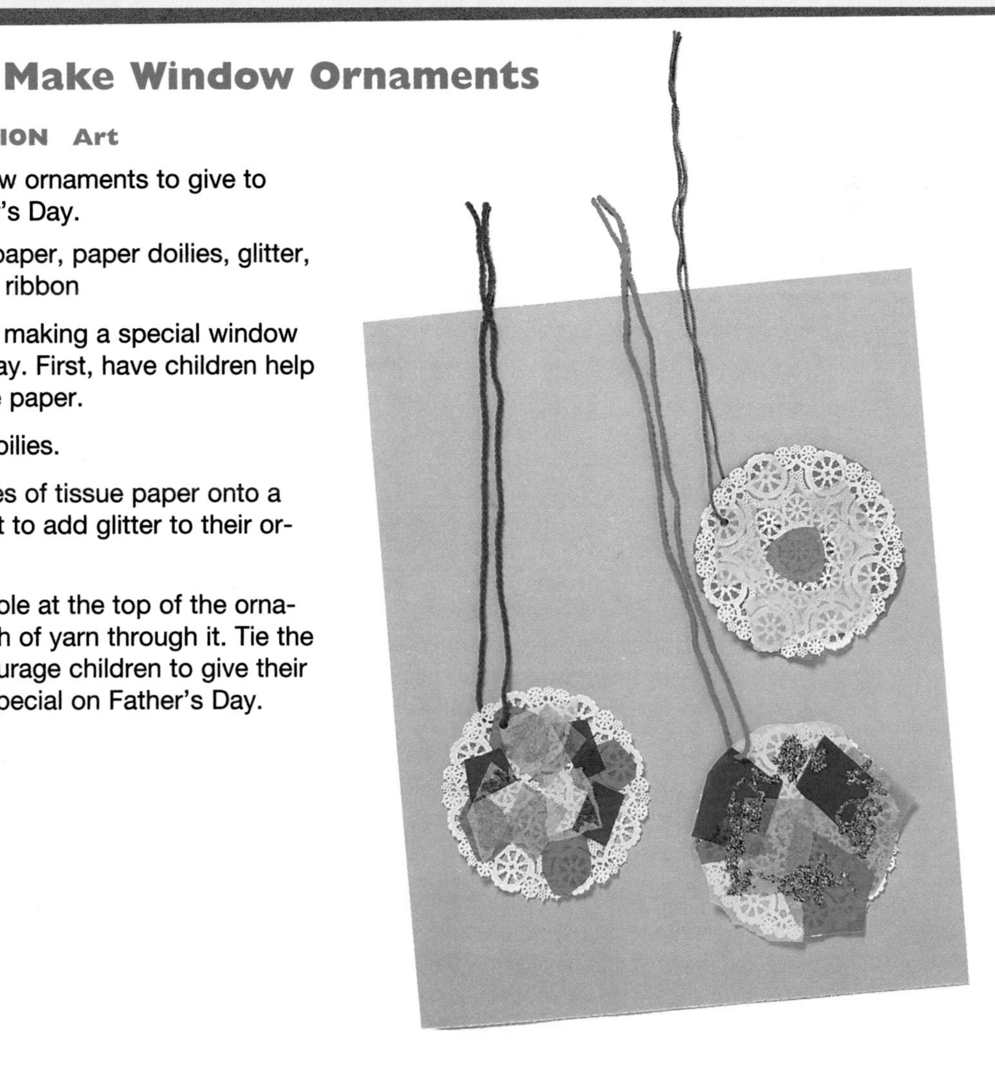

Flag Day

Use with Unit 5

Background Information

ABOUT FLAG DAY

- Flag Day marks the day in 1777 when the Continental Congress adopted a resolution to create a flag for the new United States of America. The holiday is celebrated on June 14 throughout the United States.
- The first Flag Day was celebrated on June 14, 1877, marking the 100th birthday of the flag. However, the holiday did not become official until 1949.
- Many people display the American flag in front of their homes and at their place of business on Flag Day. People may dress in red, white, and blue, sing the national anthem, and pledge allegiance to the flag on this holiday.
- We are reminded on Flag Day that the thirteen stripes on the flag represent the original thirteen states and the fifty stars represent the fifty states that currently make up the United States.
- Legend has it that Betsy Ross made the first flag, but the story has never been proven conclusively.

The Story of Our Flag

In the city of old Philadelphia,
Lived a woman named Miss Betsy Ross.
Did she make the first flag? We don't really know.
The truth of the story is lost.

But many believe that she sewed the first flag
Using fabric of red, white, and blue.
Did this really happen? We can't really know.
But I certainly hope that it's true!

Waverly Pasca

Make a Flag-Day Pinwheel

CURRICULUM CONNECTION Art

Objective: To make pinwheels to celebrate Flag Day.

Materials: white drawing paper, scissors or pinking shears, red and blue markers, one metal paper fastener and one drinking straw (per child), hole puncher, uncooked tube-variety macaroni, knife

Advance Preparation: (for each child) Cut a 6" x 6" square from white drawing paper. You may wish to use pinking shears for a fun look. Also cut one 1/4" piece of macaroni. Finally, flatten one end of a drinking straw and punch one hole through that.

1. Tell children they will be making pinwheels for Flag Day. Using red and blue markers, have children decorate one side of their squares with blue stars and the other side with red stripes. When children have finished, have them diagonally fold the square in half twice and then unfold the paper.
2. Following the diagram, help children to make a 2 1/2" cut on each fold line. Be sure they do not cut the paper in half. Punch a hole through the center of the square.
3. Have children bend one tip from each section (the same on each) just over the center hole and hold them in place. Insert a paper fastener through the four tips, the center hole, the piece of macaroni and the straw. Open the ends of the fastener to secure the pinwheel.

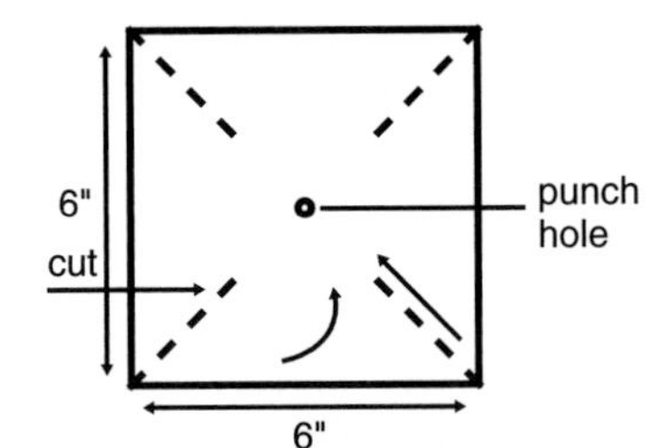

STICKERS

MACMILLAN/McGRAW-HILL

Use with Unit 1 Theme Big Book pages 6-7, 8-9

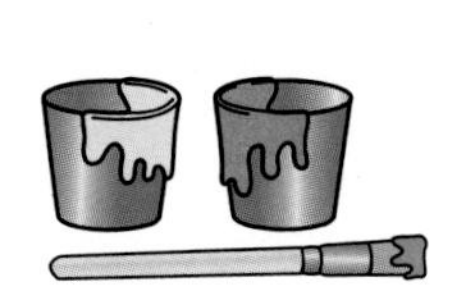
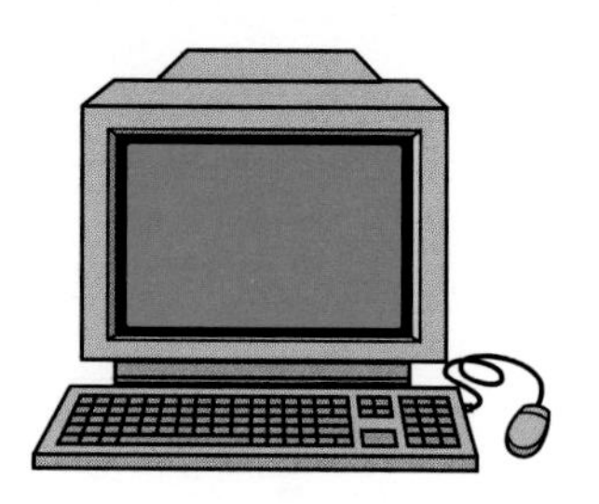

Use with Unit 1 Theme Big Book pages 8-9

MACMILLAN/McGRAW-HILL

MACMILLAN/McGRAW-HILL

SHEET 2 Stickers

Use with Unit 1 Theme Big Book pages 10-11

Use with Unit 1 Theme Big Book pages 12-13

MACMILLAN/McGRAW-HILL

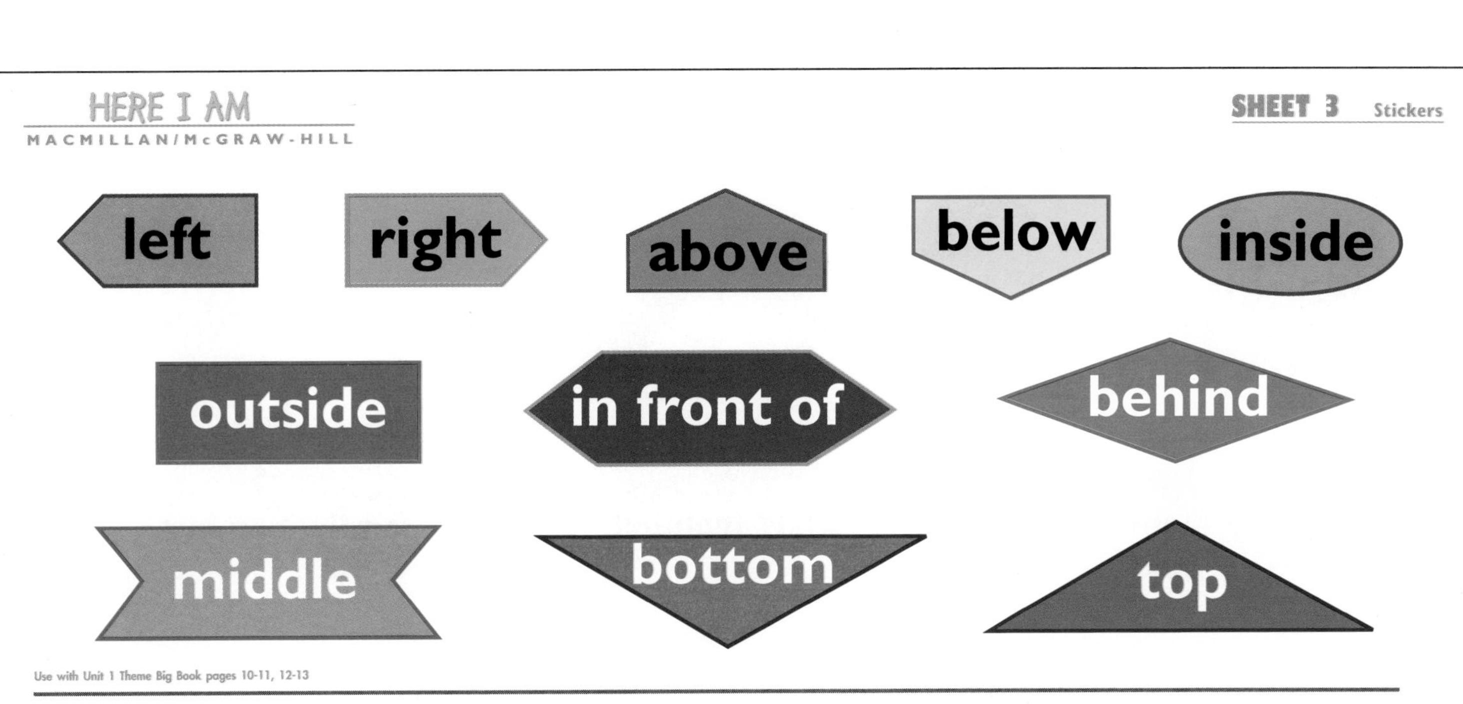

Use with Unit 1 Theme Big Book pages, 12-13

MACMILLAN/McGRAW-HILL

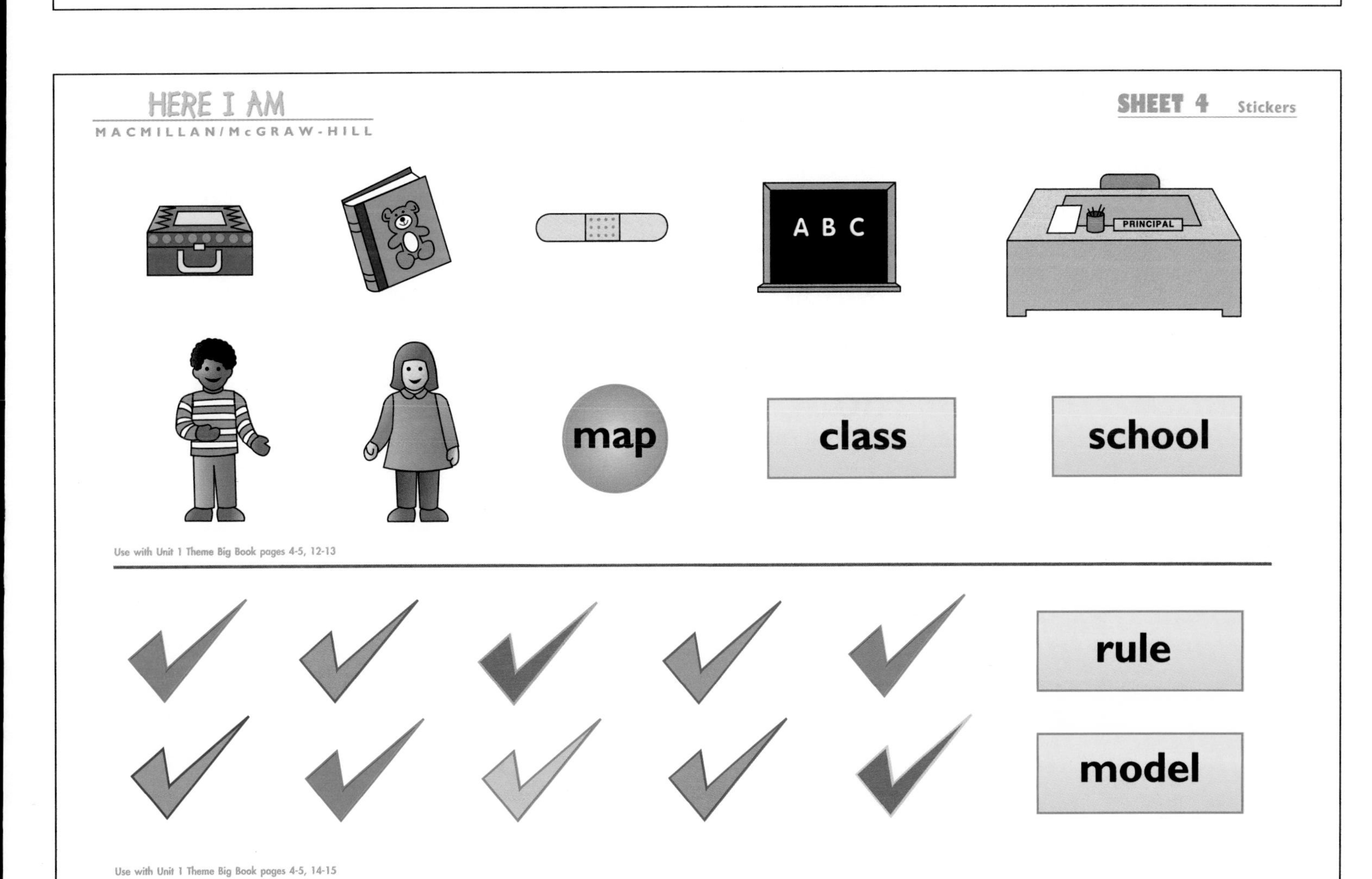

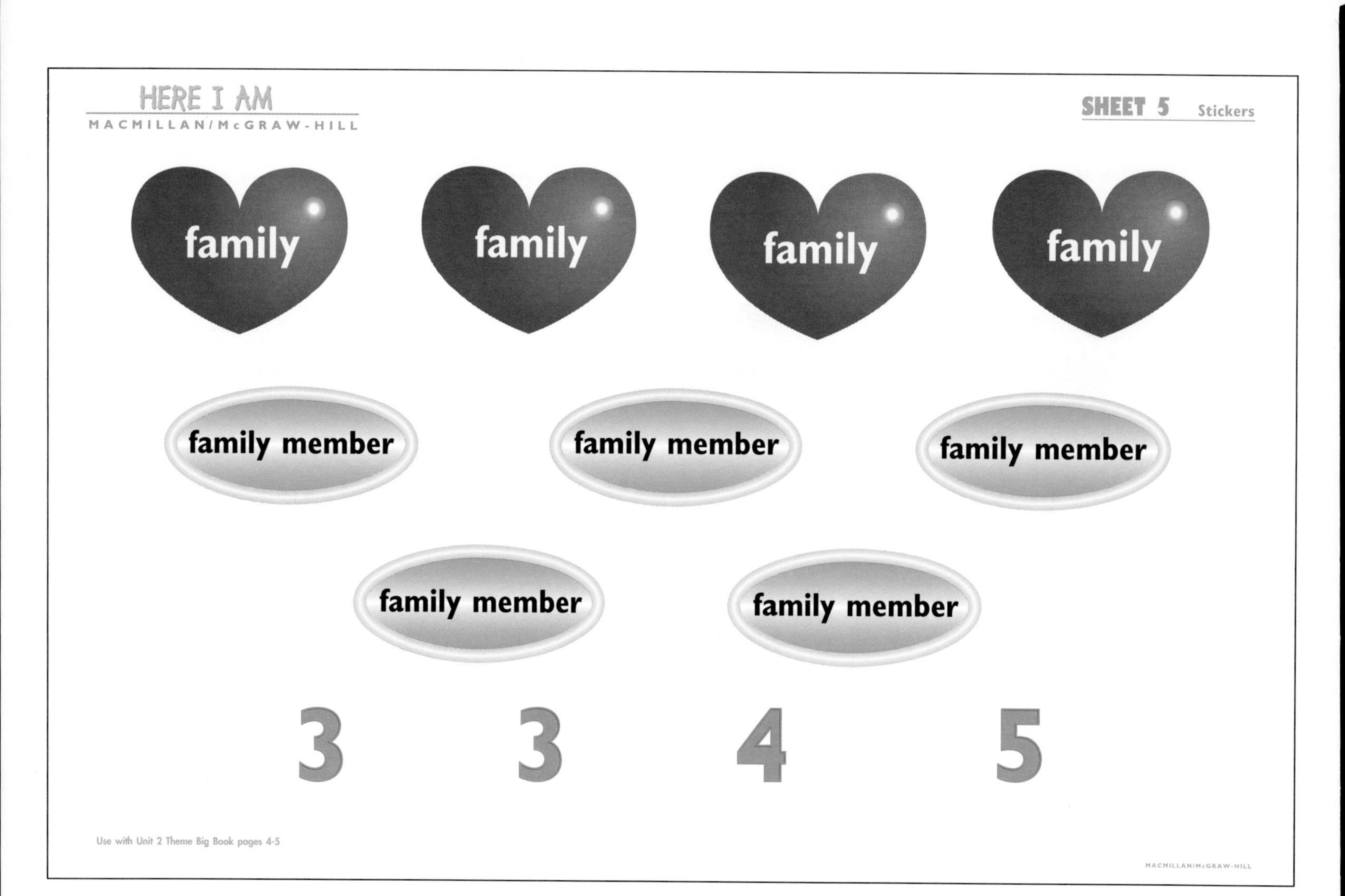
HERE I AM
MACMILLAN/McGRAW-HILL
SHEET 5 Stickers
family
family
family
family
family member
family member
family member
family member
family member
3
3
4
5
Use with Unit 2 Theme Big Book pages 4-5
MACMILLAN/McGRAW-HILL

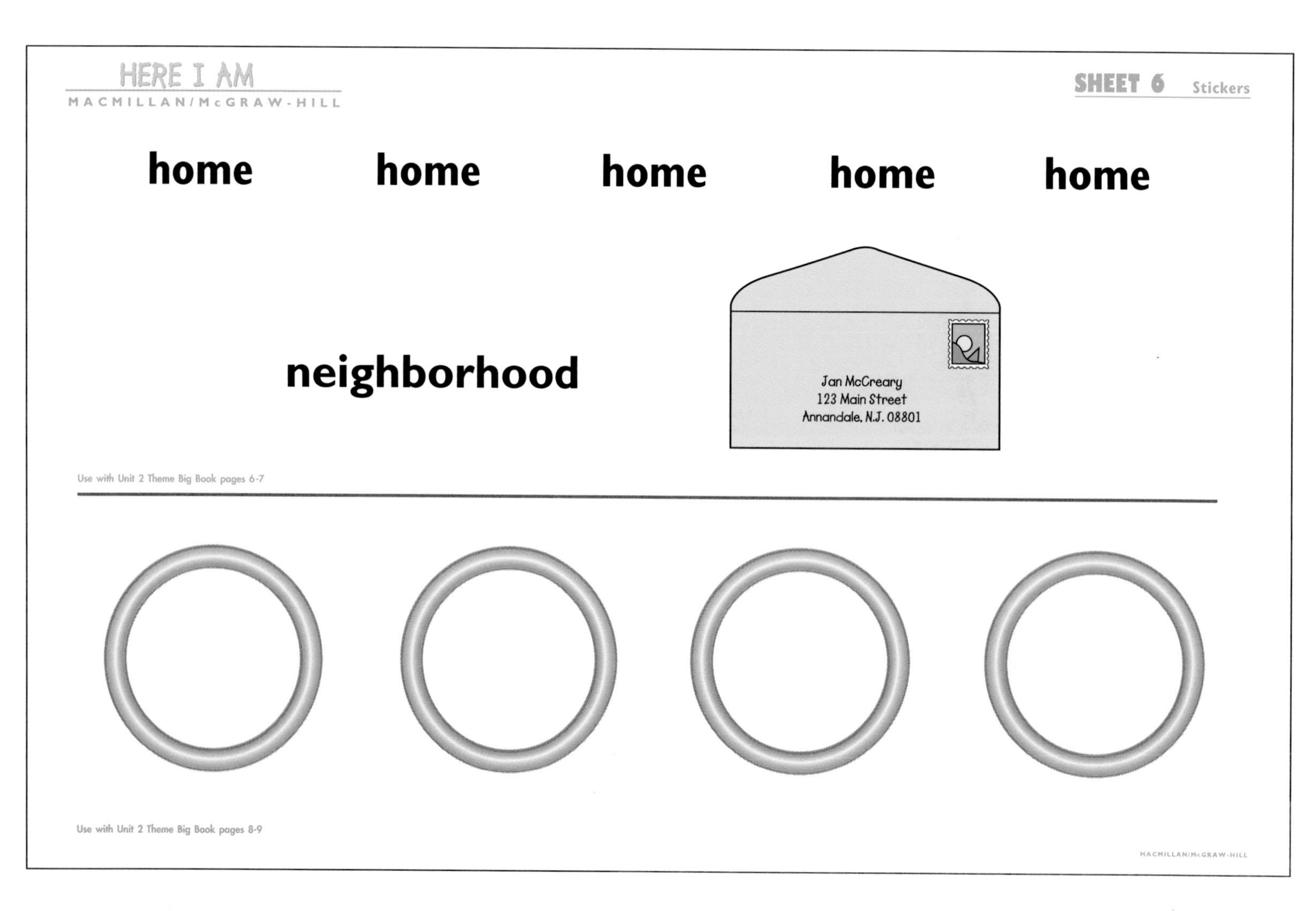
HERE I AM
MACMILLAN/McGRAW-HILL
SHEET 6 Stickers
home
home
home
home
home
neighborhood
Jan McCreary
123 Main Street
Annandale, N.J. 08801
Use with Unit 2 Theme Big Book pages 6-7
Use with Unit 2 Theme Big Book pages 8-9
MACMILLAN/McGRAW-HILL

HERE I AM

MACMILLAN/McGRAW-HILL

SHEET 7 Stickers

South Korea

The Netherlands

South Africa

Use with Unit 2 Theme Big Book pages 10-11

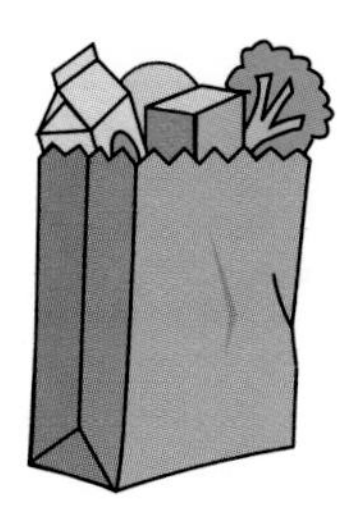

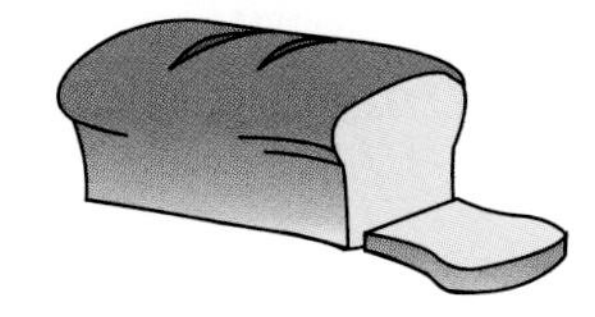

workers

Use with Unit 2 Theme Big Book pages 12-13

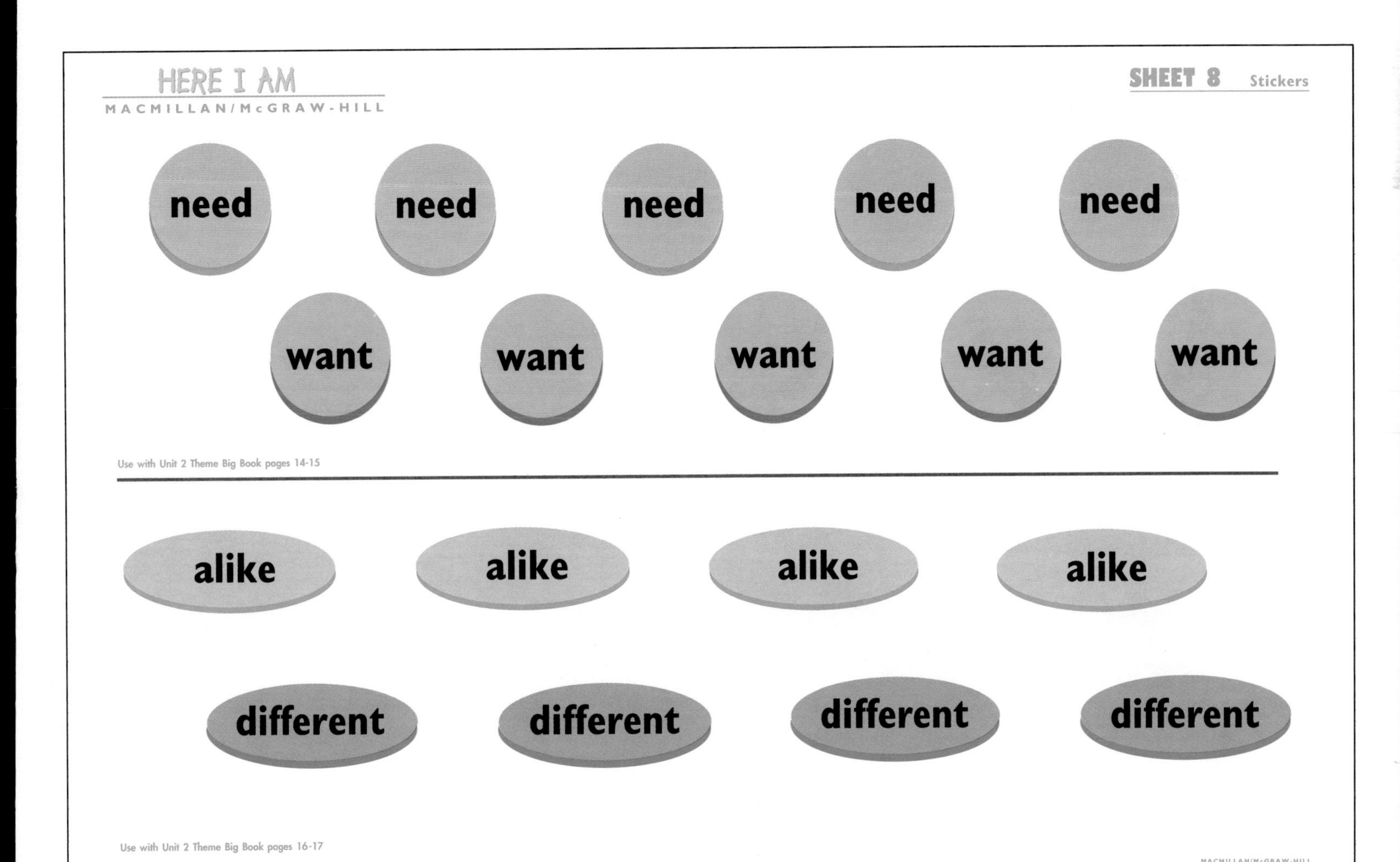

HERE I AM
MACMILLAN/McGRAW-HILL

SHEET 9 Stickers

Use with Unit 3 Theme Big Book pages 4-5

city **farm**

woods

beach

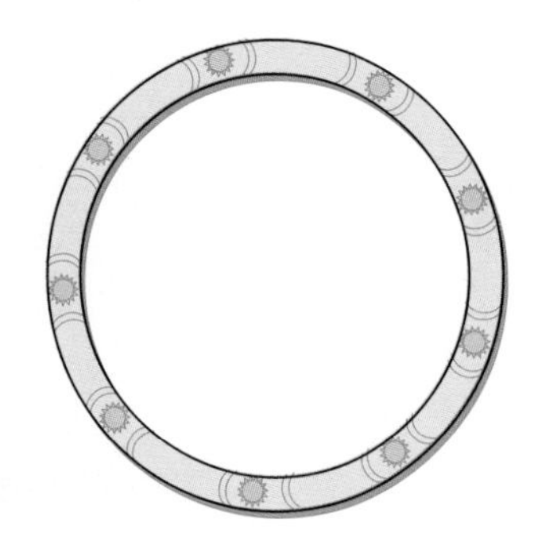
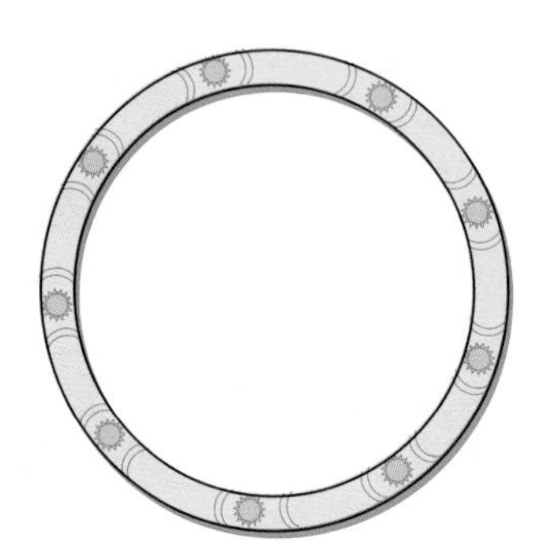
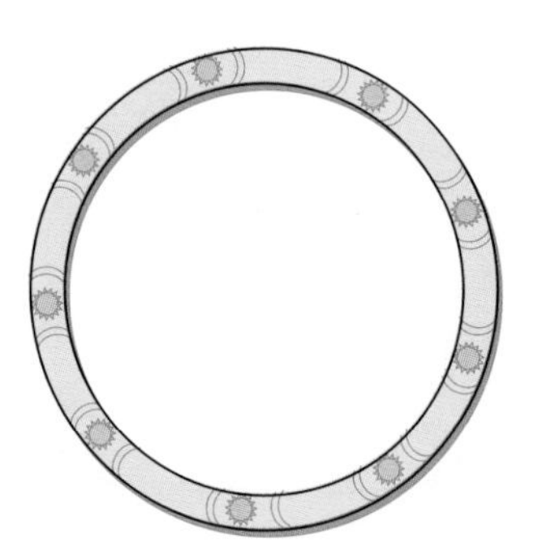

Use with Unit 3 Theme Big Book pages 2-3, 6-7

MACMILLAN/McGRAW-HILL

HERE I AM
MACMILLAN/McGRAW-HILL

SHEET 10 Stickers

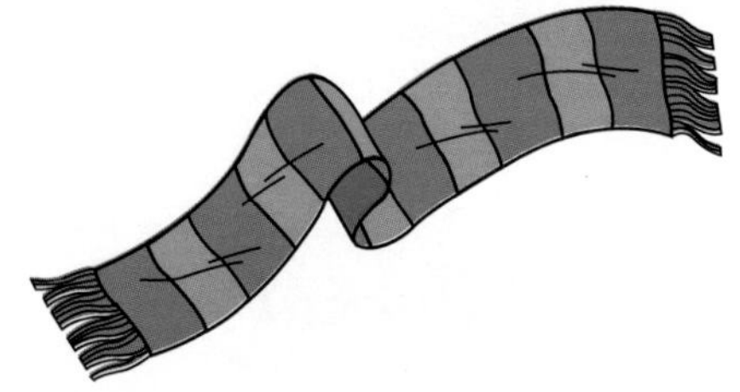

Use with Unit 3 Theme Big Book pages 6-7

MACMILLAN/McGRAW-HILL

HERE I AM

MACMILLAN/McGRAW-HILL

SHEET 11 Stickers

Use with Unit 3 Theme Big Book pages 8-9

Use with Unit 3 Theme Big Book pages 10-11

MACMILLAN/McGRAW-HILL

HERE I AM

MACMILLAN/McGRAW-HILL

SHEET 12 Stickers

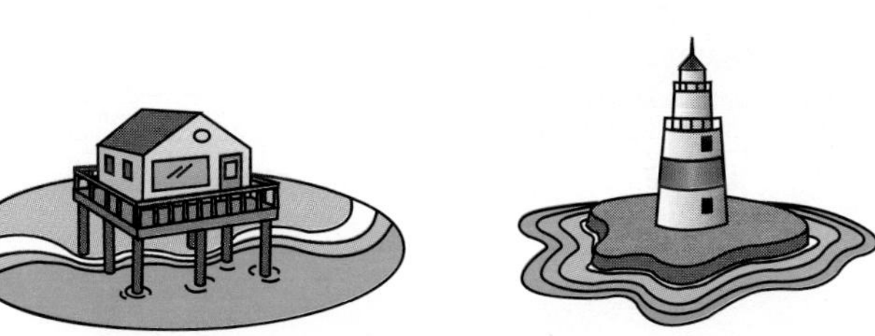

Use with Unit 3 Theme Big Book pages 12-13

Use with Unit 3 Theme Big Book pages 16-17

MACMILLAN/McGRAW-HILL

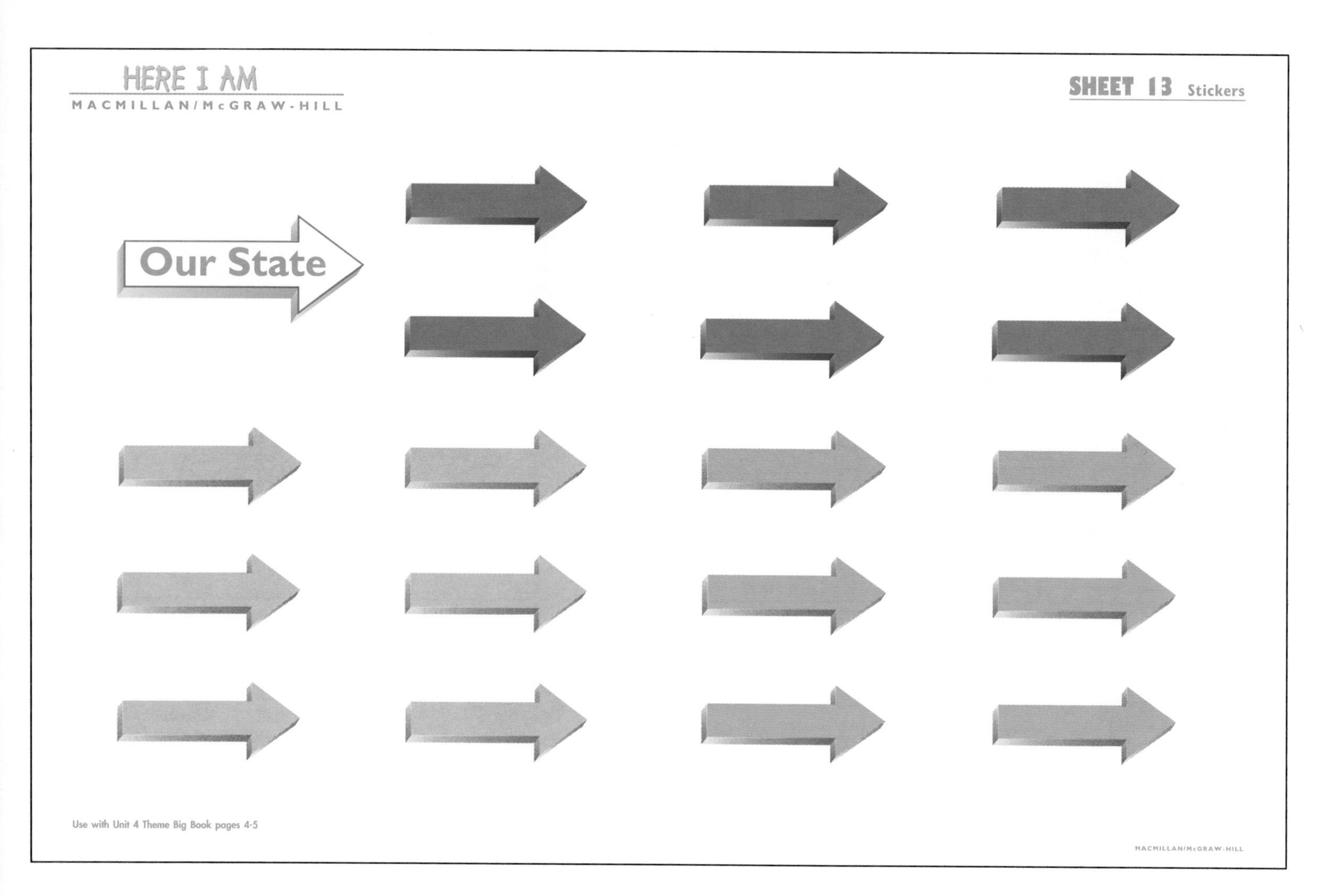
HERE I AM
MACMILLAN/McGRAW-HILL
SHEET 13 Stickers
Our State
Use with Unit 4 Theme Big Book pages 4-5
MACMILLAN/McGRAW-HILL

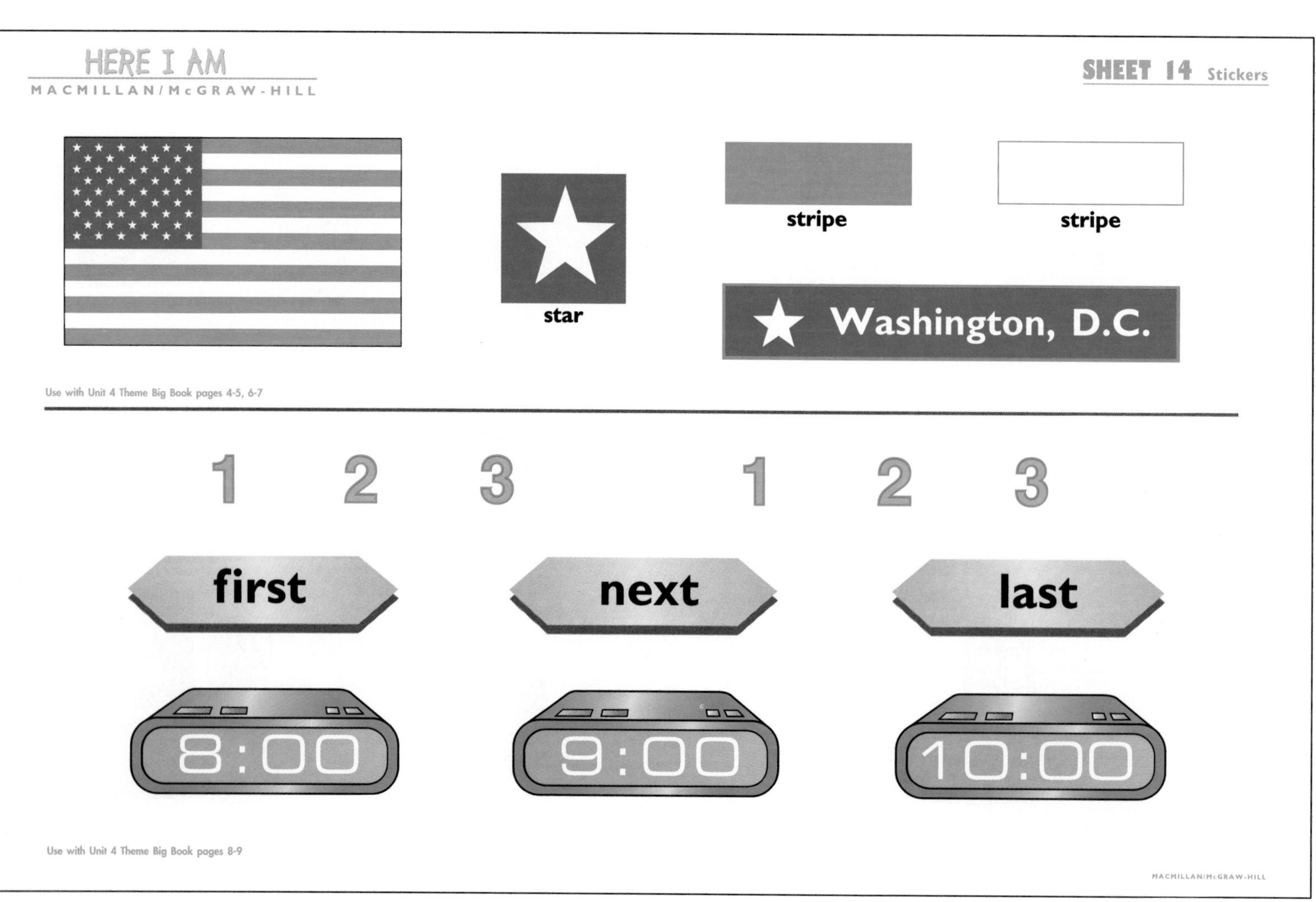
HERE I AM
MACMILLAN/McGRAW-HILL
SHEET 14 Stickers
star
stripe
stripe
Washington, D.C.
Use with Unit 4 Theme Big Book pages 4-5, 6-7
1 2 3 1 2 3
first
next
last
8:00
9:00
10:00
Use with Unit 4 Theme Big Book pages 8-9
MACMILLAN/McGRAW-HILL

SHEET 15 Stickers

river

plain

lake

hill

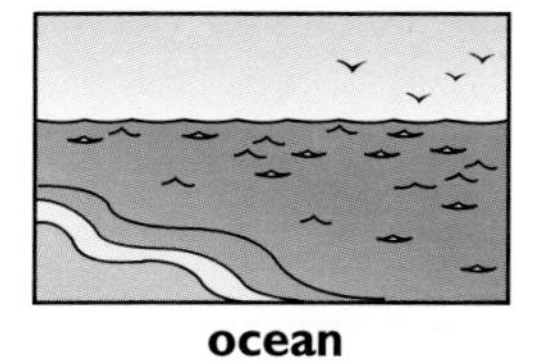
ocean

mountain

Use with Unit 4 Theme Big Book pages 10-11, 14-15

North America

South America

Europe

Africa

Asia

Australia

Antarctica

Use with Unit 4 Theme Big Book pages 12-13

SHEET 16 Stickers

Use with Unit 4 Theme Big Book pages 12-13

HERE I AM
MACMILLAN/McGRAW-HILL

SHEET 17 Stickers

holiday

birthday

Use with Unit 5 Theme Big Book pages 2-3, 4-5

Pilgrim

Wampanoag

Use with Unit 5 Theme Big Book pages 6-7, 8-9

Martin Luther King, Jr.

George Washington

Abraham Lincoln

Use with Unit 5 Theme Big Book pages 10-11, 12-13

MACMILLAN/McGRAW-HILL

HERE I AM
MACMILLAN/McGRAW-HILL

SHEET 18 Stickers

Use with Unit 5 Theme Big Book pages 8-9

Use with Unit 5 Theme Big Book pages 14-15

MACMILLAN/McGRAW-HILL

SHEET 19 Stickers

Use with Unit 5 Theme Big Book pages 16-17

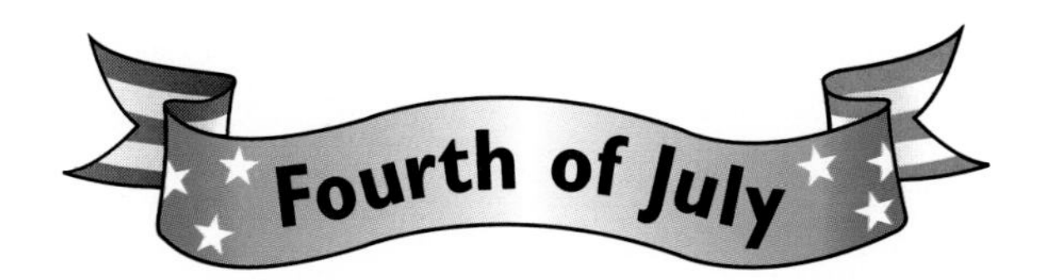

Use with Unit 5 Theme Big Book pages 18-19